The Constitution of Non-State Government: Field Guide to Texas Secession

by
T.L. Hulsey

NOTICE TO EDUCATIONAL INSTITUTIONS:
While not unlimited, a fund exists to provide free or reduced-price copies of this book when assigned to students as reading in a formal political science class. Apply at terryhulsey@terryhulsey.com.

Errata are published at terryhulsey.com/fieldguide
Suggest errata at terryhulsey@terryhulsey.com.

Produced in the Republic of South Carolina by

SHOTWELL PUBLISHING LLC
Post Office Box 2592
Columbia, So. Carolina 29202

ISBN-10: 1-947660-85-3
ISBN-13: 978-1-947660-85-4

It is only in the shadows, when some fresh wave, truly original, truly creative, breaks upon the shore, that there will be a rediscovery of the West.

– Jacques Barzun

Table of Contents

Preface

The bumptious project of this book is to return to two fateful crossroads in the history of the West and offer a comprehensive course correction to guide the inevitable secession of Texas from the larger former republic.

These two fateful crossroads were between Grotius and Althusius in the 17th century, and St. Augustine of Hippo and Pelagius in the 5th century. Specifically, the more recent crossroad was the intersection of *De jure belli ac pacis* (*Law of War and Peace*), published in 1625 by Hugo Grotius (1583-1645), with *Politica Methodice Digesta* (*Politics Methodically Defined*), published in 1603 by Johannes Althusius (1557-1638). We take the 1625 work by Grotius to be the initial theoretical blueprint of the modern state[a] whose foundation was laid on October 24, 1648, with the Treaty of Westphalia.[1] The more ancient crossroad was the intersection of the *Commentarii in epistolas S. Pauli* (*Commentaries on the letters of St. Paul*), written around 400 by Pelagius (354-418), with *Contra duas epistolas Pelagianorum* (*Against two letters of the Pelagians*), written around 420 by St. Augustine of Hippo (354-430). We take the 420 work by St. Augustine to be the doctrinal blueprint of destructive key elements in Protestant theology codified on July 17, 431, with the Council of Ephesus.[2]

The unreflective are easily blinded by the familiar.[3] Moderns fatuously equate "government" and "state." But the state form of government created in 1648 was new and unique. The state is that form of government relentlessly striving to remove every mediating institution between its power and each subject citizen, seeking legitimacy through majoritarian absolutism and the delusion of enumerated guarantees – so-called "rights" – against all encroachment, even its own.

The wrangling between the state as a dangerous *defender* of pre-existing rights and the state as a positivist *creator* of rights – more broadly, of all attempts to legitimize the state in either reason or will – is an argument far down the path of history from the more fundamental question of whether the state should be the exclusive form of government at all. The West's answer to that question constitutes a false turn taken over four centuries ago at the signpost marked "Hugo Grotius." After the state's centuries of detours – in protean

---

[a] Following the "strong definition" of Luigi Marco Bassani, "modern state" is a pleonasm for "state," as explained *infra*. [*Vide* Bassani, *Chaining Down Leviathan, op.cit. infra*, pages 12, 14.] The capitalized "State" will refer in this book to one of the 50 administrative units of the American unitary government. Similarly, "Federal" refers to that unitary government, while "federal" refers to a confederation of several sovereignties. The common definition of "state" by Max Weber – "a human community that (successfully) claims the monopoly of the legitimate use of physical force within a given territory" – Bassani shows (page 20) to be redundant in its use of "legitimate," since it is the state's monopoly of violence that establishes its "legitimacy."

metastasis as the divine right of kings, as the sovereignty of parliaments, as the expression of the "general will," as "god's will," as the apotheosis of national identity, as the midwife of communist egalitarianism, as "the end of history" – the state form of government is a spent idea that has culminated in social crisis. Its route has been steeped in the blood of human suffering and has ended in our present-day cul-de-sac from which we must retrace our steps to that fatal crossroad and reconsider Johannes Althusius.

Although ideas are the decisive causal agents in government and theology, one must be realistic about their primacy in history generally. While it is easier to draw a straight line between the abstract Pelagian dispute and its concrete resolution in favor of St. Augustine in the July 17 fifth session of the Council of Ephesus in 431, it is more difficult to do so for the abstract dispute regarding the proper form of government, however much the Treaty of Westphalia may have affirmed the principles of Grotius. To suggest the date of birth of the state on October 24, 1648 does not deny its long gestation through many contributing influences.

Nor should the return to these two fateful crossroads be understood to be some kind of nostalgia for a counter-history. The ideas of Grotius were institutionalized instead of those of Althusius, not because there was a dramatic council that decided the rightness of one over the other, but because the historical moment was ripe. There is no quixotic desire to unravel the skein of history: Like the great auk or the woolly mammoth, the state evolved inevitably in the mid-17th century, flourished, and now decomposes about us, on its way to extinction. Like the condemned man in Kafka's terrible story,[4] the West had to suffer the idea of the state inscribed into its flesh over the course of four centuries. The painful lesson is now learned; we can return to Althusius and take his blueprint to resurrect a new model of government.[b]

There were exceptions to the metastasizing state during those four centuries. Most notable was the former United States of America[c] – "former," given its *de facto* rejection of the federalism and its constitutionally established

---

[b] Of course Althusius cannot be instituted whole cloth. For example, he gave inordinate authority to the Calvinist church (page 46) and he had no doctrine of inalienable rights (page 49) – referencing Alvarado, Ruben, *The Debate that Changed the West: Grotius versus Althusius* (Pantocrator Press paperback, October 11, 2018, ISBN 978-9076660516, 282 pages).

[c] Wherever I give "United States of America," or "United States," or "USA," or "U.S.," the reader should instead read "Unitary State of America," to distinguish the current state of affairs from what was formerly meant by the United States of America, a federation of sovereign states. And following the metonymy of the puckish late Anthony de Jasay, wherever I say 'he' or 'man', I really mean 'she' or 'woman'. [*Vide* his *Social Contract, Free Ride: A Study of the Public Goods Problem* (Clarendon Press, 1989, ISBN 978-0198244745, 256 pages), page 1 footnote.]

propositional creed, which both identified its exceptionalism before the War Between the States (1861-1865). As Luigi Marco Bassani noted:

Jacksonian America [...] existed without a modern state.[5, 6]

However, a "revolution within the form" took place with the adoption of the Fourteenth Amendment on July 9, 1868, overthrowing the constitutional foundation of federalism, and setting the nation on its statist course. Jeffersonian America, which had abolished all inland[d] Federal taxes and by 1833 had paid off the national debt, perished forever.[7] Thus began the slow extinguishing of that beacon of hope to the entire world, the ideal that ordinary people can govern themselves and can assure their own prosperity, without state interference. Even in its decadence the nation achieved much. Spectacularly it demonstrated the principle that private capital makes possible the very lives of the billions of people that now inhabit the globe. There is no denying that the former federal republic defeated one form of tyranny militarily in 1945, and another ideologically in 1989. Nor is there any denying the rightful patriotism of Texans who contributed to the American achievement. But finally, neither can anyone can deny that the United States of America of this moment is a nation fallen into a rank senescence, a nation that has irretrievably lost its way.

If the United States could be retrieved from statist decomposition, a war on the front of capitalism versus socialism or of individualism versus Marxism might be practicable. But understanding three astonishing apparent contradictions will expose the futility of such an endeavor: The undying appeal of socialism despite its complete refutation by economic science, the immediate, lockstep obedience to central government edicts by every level of government during the pandemic of 2020-2021, and the triumph of individualism *simultaneously* with that of the total state. These three will be unraveled below. Only with an understanding of the state, with its complete rejection, and with a re-founding of government in a receptive corner of the world is a new way forward possible – hence the necessary sweep of this project.

Despite the forthright defense of capitalism offered in this book, this defense has little to do with capitalism in economic terms, certainly nothing to do with the usual platitudes for its efficiency and incentives, and nothing to do with its manifestation in the state. The free economy is not a mechanical device that can support just any political system, any legal system, or any cultural

---

[d] Before the War Between the States, duties on imports were "nearly synonymous with federal taxes," constituting 90% or more of all revenues. [*Vide* Gordon, John Steele, "How a Nation Born Out of a Tax Revolt Has – and Especially Hasn't – Solved the Problems of Taxing Its Citizens," (*American Heritage* magazine, May/June 1996, Volume 47, Issue 3).]

"superstructure." In short, *capitalism is not an '-ism'*, meaning that it is not just a *wertfrei* economic model. It is an organic complex that dies when transplanted out of the soil from which it flourished. Indeed the popular and academic condemnation of capitalism is more often a condemnation, not of the economic system, but of this more fundamental organic complex. This same observation applies to written constitutions, which as the American experience demonstrates, can be easily perverted from their original meaning. As Wilhelm von Humboldt observed:

> Constitutions cannot be grafted upon men as sprigs upon trees.[8]

The peculiar predicament of this book is that it must advocate technical manipulations for the restoration of institutions that are rightly organic and not subject to transformative alteration or eradication. The organic essence of society implies a need for the recognition of each individual's worth, for free association and the free exchange of the products of his labor, for the protection of property that is the expression of his being, for the bonds of family, and for structures of authority to protect these essential institutions as well as those outside the definitions of positive law and constitutions. These organic institutions have roots far deeper than economics or political philosophy: They are the foundation of our very identities. The heart of our current social breakdown is the widespread belief that these institutions can and ought to be reshaped by technocratic tinkering or by the cavalier manipulations of political operatives.

The rubric to identify the project that I propose is called *architectonics* – the method that founds the *dominium sortiens*, the society of "property, with sortition." In the briefest terms, it is the society of absolute property rights, the absence of public goods, and the sovereignty of the people in community, exercising decision-making not through oligarchic elections but through democratic sortition, which incorporates selection of offices by random lot. Architectonics is reason exercised by the living, breathing, fallible individual in the context of the *ius symbiosis*, the symbiotic right of the community first described by Althusius, a community which is as essential to individual reason and to an individual's life as the air he breathes.

Political conservatives have responded to the assault upon these organic institutions by appealing to faith, by claiming that supernaturally given scriptures provide conclusive arguments for their defense. Certainly those institutions deriving from the *ius naturale*, the natural law "which nature teaches to all animals,"[9] were once rooted in the Christian tradition. But this argument from spiritual authority concedes science and reason to their enemies, and concedes that no strictly intellectual account can be given for the very foundation of society. This concession misunderstands the very purpose of faith, which is to promulgate truth, not to substitute for it. Faith may motivate and inspire a particular policy, but no argument from authority alone, whether supernatural or otherwise, can be accepted in its defense. Accordingly, while this book will have much to say about the supernatural foundations of society, it makes no arguments from faith; it rejects the implication that the organic foundations of society have no ultimate reasoned defense.

For those libertarians and anarchists who scoff that this book is itself a venture in centralized planning, that the post-statist future must instead "evolve" – "somehow" – without a plan, I have nothing but contempt. Such a charge stamps them as dupes of a state ministry of education that teaches that all "planning" must of course mean "centralized planning." Such a willful refusal to think ahead would make sloth a virtue.

Those who enjoy the current favor of the ruling class – the metastasizing special interest groups; the holders of quotas and set-asides; the gender-dysphoric carnival freaks dignified with state-fabricated rights; the state-worshiping academics pushing their mounds of scribblings like dung beetles; the statist ciphers huddled in think tanks like the denizens of a termite mound; the cash-bulimic suppliers of 37%[10] of the world's weapons of war; the lobbyists, accountants, and lawyers worming like dermestid beetles through the state's rotting flesh as constituted by its myriad fiats and pronunciamentos; the whole squirming, vibrating mass of parasites from ghettos to C-suites – will discover, when the ravening Leviathan state runs out of prey – that "the Revolution devours its own children."[e]

Several facts contest the inevitable charge that architectonics is utopian. It hardly belongs in the class of utopias when all instances of the class to date are based on public goods, which architectonics denies. Characteristic of the class also is a longing for a primordial pure world *in illo tempore*,[11] one of spiritual presence, superabundance, and merely recreational human effort. This is the longing for reabsorption[12] – the infantile retreat from adulthood into that carefree time when food magically appeared before the child, when he was petted and indulged, when there was play only, and no work – a world supposedly made possible by the abolition of capitalism and class distinctions,[13, 14] a fantasy which architectonics denies. And if the sweep and vision of a proposal is to constitute a disqualifying fault, then let us also condemn the destructive utopias of the Club of Rome,[15] Fridays for Future,[16] and Agenda 21[17] of the

---

[e] Jacques Mallet du Pan.

United Nations. Finally, one must ask how the current failed utopia is working for you – or as it has been observed for the supposition of a benign state:

[T]he idea of a limited government that stays limited is truly Utopian.[18]

It is typical to conclude prefatory remarks with an acknowledgement of those who have assisted with the work itself. I acknowledge no one. In view of the fact that nearly all institutions of higher learning have become creatures of the state,[19] academics whom I might have acknowledged, even those with tenure, might have seen their piddling sinecures threatened by association with this book. Every line is mine alone – someone with no degree whatsoever from any university, whose loftiest state imprimatur, unique in my entire family, is a high school diploma. Thus the reader will not find in me any argument from authority. I have abundantly referenced others who might be more informed on particular matters, but ultimately the reader must face the harrowing challenge of having to think for himself. With a view to rectifying in the next edition any shortcomings here, I welcome any literate, reasoned reply which might wish to gainsay anything written here in point of fact or logic. Good luck with that.

T.L. Hulsey
Guanajuato, Mexico
February, 2022

[1] "Peace Treaties of Westphalia (October 14/24, 1648)," *The German Historical Institute* (published December 22, 2020) <https://ghdi.ghi-dc.org/sub_document.cfm?document_id=3778> accessed February 1, 2022.

[2] Chapman, John, "Council of Ephesus," *The Catholic Encyclopedia*, Vol. 5., Robert Appleton Company (last edited December 19, 2021) <http://www.newadvent.org/cathen/05491a.htm> accessed February 1, 2022.

[3] Schuessler, Jennifer, "Francis Fukuyama Predicted the End of History. It's Back (Again)," *The New York Times* (published May 10, 2022) <https://www.nytimes.com/2022/05/10/arts/francis-fukuyama-history-liberalism.html> accessed August 18, 2022. One academic, Francis Fukuyama, vacuously proclaimed in a 1989 essay the "universalization of Western liberal democracy as the final form of human government." His state-exalting utterances got him hired at the State Department's Office of Policy Planning by Paul Wolfowitz, the acclaimed genius of the the Iraq War, who opined that "Iraq has no history of ethnic conflict" [*Congressional Record*, Volume 152, Number 88, July 10, 2006, pages H4941-H4947].

[4] Kafka, Franz, "In der Strafkolonie," (RECLAM, 2017 republication of 1919 original, ISBN 978-3159612652, 64 pages).

[5] Bassani, Luigi Marco, *Chaining Down Leviathan: The American Dream of Self-Government 1776-1865* (Abbeville Institute Press, March 28, 2021, ISBN 978-1733407519, 380 pages), page 47.

[6] Ibid., page 310: Citing Donald R. Stabile and Jeffrey A. Cantor, Bassani notes that Jacksonian America was also "a period of low government expenditures and debt reduction."

[7] Abbeville Inst, "The Disintegration of Lincolnian America by Donald Livingston," (*YouTube*, length 52:52, published April 12, 2018) <https://www.youtube.com/watch?v=oC5vlcjWzpk> accessed February 10, 2022.

[8] Raico, Ralph, "The Prussian Aristocrat Who Spoke Out for Liberty," *Mises Institute* (published September 6, 2021) <https://mises.org/wire/prussian-aristocrat-who-spoke-out-liberty> accessed February 3, 2022.

[9] Rommen, Heinrich A.; Hanley, Thomas R., translator, *The Natural Law: A Study in Legal and Social History and Philosophy* from the 1936 *Ewige Wiederkehr des Naturrechts* (Liberty Fund, March 24, 1998, ISBN 978-0865971608, 278 pages), page 25, quoting Roman jurist Ulpian (†223).

[10] "US remains top arms exporter and grows market share," *BBC News* (published March 15, 2021) <https://www.bbc.com/news/business-56397601> accessed February 3, 2022.

[11] Eliade, Mircea; Trask, Willard Ropes, translator, *The Sacred and the Profane: The Nature of Religion* (Harcourt Brace Jovanovich, October 23, 1987, ISBN 978-0156792011, 256 pages), page 94: "[T]o wish to reintegrate the *time of origin* is also to wish to return to the *presence of the gods*, to recover the *strong, fresh, pure world* that existed *in illo tempore*. It is at once thirst for the *sacred* and nostalgia for *being*." [emphasis in the original]

[12] Rothbard, Murray N., "Karl Marx as Religious Eschatologist," *Mises Institute* (published October 9, 2009) <https://mises.org/library/karl-marx-religious-eschatologist#reabsorption> accessed February 3, 2022.

[13] Engels, Friedrich; Burns, Emile, translator, *Anti-Dühring* (Progress Publishers, 1947 from 1878 original) <https://www.marxists.org/archive/marx/works/1877/anti-duhring/ch24.htm> accessed February 3, 2022. According to Engels, with the abolition of class distinctions, "[t]he struggle for individual existence disappears" and then will dawn "an existence not only fully sufficient materially [...] but an existence guaranteeing to all the free development and exercise of their physical and mental faculties".

[14] "March 25," *Fridays for Future* (last edited January 31, 2022) <https://fridaysforfuture.org/March25/> accessed February 3, 2022. According to Greta Thunberg's organization: "Climate struggle is class struggle, for years, the ruling class, primarily through corporations and governments from the Global North dominated by affluent, white, heterosexual cis-males, have

exercised their power, gained through colonialism, capitalism, patriarchy, white supremacy and exploitation, to destroy the earth".

[15] Korten, David C., "Ecological Civilization: From Emergency to Emergence," *The Club of Rome* (published November, 2021) <https://www.clubofrome.org/wp-content/uploads/2021/11/Korten_EcoCiv_11032021_Updated-cover-1.pdf> accessed November 22, 2021, PDF page 7: The Club of Rome offers a description the world's problems that is itself utopian: "[T]he social structures that define the imperial era continue to feature four primary social castes determined largely by birth". These are "The Excluded Caste [who subsist on] whatever scraps are discarded by members of the three superior castes"; "The Worker Caste [whose] labor is extracted and controlled by the ruling and retainer castes"; "The Retainer Caste [who are] well compensated for their loyal service in securing and legitimating elite rule while keeping the worker caste in line and the excluded caste in its place"; and "The Ruling Caste [of] ruling families [...] headed by the world's richest billionaires". And their solution on page 17: "Break up concentrations of corporate power, including private banks"; "Replace GDP as the primary measure of economic performance"; "Eliminate financial speculation"; "Organize bioregionally defined political jurisdictions around urban hubs with strong rural-urban links that seek to optimize regional environmental and labor self-reliance. Eliminate inefficient land use by converting suburbs to rural-urban use"; "Eliminate gas powered vehicles"; "Minimize air travel"; "Strengthen non-monetized relationships between people"; "Encourage responsible community-centric parenting and child development".

[16] Rourke, Alison, "Greta Thunberg responds to Asperger's critics: 'It's a superpower'" *The Guardian* (last edited September 2 2019) <https://www.theguardian.com/environment/2019/sep/02/greta-thunberg-responds-to-aspergers-critics-its-a-superpower> accessed November 22, 2021. It is perfectly fitting that this movement should be led by the Swedish teenager Greta Thunberg, a modern-day Joan of Arc, or a leader of a Children's Crusade, threatening a screaming, kicking, breath-holding tantrum unless an all-powerful mommy and daddy set the thermostat at a pleasant level for planet earth. Fitting too – and unsettling for its proximity to the non-rational – is Thunberg's sudden international popularity, otherwise curious but for its appeal to a mythic virgin purity rebuking the dirty and sinful world of adults; further, her affliction with Asperger's syndrome seems to be embraced not just by her, but by her followers as much like a shamanistic portal to transcendent truth.

[17] "United Nations Conference on Environment & Development Rio de Janerio [sic], Brazil, 3 to 14 June 1992: AGENDA 21," *United Nations Department of Economic and Social Affairs*, Sustainable Development <https://sustainabledevelopment.un.org/content/documents/Agenda21.pdf> accessed November 22, 2021. Although the UN Agenda 21 agrees with the Club of Rome that "[p]overty and environmental degradation are closely interrelated" [¶4.3] and that "[s]pecial attention should be paid to the demand for natural resources generated by unsustainable consumption and to the efficient use of those resources consistent with the goal of minimizing depletion and reducing pollution" [¶4.5] and that "[p]articular emphasis has to be placed on the introduction of public participatory techniques, including enhancement of the role of women, youth, indigenous people and local communities." [¶18.19] – all under the wise tutelage of "coherent international and national policies" [¶4.6], the approach is quite different. Throughout the UN document, "large enterprises and transnational corporations" are to be enlisted as allies, co-opted under the watchful eye of the UN bureaucracy. They are "encouraged" to "report annually on their environmental records, as well as on their use of energy and natural resources;" [¶30.9] (The bracketed ¶ references paragraphs marked within the document.)

[18] Friedman, David, *The Machinery of Freedom: Guide to a Radical Capitalism* (Createspace Independent Publishing Platform, third edition, February 28, 2015, ISBN 978-1507785607, 378 pages), page 143.

[19] Austin University was founded in November, 2021 by prestigious academics from many fields. Although it was created specifically as an alternative to the dogmatic politicized speech of the state-captured universities, within weeks of its founding these champions of free speech fled out of fear of ostracism and other retribution – to the glee of the even more cringing mainstream media: Robertson, Derek, "It's the University of Austin Against Everyone – Including Itself," *MSN* (published November 17, 2021) <https://www.msn.com/en-us/news/us/its-the-university-of-austin-against-everyone-%e2%80%94-including-itself/ar-AAQP4iL> accessed November 17, 2021.

The Historical Context

The federal Constitution

America is said to be the "propositional nation," united not by blood ties but by an abstract creed – which along with federalism is the key characteristic of its claim of historic exceptionalism. And just what is the "proposition"? It was once thought to be that of a mass democracy united by a constitution prescribing universal rights, with equality before the law.

History has demonstrated the failure of every part of that proposition. James Madison's institutional bulwark of federalism has failed to contain the leveling forces implicit in mass democracy; the American Constitution has become a "living document" that has long abandoned natural law to instead provide color to positive law driven by the politics of the moment; and the notion of universal rights has devolved into the very things it was meant to constrain, that is, tribalism and ethnicity, whereby new "minority rights" now are minted with every election cycle so that an ever-expanding government might extend its purview in protecting them. The abstract creed has proven to be not a set of universal, fixed ideals, but instead a pliable set of slogans re-cast each political season as ideological weapons.

As for the supposedly sacred tablet of the American creed, Alexander Hamilton declared the Constitution to be a "frail and worthless fabric",[1] and though he claimed that he nonetheless labored to support it, his own actions corroborate his original charge. For just two years after its formal adoption, the First Bank of the United States was established primarily by his efforts, in spite of no enumeration of that power in the Constitution, and in spite of the explicit rejection in the Constitutional debates of any Federal powers of incorporation.[2]

Abraham Lincoln presumed State nullification of Federal laws to be illegal, yet in spite of that presumption he readily applied its bureaucratic equivalent, nonacquiescence, in ignoring the Federal Supreme Court ruling that his suspension of the writ of habeas corpus violated the Constitution.[3]

Franklin Roosevelt defied two explicit provisions in the Constitution when he issued his Executive Order 6102 on April 5, 1933, confiscating private holdings of gold by fiat without Congressional approval,[4] and outlawing contracts stipulating specie payment. Yet the Constitution could not be more plain in Article I, Section 8, stating that "Congress [not the Executive] shall have Power... to coin Money, [and] regulate the Value thereof" and Section 10, "no state... shall make any Thing but gold and silver Coin a Tender in Payment of Debts." Worse still, a politicized Supreme Court later acceded to the theft.

The Biden administration followed a policy of nonacquiescence to ignore the Federal Fifth Circuit injunction against vaccine mandates by ludicrously claiming that its "vaccine requirement" was not a mandate, despite having all the characteristics of a mandate.5

On August 3, 2021, a Biden bureaucrat at the Center for Disease Control single-handedly suspended the property rights of landlords across America by extending a moratorium on rental evictions – a decree initiated by a Republican president and sustained by a Democrat president – in brazen nonacquiescence of a Supreme Court judgment explicitly forbidding that extension.6

In fiscal 2021, U.S. Customs and Border Protection made 1.66 million arrests – *arrests*, with no accounting for undetected entries – of migrants crossing the U.S.-Mexico border illegally, the highest annual number ever recorded.7 In spite of an August, 2021 Supreme Court ruling that the Biden administration must follow the Title 42 law, the "Remain in Mexico" policy of keeping border applicants outside the United States until processed,8 it defiantly mocked that order by returning only "several hundred a month," according to the Texas Attorney General9 – all the while the mainstream media falsely reported mass suffering in Mexico as a result of that law. Brazenly lying about its true immigration policy, the Biden administration released and transported large numbers of single adult male illegal immigrants into the United States interior during the night.10 And since most of those illegal immigrants had no identification to board an airplane, it ordered the Transportation Security Administration to accept *arrest warrants* as valid identification, in further violation of law.11 By October 1, 2022, the Biden CBP had "encountered" 5,369,923 illegals nationally.12 Its policy is the moral inversion of democracy, where the *government* elects the *voters*, instead of the other way around, choosing to give free entry to those most likely to support *its* interests.

Entire executive bureaucracies routinely ignore the putative supreme law of the land. The Social Security Administration's self-scripted Acquiescence Rulings set out a shameless by-your-leave on how the agency will or will not apply decisions of the United States Courts of Appeals.13 A similar fleer is compiled by the Internal Revenue Service in its publication of Actions on Decisions.14

Examples could be multiplied, but these span all of Constitutional history, span several political parties, and demonstrate violations so incontestably, that they succinctly demonstrate that Thomas Jefferson's "chains of the Constitution"15 are really nothing more than the "frail and worthless fabric" that Hamilton said they were.

The unitary Constitution

How great a bulwark of freedom is a constitution when a government can be overthrown and a radically different one instituted under its color? This is exactly what happened with the passage of the Fourteenth Amendment on July 9,

1868. The tortured legal reasoning and the outright illegality of its proposal and passage illustrate the frailty and pliability of the Constitution, and thus more generally, the uselessness of any guarantee of rights in written positive law.

The Constitution describes the amendment process in Article V. For Congress to propose an amendment, the approval of "two thirds of both Houses" is required. During the Fourteenth Amendment's proposal in 1866, the House voted 120 to 32, with 32 abstentions – but without the 11 States of the former Confederacy, which had been denied seats. Had their 61 Representatives been included (voting against), the total would have fallen short, with only 56 percent approving. That percentage would have been even less, had the questionable status of the newly admitted States of West Virginia and Nevada been removed. In the Senate the vote was 33 to 11, with 5 abstentions. Had 22 Southern Senators been included (voting against), there would have been a tie – again, less, had West Virginia and Nevada been removed. But the Senate had not 49 Northern members, but 50 – and thus 33 was a fraction short of the necessary two thirds. Newly elected John P. Stockton of New Jersey, a Northerner who opposed the amendment, had to be illegally expelled to gain the required fraction, although he had been officially seated when Congress convened on December 5, 1865.

Passage was even more illegal than the process of proposal. 19 of 25 Union States would constitute the three-fourths majority necessary to ratify the Fourteenth Amendment; 27 of 36, if the South were included. But with the admission of Nebraska on March 1, 1867, just days before the adjournment of the Thirty-ninth Congress, the required three-fourths needed for passage became 20 of 26 Union States; 28 of 37, if the South were included. Senator Charles Sumner of Massachusetts held that the very act of seceding destroyed a State; Senator Thaddeus Stevens of Pennsylvania held that the 11 southern States were conquered provinces with no political rights. Not only was their view contradicted by the principle of a 'complete, perpetual, and indissoluble' Union under which the War was fought; it was contradicted by their sending the proposal to all 11 of those supposedly non-existent States for ratification on June 16, 1866. The border States Kentucky, Delaware, and Maryland rejected it, despite being part of the Union; although a Democrat State, California also rejected it; in Tennessee, State House members refused to appear, forcing the legislature to approve without the necessary quorum. But fatally for the amendment, New Jersey, Ohio, and Oregon rescinded their approval. The only way for the Fourteenth Amendment to pass was for the Republican Congress to disallow the three rescissions. And, completely illegally, this is what Congress did.

The Reconstruction Act of March 2, 1867 declared that "no legal state governments" existed in the ten "rebel" States that had refused to ratify the Fourteenth Amendment, so it created five military districts as the provisional government. To regain admittance to the Union that they supposedly were never capable of leaving, the States had to do the following: Have primarily black males elect delegates for drawing up new State constitutions (the majority of white "rebels," and those who had given aid and comfort to them, could not vote[16]); have the constitutions locally ratified; have the ratified constitutions approved by Congress; have the new State governments ratify the Fourteenth Amendment; and have Congress approve the ending of military rule in each district.[17]

The Act directly violated the Supreme Court's *Ex parte Milligan* ruling that martial law could not constitutionally be imposed, in the absence of war or rebellion, in areas where the civilian courts were functioning. In further contradiction, Congress in 1865 had recognized those very States with "no legal state governments" in 1867 as legitimate for their ratification of the Thirteenth Amendment – which annihilated the then-familiar concept of State citizen-ship[18] in favor of exclusively national citizenship – although their constitutions had not changed.

Through the interpretation that the Fourteenth Amendment offers substantive due process (creating rights beyond those specifically described in the first eight Amendments, with applicability to every level of government), the Supreme Court would continually expand its power,[19] issuing probably its most nationally divisive decision in 1973 with *Roe v. Wade*,[20] which was decided on the "emanations and penumbras of the Fourteenth Amendment" as imagined by Justice William O. Douglas in his majority opinion in *Griswold v. Connecticut* (1965).[21] The ruling *Cooper v. Aaron* (1958)[22] would reassert judicial supremacy of Supreme Court over all States *in all matters*, not just in State-Federal questions but even in questions formerly adjudicated between the State and its citizens, citing *Marbury v. Madison* (1803) as precedent.

In institutionalizing the Fourteenth Amendment, the northern Union played fast and loose with the idea of sovereignty: Now, in the sense of juris-diction over its rebellious southern provinces; now again, in the sense of jurisdiction over a conquered southern nation. Actually, its assertion was with a much broader idea of sovereignty: Sovereignty without intermediation over each citizen, abstracted from at least a half dozen culturally separate[f] American nations.[23] The "revolution within the form" of 1868 was legitimized as a state function as the impartial defender of universal rights[g] – when in fact it insti-

---

[f] The number and distinctness of American nations will be discussed in the section on secession.

[g] Although the Constitutional protection of individual rights extends to non-citizens within its jurisdiction, Congress enacted the International Emergency Economic Powers Act of 1977 and the Magnitsky Act of 2016, giving the president power to strip such persons of their Fourth and Fifth Amendment rights by his mere declaration and punish them without trial – all on his assertion of their violation of human rights *outside* the United States. *Vide* Napolitano, Andrew P., "Sanctions on Russia Violate the Constitution," *Antiwar.com* (published March 18, 2022) <https://original .antiwar.com/andrew-p-napolitano/2022/03/17/sanctions-on-russia-violate-the-constitution/> accessed March 18, 2022.

tuted a multinational superstate with a completely politicized judiciary. After the Fourteenth Amendment, important national issues would be decided slowly and contentiously, through the *ex post* judicial fiat of nine appointees administering universal political prescriptions, instead of promptly and consensually, through the *ex ante* legislative discussion of elected representatives administering the will of constituent local nations.

For the "propositional nation" now with no creed of federalism with universal rights univocally specified as equality before the law, what shared value would unify it? Increasingly, it became the unanimity regarding race. The universally shared value that racism is a bad thing came to form the ersatz unifying proposition for all Americans. *Yet there is not one American political constituency advocating racism.*

Paradoxically, the very thing which increasingly forms its unifying proposition is the very thing for which radicals condemn the United States. Since no constituency can be found to overtly champion racism, a "structural" racism must be discovered so that an America united behind state power can stamp it out. And when it is not found, ever more frenzied attempts must be made to find it, for it *must* exist – for how else are our goals for social harmony so persistently thwarted? If racism is universally and sincerely denied, then of course it must be *systemic*, in some structure outside the individual conscience. – Or it must be because we have defined race too narrowly: We must broaden it to include minorities that share some grievance just as debilitating as racial discrimination. Ever more groups must be included; ever more theories must be hatched by the professors of ethnic studies; ever more ruthless fines and punishments must be meted out to eradicate this oh-so-elusive menace; public sacrifices must be performed by the media priests to keep this evil spirit at bay. The careless spoken word or social media comment must be exposed even at the cost of someone's livelihood and personal humiliation, despite his abject profession of allegiance to the one uncontested shared value among Americans. And clearly the blunt, unanswerable charge of offending this value can serve only to further inflame hatred and division, which multiplies even more charges of racism.

But in fact America is divided not by race. It is divided by its hegemony over the many distinct nations within its asserted sovereignty, with a juridicized final arbiter of disputes inflaming that division.

The unitary sovereign at war

As the final arbiter of all disputes, without sovereign intermediaries,[24] the state must be extralegal, or anarchic. Since this final arbiter must be in some sense outside, or above, the law in order to be final, the inescapable true state of social affairs is not *whether* there should be anarchy, but *who* is to enjoy it in his status as final arbiter.[25] Federalism attempted to resolve this dilemma through plural, countervailing sovereignties. The smaller local anarchies of the many State powers were to check the anarchic tendency of the larger national power, which was rightly more feared. The "guarantor" of this arrangement was to be the written Constitution of 1787, and its primary role was to be the unbiased Lockean umpire of equal property rights before its law. As suggested above, the Constitution proved to be no bulwark in this primary role.

But could the unitary state be justified in the performance of another of its roles, in the absolutely necessary service of defending the lives and property of its citizens from foreign aggressors?

Once unified after the Fourteenth Amendment's destruction of federalism, the United States turned the officers and soldiers who had won the War Between the States west, for the removal of the American aboriginals from its interior – not an action in defense of American lives or property, but an aggressive genocidal war. Despite their supposedly inferior civilization, these Indians perfectly understood the meaning of treaties and the necessity of honoring one's given word. The United States held a different standard, making treaties with the aforethought of breaking them. The Supreme Court ruled in *Lone Wolf v. Hitchcock* (1903) that Congress had the right to alter or even cancel any treaty with the American Indians.[26] The ruling provided another demonstration of the fiction of "separation of powers": All three branches of unitary government form a single self-interested power.

The first war of the unitary state was the 1898 Spanish-American War – not a war in defense of American lives or property,[h] but an unprovoked imperial war. When president William McKinley took office in 1897, he stated, "We want no wars of conquest; we must avoid the temptation of territorial aggression." However, after the war provocations already planned by Senator Henry Cabot Lodge and Assistant Secretary of the Navy Theodore Roosevelt, including support for insurrectionists opposed to Spanish-held Cuba, McKinley felt compelled to send the battleship USS *Maine* to Havana harbor, where it mysteriously blew up and sank on the night of February 15, 1898. In an effort to avoid war, Spain agreed to an armistice with the insurrectionists. On April 11, McKinley asked Congress for authority to send troops to assist the insurrectionists, styled as freedom fighters, omitting mention of Spain's concession of an armistice. When the request was granted, war was inevitable. After taking Cuba in three months, United States forces proceeded to take Puerto Rico as well. In a pre-arranged coordinated action in the Far East, on May 1, Commodore George Dewey defeated a Spanish naval squadron in Manila Bay. Before the year was out, Spain signed a treaty giving the Philippines, Guam, and Puerto Rico to the United States, with Cuba under its protectorate.[27]

---

[h] Business interests in Cuba, primarily in sugar cane, were not directly threatened, and the business community wanted to avoid the disruption of war.

When World War I began in Europe in 1914, the American people "devoutly wished to avoid war."[28] Recognizing this, president Woodrow Wilson "incessantly professed love of peace".[29] Despite this profession, he intervened militarily in the Dominican Republic, Haiti, Cuba, Panama, Honduras, and Mexico, even before his request for a declaration of war against Germany on April 2, 1917.[30] Congress once again demonstrated the fiction of a "separation of powers" as a check on the consolidated, unitary state. Before the formal declaration of war with Germany, it acquiesced with the National Defense Act, authorizing the executive branch to seize any factory that refused to build war materiel on government demand, at the government's offered price.[31] Once war was declared, it passed the Lever Act, putting the executive branch in charge of the production and distribution of all food and fuel in the United States.[32] In 1913, the banner year for Congressional enabling of state power, the Sixteenth Amendment introduced four years earlier was ratified, instituting direct Federal taxation of each citizen without the intermediation of State apportionment, thereby quintupling Federal tax receipts;[33] and Congress approved the Federal Reserve Act, which gave the central bank control nationally over credit and the value of money.

Despite being fought abroad, the Great War revolutionized life in the United States, putting the former republic on a permanent war footing, with all the attendant miseries of standing armies, direct taxation, state manipulation of money and credit, perpetual government debt, legions of bureaucrats, and state indoctrination, in this case led by George Creel[34] and his 75,000 state propagandists paid to inflame hysteria against the Germans.[35] As historian Ralph Raico stated:

> Civil liberties fared no better in this war to make the world safe for democracy. In fact, "democracy" was already beginning to mean what it means today — the right of a government legitimized by formal majoritarian processes to dispose at will of the lives, liberty, and property of its subjects. Wilson sounded the keynote for the ruthless suppression of anyone who interfered with his war effort: "Woe be to the man or group of men that seeks to stand in our way in this day of high resolution."[36]

In the cases that reached the Supreme Court the state prosecution of dissenters was upheld.[37] And after the war the United States was the only country to deny amnesty to political prisoners, notoriously, to Socialist leader Eugene Debs, who had been sentenced to ten years in prison for merely giving a speech in Canton, Ohio against the war.[38] The Court also upheld the Federal income tax with its *Brushaber v. Union Pacific Railroad* (1916) ruling,[39] and has consistently refused to hear challenges to the Federal Reserve Act on the legal merits.[40] — So much for the fiction of the "separate power" of a unitary state's judiciary.

The United States entered World War II through the "colossal duplicity"[41] of president Franklin D. Roosevelt. FDR positioned "neutrality patrols" in the Atlantic to signal German U-boat locations, hoping to provoke their attack, promised "the British monarch — before the war even began — of full U.S. support in any military conflict with Germany", and "fed the hysteria by claiming that he possessed a 'secret map' showing Nazi plans to conquer South and Central America, as well as secret documents proving that Hitler planned to supplant all existing religions with a Nazi Church."[42] Provoking Japan, he froze all their assets, effectively imposing an embargo on the oil shipments vital to the Japanese economy. Congress acquiesced to FDR's initiatives, voting to arm American merchant ships, which deprived them of any immunity as neutrals, voting to permit U.S. naval vessels to enter combat zones, and voting into law the Lend-Lease Act of March 1941, providing war materiel for Stalin, a dictator even more murderous than Hitler.[43]

At the Tehran Conference of November 1943, FDR gave Stalin the gift of a Crusader's sword and refused to hear proof of Stalin's mass murder of 22,000 Polish officers and officials in Katyn Forest in the spring of 1940. FDR and Churchill agreed to give the eastern half of Poland to Stalin after the war.[44] At the Yalta conference in early February, 1945, three months before the war ended, FDR and Churchill delivered all of Eastern Europe to Stalin[45] and, in Operation Keelhaul of 1946-1947, even implemented the forced repatriation of civilians who had fled from Stalin's terror, of whom some two to five million were murdered on their return.[46] FDR and his successor Truman, who would start the Korean War entirely on his own initiative, waged total war on civilians, against all the principles of morality and the rules of war. After the war the United States did not draw down its forces to peacetime levels, but instead kept a large standing army.[47] Raico quotes conservative philosopher Richard Weaver as being revolted by

> the spectacle of young boys fresh out of Kansas and Texas turning nonmilitary Dresden into a holocaust ... pulverizing ancient shrines like Monte Cassino and Nuremberg, and bringing atomic annihilation to Hiroshima and Nagasaki.[48]

As with the First World War, the aftermath of the Second inflicted a social cost on the militarily unscathed American homeland. The Cold War (1945-1989) established the largely off-budget and unaccountable Central Intelligence Agency in 1947 more as an inept provocateur than a sentinel of American interests abroad, as witness its lack of "intelligence" prior to the fall of the Shah of Iran in January, 1978, its ignorance of the impending fall of the Soviet Union in 1989, and its clownish attempts at assassination and enemy mind control.[49] The unitary state and its intellectuals nonetheless demanded that the individual citizen recognize its competence in defending him against shadowy dangers from abroad. Even the Conservative pundit and former CIA operative William F. Buckley opined that given the

> thus-far invincible aggressiveness of the Soviet Union...we have got to accept Big Government for the duration.[50]

President Lyndon Baines Johnson concocted a supposed provocation halfway around the globe to begin the war in Vietnam in earnest. Congress approved the Gulf of Tonkin Resolution on August 7, 1964, giving the president total power "to take all necessary measures to repel any armed attack against the forces of the United States."[51]

Despite popular objections to the Gulf of Tonkin Resolution's sweeping mandate, Congress replaced it with a War Powers Act of 1973 that cited that resolution and simply codified the president's power to go to war without a Congressional declaration.[52] The Act allowed president Clinton to launch a 78-day bombing campaign in 1999 in Kosovo under NATO auspices, supposedly to prevent atrocities against Muslims by Serb leader Slobodan Milošević. But the bombing of Serbian factories, city bridges, and even the main television building in downtown Belgrade, along with anti-personnel bombing of marketplaces, hospitals, and other civilian areas, amounted to a terror campaign. Ironically, the result was an ethnic cleansing of Kosovo of non-Muslims by the Kosovo Liberation Army (KLA), whose leader Hashim Thaci – celebrated as a "freedom fighter" by Clinton – would be charged with ten counts of war crimes and crimes against humanity by an international tribunal in The Hague in 2020.[53] In 2011, president Barack Hussein Obama would cite the War Powers Act of 1973 to authorize the bombing and regime change in Libya, again under NATO auspices, despite the explicit denial of his authority to do so by Congress.[54]

True to form for presidents hectoring reluctant Americans into war, president George W. Bush campaigned in 2000 on his rejection of "nation building," then after his election in the following year discarded the pledge to begin a 20-year failed campaign of nation building in Afghanistan,[55] sustained by brazen and repeated official lying about the campaign's success.[56] His statutory foundation for waging the Afghanistan War came from the Authorization for Use of Military Force Resolution (AUMF) given to him by Congress one week after the September 11, 2001 attack on the World Trade Centers and the Pentagon. The AUMF echoed the War Powers Act of 1973, but with even broader, less defined constraints:

> [T]he President is authorized to use all necessary and appropriate force against those nations, organizations, or persons he determines planned, authorized, committed, or aided the terrorist attacks that occurred on September 11, 2001, or harbored such organizations or

persons, in order to prevent any future acts of international terrorism against the United States by such nations, organizations or persons.[57]

Two years later, Bush invaded Iraq, after having his functionary claim before Congress that its tyrant Saddam Hussein sponsored the al-Qaeda terrorists in Afghanistan,[58] that he was obtaining uranium from Niger for an atomic weapon,[59] that he possessed "weapons of mass destruction,"[60] that American cities faced a "mushroom cloud"[61] of annihilation under those weapons – every assertion of which was false. The obvious and direct way to cripple the terrorists, who despite producing nothing in trade managed to conduct expensive operations and field well-equipped armies, should have been to dry up their financial support. Saudi Arabia has long been an enthusiastic financial supporter[62, 63] of Wahhabism, an extreme form of Islam that considers all unbelievers worthy of death.[64] Osama bin Laden and all but four of the 19 hijackers in the September 11, 2001 attack were from Saudi Arabia, and all received its financial support.[65] Yet instead of working to curb that support, the United States did exactly the opposite: It embraced Saudi Arabia as an "important ally"[66] and important market for its military-industrial complex,[67] and even enlisted it to spy on American citizens.[68]

How could it be otherwise? Following president Nixon's abandonment of the world interbank gold standard on August 15, 1971, and the resulting fall of the dollar, Saudi Arabia agreed to require payment in dollars for its oil, the lifeblood commodity of the industrialized West. Should Saudi Arabia at any time require payment in Euros, Yuan, or some other currency instead, the status of the U.S. dollar as replacement of gold for the world's exchange standard would end, its wanton money printing would stop, and its economy would be crushed.[69] The unitary state had embraced, and continues to embrace, an absolutist monarchy that sponsors both a hostile form of its state religion[70] and international terrorism.

And, once again, the wars conducted with unrelenting devastation[71] abroad, supposedly for the defense of the life and property of citizens of the United States, nevertheless had devastating consequences domestically. In the war hysteria following the September 11, 2001 terrorist attack, the unitary state and its intellectuals demanded even more state power, with putative conservative Newt Gingrich even demanding a curtailment of the First Amendment.[72] Using president Wilson's sweeping Espionage Act of 1917, Bush's successor, Barack Hussein Obama, would silence dissenters by prosecuting "whistleblowers who leaked to journalists [...] more than all previous administrations combined."[73] As Edward Snowden's documentation of the National Security Agency's pervasive and illegal domestic spying proved when released on June 6, 2013 by journalist Glenn Greenwald, the United States had effectively become a police state, anarchic and absolute.[74]

The extralegal state as dispenser of rights as statutory privileges

The state thus assumed several contradictory roles: Warrior of national security, unbiased Lockean umpire of equal property rights, biased agent of civil rights. How was it to allocate public goods to effect these very different tasks?

In the last half-century in America, the Democrat Party, less out of conscious direction and more out of a blind momentum accelerating in the 1960s, stopped being the "defender of the little guy" – the modest citizen who strove to join the American Melting Pot, the figurative icon of the "propositional nation," as a self-sufficient worker – and instead based its electoral support on tribes of government dependents. It grew not as its members attained economic independence, as in the past, but as its tribes expanded in variety and size with government largesse. Under the slogan of "social justice," the ersatz "rights" of groups supplanted authentic individual rights.

The traditional American suspicion of the state as a threat to the self-sufficient individual began its final collapse in the 1960s with a state-directed three-front war: A domestic war on racial injustice, a domestic "War on Poverty,"[i] and a foreign war on communism. For the Left, apparently not even Randolph Bourne's observation that "war is the health of the state" was subject to strict interpretation: Any warlike mobilization of state power was proper and benign. The televised glamor of the Kennedy administration – a regal Camelot served by courtiers from "the best and the brightest" of Northeastern academia – provided a spectacular paradigm for the beneficent state.

The domestic war on racial injustice begun with the Civil Rights Act of 1964 did not dismantle biases institutionalized by the States (e.g., the infamous "Jim Crow" laws), but instead *undermined all local cultural norms*, whether or not canonized in law, by institutionalizing a remote, centralized power with its own biases (e.g., forced integration, affirmative action) as the final arbiter without appeal.

The foremost bias of the state became equality – an unattainable goal that would require constant and growing state intervention in the illusion of approaching it. Beyond its designation as "equality before the law," where the laws are applied equally and without favor, "equality" becomes an ambiguous notion. Should private schools be abolished in its name? Should estates be confiscated without passing to designated heirs? Should prisons be emptied of minorities beyond their percentage makeup in the community? And if some sense of "equality" is temporarily achieved at 5:00 pm, should there be a readjustment to restore it at 5:30 pm? And more: Since inequality surely stems from mental attitudes that enforce it, should there not be a policing of thought

---

[i] Inaugurated with the Economic Opportunity Act of 1964.

processes? In view of these unanswerable impracticalities, the only course was to police *equal results* – and since that too is an impossibility for individuals not inhabiting an anthill, it meant the policing of *equal results for groups*, which were statistically measurable. In other words, the state enforcement of "equality" could only mean inevitable affirmative action, quotas, race-normed employment tests, forced busing, and court-mandated "majority-minority districts" (where a single "community of color" comprises the majority) and "coalition districts" (where "communities of color" collectively comprise the majority).

These were the problems foreseen by Senator Barry Goldwater,[j] as he stated in his opposition to the Civil Rights Act on the floor of the Senate on June 18, 1964:

> I am unalterably opposed to discrimination of any sort, and I believe that though the problem is fundamentally one of the heart, some law can help — but not law that embodies features like these, provisions which fly in the face of the Constitution and which require for their effective execution the creation of a police state. [...] My concern extends beyond any single group in our society. My concern is for the entire nation, for the freedom of all who live in it and for all who were born in it.[75]

The "War on Poverty" did not create a class of self-sufficient workers among the blacks who were a prime target of its ministrations; instead, its aid to families emasculated the black man as the family provider,[76, 77] who was in fact leading his race out of poverty without state-directed aid during the 1950s.[78] Despite conceding gains made by middle-class blacks, Democrat policymakers insisted that equal opportunity was not enough, that *equality of result* must be guaranteed by the state for the black underclass. The Moynihan Report on black poverty, published in March, 1965, stated this explicitly as a state policy:

> [T]he programs that have been enacted in the first phase of the [postwar] Negro revolution [...] only make opportunities available. They cannot insure the outcome. The principal challenge of the next phase of the Negro revolution is to *make certain that **equality of results** will now follow*. If we do not, there will be no social peace in the United States for generations.[79] [emphasis added]

---

[j] Senator Goldwater could scarcely be called a racist. He integrated the staff of his family's department store in Phoenix, as well as the units under his command as an officer in the Air Force Reserve; he voted for two less intrusive civil rights laws during the Eisenhower administration; he opposed segregation in the Phoenix public schools while on the Phoenix city council; and he was a member of the NAACP. *Vide* Crispin, page 81.

The war on communism, with its duplicitous inauguration in the Gulf of Tonkin, its political assassinations, and its devastation of the local populace under its supposedly beneficent aegis, demonstrated that the cure offered by the unitary Leviathan state was far worse than the disease of communism itself. The war killed about 2 million Vietnamese civilians, 1.1 million North Vietnamese troops, 200,000 South Vietnamese troops, and some 58,000 Americans. Between 1965 and 1973, the United States dropped 8 million tons of bombs on the country; in 1969 alone, over 2.5 million acres of forest were destroyed using Agent Orange.[80]

The next Democrat president, Jimmy Carter, declared a state-directed "Moral Equivalent of War" on a national energy crisis that was actually the self-inflicted result of the declaration of a fiat dollar on August 15, 1971.[81] President Carter's "MEOW" became a lap pet to the OPEC[k] oil cartel of Gulf State oil despots, letting slip the opportunity to establish nuclear power as the basis of carbon-free energy independence.

All of these "wars" – the paradigm for statist command given to a faceless army – were worse than failures, exacerbating the very problems they intended to ameliorate.

At the Democrat Party's fatal turning in 1980, Ronald Reagan became president by convincing a majority of "little guys" that the party of their grandfathers had abandoned them. Democrats would come to corroborate his victory by re-casting the upwardly mobile segment of "little guys" as "deplorables"[82] deluded by bigoted populist politicians. Worse still, they redefined the remaining segment in ethnic terms, so that their status as a permanent underclass was propagandized as due to "systemic racism" and even "whiteness"[83] – an epithet somehow designated by statist intellectuals as not racist – instead of due to the destructive disincentives of government. This class- and race-based redefinition produced an explosive polarity that could only encourage violent destruction of the "systemic" oppressors,[84] instead of encouraging the resolution of class differences through economic policies without reference to race, gender, or ideology. At no point after 1980 was there a critical introspection among Democrat leaders to return to the roots of their former appeal, but instead a resolute march away, with dependent tribes of rootless *clientes* led by their *patroni* of world government Davos Men.[85]

While extravagant, the promises made to Democrat political tribes before votes were cast in 2020 dwindle in comparison to the party's Green New Deal announced after winning the election. Not only does the Green New Deal guarantee a "family-sustaining wage, family and medical leave, vacations, and a pension," and "safe, affordable, adequate housing," and "healthy food" to all

---

[k] Organization of Petroleum Exporting Countries.

Americans, but also "economic security" for all who are "unable or unwilling" to work, among other even more costly transformations.[86, 87] Since even a Soviet-style liquidation of the vilified upper class could not possibly finance this theft, the state has no alternative but to crush the middle class with the burden of paying for it, while at the same time enfeebling its productive ranks with similar seductions to a parasitic dependency, that is, with expanding retirement and medical benefits, disability payments, mortgage subsidies, unemployment supplements, debt cancellations, and other fictitiously "free" handouts.

The root of this malignant redirection of the Democrat Party toward group "rights" founded on statute should be obvious. Being of the Left, its most fundamental principle is that state power can be unleashed for beneficial, indeed transformative, social purposes.

The absolute state without intermediaries

The state must inevitably trend toward socialist absolutism as surely as a stone falling under the influence of gravity.

In its purely economic aspect, capitalism accounts for the market – the free interchange of factors of production so that prices may be set, whose function is to permit calculation of how scarce goods may be allocated. Calculation outside the market, whether it be a panel of socialist economic commissars or a single human mind — even if it had godlike knowledge of the countless available factors of production — would be utterly incapable of determining the optimal pattern of resource allocation.[88] Socialist economies must borrow pricing information from extant markets. Eradication of those markets would mean global mass starvation, and subsistence for the survivors.

Despite the economic demonstration of the necessity for markets by Ludwig von Mises in 1920, *the state must persist in rejecting that truth*, no matter what the misery inflicted on its subjects. It must do so because the existence of any intermediary challenges the sovereignty of the state as the final arbiter of all social disputes. This fact explains why "capitalism isn't an '-ism'": Because beyond its mechanics as an economic system, the market is the most powerful intermediary between the state and its individual subjects. It is an organic intermediary that, unlike the intermediaries of States or churches or associations, *cannot be eradicated*. The market, with its basis in private property,[1] constitutes the "anomaly" of a second center of power against the unitary state, as Anthony de Jasay explained:

> [State capitalism] ends the anomaly of armed force being centered in the state, while the ownership of capital is dispersed throughout the

---

[1] Strictly speaking, the term "private property" is a pleonasm for "property": There is no need for it as a distinction from "public property," since state expropriations through taxation are properly signified as "public goods."

civil society.[89]

The powerful tendency of the state is to fuse political and economic power

> so that the subject's whole existence shall be ruled by *one and the same command-obedience relation, with no separate public and private spheres, no divided loyalties, no countervailing centres of power, no sanctuaries and nowhere to go.*[90] [emphasis in the original]

Yet why "state capitalism" – whose purely nominal property rights in fact identifies it as fascism – instead of outright dictatorship? Because with advertised total power comes total responsibility and, with failure, total blame. The subterfuge of a sham capitalism *must* exist as a scapegoat for the inevitable failures of the state. Thus a four-year high for gasoline prices in 2022 is not caused by administrative hostility to fossil fuels[91] – no, capitalist "gouging" must be responsible; thus a 40-year high of inflation in 2022 is not caused by the state central bank creating $1.9 trillion out of thin air and giving it to individuals in March, 2020[92] – no, capitalist "greed" must be responsible. The compliant legions of "intellectuals" in the media and academe make sure that the "proper" blame is assessed in favor of the state.

Since the French Revolution these legions of "second-hand dealers in ideas,"[93] these "bourgeois ideologists,"[94] have become absolutely indispensable to state power. With the birth of mass democracy in 1789 in France, the state no longer held power by the phylacteries of church, no longer by the regalia of heredity – and certainly no longer by the force of arms. As the collapse of the Soviet Union demonstrated beginning with the fall of the Berlin Wall on November 9, 1989, a state cannot exist without the consent of some significant part of its subjects, no matter how powerful the state, no matter how numerous its tanks, guns, armies, and police. As Étienne de la Boétie[95] observed in the 16th century, the masses can easily throw off their outnumbered masters if only they awaken to the possibility. The state is certainly aware of this possibility – neurotically so, since it must incessantly blare forth propaganda affirming the "power of the people," all the while trembling in fear that someday a will-o'-the-wisp electorate, aroused by one of the revolutionary democratic credos that ground its power, might awaken and sweep it into oblivion.

And most certainly the intellectuals are aware of the possibility of some spontaneous awakening of the state's subject masses. With its drive to remove all intermediating institutions, the state had razed to the ground the former bedrock of church and monarchy upon which its claims of legitimacy stood. Nothing would provide it now, save for the intellectuals cultivated for that purpose by the state. Legitimacy is the golden article of trade of the intellectuals, the ichor and ambrosia of the godlike state that only they can provide.

In two recent mass protests the "intellectuals" – meaning the media fourth estate, of which there were four times as many Democrats as Republicans[96] – overwhelmingly supported the state, despite the legitimate grievances of the protesters and their legitimate right to peacefully protest.

At least 10,000[97] protesters and rioters stormed the capitol building in Washington, DC on January 6, 2021. Several of them did illegally possess firearms, but the fact is that the only weapon brandished and discharged was used by a state officer in the sole fatality of that day: The needless killing of rioter Ashli Babbitt.[98] Almost universally the media labeled the incident an "insurrection," despite the fact that many policemen invited the entry of the protesters into the capitol and supervised their presence there.[99]

In February, 2022, in Ottawa, the capital of Canada, a mass protest by Canadian truckers over vaccine mandates and other state restrictions garnered over $18.7 million (USD)[100] in popular support – $10 million through the crowdfunding site GoFundMe, then, after the site confiscated the money under state pressure, $8.7 million through another crowdfunding site, GiveSendGo – mostly in small donations. Despite the protest being peaceful, and despite his never addressing the protesters' concerns, the prime minister of a minority government invoked the Emergencies Act, which had never been used since becoming law in 1988, replacing the War Measures Act of World War I.[101] Although the law permits invocation for a catastrophe that "seriously endangers the lives, health or safety of Canadians" or "seriously threatens the ability of the Government of Canada to preserve [its] sovereignty," under its color the prime minister threatened fines, imprisonment, confiscation of trucker rigs, and the freezing of bank accounts.[102] In spite of the disproportionate state response, media in both Canada and the United States enthusiastically supported the Act,[103] and on February 21, Canada's parliament voted 185 to 151[104] to approve its extension.[105]

Within the state, during the COVID epidemic of 2020-2021, functionaries at every level of government, from the Federal level to local school boards, obeyed in military lockstep despite almost weekly contradictions in guidance from the state Center for Disease Control.[106] Particularly astonishing was the universal obedience of local school districts – each of them everywhere styled "*independent* school district" – to not only COVID mandates[107] but to Federal guidance on attitudinal instruction regarding race and gender[108] – areas formerly under the control of local school boards and parents.

The burgeoning growth in the number of functionaries at the Federal level – which now comprises some six percent of all employment – has been concealed in recent years by contract hiring. But once the functionary is hired, the advantages of a state sinecure would tend to encourage his obedience:

[Federal workers] receive pay that is 17 percent higher on average than private sector employees who perform comparable work, even though they work 12 percent fewer hours on average. Meanwhile, federal workers face a 0.2 percent chance of getting fired in any given year. That is more than 45 times lower than their private sector counterparts.[109]

Non-Federal public sector growth has been explosive in sectors critical to a "long march through the institutions,"[110] especially the schools. As Benjamin Scafidi observed:

> Nationwide since 1950, the number of public school administrative and non-teaching positions has soared 702 percent while the student population increased just 96 percent.[111]

Furthermore, these proliferating functionaries are heavily unionized, collective bargaining for them being illegal in only seven States.[112] Unsurprisingly, they have long been deeply connected to the Democrat Party and active in promoting Leftist ideology.[113]

Why this revolution giving state control over the mental formation of children? – And why the remarkable ignorance of parents about state indoctrination? *Because the public sector, especially in education, has become a Federal sanctuary for those groups favored by the state*, whose well-being derives from state patronage – groups whose status may not be questioned by the parents. The Parent Teacher Association is a quaint anachronism that has become "a support group for teachers and teacher unions"[114] hostile to any policy that might empower parents, such as vouchers to rebate public school taxes for private schooling. State monopolies of teacher certification assure the hiring of applicants more accomplished in state obedience than mastery of any subject,[115] and functionaries once hired seldom lose their certification, even for moral turpitude.[116] *The parents themselves have been removed as intermediaries standing between state power and their own children.*

This lockstep obedience to government edicts is one symptom in what is the most alarming, yet inevitable, development of state power: The union between the drive to totalitarianism, through the removal of all intermediating institutions, and the perennial temptation to nihilism that is inherent in the human condition. Just as we have defined capitalism in its broader, more organic sense, so the Russian mathematician Igor Shafarevich has done for socialism:

> [Socialist] Marxism is based on the same psychological foundation as nihilism – a burning hatred for surrounding life that can be vented only through complete annihilation of that life. [...] Marxism accomplished a transformation of the elemental, destructive emotions that ruled

[Mikhail] Bakunin and [Sergey] Nechayev into a structure that seemed incomparably more objective and hence convincing.[117]

In the sense used by Shafarevich, socialism is not another economic '-ism' from the 19th century. It is not an evolution from capitalism, not a development from the proletariat, and not a scientific theory.[118] It is a "doctrine and an appeal based on it, a program for changing life"[119] evident in all human history with the following program:

1. The abolition of private property
2. The abolition of the family
3. The abolition of religion
4. The abolition of individuality through radical equality.[120]

Of the last principle, he says that it "frequently gives rise to hostility toward culture as a factor contributing to spiritual and intellectual inequality and, as a result, leads to a call for the destruction of culture itself."[121] This aspect of socialism is what the economist Ludwig von Mises meant by what he termed the pathological "Fourier Complex":

> Socialist authors promise not only wealth for all, but also happiness in love for everybody, the full physical and spiritual development of each individual, the unfolding of great artistic and scientific talents in all men, etc. [...–] the kingdom of perfection, populated by completely happy supermen. All socialist literature is full of such nonsense.[122]

This same aspect of socialism is what the economist Murray Rothbard termed "reabsorption theology," which he detailed in his own account of the chiliastic writings:

> As far as I know, there is no commonly-agreed-upon name to designate this fatefully influential religion. One name is 'process theology,' but I shall rather call it 'reabsorption theology,' for the word 'reabsorption' highlights the allegedly inevitable end point of human history as well as its supposed starting point in a precreation union with God.[123]

Remarkably, although he did not know Rothbard, Shafarevich uses the same term, taken from his quotation from *Eros and Civilization* by Leftist Herbert Marcuse:

> Narcissus and Orpheus [...] symbolize 'the redemption of pleasure, the halt of time, the absorption of death; silence, sleep, night, paradise – the Nirvana principle not as death but as life.'[124]

This "absorption" that resolves the socialist's metaphysical alienation is inseparably a part of all four basic principles enumerated by Shafarevich, but especially the fourth:

The usual understanding of 'equality,' when applied to people, entails equality of rights and sometimes equality of opportunity (social welfare, pensions, grants, etc.). [... But t]he equality proclaimed in socialist ideology means identity of individualities. The hierarchy against which the doctrine fights is a hierarchy based on individual qualities – origin, wealth, education, talent and authority.[125]

Now we see why an otherwise silly current event became a pitched battle: Whether a person only outwardly indistinguishable by one gender should use a public restroom for that gender. Framed in this way, most people could care less. After all, if indistinguishable, what difference does it make? But the issue was not framed in this way. The central government reinterpreted the Title IX section of the Education Amendments of 1972[126] so that gender is not a condition fixed by nature, but a completely malleable and plastic definition, determined solely by what a person claims it to be on any given day, and enforced by the state.

The issue was not the vast sweep of the law (made more threatening by a presidential directive[127]), which applies to any educational institution receiving Federal money – in effect, every public school at every level. *The issue was not* the validity of gender claims, which most schools tried to accommodate.[128] *The issue was not* about tolerance. As demonstrated by the fury of state functionaries over the North Carolina bill that would have allowed gender-indifferent single-occupancy restrooms and private property exemption from the law,[129] they wanted to revolutionize the thoughts and behavior of the majority who find these lifestyles distasteful and immoral as a role model for children, and they are eager to compel this revolution in thought and behavior by law and police power. They want not accommodation, but a revolution in centuries-old belief and behavior, smearing dissenters as "prejudiced" and "racist." Their rejection of the North Carolina law demonstrates the revolutionary socialist agenda of the Federal unitary state, leveraging the "rights" that it has bestowed upon a group, the LGBTQIA-MOGAI[130] community, and will not rest until Christianity and other long-recognized standards of civility concede not toleration, but approval.

The issue is that compliance with the Federal law makes every public school in the land an indoctrination center for reinterpreting what lies at the core of a person's individual identity – his sexual identity – pulverizing it, and plasticizing it and the family values designed to protect it. *The individual's natural identity has been removed as an intermediary standing between state power and his very being.*[131]

How is it possible that individuality, the apotheosis of the Western tradition, could be so perverted as to destroy it? How is it possible that the Constitution of the United States that enshrined the Bill of Rights against state power could within so short a time become the very tool of individual oppression by the state? The fork taken at the fateful crossroad in the 17th century effected this ultimate result. It was the intellectual answer given to the political question that the West had grappled with since its beginning. As sociologist Robert Nisbet explained:

> The problem for Plato, as was to be the problem for Rousseau two thousand years later, was that of discovering the conditions within which the absolute freedom of the individual could be combined with the absolute justice of the [s]tate.[132]

The entire project of the West was to free the individual, to provide his autonomy, by entrusting the state with ultimately unlimited power to effect that independence. In so doing it deracinated him from the institutions that gave him his identity, leaving him alienated, an atom in the lonely crowd,[133] bowling alone.[134] The project began before the 17th century, with the undermining of the protection in natural law ambivalently offered by the Church. Nisbet quotes from R.H. Tawney's 1926 *Religion and the Rise of Capitalism*, pointing out that the Protestant Reformation, carried

> to its logical result, [...] made not only good works, but sacraments and the Church itself unnecessary.[135]

Thus *the idea of individual versus the state is a false antithesis*.[136] Tragically, with this trust in a beneficent state, the investiture of power produced a godlike creation that now presumes power over creation itself, banishing traffic deaths[137] and cancer[138] by its omnipotent fiat. After entrusting the all-powerful state with the protection of his individual rights we see that the state has devoured the very core of the citizen's identity, his gender, now stridently proclaiming to protect anything – absolutely anything, no matter how freakish, no matter how destructive to the children living under its ukase – so long as it is rooted solely in the state and not in the natural order.

❦

We have now resolved the three astonishing apparent contradictions set out above, to better justify the organic approach of architectonics. Recall that they were: The undying appeal of socialism despite its complete refutation by economic science, the immediate, lockstep obedience to central government edicts by every level of government during the pandemic of 2020-2021, and the triumph of individualism *simultaneously* with that of the total state.

We have progressively peeled back the layered pathologies of the state in the American historical context. With the particulars of this American autopsy in mind, scalpel still in hand, we are ready now to examine the state's abstract essentials.

1 "From Alexander Hamilton to Gouverneur Morris, [29 February 1802]," *National Archives Founders Online* (last edited October 11, 2021) <https://founders.archives.gov/documents/Hamilton/01-25-02-0297> accessed February 7, 2022.

2 Max Farrand, editor, "The Records of the Federal Convention of 1787, vol. 2, section 616," *Liberty Fund* republication of 1911 original (last edited January 24, 2022) <https://oll.libertyfund.org/title/farrand-the-records-of-the-federal-convention-of-1787-vol-2> accessed February 7, 2022.

3 Bomboy, Scott, "Lincoln and Taney's great writ showdown," *National Constitution Center, Constitution Daily* (published May 28, 2021) <https://constitutioncenter.org/blog/lincoln-and-taneys-great-writ-showdown> accessed February 7, 2022.

4 Ash, Adrian, "Governments Still Heavy-Handed 80 Years After FDR's Gold Confiscation," *Forbes* magazine, *Great Speculations* (published April 5, 2013) <https://www.forbes.com/sites/greatspeculations/2013/04/05/governments-still-heavy-handed-80-years-after-fdrs-gold-confiscation/?sh=499439fa16a6> accessed February 7, 2022.

5 Nelson, Steven, "White House says calling vaccine mandate a 'mandate' is 'misinformation'," *New York Post* (published November 5, 2021) <https://nypost.com/2021/11/05/white-house-calling-vaccine-policy-mandate-is-misinformation/> accessed November 8, 2021.

6 "Opinion: The CDC's eviction moratorium is almost certainly illegal," *The Washington Post* (published August 4, 2021) <https://www.washingtonpost.com/opinions/2021/08/04/cdcs-eviction-mortarium-is-almost-certainly-illegal/> accessed February 7, 2022.

7 Hackman, Michelle, "Border Patrol Makes About 1.66 Million Arrests at Southern Border in 2021 Fiscal Year: Number marks highest annual arrest total ever recorded" *The Wall Street Journal* (edited October 22, 2021) <https://www.wsj.com/articles/border-patrol-makes-about-1-66-million-arrests-at-southern-border-in-2021-fiscal-year-11634932866> accessed February 6, 2022.

8 Hansen, Claire, "Supreme Court Rules Biden Administration Must Comply with Order to Restart Trump-Era 'Remain in Mexico' Policy," *U.S. News & World Report* (published August 24, 2021) <https://www.usnews.com/news/national-news/articles/2021-08-24/supreme-court-rules-biden-administration-must-comply-with-order-to-restart-trump-era-remain-in-mexico-policy> accessed February 6, 2022.

9 Smith, Jillian, "Texas AG says Biden administration is 'making a mockery' of federal law, courts," *The National Desk* (published January 25, 2022) <https://thenationaldesk.com/news/americas-news-now/texas-ag-says-biden-administration-is-making-a-mockery-of-federal-law-courts> accessed February 6, 2022.

10 Melugin, Bill, "Fox News footage shows mass release of single adult migrants into US: More than 178,840 migrants were encountered in December," *Fox News* (published January 25, 2022) <https://www.foxnews.com/politics/texas-footage-single-adult-migrants-released-us> accessed February 6, 2022.

11 Shaw, Adam, "TSA confirms it lets illegal immigrants use arrest warrants as ID in airports," *Fox News* (published January 21, 2022) <https://www.foxnews.com/politics/tsa-confirms-allows-illegal-immigrants-arrest-warrants-id-airports> accessed February 6, 2022.

12 "Nationwide Encounters," *U.S. Customs and Border Protection* (last edited October 19, 2022) <https://www.cbp.gov/sites/default/files/assets/documents/2022-Oct/nationwide-encounters-fy20-fy22.csv> accessed October 28, 2022. The Customs and Border Protection (CPB) "encounters" comprise "apprehensions, expulsions, and inadmissibles." This national total of 5,369,923 for the first two Biden fiscal years is greater than the population of Ireland.

13 "Social Security and Acquiescence Rulings," *Social Security Administration* (last edited January 19, 2022) <https://www.ssa.gov/OP_Home/rulings/rulings-pref.html> accessed February 7, 2022.

14 "Actions on Decisions (AOD)," *Internal Revenue Service* (last edited January 4, 2022) <https://apps.irs.gov/app/picklist/list/actionsOnDecisions.html> accessed February 7, 2022.

15 "Jefferson's Fair Copy – The Papers of Thomas Jefferson, Volume 30: 1 January 1798 to 31 January 1799, pages 543-49," *Princeton University, The Papers of Thomas Jefferson* (last edited December 8, 2021) <https://jeffersonpapers.princeton.edu/selected-documents/jefferson%E2%80%99s-fair-copy> accessed February 7, 2022. "In questions of power, let no more be heard of confidence in man, but bind him down from mischief by the chains of the constitution."

16 Leigh, Philip, "Reconstruction Era Chicanery," *Abbeville Institute* (published March 2, 2022) <https://www.abbevilleinstitute.org/reconstruction-era-chicanery/> accessed March 3, 2022.

17 McDonald, Forrest, "Was the Fourteenth Amendment Constitutionally Adopted?" *Abbeville Institute* (published April 23, 2014) <https://www.abbevilleinstitute.org/was-the-fourteenth-amendment-constitutionally-adopted/> accessed February 5, 2022.

18 Bassani, Luigi Marco, *Chaining Down Leviathan: The American Dream of Self-Government 1776-1865* (Abbeville Institute Press, March 28, 2021, ISBN 978-1733407519, 380 pages), page 158: "Whenever [Jefferson] used this expression ['my country'], he always meant Virginia."

19 Merriam, Jesse, "Another Original Meaning of the Fourteenth Amendment," *Law & Liberty* (published December 14, 2021) <https://lawliberty.org/book-review/another-original-meaning-of-the-fourteenth-amendment/> accessed February 10, 2022.

20 Business Insider, "ALAN DERSHOWITZ: Why Supreme Court got Roe v. Wade wrong" (*YouTube*, length 2:33, published November 4, 2016) <https://www.youtube.com/watch?v=_yAcf-S1wEU> accessed February 8, 2022. Even the liberal Professor Dershowitz declared: "Roe versus Wade was a disaster because it weakened, politically, us, the pro-choice movement – turned it over to nine me to decide the fate of women. [...] Abortion will continue to divide America as long as this country exists."

21 Iannacci, Nicandro, "Recalling the Supreme Court's historic statement on contraception and privacy," *National Constitution Center* (published June 7, 2019) <https://constitutioncenter.org/blog/contraception-marriage-and-the-right-to-privacy> accessed February 10, 2022. Douglas: "[S]pecific guarantees in the Bill of Rights have penumbras, formed by emanations from those guarantees that help give them life and substance."

22 "William G. COOPER et al., v. John AARON et al.," *Cornell Law School, Legal Information Institute* (last edited January 19, 2022) <https://www.law.cornell.edu/supremecourt/text/74/700> accessed February 11, 2022.

23 Woodard, Colin, *American Nations: A History of the Eleven Rival Regional Cultures of North America* (Penguin, September 25, 2012, ISBN 978-0143122029, 384 pages).

24 *Op.cit.*, Bassani, *Chaining Down Leviathan*, page 24. Bassani quotes David Gross: "[B]y the mid-eighteenth century, the European states had for the most part won [...] their 'war of annihilation' against the major intermediate institutions that had survived since the Middle Ages."

25 Cuzán, Alfred G., "Do We Ever Really Get Out of Anarchy?" (*The Journal of Libertarian Studies*, Volume 3, Number 2, 1979). Online at <https://mises.org/library/do-we-ever-really-get-out-anarchy> accessed February 11, 2022.

26 "LONE WOLF, Principal Chief of the Kiowas, et al., Appts., v. ETHAN A. HITCHCOCK, Secretary of the Interior, et al.," *Cornell Law School, Legal Information Institute* (last edited November 1, 2020) <https://www.law.cornell.edu/supremecourt/text/187/553> accessed February 11, 2022.

27 Raico, Ralph, "The Conquest of the US by Spain," *Mises Institute* (published February 15, 2020) <https://mises.org/library/conquest-us-spain> accessed February 11, 2022.

28 Raico, Ralph, *Great Wars and Great Leaders: A Libertarian Rebuttal* (Mises Institute, April 2, 2015, ISBN 978-1610160964, 263 pages), pages 26-27.

29 Ibid.

30 Ibid., page 19.

31 Ibid., page 34.

32 Ibid., page 35.

33 Ibid., page 36.

34 Ibid., page 39.

35 Cull, Nicholas J., "Master of American Propaganda: How George Creel sold the Great War to America, and America to the world," *PBS* (last edited October 10, 2021) <https://www.pbs.org/wgbh/americanexperience/features/the-great-war-master-of-american-propaganda/> accessed February 13, 2022.

36 *Op.cit.*, Raico, *Great Wars and Great Leaders: A Libertarian Rebuttal*, page 38.

37 Ibid., page 39.

38 Ibid., page 41. President Harding commuted his sentence to time served on December 23, 1921, over three years after the end of the war.

39 "FRANK R. BRUSHABER, Appt., v. UNION PACIFIC RAILROAD COMPANY," *Cornell Law School, Legal Information Institute* (last edited November 28, 2021) <https://www.law.cornell.edu/supremecourt/text/240/1> accessed February 12, 2022.

40 Conti-Brown, Peter, "Is the Federal Reserve Constitutional?" *Law & Liberty* (published September 1, 2013) <https://lawliberty.org/forum/is-the-federal-reserve-constitutional/> accessed February 12, 2022.

41 *Op.cit.*, Raico, *Great Wars and Great Leaders: A Libertarian Rebuttal*, page 223.

42 Ibid.

43 Ibid., page 224.

44 Ibid., page 57.

45 Ibid., page 105.

46 Hummel, Jeffrey Rogers, "Operation Keelhaul Exposed," *Reason* magazine (November, 1974 issue) <https://reason.com/1974/11/01/totalitarianism/> accessed February 13, 2022.

47 "Ike's Warning Of Military Expansion, 50 Years Later," *NPR Radio* (published January 17, 2011) <https://www.npr.org/2011/01/17/132942244/ikes-warning-of-military-expansion-50-years-later> accessed February 16, 2022.

48 *Op.cit.*, Raico, *Great Wars and Great Leaders: A Libertarian Rebuttal*, page 142.

49 Eschner, Kat, "The CIA Experimented On Animals in the 1960s Too. Just Ask 'Acoustic Kitty'," *Smithsonian Magazine* (published August 8, 2017) <https://www.smithsonianmag.com/smart-news/cia-experimented-animals-1960s-too-just-ask-acoustic-kitty-180964313/> accessed February 13, 2022.

50 Gordon, David, "The Right's Wrong Turn," *The American Conservative* (published June 18, 2010) <https://www.theamericanconservative.com/the-rights-wrong-turn/> accessed February 13, 2022.

51 Bomboy, Scott, "The Gulf of Tonkin Resolution and the limits of presidential power," *National Constitution Center* (published August 7, 2021) <https://constitutioncenter.org/blog/the-gulf-of-tonkin-and-the-limits-of-presidential-power> accessed February 14, 2022.

52 Catalán, Jonathan M. Finegold, "A Culture of Fear," *Mises Institute* (published May 31, 2021) <https://mises.org/library/culture-fear> accessed February 14, 2022.

53 Bovard, James, "New Kosovo Indictment Is a Reminder of Bill Clinton's Serbian War Atrocities," *Mises Institute* (published July 18, 2020) <https://mises.org/wire/new-kosovo-indictment-reminder-bill-clintons-serbian-war-atrocities> accessed February 14, 2022.

54 "House of Representatives votes against US Libya role," *BBC News* (published June 24, 2011) <https://www.bbc.com/news/world-us-canada-13908202> accessed February 15, 2022.

55 Fukuyama, Francis, "Nation-Building 101," *The Atlantic* (online version of January/February 2004 print issue) <https://www.theatlantic.com/magazine/archive/2004/01/nation-building-101/302862/> accessed February 15, 2022. This person cites the reversal of Bush *fils* on "nation building" not to show its failure, but to presume its success, given an American commitment "for generations," no matter what the price in blood and treasure. *Vide* Fukuyama, Francis, *The End of History and the Last Man* (Free Press, reissue edition, March 1, 2006, ISBN 978-0743284554, 464 pages), page 48. This person, astonishingly still employed as an "expert" on international affairs at Stanford University, proclaimed the end of history as such: That is, the end-point of mankind's ideological evolution and the universalization of Western liberal democracy as the "final form of human government."

56 Greenwald, Glenn, "The U.S. Government Lied For Two Decades About Afghanistan," *Substack* (published August 16, 2021) <https://greenwald.substack.com/p/the-us-government-lied-for-two-decades> accessed February 15, 2022.

57 Crook, John R., "The War Powers Resolution – A Dim and Fading Legacy," (*Case Western Reserve Journal of International Law*, Volume 45, Issue 1, 2012), page 166. Online at <https://scholarlycommons.law.case.edu/cgi/viewcontent.cgi?article=1070&context=jil> accessed February 15, 2022.

58 Smith, R. Jeffrey, "Hussein's Prewar Ties To Al-Qaeda Discounted," *The Washington Post* (published April 6, 2007) <https://www.washingtonpost.com/wp-dyn/content/article/2007/04/05/AR2007040502263.html> accessed February 15, 2022.

59 Ross, Brian, "Niger Intelligence Came From Forged Docs," *ABC News* (published July 14, 2003) <https://abcnews.go.com/WNT/story?id=129584&page=1> accessed February 15, 2022.

60 Filkins, Dexter, "Colin Powell's Fateful Moment," *The New Yorker* (published October 18, 2021) <https://www.newyorker.com/news/daily-comment/colin-powells-fateful-moment> accessed February 15, 2022.

61 Editorial staff, "Remember That Mushroom Cloud?" *The New York Times* (published November 2, 2005) <https://www.nytimes.com/2005/11/02/opinion/remember-that-mushroom-cloud.html> accessed February 15, 2022.

62 Roth, John; Greenburg, Douglas; Wille, Serena, "Monograph on Terrorist Financing," *National Commission on Terrorist Attacks Upon the United States*, page 21. Online at <https://govinfo.library.unt.edu/911/staff_statements/911_TerrFin_Monograph.pdf> accessed February 16, 2022.

63 "Terrorism: Two Years After 9/11, Connecting the Dots," (*U.S. Government Printing Office*, Senate Hearing 108-921, September 10, 2003). Online at <https://www.govinfo.gov/content/pkg/CHRG-108shrg93083/html/CHRG-108shrg93083.htm> accessed February 15, 2022.

64 "Analysis: Wahhabism," *PBS Frontline* (last edited February 7, 2022) <https://www.pbs.org/wgbh/pages/frontline/shows/saudi/analyses/wahhabism.html> accessed February 16, 2022.

65 *Op.cit.*, "Monograph on Terrorist Financing," pages 3, 13.

66 "Analysis: U.S.-Saudi Relations," *PBS Frontline* (last edited May 10, 2021) <https://www.pbs.org/wgbh/pages/frontline/shows/saudi/analyses/ussaudi.html> accessed February 16, 2022.

67 *Op.cit.*, "Ike's Warning Of Military Expansion, 50 Years Later."

[68] Greenwald, Glenn; Hussain, Murtaza, "The NSA's New Partner in Spying: Saudi Arabia's Brutal State Police," *The Intercept* (published July 25 2014) <https://theintercept.com/2014/07/25/nsas-new-partner-spying-saudi-arabias-brutal-state-police/> accessed February 15, 2022.

[69] Wong, Andrea, "Behind Saudi Arabia's 41-Year U.S. Debt Secret," *Bloomberg* (published May 30, 2016) <https://www.bloomberg.com/news/features/2016-05-30/the-untold-story-behind-saudi-arabia-s-41-year-u-s-debt-secret> accessed February 15, 2022.

[70] Fahmy, Dalia, "5 facts about religion in Saudi Arabia," *Pew Research Center* (published April 12, 2018) <https://www.pewresearch.org/fact-tank/2018/04/12/5-facts-about-religion-in-saudi-arabia/> accessed February 15, 2022.

[71] "Iraq Body Count," *Iraq Body Count* (last edited February 12, 2022) <https://www.iraqbodycount.org/> accessed February 15, 2022. As of the access date, the total violent deaths including combatants stood at 288,000.

[72] Gerstein, Josh, "Gingrich: Free Speech Should Be Curtailed To Fight Terrorism," *The New York Sun* (published November 29, 2006) <https://www.nysun.com/national/gingrich-free-speech-should-be-curtailed-to-fight/44302/> accessed February 15, 2022.

[73] Greenberg, Jon, "CNN's Tapper: Obama has used Espionage Act more than all previous administrations," *Politifact* (published January 10, 2014) <https://www.politifact.com/factchecks/2014/jan/10/jake-tapper/cnns-tapper-obama-has-used-espionage-act-more-all-/> accessed February 15, 2022.

[74] Greenwald, Glenn, "The Case For a Pardon of Edward Snowden by President Trump," *Substack* (published December 14, 2020) <https://greenwald.substack.com/p/the-case-for-a-pardon-of-edward-snowden> accessed February 15, 2022.

[75] Sartwell, Crispin, *Extreme Virtue: Truth and Leadership in Five Great American Lives* (SUNY Press, November 20, 2003, ISBN 978-0791458808, 149 pages), page 81.

[76] Cummings, Judith, "Breakup of Black Family Imperils Gains of Decades," *The New York Times* (published November 20, 1983) <https://www.nytimes.com/1983/11/20/us/breakup-of-black-family-imperils-gains-of-decades.html> accessed February 9, 2022.
"The conservative economist George Gilder asserts that conservatives were right in their prediction that the income redistribution programs of President Johnson's 'war on poverty' would result in 'destroying the incentives and families of the poor.' In an attack this fall on what he termed 'the welfare state disaster,' Mr. Gilder wrote, 'Current programs will continue to create a criminal underclass of unlisted male welfare beneficiaries who exploit the welfare trap by living off a series of female recipients – and extend it by violence ever deeper into the heart of our cities and our national consciousness.'" Federal policies such as AFDC (later, TANF) were the primary cause of the breakup of the black family, according to George Gilder, *Wealth and Poverty* (1981), black economists Thomas Sowell, *Markets and Minorities* (1981) and Walter Williams, *The State Against Blacks* (1982), and other economists.

[77] Gilder, George, *Wealth and Poverty: A New Edition for the Twenty-First Century* (Regnery Gateway, revised edition, August 21, 2012, ISBN 978-1596988163, 256 pages), page 156: "The moral hazards of government programs are clear. Unemployment compensation promotes unemployment. Aid to Families with Dependent Children (AFDC) [later replaced by Temporary Assistance for Needy Families (TANF)] made more families dependent and fatherless".

[78] Thernstrom, Abigail; Thernstrom, Stephan, "Black Progress: How far we've come, and how far we have to go," *Brookings Institute* (published March 1, 1998) <https://www.brookings.edu/articles/black-progress-how-far-weve-come-and-how-far-we-have-to-go/> accessed February 9, 2022.
"As a consequence, with the shortage of workers in northern manufacturing plants following the outbreak of World War II, southern blacks in search of jobs boarded trains and buses in a Great Migration that lasted through the mid-1960s. They found what they were looking for: wages so strikingly high that in 1953 the average income for a black family in the North was almost twice that of those who remained in the South. And through much of the 1950s wages rose steadily and unemployment was low."

[79] "The Negro Family: The Case for National Action," *Office of Policy Planning and Research, United States Department of Labor* (published March, 1965) <https://web.stanford.edu/~mrosenfe/Moynihan%27s%20The%20Negro%20Family.pdf> accessed February 9, 2022. This document is more commonly referenced as the "Monynihan Report," after the Democrat Senator who was its principal author. Another key passage: "[T]he Negro family in the urban ghettos is crumbling. A middle-class group has managed to save itself, but for vast numbers of the unskilled, poorly educated city working class the fabric of conventional social relationships has all but disintegrated."

[80] "The Vietnam War," *BBC News* (published July 27, 2021) <https://www.bbc.co.uk/bitesize/guides/z8kw3k7/revision/11> accessed February 16, 2022.

[81] Domitrovic, Brian, "Oil Soared Because The U.S. Tanked The Dollar," *Forbes* magazine (published May 7, 2018) <https://www.forbes.com/sites/briandomitrovic/2018/05/07/oil-soared-because-the-u-s-tanked-the-dollar/?sh=487618047588> accessed February 10, 2022.

[82] Roberts, Roxanne, "Hillary Clinton's 'deplorables' speech shocked voters five years ago — but some feel it was prescient," *The Washington Post* (published August 31, 2021) <https://www.washingtonpost.com/lifestyle/2021/08/31/deplorables-basket-hillary-clinton/> accessed February 16, 2022. The phrase "basket of deplorables" was uttered by Hillary Clinton on September 9, 2016. The article approvingly cites a Clinton functionary defending Clinton's remark as a blow against racism, the "alt-right," and the "quest to preserve white maleness" in America.

[83] Wulfsohn, Joseph A., "The Root accused of racism after piece declares 'Whiteness is a Pandemic'," *New York Post* (published February 16, 2022) <https://nypost.com/2021/03/18/the-root-accused-of-racism-after-piece-declares-whiteness-is-a-pandemic/> accessed February 16, 2022. The Negro luminary Damon Young had opined: "Whiteness is a public health crisis. It shortens life expectancies, it pollutes air, it constricts equilibrium, it devastates forests, it melts ice caps, it sparks (and funds) wars, it flattens dialects, it infests consciousnesses [sic], and it kills people".

[84] "Most Voters Want Congress to Investigate the 574 Violent Riots in 2020 that resulted in over 2,000 injured police officers as well as the January 6th riot at the US Capitol," *National Police Association* (published July 21, 2021) <https://nationalpolice.org/most-voters-want-congress-to-investigate-the-574-violent-riots-in-2020-that-resulted-in-over-2000-injured-police-officers-as-well-as-the-january-6th-riot-at-the-us-capitol/> accessed February 10, 2022.

[85] Ellyatt, Holly, "Who are 'Davos Man' and 'Davos Woman'?" *CNBC* (published January 19, 2018) <https://www.cnbc.com/2018/01/19/who-are-davos-man-and-davos-woman.html> accessed February 10, 2022. As the article quotes Samuel P. Huntington from 2004: Davos Men are "'gold-collar workers' or... 'cosmocrats', [an] emerging class [...] empowered by new notions of global connectedness. It includes academics, international civil servants and executives in global companies, as well as successful high-technology entrepreneurs, [who] see national governments as residues from the past whose only useful function is to facilitate the elite's global operations."

[86] Ezrati, Milton, "The Green New Deal And The Cost Of Virtue," *Forbes* magazine (published February 19, 2019) <https://www.forbes.com/sites/miltonezrati/2019/02/19/the-green-new-deal-and-the-cost-of-virtue/?sh=5d4c429c3dec> accessed September 6, 2021.

[87] Harsanyi, David, "The 10 Most Insane Requirements Of The Green New Deal," *The Federalist* (published February 7, 2019) <https://thefederalist.com/2019/02/07/ten-most-insane-requirements-green-new-deal/> accessed September 6, 2021.

[88] Mises, Ludwig von, "Economic Calculation in the Socialist Commonwealth," *Mises Institute* (originally published January 1, 1920) <https://mises.org/library/economic-calculation-socialist-commonwealth> accessed February 18, 2022, PDF page 51. Professor Joseph T. Salerno evaluates the impact of this seminal essay on pages 49-69.

[89] de Jasay, Anthony, *The State* (Liberty Fund, illustrated edition, March 31, 1998, ISBN 978-0865971714, 330 pages), page 274.

[90] Ibid., page 277.

91 Wethe, David; Dlouhy, Jennifer A.; Natter, Ari, "Who's to Blame for the Pain at the Pump? It's Complicated," *Bloomberg* (published November 30, 2021) <https://www.bloomberg.com/news/articles/2021-11-30/fact-checking-the-finger-pointing-on-high-gasoline-prices> accessed February 17, 2022.

92 Morrow, Allison, "Who's to blame for inflation? It's complicated," *CNN Business* (last edited January 10, 2022) <https://www.cnn.com/2022/01/10/economy/inflation-blame-pandemic-biden-fed-corporations/index.html> accessed February 17, 2022.

93 Hayek, Fredrich A., *The Road to Serfdom* (Institute Of Economic Affairs, condensed paperback, August 20, 2005, ISBN 978-0255365765, 140 pages), page 105.

94 Marx, Karl; Engels, Friedrich, *Manifesto of the Communist Party* (Project Gutenberg eBook #61, published January 25, 2005) <https://www.gutenberg.org/cache/epub/61/pg61.html> accessed February 17, 2022.

95 Rothbard, Murray N., "The Political Thought of Étienne de la Boétie," *Mises Institute* (published July 20, 2005) <https://mises.org/library/political-thought-etienne-de-la-boetie> accessed February 17, 2022.

96 Cillizza, Chris, "Just 7 percent of journalists are Republicans. That's far fewer than even a decade ago," *The Washington Post* (published May 6, 2014) <https://www.washingtonpost.com/news/the-fix/wp/2014/05/06/just-7-percent-of-journalists-are-republicans-thats-far-less-than-even-a-decade-ago/> accessed February 18, 2022. In 2013, 7.1% of polled journalists identified themselves as Republicans, while 28.1% were Democrats.

97 Mascaro, Lisa; Fox, Ben; Baldor, Lolita C., "'Clear the Capitol,' Pence pleaded, timeline of riot shows," *Los Angeles Times* (published April 10, 2021) <https://www.latimes.com/world-nation/story/2021-04-10/clear-the-capitol-pence-pleaded-timeline-of-riot-shows> accessed February 19, 2022. The newspaper's report was from the Associated Press.

98 Rouan, Rick, "Fact check: Claim about FBI official who said bureau recovered no guns at Capitol riot is missing context," *USA Today* (published March 4, 2021) <https://www.usatoday.com/story/news/factcheck/2021/03/04/fact-check-fbi-says-bureau-didnt-recover-guns-capitol-riot/4578286001/> accessed February 18, 2022.

99 Mallin, Alexander; Hosenball, Alex; Rubin, Olivia, "At least 29 accused rioters say they thought it was OK to enter the Capitol," *ABC News* (published February 19, 2021) <https://abcnews.go.com/author/alexander_mallin> accessed February 18, 2022.

100 Kim, Lisa, "Canadian Protest Convoy Raises $8.7 Million As Donations Flow Into Christian Site A Day After Ontario Court Freezes Monetary Access," *Forbes magazine* (last edited February 11, 2022) <https://www.forbes.com/sites/lisakim/2022/02/11/canadian-protest-convoy-raises-87-million-as-donations-flow-into-christian-site-a-day-after-ontario-court-freezes-monetary-access/> accessed February 18, 2022.

101 "Canada's Emergencies Act: What power does it give Justin Trudeau?" *Al Jazeera* (published February 15, 2022) <https://www.aljazeera.com/news/2022/2/15/canada-emergencies-act-what-power-does-it-give-justin-trudeau> accessed February 18, 2022.

102 Eastman, Leslie, "Will Trudeau's 'Emergencies Act' Stunt Make it Through Parliament or Court?" *Legal Insurrection* (published February 15, 2022) <https://legalinsurrection.com/2022/02/will-trudeaus-emergencies-act-stunt-make-it-through-parliament-or-court/> accessed February 18, 2022.

103 Miller-Idriss, Cynthia, "Canada's 'nationwide insurrection' is bringing together an unlikely and alarming alliance," *MSNBC* (published February 9, 2022) <https://www.msnbc.com/opinion/canada-s-nationwide-insurrection-bringing-together-unlikely-alarming-alliance-n1288832> accessed February 18, 2022.

104 Berg, Augustus, "'Honk, Honk' = Heil Hitler claims Canada's Minister of Child, Family, and Social Development," *BitChute* (published February 21, 2022) <https://www.bitchute.com/video/HRz09MW6wyc3/> accessed February 21, 2022. During debate on the measure, Liberal MP Ya'ara Saks, Parliamentary Secretary to the Minister of Families, Children and Social Development, decried the truckers' sounding their horns in protest, saying that "honk honk [...] is an anacronym [sic] for 'hail [sic] Hitler'."

105 Ljunggren, David, "Canada's parliament approves Trudeau's emergency powers," *Reuters* (published February 21, 2022) <https://www.reuters.com/world/canadas-trudeau-calls-national-healing-after-truckers-blockade-over-covid-curbs-2022-02-21/> accessed February 21, 2022. Trudeau's minority Liberal government secured passage through support from left-leaning New Democrats.

106 Flood, Brian, "Contradictions from Fauci, CDC throughout COVID pandemic outlined in viral Twitter thread," *Fox News* (published July 29, 2021) <https://www.foxnews.com/media/twitter-thread-fauci-cdc-contradictions> accessed February 18, 2022.

107 Gutman, Rachel, "Mask Mandates Don't Need to Make Sense: They only need to align with communities' goals." *The Atlantic* (published February 20 2022) <https://www.theatlantic.com/health/archive/2022/02/covid-mask-mandate-washington-dc/622860/> accessed February 20, 2022.

108 Dorman, Sam, "Parents across US revolt against school boards on masks, critical race theory and gender issues," *Fox News* (published August 12, 2021) <https://www.foxnews.com/politics/parents-across-country-revolt-school-boards-masks-critical-race-theory> accessed February 18, 2022.

109 Tate, Kristin, "The sheer size of our government workforce is an alarming problem," *The Hill* (published April 14, 2019) <https://thehill.com/opinion/finance/438242-the-federal-government-is-the-largest-employer-in-the-nation> accessed September 24, 2021.

110 Kilpatrick, William, "The Long March through American institutions continues," *Catholic World Report* (published June 17, 2020) <https://www.catholicworldreport.com/2020/06/17/the-long-march-through-american-institutions-continues/> accessed February 20, 2022.

111 Perry, Mark J., "Chart of the day: Administrative bloat in US public schools," *American Enterprise Institute* (published March 9, 2013) <https://www.aei.org/carpe-diem/chart-of-the-day-administrative-bloat-in-us-public-schools/> accessed February 18, 2022.

112 Nittler, Kency, "Collective bargaining and teacher strikes," *National Council on Teacher Quality* (published March 28, 2019) <https://www.nctq.org/blog/Collective-bargaining-and-teacher-strikes> accessed February 18, 2022.

113 McDonald, Kerry, "Teachers Unions Are More Powerful Than You Realize — but That May Be Changing," *The CATO Institute* (published August 31, 2020) <https://www.cato.org/commentary/teachers-unions-are-more-powerful-you-realize-may-be-changing#> accessed February 18, 2022.

114 Haar, Charlene, "National PTA Positions Make Parent Involvement Useless," *Texas Public Policy Foundation* (published April 1, 1999) <https://www.texaspolicy.com/national-pta-positions-make-parent-involvement-useless/> accessed February 21, 2022.

115 Lyons, Gene, "Why Teachers Can't Teach," *Texas Monthly* magazine (published September, 1979) <https://www.texasmonthly.com/news-politics/why-teachers-cant-teach/> accessed February 21, 2022. In the universities, "entering freshmen who declared education as their major had the lowest mean [standardized] test scores of any entering group" and in Dallas half of those graduates fail the Wesman Personnel Classification Test.

[116] Nanette Light, Nanette; Grissom, Brandi, "Abbott signs bill cracking down on Texas' 'statewide plague' of improper student-teacher relationships," *The Dallas Morning News* (published May 25, 2017) <https://www.dallasnews.com/news/education/2017/05/25/abbott-signs-bill-cracking-down-on-texas-statewide-plague-of-improper-student-teacher-relationships/> accessed February 21, 2022. Teachers fired for moral turpitude, or who quit before firing, keep their license to teach and simply re-apply at another district.

[117] Shafarevich, Igor; Tjalsma, William, translator; Solzhenitsyn, Aleksandr I., foreword, *The Socialist Phenomenon* (Gideon House Books, October 17, 2019, ISBN 978-1943133772, 344 pages). Online at <https://drive.google.com/file/d/0B0xb4crOvCgTcHM5aU1kQkt2ZUU/> accessed February 19, 2022, PDF page 277.

[118] Ibid., pages 202-204.

[119] Ibid., page 2.

[120] Ibid., pages 195-196.

[121] Ibid., page 196.

[122] von Mises, Ludwig; Raico, Ralph, translator, *Liberalism: In The Classical Tradition* (Cobden Press and The Foundation for Economic Education, Inc., third edition, January 1, 1985, ISBN 978-0930439231, 208 pages), page 17. Online at <https://mises.org/library/liberalism-classical-tradition/html> accessed February 19, 2022.

[123] Rothbard, Murray N., "Karl Marx as Religious Eschatologist," *Mises Institute* (published October 9, 2009) <https://mises.org/library/karl-marx-religious-eschatologist#reabsorption> accessed February 3, 2022.

[124] *Op.cit.*, Shafarevich, 282.

[125] Ibid., page 261.

[126] "Title IX and Sex Discrimination," *U.S. Department of Education, Office for Civil Rights* (edited August, 2021) <https://www2.ed.gov/about/offices/list/ocr/docs/tix_dis.html> accessed February 19, 2022.

[127] Eilperin, Juliet; Brown, Emma, "Obama administration directs schools to accommodate transgender students," *The Washington Post* (published May 13, 2016) <https://www.washingtonpost.com/politics/obama-administration-to-instruct-schools-to-accommodate-transgender-students/2016/05/12/0ed1c50e-18ab-11e6-aa55-670cabef46e0_story.html> accessed February 19, 2022.

[128] Eldeib, Duaa, "Feds: Palatine district discriminated against transgender student by barring her from girls' locker room," *Chicago Tribune* (published November 03, 2015) <https://www.chicagotribune.com/news/ct-transgender-student-federal-ruling-met-20151102-story.html> accessed February 19, 2022.

[129] Campbell, Colin; Jarvis, Craig Jarvis, "LGBT protections end as NC governor signs bill," *Raleigh News & Observer* (edited October 05, 2016) <https://account.newsobserver.com/paywall/subscriber-only?resume=67731847&intcid=ab_archive> accessed February 19, 2022.

[130] "LGBTQIA Resource Center Glossary," *University of California, Davis* (last edited January 14, 2020) <https://lgbtqia.ucdavis.edu/educated/glossary> accessed February 19, 2022.

[131] Nisbet, Robert, *The Quest for Community: A Study in the Ethics of Order and Freedom* (Intercollegiate Studies Institute, July 5, 2010, ISBN 978-1935191506, 330 pages), page 133: Rousseau's "general will" demands that all citizens "surrender" to it. This "surrender" means razing to the ground any and all intermediating institutions standing between the citizen and the general will. Thus there can be no associations (page 136), no charitable institutions (page 147), no religion other than patriotism (page 138), no family (page 139), no marriage or parental authority (page

148). With the state replacing every abiding institution, the general will is the expression of a society with no institutional memory: It is a state of permanent revolution (page 140), now embodied by the absolute majoritarianism of Western democracies.

[132] Ibid., page 106.

[133] Riesman, David; Glazer, Nathan; Denney Reuel, *The Lonely Crowd: A Study of the Changing American Character* (Veritas abridged and revised edition from 1950 original, March 17, 2020, ISBN 978-0300246735, 376 pages).

[134] Putnam, Robert D., *Bowling Alone: The Collapse and Revival of American Community* (Simon & Schuster paperback, August 7, 2001, ISBN 978-0743203043, 544 pages).

[135] *Op.cit.*, Nisbet, page 96.

[136] Ibid., page 237.

[137] "U.S. Transportation Secretary Pete Buttigieg Announces Comprehensive National Roadway Safety Strategy," *U.S. Department of Transportation* (published January 27, 2022) <https://www.transportation.gov/briefing-room/us-transportation-secretary-pete-buttigieg-announces-comprehensive-national-roadway> accessed February 2, 2022.

[138] Boak, Josh, "Biden aims to reduce cancer deaths by 50% over next 25 years," *Chicago Tribune* (published February 2, 2022) <https://www.chicagotribune.com/nation-world/ct-aud-nw-biden-cancer-deaths-20220202-pohpetkbdfebxhcmtd52y667ku-story.html> accessed February 2, 2022.

1. APODICTIC FOUNDATION

Architectonics is the conceptual foundation of this system of government proposed to replace the decomposition of the modern state. Architectonics is the method that establishes the *dominium sortiens*: The society of absolute property rights, the absence of public goods, and the sovereignty of the people in community, exercising decision-making not through oligarchic elections but through democratic sortition. This society might alternately be called a kleristocracy,[m] or a sortive democracy. Architectonics modifies the symbiotic communitarianism[n] of Johannes Althusius in order to redefine it as a category of praxeology.

Writing in 1951, the economist Murray Rothbard (1926-1995) outlined four[o] known categories of praxeology[1] then offered a fifth – "Unknown" – to allow for new categories. *Architectonics is the new political science category within the field of praxeology.*

Praxeology, as designated by economist Ludwig von Mises (1881-1973), is the study of human action. Two broad objects of study are open to human reason: The study of volitional events (praxeology, whose first two categories are economic categories), and the study of nonvolitional events (e.g., physics, biology), corresponding to man's only two ways of knowing reality:

> There are for man only two principles available for a mental grasp of reality, namely, those of teleology and causality. What cannot be brought under either of these categories is absolutely hidden to the human mind. An event not open to an interpretation by one of these two principles is for man inconceivable and mysterious. Change can be conceived as the outcome either of the operation of mechanistic causality or of purposeful behavior; for the human mind there is no third way available.[2]

The following is a gloss of Mises' own account of praxeology in his 1949 masterwork, *Human Action.*

Human action is purposeful behavior. *Action* is not simply the giving of a preference. It is the choice from among limited means, rejecting other choices, and acted upon to attain a goal. It is not only doing but no less omit-

---

[m] From κλερος, or lot. The Greek favors the spelling "klerostocracy," but "kleristocracy" is current and furthermore is just one syllable removed from the familiar and easily pronounced "aristocracy." *Sors* is Latin for "lot," thus the cognate "sortition," the drawing of lots.

[n] We resist any usage of "communitarianism" for the project of this book. Despite its suggestive usefulness, it is freighted with associations to socialism and to the communitarianism of Amitai Etzioni – positions alien to architectonics. We are forced to the terms "architectonics" and "kleristocracy" not out of vanity for novelty or neologism, but in the confidence, as C.S. Peirce once suggested, that they would be "safe from kidnappers."

[o] Crusoe Economics, Catallactics (market economics), War Theory, Game Theory.

ting to do what possibly could be done, in order to remove some felt discomfort.[3] Human action is concerned only with the means to attain a goal, not the end or the goal itself (e.g., whether the goal is worthwhile or will make the actor "truly" happy by some standard), nor is it concerned with the ultimate explanations of why one action was taken instead of another (e.g., whether will is in fact only the result of mental chemistry or physiological events). Since the choice of acting to attain one goal instead of another is subjective and thus cannot be determined to be more "rational" than another, only the action itself is rational, by being volitionally directed to some goal to remove a felt discomfort.[4] Thus the opposite of action is not irrational behavior, but nonvolitional action, like the response of the body to poison or disease. *It is this subjective theory of value that provides the scientific foundation to praxeology.*[5]

Since praxeology studies means and not ends, it must assume cause and effect. Even if it must be stated that some cause only statistically results in some effect, causality exists, otherwise various means could not be evaluated as being more or less favorable to producing some desired result.[6] Causality is based on the intersubjective validity of logic common to all reasoning beings. There is no need to consider the "other minds" problem, or the possibility of beings coming to "know" by some other method, or the assumption of immortal souls. The object of study is simply purposeful behavior as the means to attain a goal.[7] Mises:

> [W]e cannot help acknowledging that our fellow men act. [...O]ur fellow men are acting beings as we ourselves are. For the comprehension of action there is but one scheme of interpretation and analysis available, namely, that provided by the cognition and analysis of our own purposeful behavior.[8]

For Mises, all praxeological analysis must begin not with empirical data, but with undeniable truths that are more fundamental than defined axioms. Yet since they provide empirically testable information about reality, and not merely tautological truths, they are in Kantian terms *synthetic a priori* truths. The *a priori* refers to the essential and necessary character of the logical structure of the human mind, to fundamental logical relations that are primary, antecedent to definition. They are ultimate unanalyzable categories that are not subject to proof or disproof, since attempting to do so would mean "thinking" in some nonhuman way.[9]

Murray Rothbard was the intellectual heir of Mises and founder of the term "Austrian economics" in its current sense as a school of thought rather than an episode in economic history.[p] His approach to praxeology did not insist on its status as a Kantian category:

> What name we apply to this method of obtaining knowledge is basically unimportant and involves irrelevant philosophical problems; thus, it may be called 'introspective,' 'empirical,' 'a priori,' or 'reflective.'[10]

For him an axiom was sufficiently true if "[t]o deny it would be absurdity."[11] The foundation of these axioms in praxeology distinguishes the Austrian school of economics, both Mises and Rothbard, as it does architectonics. However, the fundamental truths surrounding the necessity of human action are the intuitively and introspectively verified basis of all economics, even for schools that repudiate Austrian principles. For example, David Friedman, a member of the Chicago school of economics, writes:

> I do not know other people [...] well enough to incorporate their irrationalities into my analysis of the effect of legal rules on their behavior. What I do know about them is that they, like me, have purposes they wish to achieve and tend, albeit imperfectly, to correctly choose how to achieve them. That is the predictable element in human behavior, and it is on that element that economics is built.[12]

All reasoning that aspires to the status of science furthermore accepts the axiom that (non-praxeological) scientific truths are tentative, contingently held until falsified, and confirmed by collegiality – the prevailing view, asserted by Austrians, praxeologists, economists, and positivists alike.

1.1 Axioms of Government

Architectonics is a praxeological category, regardless of its Kantian status, and thus accepts the first axioms of praxeology:

- Man must act purposefully to achieve goals that allow him to live;
- Man must use reason in some sense, despite its fallibility, to achieve those goals.

To be demonstrated according to architectonics are the following axioms, among others, that define it as a unique praxeological category:

1.1a Man's goals cannot be reached without the cooperative action of others,[q] especially in shaping man's essential means of action, that is,

---

[p] Professor Joseph T. Salerno details this distinction in his 2004 introduction to the second edition of Rothbard's original 1962 *Man, Economy, and State, op.cit. infra,* and furthermore provides an excellent historical and intellectual context for the school.

[q] It should be obvious that this truth does not gainsay Crusoe Economics, whose apodictic truths apply in a different context, any more than psychiatry should gainsay the study of nerve cells.

language and reason; following Althusius, this communal action may be termed *symbiotic action*.

1.1b Human action taken by a community larger than the family requires consistent rules of mutual cooperation, whether implicit or explicit, in order to achieve communal goals, with no reference to the form of a state; following Althusius, these non-state rules for communal action may be termed *symbiotic government*.

1.1c A community that nurtures reason is more likely to reach its goals than one that does not; following Althusius, this communal nurturing of reason may be termed *symbiotic reason*.

The Corollaries

1.1.1 Government must exist, and it must enforce a guide that shapes human behavior.

> In Heaven there will be no law[;...] in Hell there will be nothing but law, and due process will be meticulously observed.
> – Grant Gilmore

Man is a rational animal whose offspring need a long period of gestation and protection requiring the cooperative behavior of others, at the very least within a family, before reaching self-sufficiency. Government[r] is the enforced guide, explicit or implicit, for this behavior outside the family. Since even in the complete absence of law and self-consciously government agents there is some implicit guide to extra-familial behavior, government must exist. To deny this is to assert that society is less than a pack of wolves, who do obey consistent rules of mutual cooperation. These consistent rules of mutual cooperation would be called government if these animals possessed the key faculty for ordering those rules: The faculty of reason.

One may fantasize a government for some creature that has no language, and that is self-sufficient after seven months, like a wolf that acquires its hunting teeth at that age. Similarly, one may imagine a Robinson Crusoe living for years alone on an island. Yet in every imagining, this person must necessarily arrive on his island equipped with language, reason, and skills forged previously in a community of other human beings. Should this person bereft of all community wash up on his island in a basket like Moses in the bulrushes, he would perish. Human existence of any kind requires community, and far more than physical sustenance, as the fatal experiment of Holy Roman Emperor Frederick II (1194-1250) with language should demonstrate. His monk Salimbene di Adam described how the emperor took five hapless infants,

---

[r] *N.B.*: Again, "government" is *not* the "state"; the state is a form of government that began in Europe in the middle of the 17th century.

bidding foster-mothers and nurses to suckle and bathe and wash the children, but in no wise to prattle or speak with them; for he would have learnt whether they would speak the Hebrew language (which had been the first), or Greek, or Latin, or Arabic, or perchance the tongue of their parents of whom they had been born. But he laboured in vain, for the children could not live without clappings of the hands, and gestures, and gladness of countenance[.][13]

One may also fantasize the "government" of this solitary Robinson Crusoe, whose "society" perishes with him, who playfully says to himself that he has been "good" or "bad," or playfully says to himself that he will be "punished" if he does not, say, dry his catch of fish by sundown. However, this is an idiosyncratic use of terms. There is no ethical "good" or "bad" for him, and no agency to enforce his behavior: The solitary Robinson Crusoe has no ethics, no morality, and no government: He has but one behavioral guide, and it is merely hygiene.[14]

As for the necessity of government to enforce consistent rules of mutual cooperation, this enforcement does not necessarily imply violence. To be sure, man's entire history is marked by violent behavior, particularly from government. But whether this violence is "innate" or not, it is also undeniably true that man is aware of nonviolent cooperation as a survival strategy, and that he is responsive to nonviolent signaling of expected behavior. Communities that employ reason in some way to limit violence, especially the organized violence of government, are more successful at reaching their goals[s] than those that do not.

1.1.2 No government can be considered good without conforming with man's nature as a rational animal. Yet since nor "good" nor "nature" nor "reason" is a univocal term, a rectification of terms establishes the second central problem: Where to locate the agency of reason.

> So convenient a thing is it to be a reasonable creature, since it enables one to find or make a reason for everything one has a mind to do.
> – Benjamin Franklin

The standard of behavior enforced by government is necessarily a standard of values. One may fantasize a government that is a completely value-free umpire, indifferent to the terms of contracts, no matter how barbaric, in which men can freely enslave, prostitute, mutilate, torture, or cannibalize themselves or mem-

---

[s] Of course an idle pettifogger can concoct the logical possibility of a society with a goal of maximizing violence or increasing suffering, achieved by botched, unreasonable means. But even that absurdity fails in that it would assume a society exclusively composed of suicidal psychopaths: Any society this side of cloud cuckoo land would at worst want to maximize violence and suffering *for those not in power*. Kleristocracy makes that unrealizable.

bers of their families, untroubled by warring enclaves or by civil war – in other words the squared circle of a "government" that "enforces" no standard of behavior whatsoever. But even this supposedly value-free government enforces a standard of values: It prefers behavior qualified solely by contract above all other behavior. Such fantasies can narrowly be termed "good," in the sense that they do provide *some* advantages of mutual cooperation, possibly for *some* members of the community. But in all senses, whether narrow or broad, a good government always enforces an ordinal set of preferred behaviors – that is, *values*, which is an inalterable fact unique to man.

There is no scientific knowledge of human nature useful for political science.
Having a universally accepted scientific knowledge of human nature would still be useless for the establishment of any axiom of government. One may claim that the human brain of 3,000 years ago works epistemologically the same way as that of the present day,[t, 15] but whether this conjecture is established by science as true or false is irrelevant for political science. The human brain is unique in its ability to form abstractions, but a government may flourish for centuries by subjecting its reasoning citizens to corvée labor scarcely different from that of brutes. The governments of the pharaohs ruled for thousands of years without an abstract knowledge of geometry, despite its value for reestablishing property boundaries after the flooding of the Nile. Whatever may have been human nature in the time of the pharaohs, or in the time before or after, it is axiomatically true that governments existed that compelled the cooperative behavior of their subjects, and even if tyrannical, may be narrowly termed "good" at the very least by virtue of their enforcement of the cooperative behavior necessary to a society larger than the family, without which the individual cannot exist.

Biosocial science or evolutionary psychology/biology is not useful for political science.
These related fields of study tend to support the principle that man is an in-nately sociable animal. For example, biosocial scientist Nicholas A. Christakis:

> Genes affect not only the structure and function of our bodies; not only the structure and function of our minds and, hence, our behaviors; but also the structure and function of our societies. [...] Natural selection has shaped our lives as social animals, guiding the evolution of what I

---

[t] One may scoff at G.K. Chesterton's rejection of evolution, but logic demands acceptance of his observation that the transition from animal to man, whenever and however it occurred, must have been sudden, not gradual. For the axiom of human nature, a brain capable of thinking in abstractions either exists or does not exist: No transitional state is possible. See the discussion "The Alleged Logical Heterogeneity of Primitive Man" in *Human Action, op.cit.*, page 36.

call a "social suite" of features priming our capacity for love, friendship, cooperation, learning[. ...W]e carry within us innate proclivities that reflect our natural social state, a state that is, as it turns out, primarily good, practically and even morally. Humans can no more make a society that is inconsistent with these positive urges than ants can suddenly make beehives. [...] Our good deeds are not just the products of Enlightenment values. They have a deeper and prehistoric origin.[16, 17]

This empirical research does not supply any material for praxeology, the study of human action.[18] And even if we suppose the principle of sociability to be demonstrably true or false, neither supposition can answer the normative question of what kind of government ought to exist. For example, one may genially assume man to be innately sociable, and yet out of an abundance of caution against his capacity for violence attempt to establish a limited government of divided powers, with numerous checks and balances. On the other hand, one may assume man to be innately wolfish, and yet in the hope of a beneficent government, establish a singular wolf to violently impose his will to prevent a "condition of Warre of every one against every one; in which case every one is governed by his own Reason".[19]

Neither morality, ethics, nor 'moral science' is useful for political science.
One may well condemn a society that practices female genital mutilation, honor killings, and the stoning of unbelievers. But that very society may reply, "So then, genital mutilation of 'dysphoric' children, sodomy, unrestricted abortion, and euthanasia are your evidence of a superior society?" Certainly in practice every society corroborates the dictum of David Hume (1711-1776) that no 'is' can necessarily imply an 'ought.' That is to say, it *is* the case that human cooperation beyond the family necessarily signifies government, which is necessary for individual existence; but beyond affirming the "goodness" of some type of order solely by virtue of its enforcement of cooperation, nothing can be implied describing how that order *ought* to be.

The American philosopher and neuroscientist Sam Harris has recently challenged that dictum. He seeks to give objective status to values with his attempt to prove the following premise: "Values reduce to facts about the well-being of conscious creatures." He argues that scientific evidence has value, specifically objective medical evidence for human well-being, saying:

I argue that the value of well-being – specifically the value of avoiding the worst possible misery for everyone – is on the same footing [as objective medical evidence....] Certain "oughts" are built right into the foundations of human thought. We need not apologize for pulling ourselves up by our bootstraps in this way.[20]

And:

> I am claiming that people's actual values and desires are fully deter-
> mined by an objective reality[21]

and, he maintains, that science can come to understand how that determination takes place. Even supposing such a moral science existed, one could
nevertheless construct a society on completely inhuman values, even one
devoid of compassion and human sympathy – as Stalinist society was. Witness
Solzhenitsyn's heartbreaking account of the girl forced to stand in the icy wind
at the Marfino *sharashka* Soviet labor camp merely for wishing that an escapee
might "have a good time."[22]

Even the values of pleasant socialists like the avuncular Bernie Sanders
must be rejected as informing political science, as well as those of Leftist academics like John Rawls. For despite their appeal to some lofty morality or
ethics, they follow a socialist model as did the Stalinists: They all assume a state
using public goods and police power to enforce *their* value system, to the
benefit of *their* preferred groups, usually under the pretense that "everybody" is
better off with a "little" coercion here and there, according to *their* fancied
standard. That standard is rooted in state power, with the pleasant socialists
differing from thoroughgoing, consistent socialists – the Stalinists – only in
degree, not in kind.

A government is termed "good" as it conforms with man's nature as a
rational animal, but beyond the universal "goodness" of providing some order
for cooperation beyond the family, without which community individual life is
impossible, that conformity is completely subjective. In contrast, the state is a
type of government prevailing over the last four centuries that makes sweeping
claims to ethical goodness – typically in terms of a deontological "equity" or
"social justice" – when in fact its claim to being "good" rests on the ethical
system chosen and enforced according to the subjective will[23] of its sovereign.
By embracing the state as their governing model, socialists – pleasant or
otherwise – have chained themselves to a boulder whose ineluctable gravitation
is toward totalitarianism.

Despite their nature as rational animals, the great mass of men are not led by
reason; they are led by Interest.
But for a meagre handful of philosophers – and this excludes the captious
pettifoggers in the state academia – I do not find anyone guided by Aristotle's
definitive characteristic for man, his reason. For the vast majority, reason is
merely rationalization – an artistic assembly of words to justify a conclusion
reached in advance by Interest. I do not say "self-interest," with its insinuation
of "selfishness," for many follow a perceived interest that is manifestly
pernicious to their own well-being. I say *Interest*, plainly and simply: The

childish wanting for something felt to be good, obtainable with the minimum of effort and the minimum of rationalization offered to contemporaries. Many proclaim, "Let reason be our guide, wherever it may lead us," and behold, the Christian speaker justifies Christianity, the Muslim justifies Mohammad, the endowed justifies his benefactor, the aggrieved justifies his violence, and the ignorant justifies his nonsense.

This Interest, so readily and naturally at odds with our reasoned well-being, becomes a fearful monster of oppression when vested with political power, as George Washington so presciently cautioned.[24] Where in the past all good men strove to "hitch their wagon to a star," meaning to attach their lives to some enduring truth, now the majority strive to "hitch their wagon to the juggernaut," the state that crushes those opposed to their Interest. The political investiture of Interest constitutes ideology. Ideology, in this pejorative sense, is the unfalsifiable, systematic rationalization of Interest.

Furthermore, the individual seldom arrives at this rationalization of Interest as an individual. A revolution in views on the culturally foundational issues of abortion[25] and marriage[26] took place within the span of a few years. Did this radical shift in majority opinion occur because each citizen soberly considered the matter and conveyed his reasoning to a legislator? No, it did not. This shift in "reasoning," like the result of every other "national dialog" on a controversial issue, was the result of a process of cultural osmosis, of repeating ideological clichés and of referencing the prevailing shibboleths of "freedom" and "equity," having little to do with reason.[27]

However, the fact of an unreasoning mass does not argue for restricting political decision-making to philosopher kings. Even they, like everyone, know only the mental landscape[u] furnished by their milieu, by their community. There is no godlike reasoning in a vacuum, no solitary soul communing in his skull with an all-knowing, supernatural being – the archetypal mental landscape of almost every political philosopher. Despite the removal of threats associated with atheism, the image of god remains from an age that truly, fearfully believed. In all the descriptions of political scientists, one can't help visualizing the solitary reasoner, the projected self, standing alone as if before

---

[u] A.O. Lovejoy described the minefield of entering the mental landscape of a past age. His warnings to the historian of ideas fully apply to contemporary ideas. He lists 1) "Unconscious mental habits," e.g., of the 18th century oversimplification of applying "reason" to social problems; 2) "[E]ndemic assumptions," especially those of the age in which one lives; 3) "Metaphysical pathos," or the appeal of a set of ideas to deep-seated feelings, e.g., "monistic pathos," the assumption of a universe comprised in a consistent, monolithic principle; 4) "Philosophical semantics," or the use of "sacred words and phrases" in contexts that make their meaning elastic, e.g., the various significations of "nature"; and 5) Focus on just the explicitly stated ideas of philosophers of the age under study, inviting the introduction of anachronistic context. Lovejoy, A.O., *The Great Chain of Being: The Study of the History of an Idea* (Harvard University Press, revised edition from 1933 original, October 1, 1971, ISBN 978-0674361539, 400 pages), pages 7ff.

the father god in judgment, attempting to account for his place in society. But unlike the homunculus in Daniel Dennett's Cartesian Theater,[28] the interior man cannot bear to be alone: There is always a symbiotic presence, whether acknowledged or not, shaping and evaluating every projected thought. Like much of atheistic thinking, there is almost always the "whiff from the empty bottle"[29] of a vanishing Christian tradition.

The only choices open to anyone for changing his mental landscape are whether to enter a community that offers more or fewer rewards for reasoning (e.g., a scientific instead of, say, an artistic community) and whether to enter a community that is wider or narrower (e.g., as a horticultural scientist instead of a local farmer). In every case, the reasoning individual may offer his syllogisms, but his premises are shaped inescapably and beyond his ken by his community – a community whose greater or lesser nurturing of dispassionate discourse constitutes its symbiotic reason.

The second[v] central problem is where to locate the agency of reason.
In spite of the insoluble difficulties with individual reason – its definition, its standard of truth, its applicability – political philosophers have relentlessly tried to introduce it as the agency for determining political choices in accordance with man's rational nature. But reason does not exist in [A] the individual in a state of nature, not in [B] reason reified in the natural law, not in [C] the general will, not in [D] a universal secular humanist ethics, not in [E] the abstracted individual of game theory – that modern-day equivalent of Scholastic casuistry, and not in [F] the individual as "informed voter."

That almost inescapable god-soul inner dialog is the basis of the greatest error in the search for political axioms, which is to search for ultimate principles positioned somehow *outside* the subject under discussion. According to this view, the subject alone cannot "pull itself up by its own bootstraps" without self-justifying circularity of argument. For example, in this view a supernatural being, outside the natural order, must provide a metaphysics that instantiates its own mental activity (e.g., John 1:1's "In the beginning was the Word, and the Word was with God, and the Word was God.") and must provide a system of ethics by revelation. If there were no supernatural agency to perform these roles, then human thought would have only a purely subjective correspondence with the physical world around it, and all ethics would be "situational," with men "making it up as they go along." However, this view merely regresses the metaphysical and ethical issues of an individual mind into the mind of the supernatural agent, whose supernatural powers, untroubled by

---

[v] The first is discussed in the following section.

the sublunary difficulties of its own creation, somehow provide a magic window into the foundational solution.

Both Hobbes and Descartes implicitly recognized the question-begging nature, the circularity, of the supernatural agent, and excluded it. Yet without it, their rationalistic reductionism left them with a nominalism that, in its political aspect that concerns us here, placed ultimate political power in the subjective will of the sovereign, as flamboyantly and explicitly stated by Hobbes (1588-1679) in *Leviathan* (1651) and casually accepted by Descartes (1596-1650) in his letter to his friend Pierre Chanut.[30] Thomas Hobbes is aggressively anti-Scholastic[31] in his admirable attempt at the rectification of terms:

> The Light of humane minds is Perspicuous Words, but by exact definitions first snuffed, and purged from ambiguity ; *Reason* is the *pace*; Encrease of *Science*, the *way* ; and the Benefit of man-kind, the *end*. And on the contrary, Metaphors, and senslesse and ambiguous words, are like *ignes fatui* ; and reasoning upon them, is wandering amongst innumerable absurdities ; and their end, contention, and sedition, or contempt.[32]

But what is his abstract man in the state of nature but a Scholastic "*ignis fatuus*"?

Even when reading the supposedly modern, atheistic accounts of how property rights were established – sometimes with the bogus[w] caveat that they are *logical* and not historically testable – one realizes how myths and legends were formed: The academic's projected self enters a Garden of Eden landscape and does some "homesteading" followed by quibbling over its legitimacy.

Let us re-examine in more detail the many misplacements of the agency of reason, in order to discard them.

1.1.2a   Man in a so-called state of nature, standing abstractly alone and apart from any community, is the kernel idea of much specious theorizing about the state, whether from Hobbesian absolutism, or Lockean liberalism, or libertarian daydreaming.

The presumed "man in a state of nature" not only has never existed historically, but cannot even be applied logically to anything human. As John C. Calhoun observed:

> [S]uch a state [of nature] is purely hypothetical. It never did, nor can exist; as it is inconsistent with the preservation and perpetuation of the race. It is, therefore, a great misnomer to call it *the state of nature*.

---

[w] For if the historical fact falsifies the logical account, then of what value is the counterfactual logical account, even as a "heuristic"? Logical accounts, including those offered by praxeology, must nevertheless survive falsifiability.

Instead of being the natural state of man, it is, of all conceivable states, the most opposed to his nature – most repugnant to his feelings, and most incompatible with his wants. His natural state is, the social and political – the one for which his Creator made him, and the only one in which he can preserve and protect his race. As, then, there never was such a state as the, so called, state of nature, and never can be, it follows, that men, instead of being born in it, are born in the social and political state; and of course, instead of being born free and equal, are born subject, not only to parental authority, but to the laws and institutions of the country where born, and under whose protection they draw their first breath.33

Notwithstanding, let us try to suppose such a man. There he stands, stooped, drooling from his prognathous mouth, wrapped in a dirty animal hide, clutching his spear. After some solitary philosophizing – miraculously, outside the context of language and family – he has realized the benefits of society and has suddenly sought out his fellows, who have simultaneously and miraculously been struck by the same epiphany. Just where did this hairy philosopher come from? He could not have come from a family, for that implies a tribal order, and with it, a rudimentary governance prior to this "state of nature." No, clearly he materialized out of thin air, for the benefit of political philosophers everywhere. Nor can one object that this creature is not a historical fact, but is simply a "heuristic" tool useful as a logical construct, or as a device to reduce a complex to its simplest parts. For wherever and however he appears, from Hobbes' brutes in perpetual "Warre [...] without a common Power to keep them all in awe"34 to de Jasay's "algebraic" placeholder,35 this construct or device invalidates everything that follows, since it is a fable with no more resemblance to anything human than Adam and Eve – and likely spawned from the same unconscious archetype. It is an archetype of fable, with no more resemblance to human nature than a hydra or a hippogriff.

1.1.2b   No discussion of the agency of reason in political science can be undertaken without a discussion of the *ius naturale*,ˣ natural law, and the work on that subject by Heinrich A. Rommen. Strikingly ironic in its development over two millennia in the West is the inversion of the expected basis of natural law in reason compared to the will: For it is the Christian thinkers who are by far the

---

ˣ Rommen notes that the terms *lex naturalis* and *ius naturale* were used interchangeably, citing only usage by Francisco Suárez and Robert Bellarmine (1542-1621) as exceptions. Their only distinction was that international violations of *lex naturalis* were not grounds for just war, while violations against *ius naturale* were. He does not take up what seems to me the more important distinction, namely the connotation of *ius* with right and *lex* with statute. *Vide* Rommen, *op.cit. infra*, pages 59-60.

greatest supporters of *lex-ratio* (the primacy of reason over will in natural law), while it is the rationalist and positivist thinkers, particularly of the Enlightenment, who are supporters of *lex-voluntas* (the primacy of will over reason).[36]

Rommen finds the beginning of Christian thinking on natural law in the Apostle Paul, especially referencing Romans 2:15, which states that Christians have the true law "written in their hearts."[37] But this is hardly discursive, since every human being has an intuitive sense of a rightness that is superior to any statute.[38] Exact thinking on natural law in the Christian tradition truly begins with the Jesuit Francisco Suárez (1548-1617) of the School of Salamanca, Spain, whom Rommen calls the "father of modern natural law",[39] stealing the honorific from Hugo Grotius. Suárez constructed a true political theory, based on Thomas Aquinas (1225-1274), elaborating his *Summa Theologiae, prima-secundae* (I-II), questions 90-108, where Aquinas himself mentions *ius naturale* just once in over 500 questions, in question 94.[40]

For Aquinas, man's very nature is a reflection of the image of god, in two respects: His reason and his free will:[41]

> As cognition is directed to being, so the will is directed to goodness[42]

> since only the good constitutes a proper *telos*, or end for man. Thus

> both in God and in man the intellect, not the will, holds primacy.[43]

For contemporary Alexander of Hales (1185-1245), god's eternal law is the seal; natural moral law is its impression on man's rational nature.[44] For Aquinas and Hales, the foundation of law is in the mind of god, with nothing to do with a speculative origin in a "state of nature."[45] And since all of creation is a manifestation of the one god, one may reason without explicit reference to revelation on matters not directly relating to the salvation of souls. Thus under the *ius naturale* reason and revelation are not mutually exclusive; instead, it provides the foundation for reason. Nor are natural law and positive law mutually exclusive, and Aquinas even enjoins obedience to an unjust law if it is for the sake of the greater good.[46] The idea of "the reign of a rational divine power in all that exists and all that comes to pass in the world"[47] is a seminal idea in all of Western philosophy from Plato forward, and it becomes the controlling idea of the Middle Ages as the Great Chain of Being.

In flamboyant and ominous contrast to the main Christian tradition stand Duns Scotus (c1265-1308) and William of Occam (c1285-1347). For Scotus, "morality depends on the will of God", and law is purely will, in the legal positivist sense.[48] For Occam, the will of god is so absolute that he can even will that human beings hate him.[49] According to Occam

> all being is founded on the mere absolute will of God without participation in His essence.[50]

Thus reason is not a reflection of, or impress from, the mind of god – it is merely the servant of the will;[y] universals are not rooted in being, in god's creation – they are a mere *flatus vocis*, a spoken breath.[51]

Rommen characterizes Occam's views as setting in motion an evolution in "the natural moral law [that] would lead to pure moral positivism, indeed to nihilism."[52] With Scotus and Occam the Great Chain of Being forged by god had been shattered, and reason unfettered from its metaphysical moorings.

The religious wars of the 16th and 17th centuries in Europe definitively shape the mental landscape of the political thinkers of that time. The French *politique*[z] Jean Bodin (1530-1596) published his *Les six livres de la République* (*The Six Books of the Republic*) in 1576, about the middle of the French religious wars (1562-1598) between the Catholics and Calvinist Hugenots. The Arminian – the Dutch equivalent of the French *politiques* – Hugo Grotius published *De jure belli ac pacis* (*Law of War and Peace*) during the Thirty Years' War, in 1625, when the entry of the Dutch widened the conflict, which was evolving into a full-scale religious war between Protestants and Catholics. Hobbes' *Leviathan* (1651) was published at the end of the English civil war, just two years after Cromwell's massacre of Irish Catholics at Drogheda, and the beheading of Catholic-leaning King Charles I, whom Hobbes ardently supported. The *Politica Methodice Digesta* (*Politics Methodically Defined*) of Calvinist Johannes Althusius was published in 1603, six years before the war of independence (1566-1609) separated the Calvinist Netherlands from Catholic Spain. The impulse of all these writers was to restrain religious war generally, and especially restrain the influence of the Catholic Church upon the Holy Roman Empire.

It is important to note that this backdrop of religious wars gave birth not only to the state in the middle of the 17th century but also to the kernel idea of the Enlightenment project: The effort to construct a single universal ethics[aa] based not on creed or doctrine but on reason. Indeed the powerful synergy of this project provided legitimacy to a state that was supposed to be simultaneously capable of omnipotence and impartiality.

Bodin's *Six livres* established him as the great theorist of absolutism, of the unlimited power of the sovereign. In the book he describes sovereignty as *la puissance absolue et perpetuelle d'une République*

---

[y] This fundamental confrontation of reason and will is taken up again in discussing the theological crossroad of Pelagius and Augustine, where in the latter the assertion of complete absolutism in the will of god finds its roots in Manicheism.

[z] The *politiques* were French intellectuals who wanted to minimize religious disputes by enhancing the power of the state.

[aa] Jean Bodin's last manuscript, *Heptaplomeres* (1683 posthumous publication), was a dialog among adherents of seven faiths, concluding in their agreement that all religions share the belief in one god and in the same universal truths.

which is subject to no earthly tribunal, a power which creates law but is not subjected to the law it creates. As well, this power is indivisible, and so cannot be divided between supreme and lesser magistrates. Sovereignty is centralized supreme power.[53]

Thus with Bodin the sovereign acquires the power to legislate, and do so absolutely – a break from the medieval limitation of the monarch as a judge, further limited by his subservience to god in the Great Chain of Being and to the *ius naturale*.

Grotius is rooted in the scholastic tradition – he relied on the *ius gentium*[bb] of Fernando Vázquez de Menchaca (1512-1569), another jurist of the Salamanca school – and his praise of Augustine marks him as an advocate of dogmatic rather than latitudinarian Christianity.[54] Nevertheless, his *De jure belli ac pacis* marks the transition from the metaphysical to the rationalist view of natural law.[55]

Despite its title, the *Law of War and Peace* concerns not just the conduct of nations, but of the individual entering society at its creation, since, as Hobbes was to do a quarter-century later, Grotius views the individual outside society as homologous to the state outside the law. The first right of all creatures to self-defense (book I, chapter II, §I; chapter III, §I) is like the right of states to engage in just war (book I, chapter II, §II-IX): Both are based in *ius naturale*; the former is private war, the latter is public war. The second right is the right of property, deriving immediately from the first (book I, chapter II, §I).[56] Grotius finds the origin of property in "division or occupation" (book II, chapter III, §I) – essentially, (social) gift or homesteading. Grotius does not mention conquest in this context, since he must elaborate the many details of the rightness of property taken by war in the final book III of the work.

Grotius is insistent on the rights of sovereignty, which he defines in book I, chapter III, §VII:

> The sovereignty or supreme authority is that authority the acts of whom are not subjected to the legal power of another [...and...] is not bound by his predecessor's decisions.[57]

His sovereignty is absolute, with no basis in sovereignty of the people or in the peoples' calling kings to account or in their consent (book I, chapter III, §VIII), for

---

[bb] The Roman *ius gentium*, law of peoples, guided their administration of subject nations within the empire; the Roman policy was to tolerate the rule of locals under their own laws, provided they paid taxes and acknowledged the *imperium*. Since this meant finding the common elements of law among disparate people, it came to be equated with *ius naturale*, even as early as Ulpian (†223). *Vide* Rommen, *op.cit. infra*, page 26.

in the case of civil government, one must stop at the supreme person or assembly because higher authority cannot keep ascending into infinity. Only God is devoted to passing judgement on the crimes of this body.[58]

Furthermore,

[w]hether an act be morally acceptable or unacceptable is not a suitable distinguishing criterion – certainly in affairs of state, in which this is often difficult to discern.[59]

The people have no right of resistance against the sovereign (book I, chapter IV, §II), and even the right of personal self-defense is curtailed against him, since one cannot kill "persons of great importance, such as rulers"[60] – not even when he is the aggressor, as his "life is of great serviceability to others."[61] The people are wholly at the mercy of the sovereign, since even when oppressed they are forbidden from appealing to a foreign power:

The desire for liberty does not entitle one to wage war, because liberty is not an attribute of people always and everywhere. When it is said that men and peoples have liberty by nature, this is referring to the law of nature prior to the advent of human society. [62]

Nor is there any appeal to a higher authority in natural law:

The natural law is not dependent on God for its content, nor for its existence, but only for its implantation in us. It would exist even if God did not exist. [63]

Thus in Grotius the fundamentals of the state are set: There is no earthly power above the state sovereign; he is the final arbiter of disputes; his authority derives solely from his will; and most significantly, his power is exercised directly upon his subjects[cc] in his role as sole guardian of their enumerated rights.

In Thomas Hobbes' *Leviathan* the absolutism of the state is set forth in histrionic style.[dd] Just as Grotius had written to vindicate king James I of England,[64] Hobbes wrote to vindicate the autocratic king Charles I,[65] even asserting that sovereigns need never obtain their subjects' consent to taxation.[66] He defines the eponymous title:

For by Art is created that great LEVIATHAN called a COMMON-WEALTH, or STATE, (in latine CIVITAS) which is but an Artificiall

---

[cc] For the 17th century at least, the power of the state stopped at the threshold of the family. Specifically in Grotius: (book II, chapter V, §I-VII).

[dd] Indeed, one hears on almost every page of *Leviathan* the voice of someone determined to "cut a dash" – the incessant booming of a tiresome blunderbuss.

Man ; though of greater stature and strength than the Naturall, for whose protection and defence it was intended ; and in which, the Sovereignty is an Artificiall Soul, as giving life and motion to the whole body[.][67]

Here Hobbes forthrightly detaches himself from the metaphysical realism of the past: The state has its foundation neither in god nor in the natural law – it is purely an artificial construct of reason. Natural law applies only to man in his supposedly warlike state of nature:

> The Right Of Nature, which Writers commonly call *Jus Naturale*, is the Liberty each man hath, to use his own power, as he will himselfe, for the preservation of his own Nature ; that is to say, of his own Life ; and consequently, of doing any thing, which in his own Judgement, and Reason, hee shall conceive to be the aptest means thereunto.[68]

In that state of private war (terminology doubtless borrowed from Grotius), each man has the right to use any means to preserve his life. But in order to form a society, all men wish to

> [get] themselves out from that miserable condition of Warre, which is necessarily consequent (as hath been shewn) to the natural Passions of men, when there is no visible Power to keep them in awe, and tye them by feare of punishment to the performance of their Covenants[. ...][69]

For Hobbes the essence of civilized life is the keeping of promises, implying the state function of courts; the threat of violence to civilized life requires the state functions of the armed forces and police power; and the only enforcer of this promise-keeping and security is one man:

> The only way to erect such a Common Power, as may be able to defend them from the invasion of Forraigners, and the injuries of one another, and thereby to secure them in such sort, as that by their owne industrie, and by the fruites of the Earth, they may nourish themselves and live contentedly : is, to conferre all their power and strength upon one Man, or upon one Assembly of men, that may reduce all their Wills, by plurality of voices unto one Will [...of the...] great Leviathan, or rather (to speake more reverently) of that *Mortall God*, to which wee owe under the *Immortall God*, our peace and defence.[70]

Hobbes makes a breathtaking number of assumptions here. Even conceding that man is more passionate than reasonable,[71] surely there is a passion for society and not just violence – which in Hobbes is more wolfish than the wolves, which do observe behavioral rules. Also, how is it that an exclusively wolfish mankind peacefully decided upon one man to put them all in awe? The elevation of this "Mortall God" clearly was established by a contract that by miraculous exception did not need a Leviathan to enforce it – destroying the premise that a state is required for the enforcement of any contract.[72, 73] And how is it that there was just *one* candidate for this very agreeable eminence? Despite mankind being described as warlike without exception, apparently just a single contender for "Mortall God" gamely stepped into the running without a struggle. Also, once chosen by acclamation – or in some mysterious way placed into his position – why should this primal contract be binding for the lifetimes of the original contractors, not to mention their descendants?[74] Hobbes may have sensed some glimmer of a problem in the last objection, since he insists that contracts made under the threat of violence are nevertheless binding[75] – but then on the very next page pronounces testimony extracted by torture to be invalid![76]

The root problem in Hobbes, who boasts mathematical pretensions for political science, is that he reduces man to a cipher. For him, all men are much alike in both body and spirit, remarking that

> as to the faculties of the mind, [...] I find yet a greater equality amongst men, than that of strength.[77]

Hobbes sees not flesh-and-blood human beings, but ciphers eager to "reduce all their Wills" into the Leviathan, in whose one will – not in natural law – is the source not only of their physical safety, but even of their right to property.[78, 79] And here Hobbes stands revealed as the prototype for the socialist intellectual, proclaiming: *Everybody else* is a cipher, but *my* daydream will rule.

In John Locke (1632-1704) the natural law establishes the inalienable rights of the individual in property, broadly defined as the rights to "life, liberty, and estate." These inalienable rights establish the law – the law does not establish them, and neither does the will of the sovereign, regardless of how the sovereign is defined.[80] For Locke the primary issue facing society is neither the inherent lawlessness of its members nor their inability to keep their word. On the contrary, all of them recognize the law as a function of their natural rights:

> [Man] hath by nature a power, not only to preserve his property, that is, his life, liberty and estate, against the injuries and attempts of other men; but to judge of, and punish the breaches of that law in others[.][81]

The problem is that there is no uniform standard for the enforcement of the law that they separately but willingly embrace. To overcome the problem, they freely contract to establish a single standard for judging breaches of the law:

And thus all private judgment of every particular member being excluded, the community comes to be umpire, by settled standing rules, indifferent, and the same to all parties[.][82]

Despite starting at the identical point as Hobbes – man in a fictional and combative "state of nature" – Locke's final arbiter of disputes seems at first glance to be not an autocratic Leviathan but a rather pleasant fellow: An impartial "umpire" who makes judgments at law with no self-interested motives such as maintaining himself in power, with no favoritism to any group, with no standard of values other than the absolute value of contracts and the preservation of property in the broadest sense of individual rights. Yet these pleasant attributes describe nothing human: Locke has invested the state with godlike qualities – which will be exercised by very real, ambitious, and biased human beings. The state for Locke merely postures as the "indifferent" guardian of private utilitarianism, in which the contractual arrangements of its members and not the state decide the greatest good for the greatest number.

Locke substitutes for the traditional idea of the natural as an order of human affairs, as a moral reflex of the metaphysical order of the universe revealed to human reason in the creation as God's will, the conception of natural law as a rather nominalistic symbol for a catalogue or bundle of individual rights that stem from individual self-interest.[83]

1.1.2c   As if to demonstrate the uselessness of reasoning from the protean idea of a "state of nature," Jean-Jacques Rousseau (1712-1778) uses it in yet another way, to found the central theme of his political philosophy:

The fundamental principle of all morality about which I have reasoned in all my writings [...] is that man is a naturally good being, loving justice and order; that there is no original perversity in the human heart, and that the first movements of nature are always right.[84]

In *The Social Contract* (1762), Rousseau describes the origin of society in a way that is far more realistic and plausible than Hobbes or Locke, stating at the outset:

The most ancient of all societies, and the only natural one, is the society of the family.[85]

Although created from loveless animal urges, the family soon evolved. The humans' initial self-interest yielded to "some gross ideas of mutual undertakings" and from "[i]narticulate cries, plenty of gestures and some imitative sounds" there developed a primitive language hardly more refined "than that of rooks or monkeys."[86] Rousseau paints a realistic and believable arcadia:

The first expansions of the human heart were the effects of a novel situation, which united husbands and wives, fathers and children, under one roof. The habit of living together soon gave rise to the finest feelings known to humanity, conjugal love and paternal affection. Every family became a little society, the more united because liberty and reciprocal attachment were the only bonds of its union.[87]

Family units joined up and soon they began singing and dancing together in penurious but joyous equality. – But immediately the cormorant[ee] of comparison alighted in this bucolic Eden:

Whoever sang or danced best, whoever was the handsomest, the strongest, the most dexterous, or the most eloquent, came to be of most consideration; and this was the first step towards inequality, and at the same time towards vice. From these first distinctions arose on the one side vanity and contempt and on the other shame and envy[.][88]

Along with envious comparison arose another inevitable curse: Property, born of the division of labor:[ff]

So long as men remained content with their rustic huts, so long as they were satisfied with clothes made of the skins of animals and sewn together with thorns and fish-bones [...]; in a word, so long as they undertook only what a single person could accomplish, and confined themselves to such arts as did not require the joint labour of several hands, they lived free, healthy, honest and happy lives [...]. But from the moment one man began to stand in need of the help of another; from the moment it appeared advantageous to any one man to have enough provisions for two, equality disappeared, property was introduced, work became indispensable, and vast forests became smiling fields, which man had to water with the sweat of his brow, and where slavery and misery were soon seen to germinate and grow up with the crops.[89]

Thus it is only with the advent of property that violence appears, and with it, the need for a final arbiter of disputes, a sovereign will, with the power to enforce his decisions:

Thus, as the most powerful or the most miserable considered their might or misery as a kind of right to the possessions of others,

---

[ee] John Milton, *Paradise Lost*, Book IV.

[ff] Rousseau's view of the principle of the division of labor stands in perverse opposition to every serious economist, who sees it as the peaceful engine of trade, unifying even otherwise mutually hostile people around the world.

equivalent, in their opinion, to that of property, the destruction of equality was attended by the most terrible disorders. Usurpations by the rich, robbery by the poor, and the unbridled passions of both, suppressed the cries of natural compassion and the still feeble voice of justice, and filled men with avarice, ambition and vice.[90]

This sovereign will need not be a monarch, and theorists of the period, including Hobbes and Locke, allowed that a legislative assembly might also be the sovereign. But for Rousseau, the sovereign will is much more diffuse and ambiguous: It is the mutual compact that each member of society has made, not to an autocratic Leviathan, but to every other member. Their collective contract constitutes the general will. According to Rousseau, it is infallible, always in the right, because it expresses what each member expresses in his private will, when "enlightened."[91] Nebulous as the idea may be, it can mean only one thing in practice:

> [A]ccording to the basic compact the only thing that can bind indi-
> viduals is the general will, and the only way to be sure that a particular
> will is in conformity with the general will is to put it to a free vote of the
> people.[92]

The majority had become the autocratic final arbiter of disputes, but far more capricious, bloody, and inhuman than any absolutist monarch, as events of the French Revolution, of which Rousseau was the leading inspiration, would grimly prove. In this way Rousseau advanced the paradigm of the modern state, providing not only the defining characteristic of majoritarian absolutism, but also its primal mandate for removing the cause of destructive envy – inequality – and for removing any absolute claim to private property.

1.1.2d   At the threshold of the 19th century, the West enjoyed an unprecedented optimism: The Industrial Revolution, capitalism, and the nascent science of economics were making possible the very lives of millions of people, by sharply reducing infant mortality and sharply increasing standards of health.[93] This demonstration of the power of science inspired the popular confidence that the mind could also resolve the problems of social organization so that all could live in peace and prosperity. Beethoven's Ninth Symphony, completed in 1824, became the anthem of this confidence in a society of universal brotherhood.

But at that moment philosophy, the vanguard of future society, faced an ominous dilemma. Confined within the box of the state as the sole model for government, it could find no place for the agency of reason in ordering the free and prosperous commonwealth – indeed it had undermined its role. The state was assumed to be necessary, but it had no basis outside the arbitrary will of the sovereign, however defined. Now, unlike in the past, the state could not exist without the consent of the swelling multitudes of citizens, who more than ever could read and think. Surely there could be devised a universal ethics based not on creed or doctrine but on reason, to which every citizen of the West could consent as the basis of society. This was the Enlightenment project: The effort to create in political science the universally accepted articulation of the Ode to Joy.

With David Hume (1711-1776), the effort to find reason in the natural law was completely abandoned. For him, reason, and morality as well, are merely the slave of the passions. He defines

> *virtue to be whatever mental action or quality gives to a spectator the pleasing sentiment of approbation*; and vice the contrary.[94] [emphasis in the original]

Morality, cut off from reason, can offer no prescriptive guide to human affairs, other than its consequential usefulness for each man or for the society at large. Here the broad avenue originally offered to reasoned objectivity by the natural law would run its logical course into the blind alley of 19th century utilitarianism. The fatal problem for utilitarianism is that whatever agency tries to implement it on behalf of the state cannot tell a good action from a bad one until *after its implementation*. As Anthony de Jasay points out, the guide of utilitarianism

> is thus no longer "maximize utility," but "maximize the expected value of utility." The instant we say this, however, we let loose an avalanche of problems, each of which is insoluble except by *recourse to authority*.[95] [emphasis in the original]

Immanuel Kant (1724-1804) accepted Hume's judgment, concluding that law and morality must be radically separate. His universal moral law stands like the peak of the Zugspitze, icy and alone, shunning the company of useful corollaries:

> Act externally in such a manner that the free exercise of thy Will may be able to coexist with the Freedom of all others, according to a universal law.[96]

Law has no moral character beyond the moral imperative as the principle of external freedom, guaranteed by force. Outside the moral imperative, all human dealings are a matter of contract and judicial agreement, and thus indifferent to any fixed moral standard. The sole motive of moral legislation is duty – obedience to the law, which in spite of its lack of a moral foundation, society must have.[97]

One response to the dilemma was to abandon the project altogether, and openly embrace the state's unavoidable absolutist tendency. One of the first intellectuals of the absolutist state was Georg Wilhelm Friedrich Hegel (1770-1831), appointed to the chair of philosophy at the University of Berlin in 1818 by the Prussian King Frederick William III, and variously honored and paid by him thereafter. The emphasis on "duty" Hegel acquired from Kant, and he did not fail in devoting it to his king. His writings would become the primer for those sycophants of the German state who would make possible its tragedy a century later. Karl Popper provided a sampler of some of Hegel's less turgid passages:

> 'The State is the Divine Idea as it exists on earth ... We must therefore worship the State as the manifestation of the Divine on earth [...] The State is the march of God through the world ... The State must be comprehended as an organism ... To the complete State belongs, essentially, consciousness and thought. The State knows what it wills [...] The State ... exists for its own sake ... The State is the actually existing, realized moral life.'[98] [unbracketed ellipses in the original][gg]

1.1.2e   Perhaps the last philosopher of the West[99] still committed to the Enlightenment[100] project and capable of producing a systematic political philosophy based on a universal ethics – uniquely and creatively redefined using game theory – was John Rawls.

Rawls begins with the familiar contract theory, but abstracted by game theory in order to strip the would-be participants in society of all characteristics except those few essential ones needed to get the game started:

> [T]he guiding idea is that the principles of justice for the basic structure of society are the object of the original agreement. They are the principles that free and rational persons concerned to further their own interests would accept in an initial position of equality as defining the fundamental terms of their association. These principles are to regulate all further agreements; they specify the kinds of social cooperation that can be entered into and the forms of government that can be established. This way of regarding the principles of justice I shall call justice as fairness.[101]

Thus Rawls asserts several axioms that he maintains as intuitively true: That all participants agree upon equality as the original position; that all are

---

[gg] More from Popper, on the same page cited: "[Hegel] represents the 'missing link,' as it were, between Plato and the modern forms of totalitarianism. Most of the modern totalitarians [...] know of their indebtedness to Hegel, and all of them have been brought up in the close atmosphere of Hegelianism. They have been taught to worship the state, history, and the nation."

free, rational, and self-interested; that all accept as "just" those propositions elaborated from these axioms, which starting point is agreed to be "fair." Importantly, Rawls requires one further initial axiom:

> The special assumption I make is that a rational individual does not suffer from envy.[102]

Before the participants deliberate on the details of a just society, their biases are supposedly stripped by their agreeing to be placed behind a "veil of ignorance" – an arrangement that actually strips them of all human identity:

> First of all, no one knows his place in society, his class position or social status; nor does he know his fortune in the distribution of natural assets and abilities, his intelligence and strength, and the like. Nor, again, does anyone know his conception of the good, the particulars of his rational plan of life, or even the special features of his psychology such as his aversion to risk or liability to optimism or pessimism. More than this, I assume that the parties do not know the particular circumstances of their own society. That is, they do not know its economic or political situation, or the level of civilization and culture it has been able to achieve. The persons in the original position have no information as to which generation they belong.[103]

From this "initial position" of equality behind the "veil of ignorance," Rawls is now ready to ask the participants to take a first step into the real world where inequality reigns. For any two-party social contract "unless there is a distribution that makes both persons better off [...], an equal distribution is to be preferred."[104] In other words, both parties must perceive themselves to gain by contracting, otherwise they do not make a contract – a case essentially no different from a market transaction. But the market cannot decide the matter of justice, according to Rawls. He asserts that for any multi-party move off the point of initial equality into real-world inequality, that move must satisfy the "difference principle":

> What, then, can possibly justify this kind of initial inequality in life prospects? According to the difference principle, it is justifiable only if the difference in expectation is to the advantage of the representative man who is worse off[.][105]

Thus the first derived principle of justice is the "maximin"[hh] that inevitable inequality is accepted as "just" only if that participant – in Rawls'

[hh] Rawls makes the distinction: "The maximin criterion is generally understood as a rule for choice under great uncertainty, whereas the difference principle is a principle of justice." *Vide A Theory of Justice*, op.cit. infra, page 72.

terminology "representative man" – who finds himself at the bottom of the social heap considers it to his advantage. Each participant will agree to this principle because his position behind the "veil of ignorance" forces the realization that the unfortunate "worse off" person might well be him. Why should the participants agree to this principle? Because, says Rawls,

> representative men do not gain at one another's expense since only reciprocal advantages are allowed.[106]

Once this principle is accepted, anything goes. Any democratic scheme of redistribution gains currency:

> [W]e may note that it is a political convention of a democratic society to appeal to the common interest. No political party publicly admits to pressing for legislation to the disadvantage of any recognized social group. But how is this convention to be understood? Surely it is something more than the principle of efficiency, and we cannot assume that government affects everyone's interest equally. Since it is impossible to maximize with respect to more than one point of view, it is natural, given the ethos of a democratic society, to single out that of the least advantaged and to further their long-term prospects in the best manner consistent with the equal liberties and fair opportunity.[107]

The failure of Rawls' effort is manifest from the outset.[ii] Even before getting to the impossibility of interpersonal comparisons implied by the notion of equality, even before confronting the problems of democratic decision-making, every one of his initial assumptions is questionable: The assumption of the value of equality of condition – *not* equality before the law – of a desire for "justice," of freedom, of rationality, and of a self-interest defined to solicit acceptance of Rawls' principles. He assumes that every participant wants to play his social justice game because, despite being unreal, it is a "heuristic" that can be discarded once the players behold the agreeable result that it produces:

> Later I shall try to show that when the principles adopted are put into practice, they lead to social arrangements in which envy and other destructive feelings are not likely to be strong. The conception of justice eliminates the conditions that give rise to disruptive attitudes. It is, therefore, inherently stable.[108]

But any theorist can play the game. From behind this "veil of ignorance" one can easily suppose a polar opposite world extremely *unjust* from the

---

[ii] For a more thorough demolition of Rawls, see de Jasay, *op.cit. infra*, pages 161-173, Richard Rorty, *op.cit. infra*, Robert Nozick (*Anarchy, State and Utopia*, part II, section II), and Robert Paul Wolff (*Understanding Rawls*, chapter XV).

Rawls point of view, yet which might be enthusiastically embraced by the participants. For example, one might suppose a laissez-faire "initial position" where the rich are fabulously richer than currently, and yet where even the least advantaged are many times more prosperous than currently. Such an "initial position" is far more plausible than that of Rawls, yet it goes without saying that his admirers would hysterically denounce it as "unjust." Why? Because once envy is allowed back into the game, even if the least-fortunate "representative man" were guaranteed to be twice as prosperous, they would reject the offer if it stipulated that the rich be four times as prosperous. Such a "difference principle" might well be enthusiastically embraced, but only in a world where "equality" is not a matter of secular dogma enforced by the Savonarola of the state – that is, in a world far from A Theory of Justice.

The acclaim for Rawls in political science with his A Theory of Justice (1971) is exactly correlative to that of John Maynard Keynes (1883-1946) in economics with his The General Theory of Employment, Interest and Money (1936): Despite their obvious fallacies, their scientific pretentions exalt the state; thus they are privileged court intellectuals – who will be forgotten oddities when the putrescent corpse of the state is finally interred.

Game theory as used by Rawls, and his "veil of ignorance," are abstract makeshifts for reducing society's multifarious and contentious individual reasoners to a symbolic reason, which is then manipulated to accept his assumptions and his presumptive notions of justice. Game theory is currently popular among political theorists because it simplifies the problem of where to locate the agency of reason. But it is a tool of dubious value. For example, the so-called "prisoners' dilemma" addresses the problem of the inaccessibility of reason for the group, even if the group is merely two people. This inaccessibility of reason prevents cooperation for mutual benefit. It is obvious that one person cannot reason with many others in a nation of 331 million people, nor can many factions reason with one another in so large a group. Conversely, it is equally obvious that reasoned exchange is more likely in a small group, especially when the small groups are eager to have it, and not artificially prevented from having it, as in the contrived and endlessly cited "prisoners' dilemma." Criticizing the use of game theory in On What Matters, by Derek Parfit – specifically, the so-called 'Trolley Problem' – Roger Scruton wrote:

> Nothing that really matters to human beings – their loves,
> responsibilities, attachments, their delights, aesthetic values, and
> spiritual needs – occurs in Parfit's interminable narrative.[109]

Even the masterful Anthony de Jasay cannot employ game theory to devise a government that protects classical liberal values: In his work The State he is trapped within the current framework of the state. He begins with a liberal democratic state with limited powers. But unsurprisingly, the consequences of his fertile deduction over the length of the book force him to admit that this state has a powerful tendency to become totalitarian.[110]

Every "rational choice" game theory approach to providing a systematic solution to social problems must necessarily fail because none addresses the first central problem of social organization: How to control destructive envy.

1.1.2f Any belief in the superstition of an "informed voter" is easily dispelled by watching interviews of voters in caucuses, on the street, or after voting. When the interviewee can cobble together a coherent – never mind grammatical – sentence, one finds that few can give a reasoned account for their vote, while most regurgitate an emotional splutter of clichés picked up from social media.

And yet the striking contradiction is that most of those same inarticulate voters, in individual conversation on non-political topics, can show sound judgment. Outside politics, there does seem to be justification for a "wisdom of crowds."[111] For example in 2014, Google launched Project Aristotle, led by researcher Julia Rozovsky, tasked to develop the perfect team. For over a year Rozovsky studied over a hundred groups assembled according to various standards, looking for the ideal "group norms," or "team culture." The greatest contrast was between Team A, a star group of exceptionally smart and efficient professionals, and Team B, a group of capable but essentially random workers. She found that Team B was more willing to "take risks" and overall performed better. These advantages were expressed in a "collective I.Q." greater than the sum of its parts because it encouraged the "psychological safety" of each member contributing to the group. Indeed the praxeological foundation of markets relies on a kind of "wisdom of crowds," but with important differences that will be made clear in the discussion below on sortition.

The absence of collective wisdom in the voting crowd has long been recognized. William Poundstone[112] has cataloged most of the methods that attempt to restore it, but the three major categories of voting methods – ordinal, cardinal, and plurality – all have defects. Although no ordinal voting method achieves the basic standard of fairness set by Nobel laureate Kenneth Arrow's "impossibility theorem," some are better than others. Ordinal variants such as range voting (also called score voting) and ranked voting have been found to be "less unfair" than other variants. However, strategic voting within range voting can eliminate the voters' overall preferred candidate; thus ranked voting is preferred by the FairVote organization[113] and was used in the 2021 New York City mayoral election.[114] Cardinal voting, in which each candidate is scored independently of the others, is difficult to tabulate and to independently verify. The plurality voting (simple majority voting, or "first past the post" voting) practiced in the United States and most Western democracies has been found to be the least fair, and invariably tends to a two-party system.[ii]

Despite all of the clever remedies suggested, there is no voting method that can possibly be devised to overcome the fatal defect: All preserve the institution of political parties. And this is exactly how the state wants it. There is a reason for the contradiction of the state's political parties who exalt the sacred "informed voter" citizen to the skies while simultaneously demanding that this same citizen be hog-tied and gagged with red tape regarding his market vote of dollars for a gas-driven automobile, a high-calorie meal, a three-gallon flush toilet, or an unthrottled shower head.[115] The reason is that the "informed voter" citizen does not exist except as a finger-painted poster child of each party's "social justice" fantasy, as the faceless "American people," while the free citizen voting with dollars to satisfy his individual ends truly does exist, and must be "reformed" into the procrustean ideology.

The political machines of the modern state have institutionalized democratic elections to simultaneously pander to the democratic ideal while narcotizing its realization. Ironically, the pathological variant on government that is the state that began as a tool to control religious wars has itself devolved into secular jihad. Outside the United States multiple splinter parties prevail. Many have their identities by coalescing voters around one of the reigning en-thusiasms of the day, e.g., climate change, gender "rights," anti-racism, etc. To maintain their influence they must keep their constituencies whipped up into alarmed activism, and above all, they must never accept that their motivating issue is tractable by reasoned solutions, lest their party and all its parasites in the grievance industry go out of existence. In the United States, the political antipathy to reason is permanently and intractably institutionalized in two major political parties. This antirationality is made permanent as two parties by plurality voting and made intractable by being rooted in the two irreducible theological replies regarding the malleability human nature: Either plastic and perfectible, or fixed and fallen. But then, as Carl Schmitt concluded:

> All significant concepts of the theory of the modern state are secu-larized theological concepts.[116, 117]

Religion, particularly Christianity until recently, has been the bulwark of the idea that human nature is fixed, unchanging, and incapable of perfection. This idea is the irreducible first principle of the Right, with the first corollary that any government that tries to reshape human nature toward perfection must fail, regardless of any force it may apply. The reverse, the idea that human nature is malleable, evolving, and perfectible is the irreducible first principle of

---

[ii] According to Duverger's Law. See Mark Fey and Daniel Bochsler, *op.cit.*, in the endnotes.

the Left, with its first corollary that government is *obligated* to help positively shape human nature, whether using the fiscal and social policy of bland populist socialism, or the gulag and killing fields of the total state – a distinction within the Left of degree, not of kind. A further critical distinction inclines the Left to ideological enthusiasms: The Right verifies its claims in the past; the Left, much like a religion, verifies its claims in the future. Thus the failures of the Left are always merely a "revolution betrayed," never a repudiation of its ideologies, which are unfalsifiable by empirical evidence, which always lies in the past. This claim to some future verification also accounts for the remorseless fury that the Left directs toward its opponents: For they do not deliver an empirical correction, for which they might be thanked; they deliver a blow to the "revolution," for which they must be crushed.

However, one should not be deceived by the apparent opposition of the Right to the Leviathan state. Politicians of both Left and Right have approved budgets that currently bring the United States national debt to over 30 trillion dollars – an incomprehensible and unrepayable figure. It is the Right that routinely magnifies the military arm of the state, whose *accounted* spending is over $732 billion a year, or more than the military spending of the next ten countries combined[118] – and this in a time when no war has been declared. The "informed voter's" reasoned choices have been constrained. As every clever parent knows, you do not ask little Johnnie what candy he wants; you ask him does he want the chocolate in the red wrapper, or the one in blue. Offering the unbounded choice may result in a tantrum when, no, he really can't have the giant éclair. But red or blue, he's electing the same deadly saccharine.

🍂

Special mention must be made of Hans-Hermann Hoppe's "argumentation[kk] ethics," although it is an anomaly in the list of attempts to provide an apodictic foundation to reason as the agency for determining political choices. It is anomalous in that Hoppe accepts[119] Hume's dictum that no empirical 'is' can necessarily imply a normative 'ought' – which might preclude any universal role for reason like those just discussed – while at the same time maintaining his ethics as the ethical foundation of capitalism – which does indeed imply universal rules for the rational ordering of society. He performs this dual feat by asserting argumentation ethics as a normative, synthetic a priori Kantian category. Insofar as he succeeds, the principle of self-ownership becomes a general theory of property.

But does he succeed? Hoppe's argument is the following:

(i) Any truth claim must be raised by argumentation, "and it must be assumed that everyone knows what it means to claim something to be true";[120]

[kk] "Argumentation" in Hoppe's usage actually means "propositional exchange" (which he himself offers as an equivalent term), not necessarily implying debate or impassioned reasoning.

(ii) "argumentation is always an activity"[121] involving the use of one's own body;

(iii) argumentation is conflict-free in the sense that the participants cooperate in arguing, even when they stridently disagree.

From these three premises Hoppe draws not only the following...

(iv) When people are engaged in argumentation each of them *ipso facto* recognizes that each has the moral right to exclusive control over his own body without aggressive interference. To deny this is to engage in a "practical contradiction" (or Hoppe's equivalent term, a "performative contradiction").

...but also more sweepingly he concludes:

Hence, one reaches the conclusion that norms must indeed be assumed to be justifiable as valid. It is simply impossible to argue otherwise, because the ability to argue so would in fact presuppose the validity of those norms which underlie any argumentation whatsoever. [...Therefore], reason can claim to yield results in determining moral laws which can be shown to be valid a priori. [...T]he ethics implied in argumentation [has] validity [that] cannot be disputed, as disputing it would implicitly have to presuppose it.[122]

[...] "Nobody has the right to uninvitedly aggress against the body of any other person and thus delimit or restrict anyone's control over his own body." This rule is implied in the concept of justification as argumentative justification. Justifying *means* justifying without having to rely on coercion. [...] With this justification of a property norm regarding a person's body it may seem that not much is won. [...] But in fact, any other norm must be logically compatible with the nonaggression principle in order to be justified itself, and, mutatis mutandis, every norm that could be shown to be incompatible with this principle would have to be considered invalid.[123] [emphasis in the original]

Property in oneself is the norm prior to all other property norms. And since property must be defined as exclusive title to a scarce good, this norm must apply to other scarce goods and their allocation; and since only the ownership of private property can non-contentiously allocate scarce goods, capitalism is justified as an a priori norm.

Any counterexample to Hoppe must show that people can argue without recognizing each other's moral right to exclusive control over his own body. Furthermore, the counterexample must be really possible, not fantastic.

Epictetus was a great stoic philosopher, who was nonetheless a slave. Does the example of the Epictetus-*dominus* relation refute Hoppe's claims? Hoppe would be right to first object that he is not talking about the slave's legal status, but his moral status. But out of whim or amusement, the *dominus* may behave *as if* Epictetus had a moral right to argue, when in fact he has only a permission. If Hoppe asserts that the moral right is nonetheless established, then the question becomes its duration or universality. Hoppe does not claim that the right endures only for the length of the exchange; he claims that once made, it is universally valid: "[T]he validity of a mathematical proof is not restricted to the moment of proving it".[124] But has the "moment of proving" the moral right occurred? It seems to be merely a permission, not a right. In that case, Hoppe seems to claim that the moral right[ll] is established as a norm by *any* instance of argumentation, regardless of the fact that both Epictetus and *dominus* agree that it is only a permission. The word "norm" attempts two logical leaps: From the provisional to the universal, and from the property in oneself (with its argumentatively-established nonaggression principle) to capitalist property titles (with their merely assumed non-contentious allocation of scarce goods). His reasoning suffers from the very weakness[mm] of the Kantian Categorical Imperative to which he claims kinship: That a "norm" is not a "proposition" to which truth or falsity can be assigned – it is a subjective assertion.

In spite of the superfluity of an a priori argument for property – we claim it to be intuitively understood as any physical agency to effect the will of the one who has title to it, which agency is the necessary condition for the exercise of all rights, natural or statutory – Professor Hoppe's reasoning does support the claim previously stated here that *capitalism is not an '-ism'*: It is not an economic model detachable from its cultural context; it is the elaboration of property, which is the very expression of our personal identity.

❦

The failure of the state form of government is most concisely stated as the failure to accommodate the agency of reason. Thomas Bridges:

> The universalist and essentialist philosophical vocabulary of the Enlightenment, the language used by liberals to explain and advocate the establishment of liberal political institutions, is now irretrievably lost. Central to the cultural project of the Enlightenment was the doctrine of the autonomy of human reason. This doctrine expressed the belief that human reason, on its own, using methods derived from an analysis of its own powers, could transcend the limits imposed by historical cir-

---

[ll] One thinks of Friedrich Schiller's play *Maria Stuart*, where the main character is beheaded after 18 years in prison. She, like Epictetus, achieves a complete inner freedom – if you like, a "property in oneself" abstracted from every external condition that impinges on the universal. But Mary, like Epictetus and martyrs of a faith, do not establish by their testimony and actions a universal "property norm in oneself"; they establish the universal principle of moral integrity.

[mm] Of course Professor Hoppe is aware of that other, more obvious, weakness in Kant's Categorical Imperative, that any ethical norm must be "universalizable," since the norm "everybody must get drunk on Sunday" might be championed just as universally as "thou shalt not steal."

cumstances and attain universally valid knowledge. It is this doctrine that simply no longer makes sense in the world that has emerged in the course of the twentieth century. In this world, we are everywhere confronted with the inescapable reality of cultural difference and the power of historical circumstance to shape belief. In this world, the particularism of the cultural assumptions underlying liberal political doctrine is also impossible to deny. In this world, liberal political institutions can no longer be credibly explained and justified by appeal to self-evident truths, universal natural law, the principles of pure practical reason or any other supposedly culture-neutral metaphysical or epistemological theory.[125]

1.1.3 The first central problem is how to address destructive envy, coterminous with inequality.

Envy is the primary problem of all government because it excludes the agency of reason in resolving social conflict.

> We believe that equality is of the devil, and that the Lord our God delights in multiplicity.
> – Hermann Borchardt

St. Thomas defines the mortal sin of envy as "sorrow for another's good," which results in "joy at another's misfortune."[126] Furthermore, as Helmut Schoeck's definitive study made evident, envy is a directed emotion with a familiar, or at least proximate, person as its target; it seeks to acquire neither a material good nor a personal advantage – it seeks the injury of the superiority of that person, whom the envier falsely evaluates as an equal and whom he perceives as the cause of his own inferiority.[127] It is obvious why John Rawls excluded the possibility of envy in his "original position": With its presence, no rational behavioral assumptions are possible, since those are outweighed by the unmeasured desire for injury to the superior.[nn]

Inequality is the conjoined twin of envy, and both are inescapable features of the human condition, growing out of man's ability to make conscious comparisons. However, it must never be forgotten that this ability forges an ambivalent tool. It must be praised for encouraging creative emulation, and for being the very source of the compassion that inspires every man to whisper in the presence of the unfortunate: "There but for the grace of god go I." Rousseau was right to see this ambivalent emotion as both the fountainhead of

---

[nn] The Russian folk tale drives the point home: A peasant is terrified by the sudden appearance of an angel in his field. The angel calms him. As a reward for his relentless toil in providing food for his people, the angel promises the fulfillment of one wish. The peasant dances for joy. "But there is one condition. Whatever you receive, your landlord will receive double." The peasant stops dancing and glumly begins to ponder. At last he snarls, "Put out one of my eyes."

civilization and as the original problem for political science.

Capitalism has certainly enabled the possibility of enormous disparities in wealth between the very rich and the very poor. It has made possible the very lives of the billions who live on earth, but it has as well become a vital source of state apparatchiks from the rich who seek to assuage their guilt for undeserved or fortuitously acquired wealth. Arthur Koestler, like many others from wealthy families, became a Communist out of that sense of undeserved superiority.[128] The *nouveaux riches* of Silicon Valley, California are the most conspicuous bankers of statist causes, surely as an envy-avoidance reflex for becoming overnight millionaires as if by a miracle of chance. And technology has made every citizen a member of the world digital village where a keyboard puts him in touch with fellow minds all over the world, yet where everyone is subject to the proximity that is the necessary condition of envy. Such is the ambivalent wonder of so much of life.

Equality inevitably becomes the principal ideology of the state, since it is nourished by the unfailing sense of fairness felt by every citizen and since the work of repairing inequality demands incessant state intervention. The state must encourage the destructive envy born of invidious comparison not only because it legitimizes its intervention, but because its threat of inflaming class hatred serves to keep the productive in submission, lest the state take a mind to seizing *all* their property in a jihad to end inequality.[129] Racial inequality and gender inequality become especially fruitful tools of state power.[130, 131]

In his study of prejudice over the twenty years immediately after World War II, Bruno Bettelheim found that the increased cultural opprobrium against racial inequality during these years had resulted in an increase in envy. He found that the suppression of hatred toward members of the out-group resulted in a more open show of envy toward prominent members of the in-group.[132] Thus by simply rewarding their minions in academe and the media to amplify accusations of racism – even untargeted "systemic" racism – the state keeps the knife of destructive envy at the throats of its potential rivals.

Traditional sex roles, especially in the middle and lower classes, once limited ruthless competition to the males, while the upper class had in every age offered opportunities for its ambitious women, although certainly with prejudice in favor of the men. Did the modern elite envy the relatively greater freedom from rivalry which women of the lower orders enjoyed? In any case, their assault on traditional sex roles removed another mediating institution standing between state power and the individual. Like the red-ink posters of Chinese women happily toiling in field and factory with a copy of Mao's *Quotations* held aloft, singing "The East Is Red," the women of the West learned to leave their children with strangers in day care, happily casting aside the fetish of monogamous marriage between a male and a female, singing Helen Reddy's "I Am Woman."

1.1.4 The third central problem is where to locate the agency of decision-making, co-terminous with public or private goods.

Belief in the existence of a common good prohibits almost nothing and permits almost anything.
– Anthony de Jasay

The problem of where to locate the agency of decision-making is inseparable from the problem of public goods. For if there are no public goods to dispose of, then the agency of decision-making is merely the expression of the community sentiment, purely advisory and without will or force. One might imagine a putative decision-making body possessing no public goods, but still with police to compel or at least threaten private property owners to the obedience of its decisions. But this too is impossible, since there would need to be some public goods at its disposal to pay the enforcing police.

Nevertheless, even though an agency having no public goods has no instrument to effect its will, it may yet wield decision-making influence, if not final power of disposal. If this agency were composed of influential and re-spected members of the community, its advice would at least be considered by property owners, otherwise they would hardly be influential and respected members of the community. Certainly for such an agency the free rider problem would not exist – or at least propertied decisions would be undertaken with acceptance or disregard of those who incidentally benefitted from, say, private construction of a dam, a lighthouse, or a road. If there were an obstructionist free rider – that is, someone withholding the use of his property from the common effort, to satisfy some ulterior purpose – either that ulterior purpose would be satisfied or community ostracism would compel him to reach some accommodation, for no one can live in the despite of the entire community. In the case of a non-resident owner taking spiteful joy in thwarting common endeavors at a distance, any enterprise undertaken on his property would suffer by public ostracism, and even his completely fallow land would lose value. In the extreme case, he would lose his property by adverse possession (squatters' taking by assumed abandonment).

When the form of government is the state, such considerations are moot, for the state cannot possibly exist without public goods. In the absence of public goods the state is without will or force, and even the all-important public intellectuals who provide its legitimacy cease to exist. For the intellectual exists solely for the purpose of haranguing the public to accept, or haranguing other state agents to favor, this or that policy decision. With no public goods, there is no policy to decide, no state-abetted advocacy, and thus the ceaselessly yawping mouth of the intellectual falls blessedly silent, and he becomes either a poor scholar or a member of a kaffeeklatsch.

In the absence of public goods for the state to dispose of, the term "politics" signifies nothing, as the master stated:

All non-unanimous politics — and unanimous politics would of course be redundant, and an oxymoron — is redistributive.[133]

Or stated in another way by Gerard Radnitzky:

"Collective decision" is short for non-unanimous decision. The expression "politics" signifies such decisions.[134]

In other words, "politics" is the allocation of public goods by some non-unanimous decision-maker. For the state, there *must* exist at least *some* public goods to be allocated that, in the economist's terms, are nonrivalrous and nonexcludable – that is, goods whose supply is not affected by the number of consumers and from which free riders can't be excluded. National defense is said to be such a public good and, it is said, only the state can provide it. However, national defense *is* rivalrous and excludable, as Hoppe has demonstrated,[135] as are police services, fire departments, and other ostensibly public functions. Before the rise of the state, notes Bassani, "the production of security was never considered a distinct institutional affair, but rather a concern of the whole community."[136] In fact there is no public good for which a rivalrous or excludable case cannot be made.[oo] An alternate definition of a public good, offered by Paul Samuelson, fails even more miserably. According to him, public goods – or "collective consumption goods" – are those "which all enjoy in common in the sense that each individual's consumption of such a good leads to no subtraction from any other individual's consumption of that good."[137] As Murray Rothbard points out, "if a good is really technologically 'collective' in Samuelson's sense, it is *not a good at all*, but a natural condition of human welfare, like air – superabundant to all, and therefore *unowned* by anyone."[138]

Thus the state cannot resolve the intractable problems of how much property is to be confiscated for use as public goods, what the policy goals should be, and who is to be the decision-maker for how public goods are disposed of to satisfy those goals. The state possesses legitimacy to the extent that it satisfies these three functions without public unrest. Of course the current state speaks in unctuous tones about its service to the "American people," but in fact it relies on popular belief in majoritarian absolutism to perform these functions in a purely subjective way, and with generous emolument to its countless leeches and parasites.

[oo] Ronald Coase suggested in *The Problem of Social Cost* (1960), that well-defined property rights could overcome the problems of externalities – one hurdle to privatization. The Coase Theorem states that if trade in an externality is possible and there are sufficiently low transaction costs, bargaining will lead to a Pareto efficient outcome regardless of the initial allocation of property.

Public goods cannot satisfy even the majority who voted for them in the political "market," to say nothing of the satisfactions of the minority. Allocation of public goods is approved by the voting majority as a package, with no final choice of each good comprising the package, and with no final choice of the individual recipients whose ends are supposedly to be satisfied by those goods. Majorities, presuming to speak in this tenuous way for millions, have declared various domestic "wars" – meaning vast mobilization of state resources for the eradication of a democratically announced problem. All of the peacetime "wars" on this or that – for example, the war on poverty and the war on illegal drugs – were so named because it is only during wartime when most citizens defer their many private ends to the single public end, the all-important end of winning the "war." The only approximation to universal satisfaction in public goods is in a war economy, when the greatest number of citizens defer their propertied ends to the "public" ends chosen by the state.

Even the majoritarian approved package itself is not final, not fixed, despite the political advertisement of its many elements. Once in office, the political party elected to allocate the package always modifies its elements to keep only the "doable" elements, according to political expediency. Therefore the majority, hoping for the best, can only decide at the very most on the administration that will distribute public goods as the administrators alone see fit. However distributed, it is impossible that the final package in its entirety will satisfy the ends of those who voted its administrators into office: Especially after its modification, parts of it will please some; other parts will displease many, even among those whose votes brought into effect the package as a whole. Inasmuch as the party platform is thought to represent that package, the indifference of party decision-makers toward their own platform – an unenforceable document – suggests that it is offered more as a cynical "bill of goods" for the purpose of getting or keeping political power than for satisfying "the will of the people," which is impossible in any case.

The above describes the scenario of direct participation in the election of administrators for enactment of a nonbinding national platform. The unavoidable logistical requirement of indirect participation to elect representative legislators presents further insurmountable problems. In the United States House, 435 members represent about 330 million citizens, that is, three-quarters of a million each. If a measure passes with a bare quorum of 218, each represents well over a million citizens. If a bare majority of that quorum passes a measure, each will have somehow spoken for three million citizens. These ratios signify a meaningless sense of "representation." But whatever the quorum or majority, what will they have enacted? The $1.5 *trillion* omnibus spending bill of 2022 was enacted into law with bipartisan support on March 10. But not a single member read the final bill before approving it. None of them could possibly have done so, since they received the final 2,741-page draft one day before its enactment.[139] In the Senate the measure likewise passed with bipartisan dispatch. In recognition of the problem, one Senator introduced a resolution to require that every bill be read aloud on the chamber floor. Had this resolution passed, this and other requirements of the resolution would have meant that the 2,741-page funding bill would have taken 137 days to be called for a vote.[140] With floor debate, passage would have taken even longer. But floor debate almost never takes place: Instead, members of both chambers typically give a histrionic declamation to an empty chamber, recorded solely for the inspiration of their constituent voting Interest, not for collegial elucidation of details within the bill. The lofty professional legislator in both chambers exists to declaim and vote; the lowly business of reading and lawgiving falls to his atelier of menials: The faceless unelected staffers who read to provide a summary – staffers who also perform the mundane task of throwing together the written statutory sausage, which will be enforced by state's armed agents of compulsion.

This haphazard process prevails throughout every branch of the state, producing a blizzard of authorizations of force. The U.S. Code is a consolidation and codification of the "general and permanent" laws of the United States, running approximately 60,000 pages.[141] This Code is a subset of the entire chronological list of laws for each session of Congress, staggeringly enumerated in the United States Statutes at Large.[142] In addition to these, and of equal force, are the rules issued by the entire administrative branch of the federal government collected in the Federal Register, which is over 70,000 pages in length.[143] Naturally, laws and rules often overlap, most conspicuously in the Tax Code, which, counting statutes, regulations, and case law, is another 70,000 pages. Behind every shred of this legal confetti stands the loaded gun of the state's police power, aimed to marshal the public goods for its enforcement.

In contrast, private goods satisfy every person who "votes" for them with the property he voluntarily surrenders during a market transaction. The word "satisfy" should not admit of cavil: A woman may become dissatisfied with the color of a dress just purchased; another may be dissatisfied that advertised features of a purchased automobile do not work; the point is that at the moment of sale, the buyer finds subjective satisfaction in the private good or otherwise he would not have parted with his property to buy it, even if it means later changing his subjective valuation or adjusting the purchase according to the terms of the sale.

Clearly then, to the extent that the agency of decision-making for community ends resides in the individual disposal of propertied goods, the more a society possesses subjective satisfaction – the only satisfaction attainable, since "objective satisfaction" would imply that the state could make continuous interpersonal comparisons of subjective valuations for each of its possibly millions of citizens, which is an impossibility.

Clearly too, elective democracy fails in its promise to empower the people; it empowers political parties; specifically, by Duverger's Law especially in the United States[144] it empowers a duopoly when employing simple elective majoritarianism as its essential agency for decision-making; thus elective democracy is not a democracy, but an oligarchy.

1.1.5 The fourth central problem is how to transfer power between regimes.

Government is force. Politics is a battle for supremacy.

– John James Ingalls

Throughout the states of the West for some two centuries, simple majoritarianism, which by Duverger's Law tends to produce a two-party system,[145] has been the uncontested mechanism for transference of political power. There is no need to discuss the problems of power transference that beset hereditary monarchy when it had legitimacy, nor the in any case obscure workings of the Russian or Chinese politburos in the matter.

As previously established, reason is not the determining factor in how a voter evaluates his own political preferences. Thus the problem under consideration must address the transference of power between regimes that employs mechanisms for manipulating non-rational factors to its favor and for suppressing rivals without igniting a challenge to regime legitimacy.

The days of Tammany Hall[146] may be over, but despite the success of state intellectuals to enshrine the myth that the sacred institution of the popular vote is without statistically significant fraud, its definition even in the United States proves to be conveniently elastic.[147] Does the Congressional franking privilege constitute an unfair benefit to incumbents, and do hyperbolic statements in the members' cost-free mailed "newsletters" constitute fraud? Why does a privately funded bribe constitute fraud, while the politically advertised publicly funded establishment of a Federal project in a Congressional district does not? Does money constitute the "mother's milk of politics"[148] for the distribution of quaint nonpartisan League of Women Voters flyers, or something much more persuasive?

In the United States, highly emotional media advertisements do not constitute fraud, and may assure successful ascent into high office. The "daisy petal" television ad[149] that first aired on September 7, 1964, may have assured the defeat of Republican candidate Barry Goldwater. It showed a three-year-old girl plucking a daisy, with her counting of petals matched with the countdown to a nuclear missile strike, followed by a blast and a mushroom cloud – a scenario that the election of Goldwater was assumed to threaten. The "Willie Horton" television ad[150] of September, 1988 may have assured the defeat of Democrat candidate Michael Dukakis. It showed a grainy mug shot of a black man who had robbed, raped, and murdered while out on "furlough" from prison – a policy approved by Dukakis, who also opposed the death penalty.

Three-quarters of all Americans favored some limitation on such expensive national advertising and other political spending, according to a Pew Research poll of 2018,[151] with a higher percentage of Democrats favoring such limitation. But in 2010, a 5-4 majority of the Supreme Court sided with plaintiff Citizens United,[152] a conservative nonprofit corporation, ruling that corporations and other outside groups can spend unlimited money on elections. Although Democrats strenuously opposed the decision, thinking it favored the supposedly better-funded Republicans, a limitation on great independent wealth would have made third-party candidates, such as Libertarian Ed Clark in 1980 and independent Ross Perot in 1992, unable to run. Perot had won 19% of the popular vote in the 1992 race, and although denied a single electoral vote, the threat of future rivals on the national "democratic" forum would be eliminated by other means. Although the bipartisan (Democrat and Republican) Commission on Presidential Debates had taken over the event from the nonpartisan League of Women Voters in 1988 because of the League's willingness to include third-party candidates, it would not repeat the 1992 mistake that had threatened the duopoly on power. The Commission simply raised the polling requirement for the next presidential debates in 1996. This would keep Perot and any future rivals from presenting an unscripted exchange of ideas in their national forum, no matter how great their independent funding.[153]

That funding hurdle could be raised higher at will, to prevent rivals from even appearing on the "official" ballot. In 2016, the Libertarian Party spent between $2.50 and $4.00 per signature for ballot access petitions, with a rejection rate of about one third, for a total cost of $841,583.78 – an amount that crippled its funding for advertising.[154] After a good showing by that party in the 2018 New York gubernatorial race, the Democrat governor established an "independent" commission that tripled the required number of signatures for the ballot access petition and moved the signature collection window into the winter, when fewer people would be in public to encounter petitioners.[155]

81% of all Americans favored term limits in 1991, according to a Pew Research poll of that year.[156] However, in March, 1995, the U.S. House overwhelmingly defeated a proposed Constitutional amendment to limit terms of office. Two months later, the Supreme Court of the United States ruled in *U.S. Term Limits, Inc. v. Thornton* (1995) that citizens are not allowed to term limit their own members of Congress using State laws, a ruling that defied the democratic will of the citizens of 23 States, whose elected representatives had enacted such laws.[157]

Clearly then, the state's ability to disburse public goods and to legally suppress its rivals' access to the public forum are central to its prevention of democratic challenges to its legitimacy at the critical juncture of regime change. However, its principal mechanism is the maintenance of the charade of "bipartisan" democracy through superficial party difference, when debate on the essential difference of the growth of state power is never in question.

1.1.6 The fifth central problem is how to guarantee the status of property, by which each person, real or legal, is to effect his will and thus maintain his life.

[T]he preservation of property [is] the end of government, and that for which men enter into society.

– John Locke

Property is intuitively understood as any physical agency to effect the will of the one who has title to it, which agency is the necessary condition for the exercise of all rights, natural or statutory. There is no need to make any reference to natural law, or Locke, or anything else to understand and accept this definition. It is pointless to pursue an infinite regress of title; the fact that property may have originated in occupation or conquest does not categorically invalidate titles, for which legal remedy is available when in question. One may well argue the validity of titles not established *ab immemorabili*, e.g., thefts of land from American aboriginals and given color of title by the central state; one may well argue the validity of intellectual property; but only an idle nattering pettifogger can contest the meaning just given. It is intuitively true because human beings are not incorporeal ghosts; they have real bodies that to remain in life must have property and its corollary rights for life's enjoyment.

The fundamental status of property comes into question when the state asserts a right to "public property." Since this term implies the contradiction of property with an undefinable right of title by all citizens of the state, the meaningful term "public goods" must be used. Since these goods are not produced by the state, they enter its domain by an asserted right to tax its subjects, validated by its assertion of final arbiter of disputes, and enforced by its monopoly on police power. The only question permitted to the state's subjects is to what extent it may seize their property for conversion to public goods.

In the case of the former American republic, the history of this question demonstrates the state's ineluctable course for the expansion of its power. Customary usage had limited the taxing power to taking less than 5% of GDP, mainly through import duties, until the collapse of federalism with the conclusion of the War Between the States on April 9, 1865, and the institution of the Fourteenth Amendment on July 9, 1868. According to Madison, the Taxing Clause of Article I, Section 8, limited the central government to spending derived from a function enumerated for it in the Constitution. Hamilton argued that the "general welfare" clause allowed spending without that restriction. The Supreme Court eventually sided with Hamilton in *United States v. Butler* (1936).[158] But could the central state enact taxation primarily to shape behavior rather than to raise revenue? After several inconclusive findings (*Bailey v. Drexel Furniture Co.* [1922], *Sonzinsky v. United States* [1937], *United States v. Kahriger* [1953]), the Supreme Court finally enshrined the obvious, that this was a distinction without a difference, saying in *NFIB v. Sebelius* (2012)[159] that "taxes that seek to influence conduct are nothing new."[160]

With no fixed percentage or fixed principle to limit its taxing power, the state's intellectuals, in their pretense as guardians of the republic, generally maintained that in principle the state could tax up to the point of infringement upon individual rights – another distinction without a difference, since the seized property is itself the foundation of all rights. In fact, the power of the state to confiscate private property for its disposal as public goods is total. Sham property rights and sham capitalism are allowed to exist solely for their function as a scapegoat for the inevitable failures of the state.

Property held by multiple owners of joint stock companies entrusted their managers with a fiduciary responsibility to make money. The standard of profit, by which the stock market assured the retirement of millions of investors the world over, is now threatened with replacement by political goals propagandized by the state: "Sustainability" trumps profit-making. It is a deceit to claim that there is no conflict between the two, since if that were so, the profit motive would achieve "sustainable" goals without political hectoring. The former chief investment officer for sustainable investing at BlackRock, for the world's largest asset management firm, called environmental, social, and governance (ESG) investing a "dangerous placebo that harms the public interest."[161]

1.1.7 Government must be sovereign over the society it governs.

The sovereign power residing in the people [...] is not a principle of discord, rancour or war: it is a principle of melioration, contentment, and peace.
– James Wilson

It is axiomatically true that for any government there must be a final arbiter of disputes over the extent of its sovereignty. For whatever its form – a monarch, a parliament, an oligarchy, a mobocracy, etc. – some arbiter must finally decide disputes, which must be defined as cases where there is a lack of unanimity over the use of property. This definition of disputes must be accepted, for only those disputes over the use of property are the concern of government; government has no role, for example, in a shouting match until there is an assault, a destruction of or impediment to property, or some threat against the ultimate property, one's life. Given these axioms, which are simply a restatement of 1.1.1 and 1.1.6 above, it must follow that the greater the amount of property subject to non-unanimous disputes, the greater the need for government power to intervene for their settlement; conversely, the greater the amount of property having unquestioned usufruct or titles of ownership, the less the need for government intervention.

In the case where there *is* unanimity over the use of property, e.g., Robinson Crusoe alone on his island, or a totally militarized society where every citizen gives total and reflexive obedience to an arbiter or some arbitrating body – the impossible fantasy of the totalitarian, approached only by a state on a war footing – there is no government, since there is no need for a final arbiter. If a society of total capitalism existed, that is, one with no public goods, where every object and every square inch of the earth were held as clearly titled property, there would be no need for government *only if the use of that property never gave rise to disputes.* This society is the fiction of modern anarchists, who blandly assume that every property owner would settle any dispute by some form of voluntary contract.

In the case of state government, public goods by definition must exist, and *a fortiori*, public policy, whose disposal must be decided with a single voice: A public road is either built or not; a tax is either imposed or not. Furthermore, as shown previously, the state has an ineluctable tendency to expand its power, to establish its legitimacy as the final arbiter of disputes over the extent of its sovereignty. The state must be sovereign in both depth and breadth over the society it governs – figuratively speaking, both vertically and horizontally. That is to say, it must strive to remove all intermediary obstacles between it and the individual subject who must work to pay the taxes that finance its operations, and it must strive to establish itself as the sole arbiter of disputes across its entire administrative extent. Otherwise, from some intermediary there might arise a "Silent Majority" or "Tea Party" inspired by some faith, or a "Moms for Liberty" or "Parents Defending Education" inspired by family values; from some "home rule" or "autonomous zone" or "State" there might arise a wealthy breakaway, a Southern Confederacy or Catalonia or Eastern Ukraine – any possibility of which might challenge its power to tax, or its very legitimacy.

The term "sovereignty of the people" has no meaning in designating the form of government, despite the often-repeated statement that democracy consists of the "sovereignty of the people." The assertion that people are sovereign because they have the right to vote is jabberwocky. We have specifically shown that plurality voting establishes an oligarchic duopoly. But even that outcome is not the exclusive result of popular voting. The sovereign people have elected dictators, monarchs, and doddering 78-year-olds. Although Mencken said that by voting, the sovereign "people know what they want, and deserve to get it good and hard",[162] it's probably more accurate to say that they do not know, and deserve better.

The term "sovereignty of the people" does have meaning in designating the ultimate veto power of the people: Violent revolution. Étienne de la Boétie is correct in observing that the greater size of a citizenry, should they awaken to their power, can enable them at any time throw off the necessarily smaller elite who enjoy their majesty at popular forbearance. And as Mises has stated:

It is impossible, in the long run, to subject men against their will to a regime that they reject.[163]

But excluding any necessary implication of a particular form of government or any particular method for establishing it, and beyond this fundamental power to overthrow a government by violent revolution, sovereignty of the people does have meaning. Just as each person is "sovereign" in his own property and achieves his own subjective satisfaction by disposing of his property as he sees fit, so too is sovereignty of the people meaningful when it signifies the achievement of subjective satisfaction through the collective choices of the entire community.[pp]

It follows from the definition of government that sovereignty cannot be divided. For if it were divided, the division would signify more than one arbiter of disputes, with each of them contending for the status of "final" – an impossibility.

History provides the familiar example of a diarchy – the failed model from early Rome in which the fratricidal Romulus removed his twin brother Remus from contention,[164] and the failed two *augusti* of Diocletian in the 4th century.[165] David Hume and John C. Calhoun[166] advocated dual executives, the latter citing the example from ancient Sparta. More recently in France in 1986, a dual executive was attempted under the rubric *cohabitation*. Socialist President François Mitterrand placed conservative leader Jacques Chirac in charge of domestic affairs as Prime Minister, keeping foreign affairs for himself. The experiment failed, especially in that it put the validity of foreign agreements in doubt, since Mitterrand was not the Prime Minister.[167] The government of Lebanon ostensibly has a divided sovereignty – which might be called a "triarchy" – whereby key arbiters are constitutionally fixed along sectarian lines. Thus the office of president, prime minister, and speaker must be split between a Maronite Christian, a Sunni Muslim, and a Shia Muslim.[168] This superficially democratic and equitable arrangement in fact has enshrined sectarian infighting at the very heart of the government, which is all but dysfunctional. Robert A. Dahl has described a "polyarchy,"[169] but his term does not describe a form of government, especially not one of divided sovereignty: It describes formal standards of greater participation and equity within the democratic model. The Swiss government could be argued with equal merit as being either "polyarchic" or "acephalous": It does not have a formal head of state. Every year, the Federal Assembly appoints one of the Federal Councillors as the president of the Swiss confederation, and so one might be tempted to call

---

pp Subjective satisfaction through the collective choices of the entire community is explained below under the discussion of symbiotic government.

this arrangement a "time-sliced sovereignty." But this would be misleading, since the president is not vested with any particular powers.[170]

What first appears to be a divided sovereignty turns out to have meaning only as a complementary division of powers. That is, the several sovereignties are final arbiters in mutually exclusive powers, jurisdictions, or territorial domains. This complementary division of powers was James Madison's brilliant innovation of federalism.[171] The federalist principle was successful in the United States for almost 73 years, from the ninth State's ratification of the federalist Constitution on June 21, 1788, until that nation's 16th president took office on March 4, 1861. Madison assumes that federalism over a large republic prevents both the tyranny of the majority and the "consolidation" of power in a centralized state. He definitively states his views in Federalist 51:[qq]

> In the extended republic of the United States, and among the great variety of interests, parties and sects which it embraces, a coalition of a majority of the whole society could seldom take place on any other principles than those of justice and the general good; and there being thus less danger to a minor from the will of the major party.[172]

In this brief passage he makes many assumptions:

a)   limited communication will maintain distance and dispersion among factions;

b)   distance and dispersion assure the formation of only "good" majorities;

c)   distance and dispersion prevent large, disruptive regional factions;

d)   distance and dispersion prevent majoritarian tyranny.

All of these assumptions are sweeping, and as history would prove even before 1860, false.

John C. Calhoun of South Carolina proposed a brilliant twist on the people voicing its ultimate sovereign veto through violent revolution: A peaceful veto on the central government by sectional interests. His idea of a "concurrent majority," described in his *Disquisition on Government*, was his answer to the problem that Madison failed to resolve: How to prevent the tyranny of the majority. His answer was that a sectional veto could be used to force supermajority approval of any nationally divisive issue. A peaceful, escalating threat would enforce the concurrent majority requirement: First by interposition, the State would prevent local application of the law, as described by Madison in his

---

qq Despite an authorship claim for Hamilton, internal evidence given by Edward G. Bourne ("The Authorship of the Federalist," *The American Historical Review*, II [April, 1897], 449–51) and other scholars strongly favors Madison.

Virginia Resolutions of 1798; then by formal nullification,[rr] the central government law would be declared null and void, as described by Jefferson in his Kentucky Resolutions of 1798; and finally by secession, the peaceful exit of the State from the Union, with the possibility of return. This mechanism would harness the threat of violent factionalism, which federalism had been unsuccessful in preventing, to tame it as the peaceful tool to preserve the Union.

Although the majoritarian control of the coercive powers of the state, along with the state's inherent impetus toward unmediated central power, put an end to the American experiment in federalism on April 9, 1865, the idea of a complementary division of powers to restrain government remains viable, especially if it contains a mechanism of self-enforcement.

1.1.8 The state form of government must tend to totalitarianism as a result of failure to address destructive envy and of Interest under the guise of personal reason, created by a deontological value system within oligarchic voting, imposed over its sovereign monopoly with the enticements of public goods, in perpetual union.

The left is not necessarily aiming at totalitarianism. But their know-it-all mindset leads repeatedly and pervasively in that direction.

– Thomas Sowell

To make egalitarianism a state ideal is to make envy a state ideal. It is simply impossible to make every citizen equal in result: The attempt merely expresses a desire to turn each unique universe that is a human soul into one of a colony of ants or termites. As Schoeck has shown, the removal of certain material differences merely sharpens the invidious focus on the remaining differences,[173] with envy especially inflamed by those remaining *ineradicable* differences,[174] that is, precisely those spiritual differences that make each human being unique.

The unattainable equal result desired by egalitarianism assures the need for constant intervention by the state: The leveler's work is never done. Even with the citizen's face removed by placement behind a state-mandated COVID mask, the eyes, the voice, the carriage all betray the inexpressible – the individual who eludes the procrustean state. The effects of the most minute racial differences must be leveled by state diktat,[175] and yet those who "identify" as one of the scientifically nonexistent[176, 177] races must be rescued from oppression by the elusive racism that everyone sincerely denies – a hateful paradox that greater state power surely will root out. Inherent gender differences

---

[rr] Calhoun's use of nullification was in fact an appeal to a supermajority whenever a contentious national issue arose – an important distinction from Jefferson's, making the step much more deliberate. If three-quarters of the states in convention according to Article V of the Constitution overruled the nullifying State, that State would have to comply with the supermajority. *Vide* Bassani, *Chaining Down Leviathan, op.cit. infra*, page 232.

are leveled by state diktat, and those who "identify" as one of the new genders sanctioned by the state will be given not just recognition but coerced acceptance,[178] if only the state roots out the hateful indoctrination of children by their own local schools and parents.

Despite its praise for the "American voter" and the "American people," the state is diminished by having those tropes suggest reasoned appraisal of policy by the individual citizen. Individual reason as a standard for the evaluation of policy is as impossible as a "national dialog" among 330 million citizens. And even if it were possible, one has only to ask: If that fictional "national dialog" were to devise a set of policies opposite to that which maintains the current regime in power, which set would be enacted? Instead, the state devises a propagandized wish list attributed to the fictional "American people," manipulating a motley of unreasoned Interests that favor the state, under the umbrella of a political party. Indeed, these various Interests (small businessmen, sexual libertines, wheat growers, racial tribes, etc., etc.) are nothing more than the "factions" described by the American Founders, while a faction of long duration is the very definition of a political party – both of which were condemned as destructive of the common good:

> The alternate domination of one faction over another, sharpened by the spirit of revenge, natural to party dissension, which in different ages and countries has perpetrated the most horrid enormities, is itself a frightful despotism. But this leads at length to a more formal and permanent despotism. The disorders and miseries which result gradually incline the minds of men to seek security and repose in the absolute power of an individual.[179]

None of the major political parties proposes a reduction in the size and power of the central state. In that sense all major political parties are variants of the total state, differing only in the laundry list of benefits offered to the Interests who elect them by plurality voting. Since each list is a farrago of rules that guide statute to reward "right" behavior and punish "wrong" behavior, claiming universal validity (if not applicability), it is ethically deontological: The rules are promoted as being not merely practical, but prescriptively "right." The history of the state demonstrates that it is not guided by any utilitarian consequentialism, which is an impossibility[180] in any case: The failures of its war on poverty,[181] its war on drugs,[182] and its war on fossil fuels[183] did not prompt any reconsideration of policy – these peacetime "wars" were deontological moral imperatives,[184] having value by being followed without consideration of consequences, no matter how counterproductive.

Echoing the assertions of Jean Bodin, Hugo Grotius, and others among its intellectual forebears, the oligarchic majoritarian total state claims absolute and perpetual sovereignty, without the possibility of secession. Clearly the

Leftist assertion that the power of the state stops at the point of infringement upon individual rights is a fiction: The judicial arm of the state, through its rulings in *Flint v. Stone Tracy Co.* (1911), *O'Malley v. Woodrough* (1939), *United States v. Sanchez* (1950), *NFIB v. Sebelius* (2012), and others,[185] sets no limit on state power to confiscate property for use as public goods, distributed as enticements that tranquilize the ultimate expression of the sovereignty of the people in rebellion. Since individual rights and property are coterminous, with no rights existing in the absence of property to realize them, the individual rights "protected" by the total state are merely provisional, rooted not in natural law or customary usage, but in the will of the sovereign as conditionally documented in positivist statute.

1.1.9 Only a non-state form of government can avoid totalitarianism, by sublimating destructive envy, diffusing Interest with symbiotic reason, avoiding the deontology/consequentialism dilemma with virtue ethics in a system of sortition, and devolving power to the sovereign people by means of the absolute right of property and the right of secession.

[Society is] a partnership not only between those who are living, but between those who are living, those who are dead, and those who are to be born.
— Edmund Burke

We do not rely on any empirically scientific or theological proof of human nature as necessary to establish either the first axiom of government that it must exist, nor the second axiom that it must conform with man's nature. We hold those not as "proofs" but merely valuable insights. What is axiomatically true, and fundamental for the discussion here, is that although assumptions about human nature may lie outside science or revelation, they must inform what is expected of government, the institution of a rational animal living in groups larger than the family.

Just as an individual man must necessarily act to achieve goals to maintain his life, so too must any human group necessarily act to achieve common goals to maintain cooperative life. But individual human action always takes place within the context of a community. To focus on individual action in order to understand human behavior and economic activity in no way vitiates either catallactics nor the necessary community context, any more than the study of a sphere vitiates the study of gravity between several planets. It is impossible for any human being to live outside a community,[ss] and like the individual – but in a very different sense – the community *must* act to achieve common goals to sustain the life of its members.

Like the individual case, the communal choice of acting to attain one goal instead of another is subjective and thus cannot be determined to be more "rational" than another. Only the communal action itself is rational, by being volitionally directed to some goal to remove a felt discomfort. Thus many varieties of communal action – kibbutz, kingship, contractual labor, indentured labor, peonage, and even widely condemned communal action such as slavery[186] and cannibalism[187] – fulfill the necessity of communal action for the maintenance of the life of the group. But unlike individual action, where the opposite of action is not irrational behavior, but nonvolitional action (e.g., a cough, a fever), the opposite of communal action is not irrational behavior, but archetypal unconscious action in response to the symbols of religion, which can be manipulated to eliminate the state ideal of radical equality, and thus reduce the envy necessarily conjoined with such an ideal. *It is this subjective theory of value for the group that provides the scientific foundation to architectonics,* asserted here as a branch of praxeology. Following the convention of Althusius, this communal action may be termed *symbiotic action. 1.1a, QED.*

While we have established by axiom the necessity of government, the necessity of a state form of government is in no way asserted. To the contrary: We have established that the state must tend ineluctably toward a central government of total power over its subjects. And while a totalitarian state absolutism certainly may rest on the previous axiom, and while the elites enjoying power in such a government certainly may want the continuance of such a communal life, we may allow their subjects a different opinion. In any case, a community larger than the family requires consistent rules of mutual cooperation, whether implicit or explicit, in order to achieve communal goals. These rules may be explicit and coercively instituted by 60,000 pages of legislation, 70,000 pages of executive fiat, and 70,000 pages of tax code; or on the other hand, they may be more subtly instituted by self-enforcing commercial rules as in the over 500-year-old Hanseatic League,[188] by custom as in the 800-year old uncodified[189] "ancient rights of Englishmen,"[tt] or by self-

---

[ss] Again, the imaginary case of Robinson Crusoe fails to provide a counterexample; nor does the case of a "Swiss family Robinson" (from the Crusoe-inspired 1812 novel *Der Schweizerische Robinson* of Johann David Wyss). In both cases, an enormous human capital from a pre-existing society keeps both the solitary man and the solitary family alive. Furthermore, the "society" of the lone Crusoe dies with him, as would the "society" of any family condemned to practice incest – the universal prohibition of mankind – for its continuance.

[tt] One looks in vain to the Magna Carta of 1215 for codification of either human rights or a constitution. The document extended some privileges to the English barons, not to English citizens, and it would see 54 drafts by the time of the death of Henry VI (1421-1471). *Vide* Graham, *op.cit. infra,* page 28.

enforcing aristocratic rules as in the 1100-year-old Venetian republic. [190] Social sovereignty is a non-contractual union that precedes political sovereignty.[191] Clearly these enduring examples – far longer than any state – of the viable power of custom demonstrate that man is not an ox or a donkey that must be beaten into productive communal action; he is a human being who recognizes the necessity and pleasure of society, and who is responsive to nonviolent signaling of expected behavior to sustain it. Following the convention of Althusius, these non-state rules for communal action may be termed *symbiotic government*. *1.1b, QED*.

We have shown that reason does not exist in (1.1.2a) the individual in a state of nature, not in (1.1.2b) reason reified in the natural law, not in (1.1.2c) the general will, not in (1.1.2d) a universal secular humanist ethics, not in (1.1.2e) the abstracted individual of game theory, and not in (1.1.2f) the individual as "informed voter." All of these attempts to employ reason – man's unique characteristic – for ordering society have failed. They have failed because neither "good" nor "nature" nor "reason" is a univocal term in the context of constructing rules for communal action.

While it is an inalterable fact unique to man that any government must enforce some ordinal set of preferred behaviors – that is, values; that is, the "good" – no one can provide a universal prescription for it; it is unanswerably subjective to the community that enforces it. How then to resolve the apparent contradiction of government necessitating a set of values, in the absence of any established set of values? Two of the three logical possibilities have already been rejected: Deontology and consequentialism. Since there is no universal prescription for the good, deontology cannot offer a guide for government, in spite of its temptation to justify state action to conduct various peacetime "wars" as moral imperatives, heedless of consequences. Consequentialism, the underlying principle of utilitarianism, cannot offer a guide for government, since it fails on two counts: The impossibility of foresight for the consequences of any suggested utility, and the impossibility of interpersonal comparisons of utilities. The only remaining possibility is the virtue ethics[uu, 192, 193] of Alasdair MacIntyre, by which a community sets its own standard of excellence, rewards it, and so achieves it in its citizens – without a prescriptive universal definition of what constitutes "excellence."

Reference to man's "nature" provides no guide to government: Left and Right remain permanently at odds because they rest upon a theological distinction of man's nature as plastic and perfectible versus fixed and fallen. Reference to "natural law" provides no guide: The foremost defender of the principle empties its content by conceding that "[a]ll men are born natural-law

---

[uu] Virtue ethics is discussed in a section below.

jurists."[194] Conceding further, he stresses that natural law is not opposed to positive law, and that while property is "in accordance with natural law," he allows the state to destroy this embodiment of individual rights by saying "this does not mean that severe restrictions on the use of property, or even expropriations for reasons of general welfare, are absolutely contrary to the natural law."[195] This emasculated use of "natural law" to defend rights, which cannot exist without property, is no better than John Locke's "proviso" – as Robert Nozick called it – which admits property rights by virtue of natural law "at least where there is enough, and as good left in common for others."[196]

It is universally recognized (although not by axiom) that "the people are sovereign," meaning that government exists for the benefit of all its members, and that they should determine how that benefit is administered. We have shown that plurality voting creates not this expression of the sovereignty of the people, but instead creates an oligarchy, typically a duopoly of two political parties. Political parties garner votes by appealing to various divisive Interests, or factions; a political party is merely a faction of long duration, amalgamating some factions, setting other factions at war with one another, to the enhancement of its own power. Clearly then, sovereignty of the people means not the mere pruning of state power, not the impossible trimming of factions or Interests, not some topiary of various electoral methods, not the fertilizing of stronger campaign finance laws for political parties – but the annihilation of the root: Popular voting. Remove voting, and factions, political Interests, politicians, and political parties – all "politicking" of every kind – go blessedly out of existence. The sovereignty of the people can only be given communal expression in the absence of voting, through the use of sortition.[vv]

Two further institutions assure the realization of meaningful sovereignty of the people and the burial of the decaying state form of government: Absolute property rights and the right of secession. As we have shown, the state cannot exist without public goods by which it enhances its power by benefiting its many parasites. A community jealous of its liberties and prosperity must drain the life blood of the state, its public goods, by striving to return public goods to titled property to the extent possible. Finally, without the right of secession, the sole ultimate veto power of the people is rebellion. Secession is the only peaceful expression of the ultimate veto power of a sovereign people. Secession is made violent only by the refusal of the central power recognize the popular will of a group seeing no reconciliation with its policies. Its recourse to violence to keep its subjects in bondage poisons the good will that would make possible any future reunion of the separated governments.

[vv] Sortition is discussed in a section below.

Symbiotic reason provides an account of the interdependence of the individual and society. It cannot be a historical account since that would require an assertion that either individual or society was prior, which is not possible: Both emerged simultaneously. In the implausible event that a scientific consensus could establish the simultaneous historical emergence of both, it would merely corroborate the logical account presented here. Since the theoretical defense of the state has been given over the course of some four centuries as resting on the primacy of the individual, the temptation is to provide a counter-theory resting on the primacy of society. But such an attempt would be equally false. The fact is that there is an interdependence of both, and since it is a truth not falsifiable by anthropogenic study or by any empirical method, it must be stated as an axiom.

Reference to man's "reason" must either be discarded under the assumption that the six enumerations exhaust its meaning – an absurd rejection of the very essence of man – or else "reason" in its practical application to government must signify the communal nurturing of reason, the necessary environment for individual reason, according to whatever subjective standard by which the community agrees to nurture it. Following the convention of Althusius, this communal nurturing of reason may be termed *symbiotic reason. 1.1c, QED.*

❦

We must now turn to constituting these general axioms in a kleristocracy, or sortive democracy. Ultimately we will breathe life into them as the kleristocratic Republic of Texas.

Who has ever seen 'the individual,' if not defined by his family, his region, his profession, his language, his inheritance, his faith? Removed from these defining characteristics the individual is an abstraction, and a political system based on an abstraction must either end in despotism or revolution.

– Juan Vazquez de Mella[197]

1.2 Kleristocracy based on architectonics

Architectonics describes a *dominium sortiens*, the society of "property, with sortition": The society of absolute property rights, the absence of public goods, and the sovereignty of the people in community, exercising decision-making not through oligarchic elections but through democratic sortition, which society might alternately be called a kleristocracy,[ww] or a sortive democracy. Architectonics is reason exercised by the living, breathing, fallible individual in the context of the *ius symbiosis*, the symbiotic right of the community first described by Althusius, a community which is as essential to individual reason and to an individual's life as the air he breathes.

1.2.1 Sublimation of destructive envy

Religion and Ethics

As stated by the axiom of symbiotic action, communal action is rational not in the sense of the rules of inference by the individual, but by the necessary consequence that man is a rational animal who must act in concert with others in a group. The opposite of communal action is not irrational behavior, but archetypal unconscious action in

This is the way the world ends, the world ends, the world ends: Not with a bang nor a whimper But with a snarl of envy.
– adapted from The Hollow Men, T.S. Eliot

response to the symbols of religion, which can be manipulated to eliminate the state ideal of radical equality, and thus reduce the envy necessarily conjoined with such an ideal. The manipulation of these symbols is the purview of theology; ethics is the purview of moral philosophy.[xx]

It is undeniable that our time in life is brief, as an infinitesimal spark in the eternal blackness before and after it. Consciousness of this fact is the ultimate foundation of all religion. The important influence of this fact on the behavior of most human beings, coupled with the complete lack of empirical evidence to specify it, has provided a rostrum for saints and charlatans since

---

ww From κλερος, or lot. The Greek favors the spelling "klerostocracy," but "kleristocracy" is current and furthermore is just one syllable removed from the familiar and easily pronounced "aristocracy." *Sors* is Latin for "lot," thus the cognate "sortition," the drawing of lots.

xx It should be obvious that ethics in theology is wholly derivative from moral philosophy, since Aristotle indebted Aquinas, just as Sartre did Paul Tillich, as Martin Heidegger did Rudolf Bultmann, as William James did Reinhold Niebuhr, and as Alasdair MacIntyre did Stanley Hauerwas.

the dawn of man. This fact is impressive enough upon most human beings that they have sought moral guides rooted in the fear of oblivion, not only for their own proper psychic behavior, but also for enforcing proper mutual behavior, the former being addressed in the cure of souls and the latter being addressed in ethics. In the Western world, Christianity arose to address that first "salvific" function, without any formal statement of an ethical function.

The formal "ethics" commonly appended to Christianity, altruism, in fact has no ethical content. Christianity's two universal and unconditional prescriptions define the good as obedience to god and happiness as the happiness of others.[198] Since both these prescriptions must be obeyed without regard for consequences, and since it attempts to achieve objectivity by placing the ethical prescriptions outside the moral agent (in god and others, respectively), the ethical standard is deontological, and thus the generic critique of that position applies to it. Second, it fails because *both sides of any moral issue can claim altruistic motives.* For example, the pro-life opponents of abortion can demand altruistic sacrifice for the baby from the mother and from the community that "should" support mother and child; while the pro-choice advocates of abortion can demand the altruistic sacrifice for the mother and the community from the baby. Another example: Those who oppose the U.S. war on Middle East countries in response to the September 11, 2001 attacks can demand altruistic sacrifice for the sake of world peace from American citizens in terms of their forbearance; while the war's advocates can demand altruistic sacrifice for the sake of world peace from American citizens in terms of expenditure of their blood and treasure. Third, altruism is empty of ethical content because *it only specifies the beneficiary of a moral act;*[199] it offers no moral system and no prescriptive action but one: An act acquires universal ethical value only if it is performed for the benefit of some interest or some person other than the self. Altruism thus offers its deontological prescription, not to guide individual action, but to empower those who can make the most authoritarian claims, using its sanction on behalf of those "others." The terrifying implications of that sanction should be clear: Although certainly not Christian, every murderous tyrant of the last century was consistently altruistic, whether the appeal for sacrifice for socialism was that of Stalin, Mao, or Pol Pot.

American Religiosity
Diverse claims have been made regarding the religiosity of the Founders of the former American republic. George Washington was a devout Christian, although his public pronouncements referenced a generic Providence, and his promotion of the value of religion was not exclusively Christian. Thomas Jefferson, John Adams, James Madison, Benjamin Franklin, and Thomas Paine might best be labeled deists. Pew Research Center polling from 2018 and 2019 shows that 4% of American adults say they are atheists, up from 2% in 2009.

An additional 5% of Americans call themselves agnostics, up from 3% a decade ago. 43% are Protestants, down from 51% in 2009, and 20% are Catholic, down from 23% in 2009. This same polling nevertheless indicates that Americans as a whole are far more religious than Europeans.[200] But these numbers are utterly meaningless. The terms "more religious" or "less religious" provide no comparison for the remarkable devolution of the meaning of Christianity and of its theology over the course of a single generation.

Obedient to the individualistic philosophy of the day, the Christian church, especially the wildly fissiparous Protestants, has been atomized into a mist of love, love, love, love, with no creedal distinction beyond who is to receive the chosen sect's happy-face badge. For the Catholics, the Second Vatican Council (1962-1965) had the priest celebrant turn his back on the fearful and demanding crucified god behind the altar, to face a community ready to get happy according to this single emotional law of love. Catholic theology has passed from Pius IX[201] to Pope Francis.[202] Lutheran theology has passed from Dietrich Bonhoeffer[203] to Nadia Bolz-Weber.[204, 205] Presbyterian theology has passed from John Knox[206] to Mark Achtemeier.[207] The ascendant trend in Christian theology is the "emergent theology"[208] of those like Brian McLaren.[209] The latter believes in a Christian faith "without objective, propositional truth," without "objective hermeneutics," and without a creed, while being very jazzed on gentleness, caring, and acceptance. Even the Southern Baptist Convention, America's largest Protestant denomination, with more than 47,000 congregations, advocates positions having little or nothing to do with the Christian mission of salvation, and everything to do with pulverizing the body of Christ into warring political factions.[210]

Drawing upon St. Augustine, Luther initiated this final dissolution of Christian moral authority:

> The doctrine (Lutheran) of justification by faith was an egregious example of putting absolute trust in the assumptions of emotionalism, indeed was the first step towards transferring the basis of faith from the preaching of the word to the so-called testimony of experience.[211]

However, the greatest modern religious emotionalism is not in the fatuous love-creed practiced within the walls of the mainline churches: It has moved to social media. Social media pretend to provide to millions across the globe the services of instantaneous information and very basic social interaction. Instead they have indiscriminately "platformed," or given a megaphone, to everyone to spew forth opinions that, in a more collegial forum, might easily be shown to be baseless and ignorant, without embarrassment to the author of such opinions. Given the nature of these media – brief, sensational, without true dialog – it is issues of absolute justice, screamed with Manichean righteousness, that dominate. Social media have created a generation that is prey to secularized religious passion, a generation incapable[yy] of rationally considering the trade-offs that are the mundane nature of every course of human activity – a generation ignorant of the science of trade-offs, economics.

Evaluation of neither the supernatural claims of religion nor its political claims is a prerequisite to understanding its role in social life. Such a prerequisite would face several insurmountable hurdles. Even if the symbiotic government were to establish a church within its bounds, to assure that the elected church would not deviate from the prescribed creed it would need to meddle directly in church affairs – a policy that, even if practicable, would doubtless force the church to be ejected from the larger confession of which it was a member. Furthermore, as a practical matter, it would not know what creed it was getting. For every Christian religion in America, the current canonical statement of creed is often at odds not only with the actual belief of the laity but with the creedal statement of its founding – a contradiction that presents the quandary of determining which is "authentic." And finally, all of these religions are beset with mutually contradictory political views among and between lay and clergy – views all robed in the sanctity of holy writ.

Clearly then, the role of the symbiotic government is not to arbitrate among the many Christian creeds, which as just illustrated, are variants on a vacuous creed of "love" in any case. Assuming this power of arbitration among creeds was the inaugural error of the state in the 17th century.

The Control of Envy

Again, the opposite of symbiotic action is not irrational behavior, but archetypal unconscious action in response to the symbols of religion. In addition to the cure of souls, which is outside any political consideration, manipulation of these symbols is the purview of theology; and this latter function is of vital concern to the symbiotic government. Government is indifferent to supernatural claims: Its concerns begin with the truth that a religious claim may be objectively false, and yet architectonically true. That is to say, a religious claim may be falsified by historical or scientific evidence, and yet still provide social benefits.

For example, a central tenet of most religions, especially Christianity, is that each person is the equal of any other. Morally, this is true: Each person deserves dignity and respect, and anyone exalted in riches, beauty, intelligence, or other gifts can acknowledge some luck in having them, without any sense of guilt or inhibition in flourishing in those gifts. Beyond that, all claims to equality are in fact not true. Some people may have better genetic endowment, may have attended better schools, may have had better surroundings, better

---

[yy] Can anyone imagine a young user of social media listening attentively – standing all the while – to one of the Lincoln-Douglas debates?

nutrition, better opportunities, and may have used these gifts to flourish in life. Should they be penalized so that less fortunate others have perfectly equal opportunities to rise, especially if the flourishing of the more fortunate benefitted the society at large? That is to say, should a society institutionalize envy under the name of perfect justice?

Explicit Church condemnation of the radical egalitarianism that is coterminous with envy has not been effective, in part because of the general hostility toward any ethical claims emanating from capitalism, in part because of the general ignorance of economics among clerics, and most significantly because of deliberate doctrinal ambiguity. While the Church has never endorsed laissez-faire capitalism, it does affirm that free markets help ensure both material well-being and human liberty, even going so far as to say that "no Catholic could subscribe even to moderate Socialism."[212] It has consistently held these principles in its three main encyclicals on economics: *Rerum Novarum* (1891), *Quadragesimo Anno* (1931), and *Centesimus Annus* (1991).[213] Yet in spite of doctrine, one of the first acts of Pope Francis on assuming office was to invite Gustavo Gutierrez, one of the founders of liberation theology (another product of the Second Vatican Council), to a meeting to signal acceptance of socialist views.[214] In any case, interference in doctrine is not the proper purview of symbiotic government.

What most certainly is the concern of government is the reduction of envy. In that capacity it should encourage those churches that use the symbols of religion to eliminate the ideal of radical equality. In the Christian context, the church must be encouraged to dispose of the image of Jesus the lower-class victim – a tendentious image that is all too easily transposed to statist political ends – and instead to portray the Scripturally true image of Jesus of the upper-class elite who made a willing sacrifice, as Erik von Kuehnelt-Leddihin iconoclastically points out:

> As for the 'Son of the carpenter,' *tekton* in Greek means carpenter but also house-builder, architect, contractor. Joseph, moreover, was not an 'ordinary Jew,' but as a descendant of David he was of royal blood and, therefore, in the eyes of his compatriots, a potential heir to the Throne of Judea. The angel characteristically addressed him as 'son of David.' (Christ too was addressed as 'Son of David').[215]

The current Christology of Jesus *patibilis*, the lower-class victim, is probably the reason that an ethically sanctioned anti-market, anti-property bias still has popular warrant, despite the repeated demonstration in economics that such a bias inflicts the greatest suffering on the great mass of people who are not rich.

A new book by Robert Grözinger confronts the Christology of Jesus the lower-class victim head-on by making the case that Jesus was a capitalist. He clarifies many parables to demonstrate a capitalistic Christ. He cites the parable of the talents (Matthew 25:14-30) as the only time Jesus spoke about interest, and did so not only in its favor, but also to recommend both the "from each" and the "to each" as belonging to the one of superior ability.[216] In the parable of the rich young man (Mark 10:17-31; Luke 18:18-30) Christ counsels the morally confused youth to give everything to the poor and follow him, since it is easier for a camel to pass through the eye of a needle than for a rich man to enter the kingdom of god. Here Grözinger points out that Christ is advising a young ruler who doesn't know what to do with his wealth; he is not providing a universal rule for all rich people.[217] Regarding Matthew 21:12-13, which gives the story of Jesus driving "moneychangers" from the Temple in Jerusalem – the only time Jesus physically chastised someone – he points out that "moneychangers" more aptly fits today's central bankers, not capitalists, and that in any case those who wanted branch banking in a church deserved chastisement.[218] Most importantly of all, Christ is steadfastly against the scourge of civilized life, destructive envy. In the parable of the vineyard workers (Matthew 20:1–16) the "lord of the vineyard" pays laborers at different rates. When one complains that he should get as much as another, the vineyard master fires him on the spot and delivers the following rebuke to the envious in verse 15:

> Is it not lawful for me to do what I will with mine own? Is thine eye evil, because I am good?[219]

Another rebuke to the envious is given in the parable of the rich fool (Luke 12:13-15) who wants Christ to force his brother to include him in his inheritance. Here we catch a glimpse of the real Jesus – not the sentimental Jesus as a tall, wheyfaced, laconic Northern European, meekly submitting to the indignities of unbelievers, with his head perpetually, anoptically cocked to the Great Kibitzer on high, with a nondescript, common bearing, but the self-confident aristocrat: The short, dark-skinned, *baredevdik* Jew of Isaiah 53:2,[zz] pugnaciously snapping his reply:

> Man, who made me a judge or a divider over you? And he said unto them, Take heed, and beware of covetousness: for a man's life con-sisteth not in the abundance of the things which he possesseth.[220]

This new narrative is not a capitalist reaction. It is not even a "new" narrative at all. It is a return to the true narrative that denies Christ's sufferings as the warrant for victimhood, and instead portrays his sufferings as the

---

[zz] For he shall grow up before him as a tender plant, and as a root out of a dry ground: he hath no form nor comeliness; and when we shall see him, there is no beauty that we should desire him.

nazar[aaa] against envy. It is an aristocratic Christ whose willing sacrifice becomes an icon of proof that to enviously gloat over the crucifixion of the superior being, of the perfect man, is an intolerable blasphemy. It is an aristocratic Christ who, by way of that profound and undying fascination with royalty, sublimates envy,[221] the perennial threat to all civilized society.

The deadly threat of religion is that it can exalt an imagined happiness that is outside any appeal of reason. But at least as deadly is the threat of envy in a fully secularized society that has either forgotten the architectonic leash on this passion formerly provided by religion, or has deliberately unleashed it to politically manipulate the lower classes. Any government that allows itself to become fully secularized in this way, or to "immanentize the eschaton"[222] (e.g., of Hong Xiuquan, Joachim of Fiore, Thomas Müntzer, and other "reabsorptionists")[223] will have exalted a destructive passion that is similarly outside any appeal of reason.

1.2.2 Diffusing Interest with symbiotic reason

Symbiotic reason is similar to the practical reason distinguished by Aristotle, since both are directly concerned with human action, its purposed end, and the maximization of benefit over time. R. Jay Wallace provides generic definitions:

Multiply your associations and be free.

– Pierre-Joseph Proudhon

> [P]ractical reason gives rise to action; [...] it is practical not only in its subject matter, but also in its issue.[224]

Furthermore, the purposive ends of action are subjective:

> A world that is shorn of objective values or norms leaves no room for rational criticism of peoples' ends, but only for Weberian *Zweckrationalität*: the rational determination of means to the realization of ends that are taken to be given, as a matter of human psychological fact.[225]

Furthermore, those who act seek to maximize those ends – or in economic parlance, people prefer more to less:

> According to the maximizing conception, the fundamental task of practical reason is to determine which course of action would optimally advance the agent's complete set of ends.[226]

[aaa] A *nazar* is a glass amulet, usually round and blue with a black dot in the middle to resemble an eye, common in the Near East, said to ward off the evil eye. The term is used to emphasize the iconic envy-suppressing function of the Cross, not to imply a graven image.

Furthermore, all action must evaluate the dimension of time – or in economic terms, time preference affects the subjective valuation of a good:

> The first and perhaps most common of these [determinations of aims or goals] takes the subjective utility of alternative actions to be determined by the agent's preferences at the time of deliberation. [...] A second and quite different interpretation results if we expand the set of desires that determine the subjective utilities of outcomes to include the totality of the agent's preferences over time.[227]

The embodiment of symbiotic reason for any community is those men endowed with the genius of practical reason. True enough, this statement may seem much like saying "find the wisest men." The point is that some communities prize and nurture such men, while others, like the current American regime, institutionally exclude them. In the United States elections are won not by wise statesmen, but by those best able to conjure votes – an undefinable knack much like the ability to perform perverse and astonishing parlor tricks.[228]

Symbiotic reason is different from practical reason in that it rests on a praxeological category and in that it signifies the nurturing of reason among the whole community according to some discursive process, that is, without appeal to any supernatural or "intuited" or "revealed" authority. Beyond that exclusion, the process may be called subjective. Of course "subjective" does not mean irrational; it simply means that there is no way to establish one universal objective process: Each community will nurture it as best befits that community. The appeal to a non-discursive authority must be excluded simply because the very meaning of reason signifies "giving an account," that is, giving an account open to argumentation. To assert that a proposition is true or that an action must be undertaken simply because one has heard god's voice in a cave or on a mountain commanding it, or because one has heard it from stones at the bottom of a hat,bbb is to place oneself in hostile separation from, or violent opposition to, everyone in the community, each of whom can bark his own unanswerable assertion in reply.

It is easy to be misled by claims of univocal reason and objectivity in what should guide the actions of a community. To the bombastic proclamation that Western elective democracy is the "final form of human government"[229] one can ask the deflating question:

Why should there be majority rule?

It has been shown that elective democracy is the root from which grows the trunk of Interests, from which branch factions, political parties, politicians

---

bbb Muhammad, Moses, and Joseph Smith, respectively – arbitrarily drawn examples.

– the entire poisonous sumac of oligarchic state absolutism. Even if the problems associated with representative agents of the democratic mass were eliminated by online direct democracy, the problems stemming from Interest would still be fatal: For, to say it yet again, there is no individual reason outside the community; individual "reasoners" would necessarily congeal according to some symbiotic reason – in the current case, the vitriolic cauldron of social media, which does not nurture a discursive exchange of ideas.

The previously cited examples of the over 500-year-old Hanseatic League and the 1100-year-old Venetian republic demonstrate that peaceful and prosperous societies can flourish without majority rule, without a formal constitution, and far longer than any state. Popular voting and the sovereignty of the people are not coterminous. The sovereignty of the people is meaningful when it signifies the achievement of subjective satisfaction through the collective choices of the entire community, however constituted by symbiotic reason. It is more likely that the great mass of people in any society would exchange the fetish of voting in favor of long-term peace and prosperity, rather than ideologically cling to it to their own enslavement and ruin. The contentedness of the populace in these two historical examples is evidence of that likelihood. Ideology is the pole star and cudgel of the state oligarchs and their sycophant intellectuals, not their subject masses.

The symbiotic reason of the Hanseatic League consisted of self-enforcing commercial rules. It would be misleading to describe the Hansa simply as a city league, which were not uncommon in Germany as well as Italy between 1159 (the founding of the principal Hansa city of Lübeck) and 1669 (the date of the last Hanseatic diet in Lübeck). None of those leagues lasted so long or grew to such an extent as the Hansa. Philippe Dollinger describes it:

> In its heyday it comprised nearly 200 maritime and inland towns, stretching from the Zuyder Zee in the west to the Gulf of Finland in the east and from Thuringia in the south to the Baltic in the north. The Hansa remained, however, an anomalous institution which puzzled contemporary jurists. It was not a sovereign power, for it remained within the framework of the [Holy Roman] Empire and its members continued to owe some measure of allegiance to many different overlords, ecclesiastical or lay. It was an amorphous organisation, lacking legal status, having at its disposal neither finances of its own nor an army or a fleet. It did not even have a common seal or officials and institutions of its own, except for the Hanseatic diet or *Hansetag*, and even that met rarely, at irregular intervals and never at full strength. But in spite of these structural weaknesses and the conflicting interests inevitable in an association of towns so different and so distant from

one another, the Hansa was able to hold its own for nearly[ccc] five hundred years. The secret of its long life is to be found not in coercion, which played no appreciable role, but in the realisation of common interests which bound the members of the community together.[230]

Members of the League did not comprise the government of their respective towns, although members often served in both capacities. Their definitive body was the *Kontor*, or mercantile concession, epitomized in the *Kontor* of Bergen, in present-day Norway. Although the word may mean "office," in fact large and established German communities lived within the foreign *Kontore* like that in Bergen. Although the concession was sharply defined and usually walled, the members shared in the life of the local community, which welcomed them because their trading wealth meant prosperity for the community as a whole. The sprawling League was divided into Hanseatic thirds, basically in the areas around Cologne, Lübeck, and Riga, where their local matters were decided. But matters concerning the whole League required a *Hansetag* of all members. Plainly, local solutions were preferred. The number of meetings where all three thirds attended (typically at the centrally located Lübeck) were only: 27 between 1356 and 1400, 12 between 1400 and 1440, and 7 between 1440 and 1480.[231]

The two critical points for the discussion here are the League's methods for intramural and intermural settlement of disputes. For the League the central problem of majoritarianism – non-univocal decision-making – did not arise for a simple reason: All *Hansetag* decisions had to be unanimous.[232] This policy forced a discursive presentation of reasoning in order to reach unanimity; it forced solidarity of action, since no oligarchy could make decisions binding on all; and it forced circumspection, since the commercial prosperity of all trumped the vainglory of a few. For disputes with surrounding nations, the League preferred diplomacy; failing that, it could enforce a boycott by all members against the offending country, which almost always brought a peaceful resolution; and most reluctantly, it could engage the resources of the entire League in war. Despite its long history, rare was its recourse to war, the pastime of vain kings and pompous saber-rattlers.

The symbiotic reason of the Hanseatic League championed geniuses of practical reason like Jakob Pleskow of Lübeck and Wulf Wulflam of Stalsund, whose tact and skill kept it out of war at the end of the 14th century.[233]

The symbiotic reason of the Venetian republic consisted of self-enforcing aristocratic rules. The republic is usually dated from the election of the first doge in 697 until its conquest by Napoleon in 1797 – 1100 years. Its

---

[ccc] Dollinger possibly says "nearly five hundred years" by counting from 1226, when Holy Roman Emperor Frederick II made Lübeck an imperial free city. With the end date of 1669, that would be 483 years. In either counting, the date of its demise coincides with the birth of the state.

prosperity attracted people from all over Europe, so that from 1050 to 1650, Venice was one of the five most populous cities in Europe.[234] Daniel J. Smith describes it:

> Venice had no formal documented constitution[; however, informal] constitutional constraints included the dispersion of power through overlapping committees, complex election procedures, strict term limits, and a ducal oath of office. [...]
>
> The Great Council was established in 1171 and served as the primary governing body of in [sic] Venice, especially when it came to matters of constitutional importance, meeting every week with high attendance rates. The Great Council was responsible for electing the doge, magistrates, judges, ambassadors, and other governmental positions. The Great Council's ratification was also required for major constitutional, military, and economic decisions. The Great Council's membership, representing all of the parishes across Venice, comprised all Venetian patriciates over the age of 25. Like membership in the patriciate, membership in the Great Council was passed down hereditarily. Only members of the Great Council were eligible for prominent public offices. Membership of the Great Council was expanded at times to include males from families that had acquired new wealth or to reward military leadership, especially when under pressure from the popular body of citizens, the Arengo. New members were approved by the Great Council and required the candidate to secure members of the Great Council to serve as pledges for them.[235]

An array of complex self-enforcing checks were imposed on every office:

> Nominators for electing patricians to office were selected at random from the patricians and served as pledges for successfully elected candidates they nominated. Pledges were obligated to pay the unpaid restitution and fines for any criminal or constitutional misconduct performed by the candidate they nominated for office. If elected, patricians were obligated to serve in that office and faced severe fines for refusing, resigning from, or neglecting their elected position. To inhibit the formation of special interest groups, patricians set up an anonymous and randomized electoral procedure and forbade all electoral campaigning. To ensure that elected officials were monitored, patricians elected state prosecutors to sit on all governing committees, including committees in charge of monitoring elections, to monitor for constitutional compliance. Finally, the patricians offered rewards for any patrician or common citizen reporting illegal activity. These re-

wards were even extended, along with clemency, to individuals complicit in the crime.[236]

Although the doge enjoyed a lifetime office, held final judicial authority, and could set the Senate's agenda and preside over it, his powers were closely watched. A 60-man Venetian Senate, the Consiglio dei Pregadi, introduced in the 13th century, met every two or three days to provide day-to-day legislative and judicial functions. The Senate created a smaller executive council, the Collegio, whose approval was required to initiate legislation but not to enact it – a limitation on the authority of the doge, who furthermore was forbidden from conducting most state business without at least four ducal councilors present.[237] Randomized selection must have worked successfully for patrician offices, for between 1172 and 1268,[238] the process was applied to the doge, as a check on the corrupting influence of voting.

The Venetian republic curbed elective majoritarianism with the use of sortition – random selection of officeholders. In its particular case, it was done by drawing the names of candidates from an urn, a process hedged about with other complex checks. The problem that confronts sortition – the possibility that total incompetents might be randomly selected – did not arise because the initial pool was all aristocrats. Certainly any pool of aristocrats is not devoid of incompetents or criminals, but those were eliminated by third-party pledges of their integrity, by term limits, and by rewards to whistleblowers – and of course all of them "had skin in the game": They could lose everything not just of their own but of their entire family if their stupidity led to Venice being defeated and sacked. As for the republic's intermural settlement of disputes, diplomacy was the preferred response: The peace and prosperity of Venice rested with practical-minded merchants who were reluctant to squander their wealth in war.

The symbiotic reason of the Venetian republic also had its geniuses of practical reason, including Leonardo Loredan, who was doge from 1501 until his death in 1521. In 1503, he stopped Ottoman Turk harassments in the eastern Mediterranean by concluding a peace treaty with them; in 1509, he recovered the Venetian strategic inland city of Padua from the Habsburg Holy Roman Emperor Maximilian I; in 1513, he concluded a defense treaty with the French King Louis XII, turning aside the threat from the "Warrior Pope" Julius II. These treaties involved the payment of tribute, which the Venetians gave without embarrassment, preferring that to war.

Other examples of successful non-state governments could be cited, but these two sufficiently demonstrate that Interest, especially common economic interests, can be used to bind community action by symbiotic reason, thus diffusing antagonistic Interests, rather than divide it by a cynical oligarchy that pits Interests against one another, concentrating its own power.

1.2.3 Virtue ethics

As previously stated, the great project of the Enlightenment was to create one universal ethics based not on creed or doctrine but on reason, to which every citizen of the West could consent as the basis of society, the guide to common group action beyond the family. Yet the conditions of human life

The flourishing of the virtues requires and in turn sustains a certain kind of community, necessarily a small-scale community.

– Alasdair MacIntyre

are so varied that offering a catalog of every possible occasion for action, or offering any prescription for action that applies universally and unconditionally (deontology), or offering a prescription for any action that has a beneficial result (consequentialism or utilitarianism) all have shortcomings. Very few universally and unconditionally true prescriptions can be offered: No one will obey a universal prescription to never tell a lie when a murderer asks you where you have hidden his intended victim. Savage means cannot justify beneficial ends: No one will obey a prescription to kill a grandmother even if her family will be somehow better off consequently.

The morality guiding the vast majority of those living in the West for the past two millennia has been Christianity. Its two universal and unconditional prescriptions define the good as obedience to god and happiness as the happiness of others.[239] In both these prescriptions the ethical standard is completely outside oneself. These prescriptions have been pressed into the deontological ethical code named altruism.

The practical meaning of an ethical standard "completely outside oneself" is that it is completely outside evaluation by reason. For if one's own reason can establish values as true or false, what's the need of a supernatural, god-given ethical standard? At this impasse Immanuel Kant stepped forward with the self-conscious goal of saving religion, particularly Christianity, from reason. True, he conceded, we can have no knowledge ("cognition," *Erkenntnis*) of anything outside of experience, meaning that we can't prove the existence of god, or verify miracles: They are outside the phenomenal world. But though the fact of religious doctrines – their truth or falsity – cannot possibly be known, we can still think about supersensible objects so long as they are not self-contradictory. If we could not think about supersensible objects we could not conceive of values, for according to Kant, pure reason, looking at the phenomenal world, can only establish facts, not normative (value) claims. The "needs of practical reason" do that, and they do so by faith, which is a mode of holding-to-be-true (*Fürwahrhalten*) that is just as legitimate as pure reason, when confined to the realm of values.[240]

Kant's fact/value distinction thus provided sanctuary for Christianity's ethical prescriptions, but at a price: It cornered them in the logical dead-end of fideism:[241] Prescriptions defended from that sanctuary were certain by faith and thus unassailable by reason, yes, but at the same time were utterly non-

rational, subjective, and no more valid than any other normative pronouncement, no matter how destructive or barbaric: A prescription to fire bomb a city
was just as valid as a prescription to feed the hungry.

Thus the impasse remained, not just for Christian apologetics, but for
the greater project that engaged even non-Christians: How to provide an ethical
code free of the dilemma of deontology and consequentialism. A way out was
provided by Alasdair MacIntyre, in his remarkable 1981 book entitled *After
Virtue: A Study in Moral Theory*.[242] MacIntyre reached back before the
Christian era to revive Aristotle's understanding of ethics in terms of virtue. For
MacIntyre ethics is not a set of universal rules to equip an isolated conscience
in confronting abstract moral obstacles with the goal of gaining an afterlife –
the goal, or *telos*, for Christians in any case. Instead he revives Aristotle's view
that we should set as our goal *eudaimonia* – happiness born of habits according to our reasoned nature, in the context of a lifetime and in the context of a
community that shares the same narrative about what constitutes human
excellence – excellence, and not resurrection, being the true *telos*. This is virtue
ethics: *Eudaimonia* offered as the alternative to the dead end of the deon-
tology/consequentialism dilemma.

At first glance, MacIntyre's virtue ethics seems completely incompatible with Christianity. The attempt of the theologian from Texas Stanley
Hauerwas to Christianize virtue ethics is illustrative of this failure. He maintains that "[e]thics is a function of the *telos*, the end",[243] but he cannot, like the
atheist MacIntyre, embrace a *telos* or goal culminating in worldly excellence.
First, he is forced to define ethics in terms of a narrated journey to the eschaton
– the divinely ordained climax of history. [244] Second, he is shackled to
Christianity's claim that there is no human excellence of any kind that merits
god's "free gift" of salvation.[ddd] Third, he allows himself to be shackled to
current Christianity's two deontological prescriptions by supposing Christ's two
commandments constituted the ethical system of altruism. Any "virtue ethics"
proposed to exist in these fetters is peculiar indeed.

However, the apparent incompatibility between virtue ethics and
Christianity is rectified with a single distinction: The separation of Christianity's "salvific" function in the cure of individual souls from the false assertion that Christ's two commandments constitute an ethical system. Any
attempt to force an ethical system onto these two passages must result in the
failed system of altruism. This distinction of functions means a re-thinking of
the first function with the previously-described (page 101) aristocratic
Christology, and a re-thinking of the second function with an ecclesi-
ology/theology explicitly rejecting the entire deontological altruistic moral

---

[ddd] Ephesians 2:8-9; Romans 6:23; Romans 5:1; 1 Peter 1:18-19.

code. With this distinction, the Christian *telos* of resurrection and the "free gift" of salvation become meaningful only in the context of the faith's "salvific" function. Christian ethics incorporates virtue ethics only with the understanding of Christ's commandments in the following way:

> First commandment, properly understood: God never enjoins a duty contrary to one's ultimate happiness, which is knowable by reason.

> Second commandment, properly understood: Knowledge of the beneficiary can never substitute for knowledge of the benefit.

The muddling of these two necessarily distinct functions, which allowed the disastrous association of Christianity with altruism, began with St. Augustine.

The influence of Augustine on Christian theology has been to divert doctrine decidedly away from reason. For conciseness and focus we provide the date of July 17, 431, at the fifth session of the Council of Ephesus as the crossroads of this diversion, for it was at this moment when key Augustinian doctrines became articles of faith, binding on all Christians. Before 431, Pelagianism was not officially anathema, even though one of the African councils – none of which were ecumenical and thus not binding on the universal Church – condemned it in 418.

At the instigation of Augustine, North African bishops had begun a campaign against Pelagius. Pope Innocent I had sided with Augustine, but when Innocent I died in March, 417, the new Pope Zosimus had the sense of justice to interview in person Caelestius, one leader of the position, and to read Pelagius' detailed letter in his own defense. Zosimus found their views not contrary to Christian doctrine; he stopped the persecution of Pelagius and ruled that the Africans should immediately come before him in Rome to present their side of the issue. They wrote back, begging that he uphold Innocent's judgment; in reply, Zosimus allowed them to hold a synod, which they did in Carthage on May 1, 418.[245] Unsurprisingly, the Council of Carthage branded Pelagianism as a heresy in eight (or nine) "true" canons, summarized as follows by an authority on dogmatic theology, Monsignor Joseph Pohle:

1. Death did not come to Adam from a physical necessity, but through sin.
2. New-born children must be baptized on account of original sin.
3. Justifying grace not only avails for the forgiveness of past sins, but also gives assistance for the avoidance of future sins.
4. The grace of Christ not only discloses the knowledge of God's commandments, but also imparts strength to will and execute them.
5. Without God's grace it is not merely more difficult, but absolutely impossible to perform good works.

6. Not out of humility, but in truth must we confess ourselves to be sinners.

7. The saints refer the petition of the Our Father, "Forgive us our trespasses", not only to others, but also to themselves.

8. The saints pronounce the same supplication not from mere humility, but from truthfulness.

9. [...] Children dying without baptism do not go to a "middle place" (*medius locus*), since the non-reception of baptism excludes [them] both from the "kingdom of heaven" and from "eternal life".[246]

With the exception of the consignment of unbaptized children to hell in canon nine, the list became articles of faith in 431. Although Msgr. Pohle says that "These clearly worded canons [...] gave the death blow to Pelagianism; sooner or later it would bleed to death," a more accurate statement would substitute "Christianity" for his word "Pelagianism." In these eight canons we see the doctrines of original sin, the justification by faith alone, and the worthlessness of "good works" to merit god's "free gift" of salvation. The most forceful, indeed vitriolic, statement of the hostility to reason of these doctrines is given by Ayn Rand. The fact that her remarks tend to inspire not an amused, orderly refutation but instead a sniping, spluttering rage tends to corroborate their truth:

> What is the nature of the guilt that your teachers call his Original Sin? What are the evils man acquired when he fell from a state they consider perfection? Their myth declares that he ate the fruit of the tree of knowledge — he acquired a mind and became a rational being. It was the knowledge of good and evil — he became a moral being. He was sentenced to earn his bread by his labor — he became a productive being. He was sentenced to experience desire — he acquired the capacity of sexual enjoyment. The evils for which they damn him are reason, morality, creativeness, joy — all the cardinal values of his existence. It is not his vices that their myth of man's fall is designed to explain and condemn, it is not his errors that they hold as his guilt, but the essence of his nature as man. Whatever he was — that robot in the Garden of Eden, who existed without mind, without values, without labor, without love — he was not man.[247]

Christian theology is not the interest of architectonics, except within the context of Carl Schmitt's observation that all significant concepts regarding the state are secularized theological concepts, the context of America's political duopoly that rests upon a theological distinction of man's nature as plastic and perfectible (the Left) versus fixed and fallen (the Right), and the context of government encouragement of religious symbols that reduce destructive envy.

It is not for us, but for some genius of the Christian tradition, a theologian of the stature of St. Thomas Aquinas, to restore the Church as a welcoming, nurturing home for reason. He will begin with the demolition of St. Augustine, with the Christology of the aristocratic Christ, and with the canonization of virtue ethics.

1.2.4 Sortition

The pilot will judge better of a rudder than the carpenter, and the guest will judge better of a feast than the cook.
– Aristotle

[T]he appointment of magistrates by lot is thought to be democratical [sic], and the election of them oligarchical.[248]

Aristotle's observation associating popular election with oligarchy has been confirmed. But 2,372 years after the writing of his *Politics*, can the selection of officeholders by lot – that is, by sortition, randomly – be democratic?

Randomness seems at first a very simple concept, as simple as drawing a name out of a hat. In fact it is a very complex concept, and only recently has truly random number generation been possible, as a practical application of quantum mechanics.[249] Nature strives for pattern, not randomness; man even more so.[250] The most unnatural thing possible is randomness.

And yet this most unnatural thing, randomness, is prized in many practical applications: Cryptography, gambling, statistical sampling, computer simulation – and sortition. For sortition – and rather paradoxically for our quest to apply reason to political science – it offers the great prize of the exclusion of rational agency. Oliver Dowlen explains:

> I identify[eee] the defining feature and chief operating characteristic of all lotteries as the 'blind break'. This is the zone at the centre of the lottery from which all rational activity is deliberately excluded. I therefore characterise the blind break as 'arational' to distinguish it from the operation of both the rational *and* the irrational. It is in this central feature that the potential of sortition lies[.][251]

And more philosophically:

> [T]he lottery is a complex phenomenon[. ...] A lottery decision is impartial, unpredictable, amoral, arational, unemotional, anonymous – to take but a few items from the 'box of possible epithets'. [...I]t denies the operation of the human qualities of thought, intention, will and morality. It is linked to the idea that there are some times when choices

---

[eee] His "blind break" and "arationality" are unowned terms in sortition; they are common to Peter Stone, Jon Elster, and many others.

can (perhaps should) be taken out of our own hands, and as such stands at the threshold of some of the most profound areas of human speculative thought.[252]

In ancient Athens, the birthplace of the forgotten true democracy, its citizens were so convinced of the value of sortitioned democracy that by 477 BC they had adopted it for every public office but one:

> [T]he whole administration of the state was in the hands of men appointed by lot: the serious work of the law courts, of the execution of the laws, of police, of public finance, in short of every department (with the exception of actual commands in the army) was done by officials so chosen.[253]

Of course the very mention of the Athenian example elicits a deafening howl from the intellectual sycophants of the state who are paid to defend its ideology of radical equality: "But slaves and women were excluded from this so-called democracy!" The nature of the Athenian democracy – however "unequal," "unjust," "racist," etc., etc. – is more reasonably stated by saying that *its initial random pool offered candidates whose particular selection was a matter of indifference to the quality of the result.*

The ideal of radical equality, now an article of secular religious fanaticism, demands representativeness as a necessary characteristic of legitimate democracy. But "representativeness" is the insurmountable contradiction at the heart of any majoritarian elective system with non-unanimous decision makers. Recent experiments in sortition that attempt to incorporate this alien characteristic by means of statistical stratification[fff] dramatically expose the failure that has always existed.

Although theoretical evaluation of sortition began at least as early as the Florentines Niccolò Machiavelli (1469-1527) and Francesco Guicciardini[ggg] (1483-1540), the subject has attracted extensive scholarly interest recently. Unlike more established disciplines such as economics, which has developed an accepted jargon, sortition requires before any discussion a rectification of terms.[254] Thus "juries," "citizen assemblies," "citizen engagement bodies," "mini-publics," "*minipopuli*," "governance-driven democratization," etc., can mean different things to different scholars. Similarly, the *type* of allotted body can indicate a judicial jury (in the conventional sense of deciding criminal guilt or innocence), an administrative jury (permanently seated to implement

---

[fff] Stratified random sampling, also called proportional random sampling or quota random sampling, divides a population into smaller sub-groups known as strata, in order to achieve representativeness for the population as a whole.

[ggg] Dowlen, *op.cit. infra*, calls Guicciardini "one of the few writers in the European tradition to take the issue [of sortition] seriously".

policy), or a legislative jury (temporarily or permanently seated to decide public policy); for the latter type, the *power* of the allotted body can extend to a purely advisory capacity, a veto capacity, or a lawmaking capacity (rarely given; one that does is CrowdLaw[255]); the body's *stage* determines its time of application, that is, whether its activity occurs prior to any deliberation (polling), at the beginning (agenda setting), at the middle (suggesting and deliberating upon any proposals, expert or otherwise), or at the end (judging and approving expert proposals); and *implementation* can mean anything from James Fishkin's Deliberative Polling®[256] (coaching ordinary citizens on single issues), to Hélène Landemore's crowdsourcing[257] of motivated experts, to Heather Marsh's total society of "stigmergy"[258] as a sweeping alternative not only to representation, but to personality, hierarchy, and group consensus.

For kleristocracy, "jury" and "allotted body" are used interchangeably to indicate any group of decision-makers selected by some process of sortition (random lot), selecting a permanent legislative body with the power to make law at any stage of the lawmaking process, with expert capacities.

Several recent experiments with sortition have been conducted at the level of state government. (1) The American James Fishkin's previously-mentioned *Deliberative Polling®* has had beginning-stage success in at least seven international applications since 2007. (2) In Ireland, there were the middle-stage *2015 Irish Constitutional Convention* on "marriage equity" comprised of 66 citizens and 33 politicians (four from Northern Ireland); and the end-stage *2018 Irish Citizens' Assembly* primarily on abortion, comprised of 99 citizens excluding politicians, which on May 25, 2018, approved as law the removal of the ban on all abortions.[259] (3) In France, the middle-stage *French citizens' climate assembly* of 2019-2020 comprised 150 jurists, with demographic stratifications, including one for location that represented the entire overseas French commonwealth with four members. It failed because, as one randomly-chosen member stated, "The government said they wanted us to deliver solutions but then they just picked what they wanted,"[260] and, as a member of the group Démocratie Ouverte that helped organize the convention said, the assembly was merely a state attempt to defuse the violent *gilet jaune* street protests. (4) In the United Kingdom, Brett Hennig's Sortition Foundation assembled the middle-stage *UK Climate Assembly* of 2019-2020 with 110 jurists to decide *how*, not *whether*, to attain net-zero greenhouse gas emissions by 2050.[261] Since, according to Henning, "completely random selection would have skewed the responses toward people with higher incomes," he skewed for what in his opinion were the "most deprived areas," reserving 20% of the jury for them; then, without detailing exactly how, he matched jurists for seven categories: "Gender identity," age, ethnicity, educational attainment, location, description of their residence as urban or rural, and level of concern about climate change. His stated greatest difficulty was how to take into account those lacking motivated views; to adjust for that he confessed to having "slightly over sampled" certain demographics. Hélène Landemore directed two middle-stage sortition experiments with limited success, using crowdsourcing. (5) In 2010-2013, Iceland made a (poorly advertised) online appeal to rewrite the *Icelandic constitution* using crowdsourcing.[262] This approach was rejected by the government, although almost 10% of the proposals from the public generated a change in the draft text of the constitution. (6) In 2013, Finland wanted citizen input in formulating *Finnish off-road traffic laws*, and so made an appeal to snow-mobile users to rewrite the laws governing those vehicles, using Landemore's crowdsourcing principles. After contention between users and government, the experiment was abandoned.[263] However, there still exists the Finnish Avoin Ministeriö (Open Ministry), a web portal where citizens can debate public initiatives.

All of the state-sponsored experiments above had the following common characteristics:

- They were legislative juries,
- deliberating as a group,
- composed of about 100 members,
- chosen by lot but stratified,
- with strictly demographic stratification, starting with age, location, gender, and income,
- temporarily seated for a specific issue,
- giving purely advisory decisions, and
- whose conclusions were Leftist whenever a political issue was to be decided.

Not only did these characteristics present no challenge whatever to the state's elective majoritarianism, the use of strictly demographic stratification actually enhanced the state's manipulation of political factions. The kernel problem is this: The benefit of sortition (the annihilation of politics) proceeds from its *arationality*; the chimerical benefit of stratification (to achieve representativeness) proceeds from its interpretive and presumptive *rationality*. It is simply impossible to reconcile this contradiction.

Stratification merely exposes the failure of representativeness that was always present in any majoritarian elective system with non-unanimous decision makers. Consider: Every one of the seemingly innocuous demographic categories is suspect, regardless of use in elective or in sortive schemes:

- **Age**: Those most apt to participate in sortition experiments are the young. The young tend more to Leftist views, and they are highly motivated by issues fueled by social media. Youth between 16 and 24 years of age spend approximately three hours a day on social media[264] – forums which do not promote a discursive exchange of ideas. Because of their spirited involvement in activist causes, the young are especially proselytized by Leftist think tanks (in Europe: Demos, the IPPR, the Fabian Society, Progress, Catalyst, the New Economics Foundation, the Club of Madrid, etc.) and by Leftist philanthropies, most notably the Philanthropists For Active Civic Engagement (PACE), whose membership reads like a who's who of endowment cash (The Bill & Melinda Gates Foundation, The Ford Foundation, the Rockefeller Brothers Fund, etc.).[265] Many of the philanthropies are well-intentioned, but many are captives of a "radical chic" inspired by fashionable enthusiasms. Had social media been around in the 1970s, it is easy to believe that not global warming, but global cooling would have been the "existential crisis" of the season, as articles by *Newsweek*,[266] *Time*,[267] *Science & Mechanics*[268] and many others[269] demonstrate – in spite of a recent mendacious failed attempt[270] to "debunk" the printed facts.

> • **Location**: It is well known the world over that rural voters are more conservative, just as urban voters are more Leftist, e.g., as voting for the Irish abortion referendum shows. Any attempt to "compensate" in either direction constitutes a bias.

> • **Gender**: Gender "identity," not biological sex, was used in Hennig's *UK Climate Assembly*. How is "identifying" in that sense any different from "identifying" as young, or rich, or by any other category?

> • **Education level**: Should jury membership be skewed to favor the ignorant or the uninformed?

> • **Income**: Is this a circumlocution to diminish the better educated 1%? In effect, people with less competence in managing their own affairs are suddenly presumed to be adept in managing the public affairs of others.

> • **Ethnicity**: Should someone blacker than another count double for Negro representation? Should someone with a multi-ethnic background get a vote for each ethnicity? And if "transgender" participants are not excluded, why should "transracial" participants like Rachel Dolezal, Jessica Krug, Hilaria Baldwin, Sacheen Littlefeather,[271] and other ethnic poseurs be excluded? Ethnic stratification is the last resort of a society with explosively irreconcilable group differences based on race. If such demographic categories are valid for sortition, they should logically be valid for permanent ethnic set-asides. India has a "reservation system," whereby certain ethnic groups are guaranteed representation, apart from any electoral choices. Lebanon's constitution, as previously cited (page 87), set aside a Christian president, a Sunni prime minister, a Shiite speaker, and a Greek Orthodox vice-minister. Of course such arrangements only exacerbate ethnic tensions, as they especially would in the West, where numerous ethnicities would declare a political war for set-aside status.

> • **Motivation**: Is not an indifferent person thereby willing to accept any outcome? Voter apathy is in fact a good thing: It is the indicator of political stability. High voter turnout likely means that political upheaval is underway, as witness the high turnouts in 1960 and 2016. On the other hand, highly

motivated participants may be inspired by Interest, not by the reasoned good for all. Any attempt to "compensate" in either direction constitutes a bias.

The application of any demographic category constitutes a rational bias. But no demonstration can possibly be made that one demographic group is better or worse "represented" under the administration of any randomly chosen demographic – unless that group constitutes a separate species incapable of common human sympathy. The Civil Rights Act of 1964 was enacted without black "representation"; Title VII of that law prohibited employment discrimination against women, although only 14[272] of the 535 members of Congress were women at the time; and many laws are passed without prejudice to the blind, the stutterers, the red-haired, or the left-handed. As Duke University professor of mathematics Dr. Jonathan Mattingly asks:

> Who's determining which categories inform decision-making? [...]
> How do we know which factors account for clarity, empathy and decisiveness?[273]

The purpose of demographic stratification seems to be state legitimization through the promise of equal representation. But this promise cannot be separated from social justice preconceptions, which are completely subjective – "hollow incantations," as Friedrich Hayek put it.[274] Demographic stratification is only a deception to mask these subjective preconceptions, manipulated by the state to form the serviceable voting factions that maintain its power.

The original impulse to support sortition because it would overcome the politicians' perversion of the popular will[275] is admirable. For example, black people overwhelmingly oppose defunding of the police,[276] while their political leaders support it. But invariably the demographic stratification is "tweaked" to favor a predetermined Leftist outcome.

Demographic stratification may be irremediable, but what about other stratifications? It would seem that if stratification cannot be redeemed in some way, then no sampling can assign meaning to representativeness.

A. Phillips Griffiths of the University of Warwick defines four categories of representation:[277]

- DESCRIPTIVE: Likeness between the representative and those represented; e.g., demographics.
- SYMBOLIC: Representative is the "focus of attitudes" of those represented, e.g., a monarch.
- ASCRIPTIVE: Representative is unlike those represented, who are responsible nonetheless for the representative's choices, e.g., Congressmen whose choices impose taxes their constituents.
- INTERESTED: Representative is the voice of a subset faction, e.g., Congressmen who obey lobbyists.

Griffiths trenchantly dismisses demographics, saying of the DESCRIP-TIVE category that "we should not allow lunatics to be represented by lunatics". He dismisses SYMBOLIC as non-functional. He claims that deliberative democracy depends on the latter two. Yet it is precisely those two categories that demonstrate the failure of representativeness in any majoritarian elective system with non-unanimous decision makers. Furthermore, in such a system, the impossibility of direct democracy demands intermediaries – even in the absence of their "representativeness" – and thus tends to affirm Robert Michels' "iron law of oligarchy."[278]

It should be obvious that the failure of demographic stratification in sortition illustrates a like failure in elective majoritarianism, whose factions are composed of these very same groups.

Griffiths' four categories of representation may fail to define its meaning, but what about other stratifications outside that narrow box? – For example, the following:

• **Stratify for posterity**. To better offer political representation for future generations, Andrew Dobson of Keele University in the United Kingdom proposes a "restricted franchise model," in which some seats in legislative assemblies are reserved for those who represent future generations – his "F-representatives."[279] However, the presumption of clairvoyance of the political needs of an unborn generation is manifest in Dobson himself: He would restrict membership to environmentalists.

• **Stratify for function or skill**. Terrill Bouricius envisions "an interconnected network of minipublics, each with a specific legislative function and a specific topic or issue."[280] Thus there would be not a monolithic allotted legislative body, but instead many, assigned according to task: An Agenda Council, a Review Panel, a Policy Jury, a Rules Council, and an Oversight Council. However, it would seem that under this scheme all of the selection issues confronting a single body would simply be multiplied *in parvo*.

• **Stratify for wisdom**. We assume universal agreement that wisdom is a characteristic equally prized among members of any social grouping of any kind. Although there is no standardized test for wisdom[281] – fortunately or unfortunately, as the unknowable case may be – wisdom is the familiar term for, and the very essence of, practical reason.

It seems that making institutional arrangements for wisdom would need to begin with a relatively small community, since even in the very unlikely event that the wise choices applied equally, say, to rural Northern Californians as well to as those in Los Angeles, any bad judgments would still need to be compartmentalized, not afflicting an entire region. Further, there would seem to be a need to identify abiding communities for which abiding judgments would be made, since any judgments should avoid being made on the basis of alarmism[282] or ephemeral political fashion.

George F. Kennan (1904-2005), the renowned diplomat, suggested creating for the United States a "Council of State" composed of nine permanent members sitting in the nation's capital to consider no more than three national issues at a time, offering "guidelines for governmental action, not [...] recommendations for specific measures."[283] To ensure that the Council would be apolitical and drawn from wise experts, he elaborated the composition of a selection panel composed of all the State governors "together with [each S]tate's highest judicial figure, and one layman to be chosen by the two of them."[284]

Although he does not mention Althusius in his book, Kennan's words could well serve as the modern paradigm of that 17th century scholar:

> There is a preference for the small over the great, particularly in the
> case of the human political community. There is a preference for the
> qualitative over the quantitative, for the personal over the impersonal,
> for the discriminate over the indiscriminate, and for the varied over the
> uniform [...]. With particular relation to the habits and practices of
> governments, there is an aversion to the American tradition of the
> treatment of social and political problems by great, all-inclusive
> categories (that is, by abstract and rigid legal definitions with theo-
> retically wide-ranging applicability) and a longing for intelligent dis-
> crimination in the treatment of both persons and situations [...].[285]

Therefore, the application of sortition must begin with the several assumptions just discussed: The rejection of demographic stratification in favor of a bias toward wisdom, and the requirement of a small community with an abiding sense of identity.

The cantons of Switzerland have had an abiding sense of identity since 1291. Excluding its cities with populations of over a million (Zürich and Bern), the average population of the remaining 24 cantons is about a quarter-million.[286] Largest of the 24 is the canton of Vaud, which contains the city of Lausanne, with a population of over 800,000. The example of Vaud illustrates that no abstract and rigid size requirement can be imposed for defining "small and abiding community." One can only say that there must exist some maximum of size beyond which the notion of community is meaningless. So if this arbitrary limit of 250,000 is applied to the State of Texas, we find that only 13 of its 254 counties currently violate that limit (rounding up from 1.5 when dividing county population by 250,000).[287] In other words, 241 existing counties may be considered "small and abiding communities"; the remaining large counties have towns and suburbs – existing natural divisions – which would constitute such communities, partitioning into an additional 71 for a total of 312. Once divided, the 13 current large counties would be abolished. The previously mentioned panel for installing the first Consilium (the last-serving State Senate, State House, and State Governor; the State Supreme

Court; and the last-serving Federal Senators) could perform this division. Although canton and county are not synonymous, we arbitrarily name a county of less than a quarter million as the unit of government that typifies a "small and abiding community."

Then what precisely is a "community"? There is no "precisely"; in general, it is some small and abiding group having a set of shared values that constitute its identity. As we have demonstrated (1.1a, symbiotic action, page 92), community action in accordance with those shared values is and must be completely subjective; it is the sustaining myth of the state that it can know and defend a universal, objective, non-communitarian set of values. The community provides formal and informal rules for enforcing those values (1.1b, symbiotic government, page 93), rules derived from its own sense of what is reasonable (1.1c, symbiotic reason, page 95).

As we have shown, demographically stratified sortition fails on a contradiction: Its impossibility of joining the arational benefit of sortition (the annihilation of politics) with the presumptive rational benefit of stratification (to achieve representativeness). It fails in three ways.

First, it fails because it insists that its standard (demographics) is self-evidently, objectively, and universally rational, when in fact *it is a standard of social justice*, and as all group standards are rooted in the axiom of symbiotic action, it is necessarily subjective.

Second, it fails because *group deliberation thwarts the wisdom of crowds*. As Adam Grant points out:

> According to decades of research, you get more and better ideas if people are working alone in separate rooms than if they're brainstorming in a group. When people generate ideas together, many of the best ones never get shared. Some members dominate the conversation, others hold back to avoid looking foolish, and the whole group tends to conform to the majority's taste.[288]

This observation is corroborated by the behavioral economist and Nobel laurate Daniel Kahneman:

> [W]hile multiple independent opinions, properly aggregated, can be strikingly accurate, even a little social influence can produce a kind of herding that undermines the wisdom of the crowds. [...Thus] independence is a prerequisite for the wisdom of crowds.[289]

Third, it fails because *the order is exactly wrong*: It places the arational formation of the pool first, followed by the application of the presumptively rational (but in fact subjective) standard.

Sortition in its application in a kleristocratic government corrects the contradiction at the heart of demographically stratified sortition. It has the randomly selected agents deliberate separately. It places the admittedly sub-jective standard first, followed by the arational formation of the initial random pool. Without this order, the formation of the initial pool presents an in-surmountable problem: If it is random, it is crippled by the possibility that not only an incompetent is chosen to govern but that the entire pool is composed of incompetents. By applying the standard first, it guarantees that *its initial random pool offers candidates whose particular selection is a matter of indifference to the quality of the result.*

With these givens, sortition might be implemented as follows:

Any candidate for county office would first be required to take an oath to use his office to reduce public goods and to promote the autonomy of the county; second, he must be a citizen of the county; and third, he must post a performance bond, with the assistance of unnamed pledges, who may pledge for more than one candidate. The amount of the bond might be equal to a year's salary for the desired office. At the end of the served term, a referendum by the citizens of the county would provide a percentage of approval for that candi-date's term of service, evaluating his general competence, but most especially, evaluating his honoring the oath of office. If the approval is 66%, the bond is returned in its entirety to the officeholder and his pledges; for each percentage point lower, down to 33%, three percent of the bond is forfeited to the county, so that a possible 99% loss of the bond is suffered; for each percentage point higher, up to 99%, three percent of the value of the bond is added as a bonus, so that a possible 199% return is rewarded.

It should go without saying that a referendum is not dogmatically condemned as a species of voting: It is a polling of community opinion, not a factional contest for political spoils.

The county administration would draw up a list of further detailed requirements for these bonded candidates for county office, specifying not only the desired skills, but more importantly, the character excellence expected by the community. It could draw up an alternate list or lists, or possibly allow publicly-submitted lists; and the list(s) would be submitted to the county for approval in a referendum. That approved standard, to be absolutely unequi-vocal, is subjective. The requirements for a Mormon community might require only Mormon candidates; one for an agricultural community might require ownership of a farm within the county; one might require a degree in ac-counting or legal competence as a member of the State bar; one might impose county property ownership at a certain level; one might exclude women or undesirables, however arbitrarily defined. I mention these possibilities more for the dulcet anticipation of the apoplectic howl from the statist clerisy than for their realization. Of course no sovereign people of any county will stupidly approve any requirements that cripple its appeal to business, or that impose foolish restrictions on those working to serve them. Yes, it is entirely possible that a county might impose something asinine – for example, that its secretary for health be a man who smears makeup on himself and calls himself a woman, or that its secretary of Indian affairs be 1/1024 Cherokee, or that its director of the bureau of land management be an eco-terrorist[hhh] – but its buffoonery will stop at the county line and not pervert the entire nation.

This is the heart of the matter: There must be some final arbiter of disputes in any society, and it must be perforce anarchic by virtue of standing above the disputes it arbitrates; the only question is the administrative extent of that arbiter. Either there will exist a centralized arbiter from whose police power there is no escape, or there will exist many dispersed arbiters limited by the threat of abandonment. No amount of hysterically advertised squealing by the fourth estate over some subjective choice by some random county can controvert the force of this logic.

Office candidates qualifying for this initial pool of would be assigned a true random number.[iii] One additional random number would be drawn to provide a tell to determine the electors of the first sortition, that is, by selecting those candidate numbers nearest to the tell – proximate for a few electors, less proximate to obtain more electors. These electors would become ineligible for office but would *separately and without consulting the other electors* provide a blind evaluation of the remaining candidates, whose résumés would be divided equally among them, rejecting at least 50% of them but no more than 90%. These divisions can vary by needed size, and multiple sortitions[iii] can be conducted in order to select the best of the best qualified. From that final pool, the required officeholder(s) would be selected by his (their) proximity to another newly drawn tell. The selected candidate(s) would be ineligible for the next term's drawing for that same office, thus skipping one term, although he (they) could enter immediately for some other office.

As in Athenian sortition, the kleristocratic scheme applies to most offices. That is, while its primary purpose is to annihilate the election of representatives necessary to non-unanimous majoritarian absolutism, it also serves to replace the discretionary power of appointments held by state administrators.

To further empower the sovereignty of the people, and to reduce the cost and cumbersomeness of referenda, the county should create for its citizens an online portal for these services. This is already being done in complete se-

---

[hhh] A gift to those for whom the penny just won't drop: The references are to the state luminaries Admiral "Rachel" L. Levine, Senator Elizabeth Ann Warren, and Tracy Stone-Manning, respectively.

[iii] The number may be obtained from companies providing true quantum random number generation, e.g., QuintessenceLabs Pty. Ltd. (Australia), IdQuantique (Switzerland), TeskaLabs (UK), Quantum Dice (UK), Quside (Spain), Crypta Labs (UK), etc.

[iii] This would be similar to David Hume's advocacy of multiple election rounds for each high office. *Vide* F.H. Buckley, *op.cit. infra*, page 49.

curity, properly identifying each unique voting citizen, by Estonia, which labels itself "the world's most advanced digital society," with the following services[290] – all highly recommended for kleristocracy:

EIS – platform for public consultation on all draft laws.
VOLIS – an online decision-making platform for local authorities.
Rahvaalgatus.ee – a portal that enables citizens to compose and send collective initiatives to the Estonian Parliament.
e-Election – a secure online voting system by Helmes.

According to Althusius, there can be no sovereignty of the individual that somehow has been ceded to the state to obtain the benefits of society; sovereignty is of the community as a whole, not its aggregated individuals.[291] Sovereignty cannot belong to the individual, since no man has ever entered life outside some legal authority, which authority would therefore have original sovereignty.[292] To say that an individual is "sovereign" over himself is to speak in an idiosyncratic way, as in the previously-mentioned Robinson Crusoe somehow having a "government" or a "society," over which he is the "supreme power." Also, what could be the meaning of sovereignty's ultimate right of violent revolution for the lone individual? The individual has *self-ownership*, meaning life as his original property, not "sovereignty"; the individual has the primary right of *self-defense*, meaning the right to defend that property, not "revolution." Nor can "representativeness" define sovereignty of the people: We have just seen its meaning dissolve as every demographic category was eliminated. It is kleristocratic sortition that dispenses with the shibboleth of "representativeness" and gives the sovereignty of the people true meaning: Their peace and prosperity as secured by officeholders chosen for their ability and community values, and not for telegenic glibness.

1.2.5 Property

The personal being of man exists as a datum prior to all positive law.
– Heinrich A. Rommen

As previously stated (1.1.6, page 84), property is intuitively understood as any physical agency to effect the will of the one who has title to it, including the person, which agency is the necessary condition for the exercise of all rights. The right to property is intuitively valid because human beings are not incorporeal ghosts; they have real bodies that to remain in life must have property and its corollary rights for life's enjoyment.

Scholastic maunderings about the number of angels that can dance on the head of a pin pale in comparison with the casuistical zeal of moderns about property rights, of unemployed political science graduates blogging angrily in their parents' spare bedroom. As Murray Rothbard points out, addressing the casuistry that a drowning man has a right to violate the property of another by encroaching on his lifeboat or his plank, it is a mistake to weaken property rights

> on behalf of the "contextualist" contention that, given a choice between his life and aggressing against someone else's property or even life, it is moral for him to commit the aggression *and* that therefore in such a situation, these property rights cease to exist. The error here on the part of the "contextualist" libertarians is to confuse the question of the *moral* course of action for the person in such a tragic situation with the totally separate question of whether or not his seizing of lifeboat or plank space by force constitutes an invasion of someone else's property right. For we are not, in constructing a theory of liberty and property, i.e., a "political" ethic, concerned with all *personal* moral principles.[293] [emphasis in the original]

In other words, as David Gordon clearly summarizes: "[A]n emergency suspension of a right [cannot constitute] the elimination of that right."[294]

Natural law may be referenced to establish the primacy of property, but only with the important caveat that intuition alone establishes its claims. This caveat avoids the criticism that natural law introduces subjectivism into the law and dualism in contention with positive law.[295] Thus there is no "second" or "alternate" source of law: The intuitively established primacy of property underlies *all* law, as a single, integral fundamental.[kkk] Rommen:

> For precisely this state of being a person, this state of being an end in oneself, is the first fact, and in it lies the original germ of right. [...] Prior to the state, then, there exist rights of the person. [...] There exists a *suum*, a right, which comes into existence with us. This is, in the first place, the right to life and property. The *conservatio sui ipsius seu membrorum suorum*[lll] is not peculiar to Hobbes; on it rests the right of self-defense. [...] The integrity of this sphere of personal being, this first circle of right of one's life, is an absolute presupposition of the legal order.[296]

Furthermore, the denial of the primacy of property in one's self and the material means of effecting the will results in absurdities. By what reasoning could another person justify a claim to ownership in one's self? Any such justification would also establish a claim against that usurper himself. Also, to

---

kkk The imprecision and supernatural assumptions of the term "natural law" must be avoided. Grotius himself seems to recognize this when he asserts that natural law is the law of human nature, and famously says that natural law would exist even if god did not. See Alvarado, *op.cit. infra*, page 68.

lll The preservation of one's self and what pertains to it.

assert that one has property in one's self, but that all the material means of effecting the will belong to someone else encounters the same absurdity, and results in the further absurdity that one holds life at the forbearance or indulgence of someone who supplies at his whim the material means of realizing it.

Jeremy Bentham denies the notion of property inhering in the very being of the person, on the simple assertion that property is vulnerable unless protected by the state's police power:

> Before the laws, there was no property: take away the laws, all property ceases.[297]

Not only does he fail to address the aforementioned absurdities resulting from the denial of self-ownership, he is laughably blind to the predations against property by the state itself. These predations are glaringly obvious today in the state's abuse of asset forfeiture – a principle that pretends to skirt violation of the Fourth Amendment by asserting that property is not inherent in the person, but is radically distinct:[mmm] So much so that on the basis of a hearsay allegation, a crime can be charged *in rem*, against the *property* instrumental to the crime, and not its owner, who must prove his innocence to recover his confiscated property.[298]

The status of property is not an issue for kleristocracy; it is an issue for social justice advocates, for whom it stands as an obstruction to the state's acquisition of public goods, who must undermine its status in order to realize their ideological daydreams.

Kleristocracy provisionally[nnn] accepts the individual rights given in the Article I Bill of Rights of the Texas Constitution as corollaries of the antecedent right to property. There is no need to codify these corollary rights, any more than there is a need to write an English "constitution": Scholarship from American and English jurists is certainly useful to place a given case in the context of customary usage, but that usage, not the codification, prevails.

[mmm] As with Charles Beard's separation of "rights of person" from "rights of property" (*vide* Bassani, *Chaining Down Leviathan, op.cit. infra*, page 108), this ideological cleavage is a key tactic for those who wish to undermine the rights of property.

[nnn] As of November 2, 2021, 35 sections constitute the Texas Bill of Rights. We must "provisionally" accept it for several reasons: Some sections should be wholeheartedly embraced (e.g., Section 2, the sovereignty of the people; Sections 11a, b, c, conditions for denial of bail; Section 18, no imprisonment for debt; Section 31, compensation of victims of a crime; Section 31, traditional definition of marriage); while others are curiosities and Section 4 (no religious test for office) is self-contradictory of its protection of conscience in that it forbids atheism; and others directly conflict with kleristocratic provisions (e.g., Section 20, forbidding outlawry of a citizen). Section 31 was likely adopted because compensation for victims (a policy endorsed by the American Bar Association) currently is paid out of public funds, not by the offender as should be done, of which lawyers typically get 15%. *Vide* Benson, *op.cit. infra*, page 153. Aside from these considerations, and most importantly, any codification of rights cannot exclude others rooted in longstanding custom.

The intuited understanding of the right to property and its corollaries is made more precise by the question of what agency is to enforce those rights and by its contrast with public goods.

Enforcement of property rights, proposed and historical
Kleristocracy does not take place within political science game theory, and not from scratch on some anarchic *tabula rasa*; it will be realized on the remnants of the currently surviving state. That is to say, the revolutionary adoption of the kleristocratic constitution will nevertheless use the state apparatus for the enforcement of rights until that apparatus can be prudently dismantled. As previously shown, the so-called "balance of powers" in a legislature, an administration, and a judiciary is a purely formal distinction in the monolithic power of the state. These would be dismantled in the following descending order of speed: Its legislative arm will be annihilated by sortition; its administrative arm will be progressively atrophied by devolution to the counties; and its judicial arm will be gradually replaced by a polycentric legal order. All three stages require specification in the concrete task before us: The restoration of the Republic of Texas. Although the first has been sufficiently described for this abstract context, some mention must be made of devolution and legal polycentrism.

Devolution of state power to the counties is not only a powerful defense of property; county government is the very locus of symbiotic government. It selects by sortition its agent to serve in the Republic legislature (this designation replacing the former State legislature, convening in the same capitol). The workings of the county governments are detailed below (section 2.2).

A standing legislature is in effect no different from a standing army, in that both are the poised, imminent threat of force, set to intervene in peaceful affairs at the whim of the sovereign. Texas is blessed with a Constitution that halves this threat by establishing a biennial legislature – a system implemented only in the three other American States of Montana, Nevada, and North Dakota, and all in the odd-numbered year. It is a system that especially favors kleristocracy's unique restraint on central power: The 10-member Consilium.

The Consilium resembles the ephors of Althusius, the ephors of Sparta, or the Venetian Collegio. But most of all, in its consultative function it is like Kennan's Council of State, and in its administrative function it is like the seven-member Swiss Federal Council. The Consilium functions first as a non-political guide to the Republic's legislators chosen by sortition, as previously described. It has no direct legislative power, and it is not present in the capitol when the legislature is in session during odd-numbered years. During its private deliberations in even-numbered years, it alone sets the agenda for the legislature sitting in the following year, although it will be available remotely to immediately consider additions to the agenda, as proposed by a majority of the legislature in session. The legislature cannot initiate legislation without Consilium approval, where a tie vote of its 10 members equates to approval. The Consilium alone assigns House committee chairs from the 312 legislators chosen by sortition (1.2.4, page 113), whose complete résumés are sent to it immediately after their selection. Also from those résumés it selects the legislature's Senate, subject to challenge individually, not as a slate, by the House. It also provides expert staff for crafting unambiguous law, whom the legislators may supplement at their own expense.

The Consilium also is the personification of the Republic in its dealings with other governments. It alone maintains an expert chancery staff, and it appoints ambassadors and embassy personnel (or ministers and legations until the government is fully recognized).

The 10 members of the Consilium, called Consuls, would be selected from the Republic's citizens in the following way. For its first instantiation, each of the following would select two candidates (with at least two alternates): The last-serving State Senate, the last-serving State House, the last-serving State Governor, the State Supreme Court; and each of the last-serving Federal Senators would select one candidate (with alternates). At the conclusion of the legislature's session in the odd-numbered year, it will elect two new Consuls (or an additional number if the Consilium has fallen to less than eight members, to ultimately restore the 10). If the two additions would constitute 12, the currently-serving 10 would vote among themselves to dismiss two of their number. As with the county's sortively-elected officers, each Consul must take an oath to use his office to reduce public goods and to promote the autonomy of the counties; second, he must post a performance bond, with the assistance of unnamed pledges, who may pledge for more than one candidate. The amount of the bond must be at least equal to a Consul's yearly salary (an amount determined by the legislature). Any outgoing legislature can by majority vote recommend the dismissal of any Consul(s) for any reason, on compelling evidence received from any source; the legislature of the following (odd-numbered) session will, as its penultimate business (the election of new Consuls being its final business), vote to dismiss if at least 66% so sanction (each Consul considered separately). Similar to the previously-described bond scheme, starting at a 66% sanction where the forfeiture is 100% of the bond, an additional 3% penalty is inflicted for each higher percentage, so that a possible 199% loss of the bond is suffered. Like the Swiss "head of state," who is really just a "first among equals" who rotate the position among themselves,[299] one of the 10 Consuls would be chosen by sortition every two years to serve as this chief administrator, with no repetitions until each has served, and this administrator would, in effect, replace the current State governor.

It should go without saying that "polycentric legal order" does not mean anarchism,[300] since the very tradition of the West is one of multiple legal systems,[301] including canon law, feudal law, tribal law, maritime law, administrative law, and tax law, to name a few. Already for some 40 years in Texas and in the United States the application of alternative dispute resolution (ADR) has been rapidly accelerating,[302] in spite of the scoffing that it was "a little on the edge"[303] when first introduced in Texas. Today, only about one percent of all civil cases filed in federal court are resolved by trial, despite a dramatic increase in civil dispositions over the last 40 years.[304]

In the 1980s, the U.S. Supreme Court broadened the applicability of the 1925 Federal Arbitration Act (FAA), which was written specifically to make arbitration agreements "valid, irrevocable, and enforceable, save on such grounds as exist in law or in equity for the revocation of any contract."[305] The law first applied only to commercial disputes within Federal jurisdiction. Then with *Southland Corp. v. Keating* (1984),[306] the FAA was declared superior to all State ADR laws. A 1985 ruling widened the FAA's scope from commercial disputes to include statutory disputes, and a 1991 ruling further widened its scope to apply to employment contracts, and to recognize the validity of mandatory arbitration. On the principle of "severability," the U.S. Supreme Court holds that even when a contract is vitiated by fraud, such a dispute can be arbitrated. It's obvious why litigants embrace arbitration: According to a recent study, by using ADR, "[Assistant United States Attorneys] spent an average of $869 in neutral fees and estimated that the process saved $10,735 in litigation expenses per case."[307] Of course the state has accelerated the use of ADRs not to save litigants' money or to diminish its power, as the *Southland* case demonstrates; its purpose is to prevent a litigious society from overwhelming its formal court system.

After deferral to the central state's FAA, the State of Texas administers ADR primarily through two laws: The Alternative Dispute Resolution Act of 1987, governing mediation – by far the most used application of ADR – and the Texas Arbitration Act of 1965, governing arbitration. As the guidebook from the Texas bar states: "The [Alternative Dispute Resolution] Act lists five ADR procedures available to Texas citizens: mediation, mini-trial, moderated settlement conference, summary jury trial, and nonbinding arbitration. In addition, variations or combinations of the five basic procedures can be used if acceptable to parties and to the court."[308] As for the 1965 Act: "Unlike other forms of alternative dispute resolution, arbitration does not allow the parties to discuss and evaluate the case and come to a resolution but places the resolution in the hands of a neutral decision maker. [...J]udicial review of arbitration awards is rare, and usually only for limited circumstances."[309]

One must not make the mistake of assuming that mediation and arbitration can work only in the context of authoritarian law. As legal philosopher Lon L. Fuller wrote, "mediation is commonly directed, not toward achieving conformity to norms, but toward the creation of the relevant norms themselves."[310] And, according to law economist Bruce L. Benson, "enforceable rights and duties derive from a contract just as they do from the provisions of a statute."[311] And after all, legislation is not the sole source of law: A great amount law is created – not just revised – from adjudication.[312]

In spite of the state's reliance on the severability principle to distance ADR from criminal law, obviously there are cases where civil and criminal law overlap. This hesitancy in the introduction of private providers into criminal law is misplaced. As economist David D. Friedman puts it: If one says that private prosecution of crimes is a mistake, one implies that private prosecution of civil torts under mediation and arbitration also is a mistake.[313] This hesitancy is based on the misconception that the law is concerned not only with consequences (which civil law might well address), but supremely with justice (which criminal law must punish even if the consequences are slight): That is, justice trumps efficiency. But Friedman's study of the law finds "a surprising correspondence between justice and efficiency."[314] By that he means that consequences resulting from the application of justice cannot be immune from an economic evaluation of their efficiency. He cites the more general principle from Ronald Coase:

> All solutions have costs and there is no reason so suppose that government regulation is called for simply because the problem is not well handled by the market or the firm.[315]

Justice should be blind to the status of persons, not to the externalities of its actions:

> *Legal rules are to be judged by the structure of incentives they establish and the consequences of people altering their behavior in response to those incentives.*[316] [emphasis in the original]

To fully preclude judicial invasion of property rights, where in criminal cases the victim is excluded as a party, the application of ADR into criminal law must be promoted. (Note that ADR in criminal law has nothing to do with plea bargaining, where currently over 90% of criminal cases avoid trial through its abuse.[317]) Polycentric legal alternatives here would introduce market alternatives[ooo] that take the rights of the victim into greater account and place the restitution of his loss on the offender instead of on the general public. Current law can be the default law until customary law is restored through private law alternatives. In the context of market incentives from the availability of other providers, it could be that current law is never completely removed.

[ooo] *Vide* Bruce L. Benson, *op.cit. infra*, chapters 8 and 9. Also Friedman, *Law's Order, op.cit. infra,* especially for refuting objections supposedly fatal for private criminal law such as defenseless indigents (page 265) and judgment-proof defendants (page 304).

The fundamental misconception about property and its corollary rights is rooted in the persistent myth of state power as the safeguard of the radically alone individual, threatened with destitution and menaced by other initially asocial individuals. According to this myth, the individual is a packet of potential rights that can be actualized only upon the arrival of the state. The myth is even shared by proponents of the classical liberal "night watchman state" or the libertarian "minarchist state" – a state which supposedly provides the indispensable public goods: The courts (creating common and statutory law), the police (enforcing the laws against criminals), and the military (providing national defense). Only on this presumed foundation does the individual's flourishing rights result in society – a society with no common values other than those "spontaneously" derived from voluntary contracts between individuals.

But such a myth has no basis in history. Government prior to the state never provided courts, police, or military; the community did. With its evolution, the state provided courts, police, and military functions not out of its beneficence as a godlike, impartial umpire, but out of its essential tendency to augment its own power. This myth requires the fantasy of a primordial "sovereign individual" in a Garden of Evil in order to sustain its first premise: The "social contract" theory. Only by this myth can study of the organic development of symbiotic life be banished. Symbiotic life originated in the family; the state originated in war.[318] Law for the community originated in custom;[319] law for the state became the subjective will of the sovereign – including the majoritarian sovereign. And the bitterest irony of all: The myth of the heroic individual in a centuries-long battle with the naked power of the tyrannical sovereign. Robert Nisbet:

> The modern [s]tate and the whole ideology of the political community have become significant, influential, not through worship of naked power but because of the promise which seemed to lie in political power for the salvation of man – for the attainment of moral goals that had eluded mankind for thousands of years. Not to the writings of power worshipers or reactionaries must we look for the source and diffusion of the ideology of the political community [...].[320]

The provision of security and law was not initially provided by the monarch or the state.[321] How could it be otherwise? In the Anglo-Saxon context, the monarch was remote, and police did not exist until the 19th century. It was up to the local hundreds – the community covering an extent of land needed to sustain 100 families – to "raise hue and cry" to alert everyone in the event of a crime and to detain the accused for the "tithing," or group of neighbors serving as a cooperative protection and law enforcement association.[322] The victim was the plaintiff in bringing suit against the criminally accused – an English right until the turn of the 20th century[323] – whose purpose at law was restitution from the criminal, not social punishment beyond that restitution.[324] How could it be otherwise? There were no prisons in the sense of penal institutions, only jails for temporary detention until trial, and even if there were, in penal confinement the criminal would be idle, unable to work to make the victim whole. The laws of the hundreds were customary, not statutory, and "very concerned with protection of individuals and their property."[325] Henry I (1068-1135), the second Norman king of England after William the Conqueror (1028-1087), expanded the intrusion of authoritarian law into the affairs of the hundreds such that in the codification of Anglo-Saxon customary law it was written that

> These law books have [...] one main theme. [...] An offense, probably some violent offense, has been committed. Who then is to get money, and how much money, out of the offender.[326]

The Norman kings also introduced the notion of local appeal to the "king's peace" in whose court were levied fees for this royal service, and the notion of felony, the betrayal of a feudal lord, a crime punishable by death and the confiscation of the felon's property. The confiscations initially went to the offended lord, but later they went to the king, and more felonious crimes were added throughout the 12th century.[327] Eventually the crime of "theftbote" was introduced, criminalizing the *victim* if he accepted restitution from the tortfeasor before the pronouncement of a judgment from the king's court.[328]

Private prisons arose during the reign of Henry III (1207-1272) to induce the prisoner to pay a fine, not to serve a sentence meted out at justice.[329] Elizabeth I (1533-1603) instituted "houses of correction" for "sturdy beggars" who refused to work, but the preferred punishment for crime was transportation abroad, also instituted during her reign in 1597, and remained so until the end of the 18th century, when criminals began to be confined in hulks along the Thames in order to perform the hard labor of dredging the river.[330]

The provision of armies for protection from violent invaders is inextricably tied with the taxing power. Standing armies could not possibly have existed before the advent of the state simply because there was no medieval taxation to sustain them.[331] Armies are expensive: When not hard at work destroying lives and property, they are idle, producing nothing, eating all the while, commonly despoiling property for miles about, worse than a cloud of locusts. Before the Hundred Years War (1337-1453), armies were ad hoc affairs, raised by medieval levies legitimized by feudal obligations. Only with the French Revolution (1789-1799) did mass standing armies, uniformed and ideologically driven to total war, come into existence.

And once again we are compelled to slay the myth of a legislature, its constitution heroically raised, confronting the naked power of the tyrant. The "three branches of government" constituting "checks and balances" are a purely formal distinction within the monolithic state:

> The [English] crown had never been sovereign by itself, for before the days of parliament that was no real sovereignty at all: sovereignty was only achieved by the energy of the crown in parliament, and the fruits of conquest were enjoyed in common.[332]

Indeed, the persistence of the state despite its disastrous failings is explained not by its police outfitted in military gear, not by its legion parasites engaged in domestic surveillance, and not by its threat to destroy by taxation; it persists exactly because of the forbearance written in the hearts of its citizens, who need no document to attest to their inherent desire for peaceful mutual cooperation.

Property versus public goods
The fundamental status of property comes into question when the state asserts a right to "public property." Since this term implies the contradiction of property with an undefinable right of title by all citizens of the state, the term "public goods" must be used. Since these goods are not produced by the state, they enter its domain by an asserted right to tax its subjects, validated in its courts by its assertion of final arbiter of disputes, and enforced by its monopoly of police power. This lack of titled property by which it can assert its power explains the very nature of the state:

> The purpose of government is generally the coercive transfer of property rights.[333]

However, state provision of public goods cannot escape the difficulties associated with the nature of those goods as untitled property. First, there can be no "just" or "equitable" standard for the distribution of public goods because of the aforementioned impossibility of interpersonal comparisons of utilities; public goods are ordered and distributed according to the influence of the interest groups and according to the subjective merit attached to their claims by the prevailing administration. Second, the distribution of those public goods requires the creation of an ever-growing bureaucracy, which becomes an influential interest group in itself. Third, their status as public goods makes them subject to the "problem of the commons": Having no market price, the public goods – police, courts, medical care, etc. – are inefficiently used because they are seen as "free," or in any case less valued than market-provided goods, whose price forces the user to evaluate their worth and make comparisons with alternatives.[334] Fourth, there is no provision of public goods without unforeseen side effects: E.g., the previously discussed explosive increase in fatherlessness among families receiving goods resulting from the "War on Poverty"; the explosive increase in criminal gangs as providers of drugs resulting from their illegality under the "War on Drugs." Or as Gordon Tullock, one of the pioneers of public choice economics demonstrated, government provision of public goods creates external costs[335] – an inescapable fact of any policy choice. Policy makers are blind to this fact because they live outside the market where choices have an associated price: They live in the world of public goods.

These irreparable inherent defects of public goods are the reason that all officeholders in the kleristocracy take as their primary oath of office the pledge to reduce them. This reason should make clear the need to remove the state from the most valuable property other than life itself: The individual's real property in land. This property can only be assured in his possession of allodial title to real property, that is, held free and clear of any superior landlord, not subject to taxation, eminent domain, or any assertion of superior right.

In 2022, the State of Texas had the third highest property taxes in the nation, with each property losing an average of 1.81% of its value every year.[336] Texas counties collect taxes on behalf of about a half-dozen taxing units. The tax rates of the several taxing units within each county vary wildly, so comparisons are difficult; however, the "independent" school district within each county receives the lion's share of taxes (typically well over 50%), followed by city taxes (typically around 20%), county taxes (typically around 20%), county hospital taxes (typically less than 10%), and special taxing units such as a community college.[337] At the State level, Texas receives about 25% of its revenues from the general sales tax, 35% from the Federal government for administration of its mandated programs, less than 10% from licenses and fees, and less than 5% each from a welter of other sources. The joint tasks of privatization and secession imply a sweeping reordering of these budgets. Funding the transition to the new state of affairs might possibly require of citizens a one-time payment of their last Federal IRS personal income tax amount to the Republic of Texas in the year of its re-founding, with that amount progressively halved in the following three years, and eliminated in the fourth.

The primary good of the symbiotic government is not its public goods. Its goods consist in its collective right of association, which expresses the freedom of association held individually by its citizens, and in its discretionary right of citizenship granted to members of its community in accordance with the virtues they share collectively. The *ius symbiosis*, the symbiotic right of the community first described by Althusius, maintains civil rights, but in a sense completely alien to current usage. Currently the term "civil rights" signifies additional individual rights bestowed by the state on some individuals and not others, according to its political advantage. Thus "people of color" acquire the enjoyment of racial quotas, "LGTBQIA2S+"[ppp] acquire protections as an "alternate gender," and women, who constitute a majority in nearly every Western society, bizarrely acquire protections as a minority. But civil rights are not factional Interests given legal sanction equivalent to individual rights; civil rights are the contingent rights bestowed by the community as a whole to favor its communal well-being. Civil rights are the rights bestowed by a community by virtue of its *ius symbiosis* on individuals in the form of citizenship specific to that county alone, after acquisition of citizenship in the Republic of Texas. Each county recognizes the prerequisite citizenship conferred by the Republic, but adds requirements entirely at its discretion for participation in its community life. It prescribes its own county residency requirement, its militia exemptions, its own property requirements (if any), its own citizenship test (if any), its own oath of citizenship (if any), and any other stipulation without restriction.

The prerequisite citizenship of the Republic is conferred on the basis of *ius sanguinis* and not *ius soli*; that is, its citizenship is conferred on anyone who has lived in any Texas county for a total of 35 years, disregarding any hiatus, or on anyone who can document lineal descent to, or adoption by, an ancestor who has lived in any Texas county for a total of 35 years, disregarding any hiatus. With this residency requirement and with the oath of citizenship in the Republic of Texas (described in its section below), citizenship is automatic, unlike the conditional county citizenship.

County citizenship is a desirable good because it authorizes access to the community surplus, called the *bonum sociale*, created by voluntary contributions. The amassing and distribution of this voluntary surplus will be detailed below (section 2.2), but in general it replaces the redistributive schemes of the state and the moral fiction[qqq] that sustains such schemes. The monolithic and immoral state scheme of redistribution according to the subjective will of the majoritarian sovereign is thus replaced by the distributive justice of the county, according to the voluntary and thus moral subjective will of its local citizens. County citizenship is also a prerequisite for holding allodial title, over which the county has the power of defining further conditions for holding such title, such as any residency requirements separate from citizenship. Loss of citizenship is an undesirable detriment not only because it forfeits access to this surplus, but because it is the precondition of loss of allodial title

---

[ppp] Lesbian, Gay, Bisexual, Transgender, Queer and/or Questioning, Intersex, Asexual, Two-Spirit, etc. – none of which have sprouted a z chromosome to create an additional gender. Possibly the "plus" will one day accommodate pedophilia, bestiality, and necrophilia, which currently endure cruel discrimination in the absence of state protections. A pioneering effort has begun with the re-labeling of pedophiles as "minor-attracted persons" (MAPs).

[qqq] Any action loses moral value when coerced because it lacks the elements of personal intention and will, which are the essence of morality. The state holds no property by which it can perform any action, other than public goods extracted from property owners by coercion, threatened or applied.

status, of outlawry, and of banishment – other powers held by the symbiotic government (see page 191). The benefits and detriments apply not only to the individual citizen, but also to the corporate personae of resident enterprises.

Madison's attempt to apply federalism over an extended mass democracy failed for two reasons: It did not provide a mechanism to devolve the consolidation of central state power, and it did not provide a check on political factions. Federalism in the context of oligarchic elections exacerbates state consolidation and factions, therefore must fail; federalism in the context of symbiotic government, which devolves power, and of democratic sortition, which annihilates factions, therefore necessarily succeeds.

1.2.6 Secession

The subject of secession commonly evokes a visceral negative response. In the American context, a completely ahistorical repugnance to secession has been indoctrinated in public school students by obedient drudges following the court historians of a unitary state whose very founding was in secession from Great Britain.

> [T]he smaller the domain where choices among alternatives are made collectively, the smaller will be the probability that any individual's preference gets overruled.
> – Anthony de Jasay

Even if there could be conceded a case against secession, its reasonable opponents must admit several advantages in preparing for it:

- The preparation itself may alert the union that it should moderate its claims against the States;
- since union collapse could come at any time, prudence demands preparation for the safety of all;
- the preparation may avoid errors otherwise inflicted by trial and error during an involuntary breakup;
- if secession is an evil, open discussion can expose it as such.

America was never a nation. It had always been a motley of radically different cultures and of sovereign nations, just as the secession document from Great Britain, the 1783 Treaty of Paris, would separately enumerate them, writing out each of the States by name as 13 nations.[338]

Born of secession, America's history would demonstrate the repeated assertion of its founding principle, ultimately by every state[rrr] and region that comprised it. Only an all-powerful centralized state nowhere described in its federal Constitution could force this motley into a union, pinned together by a million bayonets, as its War Between the States would demonstrate. Now, in an

---

[rrr] See in the appendix: A History of Secession in All 50 American States.

age when brute force has shed any pretense of needing moral authority in the arbitration of political disputes,[339] the mask of idealized unity has fallen. But the state's increasing displays of naked power to maintain the artificial union will only accelerate its inevitable disintegration. No amount of saber-rattling, no appeal to faith, and no unreasoning emotionalism can prevent this disintegration; no childish stamping of feet or pouting denials can stop it. The only option remaining is whether the secession of its parts will be conducted rationally for their mutual benefit, or whether those lustful for power will choose to baptize the inevitable in blood, ensuring only that their grandchildren endure an era of hostility, mutual bitterness, and suffering.

No one can predict the crisis that will prompt the final self-destruction of the American Empire. No overt action by the Republic of Texas should give credence to the accusation that its peaceful preparations gave any occasion to that self-destruction. That fatal crisis, entirely of the Empire's own making, might be ignited by the replacement of the dollar as the primary world reserve currency,[340] a forced drastic reduction of Social Security benefits,[341] a market reassertion of interest rates above the central bank fixing,[342] a hyperinflation, a comprehensive state attempt at retail price fixing, a cracking of blockchained operations by quantum computing[343] – no one can predict the inceptive event. But as much as the immediate trigger is unknowable, so must our readiness to respond be set forth in a program as detailed as possible. It is essential that the program be studied, its points of disagreement be resolved, and every citizen become aware of his role in the revitalization to come. Only this preparation can minimize the inevitable difficulties of the inevitable transition.

The Constitutional evidence for secession

The very genius of American federalism, a principle now forgotten, is that the central government is permitted to perform only those 17 enumerated powers[344, 345] detailed in the U.S. Constitution; all other powers belong to the people or to the States, as the Ninth and Tenth Amendments make clear, including the power of secession. To claim that secession is illegal because "it's not in the Constitution" is therefore either an admission of ignorance of the Constitution or a denial that the United States is a federal republic. Even the most stilted reading of the debates in convention in 1787 and the printed ratification advocacy must admit that every contemporary accepted the sovereignty of each State and therefore its right of secession. How could it be otherwise? Any denial of secession would necessarily imply either the return of the United States to the British government from which it seceded, or that there was no secession in 1776, but instead a war of conquest against the British government.

Alexander Hamilton was probably the strongest supporter of centralized government among the Founders. In his Federalist 15 he describes federalism as "the political monster of an *imperium in imperio*" – meaning that divided sovereignty is impossible. We have already discussed (1.1.7, page 88) the failure of Madison's implementation of federalism. Hamilton's true inclinations were revealed in his famous six-hour speech delivered to the convention on June 18, 1787, in which he advocated an "elective Monarch" (as Madison put it) serving for life, with the power to appoint all the State governors. So, although one might reasonably charge him with duplicity in Federalist 32, his words there are at least a confession that his true designs would fail without lip service to the true meaning of federalism, which meant the sovereignty of the States:

> [T]he plan of the convention aims only at a partial union or consolidation, the State governments would clearly retain all the rights of sovereignty which they before had, and which were not, by that act, EXCLUSIVELY delegated to the United States.[346]

It is obvious that the States did not surrender their *entire* sovereignty in forming the federal republic, but only *partially*, yielding only to those 17 enumerated powers of the central government,[sss] and even then, *contingently*. This is true not only as a matter of logic – since total loss of sovereignty would no longer signify federalism in any sense – but also as a matter of stated reservation: Three States explicitly affirmed only a *contingent* acceptance of the union when they ratified the Constitution.

> New York:
> We, the delegates of the people of the state of New York, [...] Do declare and make known, [...] That the powers of government may be reassumed by the people whensoever it shall become necessary to their happiness;[347]

> Rhode Island:
> We, the delegates of the people of the state of Rhode Island and Providence Plantations, [...] do declare and make known, [...] That the powers of government may be reassumed by the people whensoever it shall become necessary to their happiness.[348]

> Virginia:
> WE the Delegates of the people of Virginia, [...] DO in the name and in behalf of the people of Virginia, declare and make known that the powers granted under the Constitution, being derived from the people of the United States may be resumed by them whensoever the same

---

[sss] As John Taylor of Caroline put it: "The owners of a loaf of bread divide it between two persons. The donation of one half, does not imply a right to eat up the other half." From his *New Views on the Constitution*, 1823, pages 66-68.

shall be perverted to their injury or oppression, and that every power not granted thereby remains with them and at their will[.][349]

Now, if these caveats *are not* valid, then the State's ratification document is invalid and these States never officially joined the United States, and thus retain their original sovereignty as independent nations; and the original sovereignty of all the other States is thereby validated. If, however, these caveats *are* valid, then either these three States alone enjoy the right of secession that is nowhere recognized or assented to as uniquely theirs by any of the other States, or else all of the States as equally-titled signatories to the same document enjoy the right of secession. If it is asserted that these three States alone enjoy the right of secession, then it is no longer a right, but a *privilege*, given in negation of their claim that it is a *right* deriving from the sovereignty of the people – the assertion that it is a privilege resting on an absurd and unstated power to cherry-pick[ttt] the valid parts of the State's ratification document.

All of the State ratifications of the Constitution were the documentation of the sovereignty of the people *in convention*, as required by Article VII. Although the ratification of Amendments either by the State legislatures or by the people in convention was equally valid under Article V, the distinction between the two methods seems to have been significant to the Framers. That distinction seems to be primarily that the voice of the people in convention – however arbitrarily convened, since the Constitution does not specify – is the more fundamental expression of their sovereignty, since it is voiced for the document as a whole, and not necessarily for its appendages.

Following this reasoning then, there would be three logical possibilities for using the State convention to approve secession, assuming that secession is of such weighty consequence that it demands this more fundamental expression of the people's will. One is that since the secession of one member affects all, every other State must in some way have a voice in its separation; another is that since secession is a reassertion of original sovereignty, the voice of every other State is irrelevant to the self-determination of the separating State; and another is that both of the foregoing can be taken into account. Each of these positions has an advocate.

F.H. Buckley, an admitted unionist,[350] nevertheless draws attention to George Mason's insistence on the provision in Article V in the 1787 Convention that in effect gives the sovereign people a right to revolution within a government without first overthrowing it.[351] Buckley then references the Canadian

---

[ttt] A similar tactic was employed by Lincoln and Joseph Story to maintain that the Constitution is "perpetual," although no suggestion of perpetuity appears in the document. They derive the notion from the Articles of Confederation, Article 13, yet are somehow blind to its preeminent Article 2: "Each State retains its sovereignty". *Vide* Graham, John Remington, *op.cit. infra*, page 97.

Supreme Court's answer to the question of whether the province of Québec could constitutionally secede from Canada, as it tried to do by referenda in 1980 and 1995. Ruling in advance of any litigated complaint, as Canadian law permits, it rejected a unilateral secession, but stated that a vote by Québec citizens to approve of secession "would confer democratic legitimacy on the secession initiative which all of the other participants in Confederation would have to recognize" and proceed to negotiate the terms of disunion, with particular attention to the rights of minorities.[352] According to Buckley, any infringement upon the rights of citizens in the seceding State would disqualify the secession – an argument also made by Allen Buchanan.[353] This argument is invalid on two counts. First, on what pretext, moral or legal, is the larger state the arbiter of rights or justice in the smaller state? It is exactly against this presumptuous arrogance of power that the smaller state is seceding. And if the larger state is the self-anointed final arbiter of rights and justice, would not its authority extend to, say, Algeria and Zimbabwe as well? Second, if the high-minded larger state has the interests of some groups within the smaller state at heart, how can it weigh those interests against the consequences[354, 355] injurious to them by violently maintaining its right to disqualify the secession?

John R. Graham acknowledges the "Conventions" clause in Articles V and VII as the very expression of the sovereignty of the people, tracing it to the Convention Parliament of February 13, 1689,[356] effecting the Glorious Revolution by deposing the legitimate sovereign James II in favor of a Dutchman, William of Orange (although his wife, Mary II, was in the line of succession from James II). The 1689 Convention ended the right of succession and the divine right of kings in England, and established Parliament as the true English sovereign. Or as Blackstone famously pronounced, it was above every power on earth, could neither do nor intend wrong, was perpetual, and could do anything in law not naturally impossible.[357] Or in Jean-Louis de Lolme's more colorful statement, "Parliament can do every thing, except making a Woman a Man, or a Man a Woman."[358, uuu] As previously noted from Jouvenel, throughout the medieval period, "sovereignty was only achieved by the energy of the crown in parliament," by which joint meeting the king was able to prudently draw on feudal obligations rather than arouse hostility by solely asserting royal prerogatives. The American colonists inherited these vast powers of parliament, especially in convention as the formal expression of the sovereignty of the people, when King James I gave them the rights of Englishmen when he chartered the colonies in 1606.[359] Both Rhode Island and Virginia specifically referenced the Convention Parliament of 1689, when their ratifying conventions met in May, 1776.[360] Graham quotes Madison's remarks given in

---

uuu This is clearly an understatement, in view of the fact that Parliament assumed even that power with the Gender Recognition Act of 2004.

convention on June 19, 1787, to claim that the Constitution is a compact at will, meaning that "[i]f a contract has been materially breached, the injured party may elect to rescind"[361] – meaning of course that the sovereign States jointly entered into a contract, which if broken allows the injured State to secede, without the consultation of any other State.

John C. Calhoun, as previously discussed, incorporated these two positions as step two and step three of his idea of a "concurrent majority."[362] That is, after the first step of *interposition*, or local non-compliance with a national law, the States next would be required to meet in convention to consider the injured State's formal *nullification* of the offending law; if a supermajority of States rejected the nullification, the State would be forced to comply, or else unilaterally pursue the sovereign option of *secession*.

Therefore, if any of the ratification documents of New York, Rhode Island, or Virginia are valid with their explicit, contingent caveats, then the Texas Treaty of Annexation of April 12, 1844, and its 1845 constitution – both approved by its citizens in convention – are equally valid. Article I of the annexation treaty reads in part:

> The Republic of Texas, acting in conformity with the wishes of the people and every department of its government, cedes to the United States all its territories, to be held by them [the people of Texas] in full property and sovereignty[.][363]

Article I, Section 1 of the Texas Constitution of 1845, adopted just before annexation, reads:

> All political power is inherent in the people, and all free governments are founded on their authority, and instituted for their benefit; and they have at all times the unalienable right to alter, reform, or abolish their form of government, in such manner as they may think expedient.[364]

Also, like the original 13 colonies and no other States, Texas was the only State to enter the Union with control over its public land.[365]

Therefore, provided that the seceding State declares its separation through a convention of the people, however constituted, secession is constitutional.[366]

But is secession unconstitutional in that it constitutes treason? The Framers, who knew how easily the charge of treason could be slung at political enemies, carefully limited its meaning in Article III, Section 3:

> Treason against the United States, shall consist only in levying War against them, or in adhering to their Enemies, giving them Aid and Comfort. No Person shall be convicted of Treason unless on the

Testimony of two Witnesses to the same overt Act, or on Confession in open Court.[367]

The people of the seceding State choose secession, not for war or violent revolution, but for the very opposite: A peaceful parting of ways; 'adhering to enemies' implies a third party hostile to the national union, which does not exist under secession; and thus no 'aid and comfort' can be given to a nonexistent enemy. Nor can the term 'enemy' be made elastic to include anyone that the consolidated state dislikes: The context demands 'enemy' in the sense of a foreign power in a state of war against it. Without this context, Section 3 can be perverted to a use exactly opposite to its stated intent. Clearly, secession is not treason.

But is secession unconstitutional by virtue of the U.S. Supreme Court ruling in *Texas v. White* (1869)? Obviously those who parrot that the ruling forbids secession, either have simply not read the document, or choose to willfully misconstrue it. Paragraph 101 reads:

> The union between Texas and the other States was as complete, as perpetual, and as indissoluble as the union between the original States. There was no place for reconsideration, or revocation, except through revolution, or through consent of the States.[368]

Since the "union between the original States" has no perpetual or indissoluble basis, the Texas union cannot be perpetual, unless one asserts that the Texas union is somehow *more* perpetual or indissoluble than that of other States, contrary to this ruling. Notwithstanding that argument, the ruling clearly provides for separation through two options: Revolution or a convention of States. The suggestion of revolution is merely a taunt, of no logical consequence. While revolution is certainly the ultimate right of any sovereign people, secession explicitly rejects it: The seceding State has no interest whatever in the larger government, any more than George Washington had an interest in conquering the Palace of Westminster, or Jefferson Davis had an interest in conquering Washington, DC[369] – the seceding State simply wishes to go its own way in peace. The only argument remaining is whether the necessary convention of the people requires the consent of three-fourths of *all* States, or whether the convention of the seceding State *alone* is sufficient for a reassertion of its original sovereignty. Reasoning for a convention of all states we have already shown to be fallacious (page 139).

But is secession unconstitutional by reference to some other standard? In F.H. Buckley's account of the two attempted secessions of Québec, he says of its claim of a right of secession:

> Such a right might exist when its government represents the whole of its people, on a basis of equality and without discrimination, and when

it is oppressed by a colonial power. That's what the United Nations favors[.][370]

Such "standards" are hopelessly vague, and are clearly founded on the hollow incantations of social justice: They mean anything that the "standard-giver" wants them to mean. The vagaries of "representation" and "equality" have already been discussed; but does "the whole of its people" mean total unanimity? If that were so, then the voice of a tiny minority could thwart the purposes of a vast majority. As for "discrimination," is there a single nation on the face of the earth where not one faction can claim "discrimination"? Finally, in what sense are murder, torture, and violation of rights any different at the hands of a native oppressor, compared to that of a colonial power? Is murder less final, torture less painful, or violation of rights less oppressive in one case and not the other? The United Nations asserts "the right of self-determination of peoples," in Article 1 of Chapter 1 of its charter, but then in Article 2.4 it plainly insists that the integrity of states is vital.[371] The "integrity of states" assumes a world of unchanging borders, an obviously false assumption. When the UN was founded in 1945, there were 51[372] nations; currently there are almost 200.[373] This nearly four-fold increase in nations could not possibly have happened without the repeated and extensive alteration of national borders – which secession makes possible without violence. Clearly such bureaucratic dithering would be laughable – except that it is a formula that *guarantees* the death and suffering of millions of people.

In 1967, the Igbo people of southeast Nigeria declared themselves the Republic of Biafra. They were Christians, and the most industrious and prosperous of the Nigerians, who had had enough of exploitation by the Muslims constituting most of the rest of the country. The United Nations had recognized Nigeria's secession from the Commonwealth of Great Britain only seven years earlier, but it refused to recognize the secession of Biafra. After almost three years of fighting, after enduring a starvation blockade that fell mostly on the children, and after suffering indiscriminate atrocities, the Igbos surrendered and returned to their previous subjection. Over a million people had died.[374]

To any man who is so immoral as to hold "Union" as his fixed ideal, let there be one word in reply: "Biafra."

The historical evidence for secession
If there is no objection to Texas seceding from Mexico because of Santa Anna's violations of the Constitution of 1824 – primarily for his making the federal republic a centralized, unitary state – then why should there be objection to Texans seceding today for that same reason?

In fact there have been many other successful secessions in recent history that no one would think to condemn:

- Norway seceded from Sweden in 1905;
- Iceland seceded from Denmark in 1944 (after home rule from 1874);
- The city-state of Singapore seceded from Malaysia in 1965;
- Bangladesh seceded from Pakistan in March, 1971, which secession was enforced by India at the end of that year.
- The Czech Republic and Slovakia seceded from Czechoslovakia, splitting that country, in 1991.
- Bosnia/Herzegovina, Croatia, Macedonia, Montenegro, Serbia, and Slovenia seceded from Yugoslavia in 1991.
- 15 nations (Armenia, Azerbaijan, Belarus, Estonia, Georgia, Kazakhstan, Kyrgyzstan, Latvia, Lithuania, Moldova, Russia, Tajikistan, Turkmenistan, Ukraine, and Uzbekistan) seceded from the former Soviet Union between 1990 and 1991.

With the exception of Yugoslavia, where ethnic conflicts led to war, these secessions were peaceful, since avoidance of violence is the very intent of secession.[vvv] A rejection of the principle of secession would require that the United States revoke its recognition of all the nations above, particularly the 15 states that seceded from the Soviet Union – as did the statist court historian Eric Foner, a past president of both the American Historical Association and the Organization of American Historians, on March 23, 1990, declaring:

> There really is a genuine parallel between Lincoln and Gorbachev. Lincoln's position, like Gorbachev's, was that a union, no matter how it was formed, cannot be abandoned.[375]

Most of the recent mushrooming of books and articles about secession is rooted in this mindless worship of Union. But whether mournful or alarmist, elegiac or apocalyptic, they are all totally ignorant of the fact that *secession is the essence of the Jeffersonian federalism that flourished in the 73 years between 1788 and 1861.*

A growing free republic based on the sovereignty of the people *must champion the principle of secession to avoid becoming an empire*, as Professor Donald Livingston points out:

> [8:43 mark] Jeffersonians were serious about the classical republican teaching that *republics should be small.* Virginia had conquered the vast Northwest Territory – today the States of Illinois, Ohio, Wisconsin, Indiana, parts of Michigan and Minnesota – and they belonged to

---

[vvv] As always, the violence is imposed by states seeking to suppress the secessionists, e.g., secessionists in Abkhazia, Artskh, Chechnya, Crimea, Donetsk, Gaguzia, Luhansk, South Ossetia, Talysh-Mughan, Tatarstan, and Transnistria.

Virginia. Virginians told themselves that they could not both enjoy republican life and control territory of that vast size: It would become an empire. So, they gave it away. [...] They gave it to the Confederation, to enable new republics to be formed through secession of the people. [9:34 mark] By this principle, States also could divide through secession when they became too large in population for self government. So the western counties of Virginia seceded and formed the State of Kentucky; Tennessee seceded from North Carolina; Maine seceded from Massachusetts; and so it went.

But Jefferson went further. [10:00 mark] For 2,000 years, republics seldom went beyond 300,000 in population. That gives you an idea of what [Jeffersonians] meant by small. So Jefferson argued that Virginia should be divided into small "ward republics," each having considerable sovereignty over local matters.[376]

The kernel idea of American history is that the nation championed the principle of secession; the dogma that the arrival of its first settlers inaugurated the historical inevitability of a single, continent-spanning union is a gross anachronism, indoctrinated by state-controlled public education. As Calhoun stated: The United States is an "assemblage of nations,"[377] or as the modern historian Colin Woodard stated:

There isn't and never has been one America, but rather several Americas.[378]

Or as Richard Kreitner states:

For a century and a half, the colonies had acted as if they were independent nations with little more in common than the wish to remain apart.[379]

In fact, as Professor David C. Hendrickson points out, the United States Constitution actually came about more as a "peace pact"[380, 381] to avoid civil war among its diverse nations. Kreitner's study of American history points out the difficulty of forging even a small union from such a motley:

In 1643, delegates from the colonies of Massachusetts Bay, Plymouth, Connecticut, and New Haven met in Boston to draw up terms of union. [Nine years later, t]he union collapsed into dissension and disuse.[382]

Even a temporary emergency union for common defense against Indians was difficult. In 1695, five years after the Indian massacre of settlers in Schenectady, William Penn proposed a "Briefe and Plaine Scheam" for just that purpose of common defense, but it went nowhere.[383] In June 1754, the Albany Congress convened to consider mutual cooperation strictly for Indian affairs.

Pennsylvanian Richard Peters proposed that the colonies separate into four divisions, reasoning that smaller divisions would have more coherence. Benjamin Franklin, on the other hand, drawing inspiration from his study of Cadwallader Colden's *The History of the Five Indian Nations* (1727) and their unity, proposed a similar and more lasting union – his Albany Plan – modeled on the Iroquois' congress of 48 representatives. But his proposals went nowhere:

> Only in Massachusetts, where Governor Shirley supported Franklin's plan, was the idea seriously debated. There, too, however, legislators objected to the "perpetuity of the proposed Union" – they preferred a temporary association to deal only with the immediate emergency.[384]

Franklin concluded that only "the most grievous Tyranny and Opposition" would ever unite a people as diverse as the Colonial immigrants.[385] But even that assumption was asking too much:

> The Stamp Act Congress, like the Albany meeting of 1754, is often described as a landmark on the road to the Constitution. What it actually revealed were the conflicts and violence usually associated with later periods.[386]

Even when facing a more dire peril, unified action was difficult. In September, 1774, 45 men from twelve colonies gathered at the City Tavern in Philadelphia to form the First Continental Congress. Kreitner explains, citing John Adams:

> The delegates were a motley crew. "Here is a Diversity of Religions, Educations, Manners, Interests, Such as it would Seem almost impossible to unite in any one Plan of Conduct," Adams reported to his law partner in Boston[. It was l]ess a conclave of comrades than a meeting "of Ambassadors from a dozen belligerent Powers of Europe"[.][387]

The nation's first constitution, the Articles of Confederation of 1776, forged under the need for union during wartime, took five years to be ratified. News of the fall of Charleston in 1780 did not secure ratification; that came about only because the holdout State (Maryland) was bribed by a foreign power: The French envoy in Philadelphia, Anne-César de La Luzerne, obtained the State's ratification by offering French ships for its defense.[388]

The schoolbook saga of Ethan Allen's Green Mountain Boys fighting the British did not tell the whole story. Allen, piqued by New York's refusal to recognize Vermont statehood, told the governor-general of Québec in 1782, "I shall do everything in my power to render this state a British province."[389] The territories west of the Alleghenies were open to becoming Spanish citizens, since their commerce did not flow east, but south to the Spanish-held port of New Orleans.[390]

Even after the 1781 victory at Yorktown and the 1783 Treaty of Paris, dissolution remained a live option. In 1842, 46 businessmen of Haverhill, Massachusetts petitioned to dissolve the United States.[391] The Aaron Burr-James Wilkinson plot to rule the West was not an exception to the thinking of the time. Kreitner explodes the myth hatched in Kennedy's (or Ted Sorensen's) 1956 *Profiles in Courage* of Sam Houston's support of the Union: In fact he favored a *Texas* empire reaching from Oregon to Cuba.[392]

Consider the main secessionist impulses from the founding of the United States to just before the War Between the States, keeping in mind that *none of them were in the South*:

- The Vermont Republic (1777-1791);[393]
- The New York proposal by its Senator Rufus King and Oliver Ellsworth to dissolve the Union (1794);[394]
- The opponents of Jefferson's 1803 Louisiana Purchase, notably Josiah Quincy III[395] and Timothy Pickering;[396]
- The New England secessionists during the War of 1812;[397]
- The Hartford,[398] Connecticut secessionists and their supporters in the Essex Junto (1814-15);[399]
- The secessionism of Federalist and former president John Quincy Adams (1839);[400]
- Abolitionist William Lloyd Garrison and the New England Anti-Slavery Conventions (1834, 1844, 1858);[401]
- The "Central Confederacy" of Virginia, Maryland, Delaware, New Jersey, New York, Ohio, Indiana, Pennsylvania, Kentucky, Tennessee, and Arkansas (1850s);[402]
- The secession movements of five Middle Atlantic States (1860).[403]

The historical fact is that every State in the United States, true to the tradition of the nation's founding, has experienced some movement for secession.[www]

'Practical' considerations regarding secession

There is nothing more practical than the truth. To concede that an argument is true, but that it must be rejected for "practical" considerations is to admit moral cowardice; it is to reject the results of a free and open debate, or to admit that one's opinion trumps reason; it is to pronounce oneself unfit for the democratic exchange of ideas. Either an argument is true, and must be accepted, or it is false, based on reasoned evidence. The "practical" consideration cannot be true without also showing the foregoing arguments to be false.

[www] See the appendix: A History of Secession in All 50 States.

The most commonly given "practical" reason for rejecting secession is that the principle was "settled by the War Between the States." This bare assertion implies that violence initiated by the state has moral precedence over any reasoned argument. It completely fails to address the reasoning and the historical facts demonstrating secession as a peaceful resolution to otherwise irreconcilable group conflicts.

Another argument, less often heard, is that the United States is currently at a tenuous balance between two irreconcilably opposed political parties, much like the period just before the War Between the States, and just as explosive. The secession of one State, especially a large State like Texas or California, would be like pulling one thread on a knit sweater: It would unravel this precarious balance, and signify the breakup of the entire United States. This objection must be conceded as at least very likely. But of itself, this argument proves nothing, since it fails to consider whether such a breakup might be a very good thing; it must be followed by the next argument.

This next argument is that once broken up, the United States will lose all the advantages of being big. Advantages? The entire history of attempts to introduce democratic principles into a large unitary state demonstrates that they have so far not succeeded. The example of the United States shows that the initially democratic state becomes an empire, with all the disadvantages of an empire, as witness its failures in the Philippines, Vietnam, North Africa, Iraq, and Afghanistan. It is true that at the moment the superpower size of the United States enforces recognition of its currency as the primary world reserve currency. But this "blessing," which is by no means guaranteed to be permanent, has led its lawmakers to saddle its citizens with a national debt of over 30 *trillion* dollars – an incomprehensible, unrepayable sum. As Kreitner noted: "The [S]tates could be either closely united or democratic – not both."[404] That is, you can have coerced union, or separatist liberty – but never both in a country as large and diverse as the United States. On the other hand, a great many advantages derive from smallness, not the least of which is small government, under local control. Switzerland has been free and prosperous since its founding in 1291; Liechtenstein, Singapore, and Hong Kong (at least before being swallowed by mainland China) are relatively tiny nations that have prospered in the absence of a large unitary state.

Then there is the argument that secession is a principle that cannot be limited. That is to say, if you allow secession, where does it stop? The War Between the States was fought over secession to form two states; Colin Woodard advocated 11; George F. Kennan, 12;[405] Kirkpatrick Sale, 63;[406] Thomas Jefferson, thousands;[407, 408] Ludwig von Mises, innumerable:

> The right of self-determination [...] thus means: whenever the in-
> habitants of a particular territory, whether it be a single village, a whole

district, or a series of adjacent districts, make it known, by a freely conducted plebiscite, they no longer wish to remain united to the state to which they belong at the time [...] their wishes are to be respected and complied with. [409]

Furthermore – not shrinking from the logical implication – the right

extends to the inhabitants of every territory large enough to form an independent administrative unit. If it were in any way possible to grant this right of self-determination to every individual person, it would have to be done.[410]

But the principle of secession is limited either by the unlikelihood of its being applied to caricature, or by the nature of symbiotic government. The position of Mises, which we reject, accepts no limitation, but reposes in the confidence that no one is so stupid as to declare himself a country and thereby cast himself out of society. His sanguinity may underestimate the ignorant. Note that our rejection argues neither against the individual's primal property in himself, nor against the elimination of the state as represented by its public goods; it argues against the state without reservation, in this case when declared in himself by some lone, confused libertarian, who does not possess civil rights in any case. The symbiotic government of kleristocracy recognizes the power of the community to bestow civil rights, particularly in the form of citizenship. As a practical matter, under kleristocracy that smallest community is identified with the county. There is nothing to stop the creation of a polygamous cult from a Texas county; nothing to stop aggressive men and compliant women from controlling a county where the latter must go about in public in a black bag – and nothing to stop either of them from seceding from the Texas Republic. However, since that community is necessarily within a wider Texas community of counties, the neighboring counties must have some say-so over the choice. Thus a county secession must be approved by a simple majority referendum approval by all adjacent counties (including those diagonally adjacent at a single point), along with a simple majority approval by the Republic's legislature. This method is more reasonable than the suggestion (refuted in any case on page 139) of F.H. Buckley and (possibly) Justice Salmon P. Chase in *Texas v. White*, paragraph 101, who offer the insuperable requirement that three-fourths of all States, no matter how remote from the seceding State, approve a secession from the Federal Union in a convention of States.

Another argument is that, whatever the merits of secession, the disruption of bringing it into effect will be devastating. This argument is easily disposed of. The previously mentioned secessions did not cause undue disruption. And in spite of the apocalyptic warnings from the losers of the Brexit vote in Great Britain, neither has there been undue disruption there, in spite of the added challenge of occurring during the crisis of a pandemic. Many of the difficulties have come from cross-border regulations and paperwork, where the inflexibility of the European Union, which fiercely opposed Brexit, has caused delays. The London financial sector did lose some six billion euros as some institutions moved to Amsterdam or Paris, but the alarmism over food and medicine shortages proved exaggerated.[411]

The most muddled arguments of all surround the apportionment of the national debt upon the seceding State. It is muddled not only because of the difficulties of finding a "just" portion of the debt to be imposed, but also because demands for payment often mask ulterior motives. But let us assume for the moment that both parties are at least trying to negotiate in good faith.

As part of that good faith reckoning, future values, intangibles, and "goodwill" would be excluded as too arbitrary, with the focus strictly on national debt accumulated in the past. However, even that amount has no straightforward accounting. One must assume the continuation of totalization agreements between the Federal government and the seceding State, so that those having paid into Medicare and Social Security receive proportional coverage and disbursement, respectively. But if that is so, then there must be a consideration of the debt from unfunded Federal liabilities, the most significant of which are Medicare and Social Security. The net present value of the U.S. government's 75-year future liability for Medicare and Social Security amounts to an *additional* $46.7 *trillion* on top of the familiar $30 *trillion* national debt.[412] These amounts are so vast as to have no meaning, and simply cannot be paid by any government, including the United States. They can only have significance as threats, and are thus null and void since they amount to "odious debt," under its definition as "hostile debts":

> "Hostile debts" can be defined as debts incurred to suppress seces-
> sionist movements[.][413]

Under the concept of odious debt, none of the states in Africa that seceded from colonial powers paid any part of their national debts. Certainly any accounting should not run exclusively against the seceding state. If it is true that these states were exploited, then quite the contrary: The colonial powers subtracted from the new states' national wealth and should repay it – which of course has not been done. In any case, the seceding states repudiated the debt under another definition of odious debt – that it was

> clearly in contradiction to the interests of the people of the entirety of
> the former State or a part thereof [...and that...] the creditors, at the
> moment of paying out the loan, were aware of its odious purpose.[414]

The concept of odious debt is not a spurious notion, but is one in principled contention with the established one of *pacta sunt servanda* (contracts must be honored). Article 38 of the 1983 *Vienna Convention on Succession of States in Respect of State Property, Archives and Debts* reads in part:

> When the successor State is a newly independent State, no state debt of the predecessor State shall pass to the newly independent State, unless an agreement between them provides otherwise[.][415]

Nor is this concept a product of modern scholarship, e.g., Éric Toussaint (2019), Michael Kremer and Seema Jayachandran (2006), Alexander Nahun Sack (1927); it has an intellectual pedigree of 400 years:

> Grotius (1625) held that contracts made by the sovereign that are of no advantage and harmful to the State should not be honoured[.][416]

The history of past secessions is a muddled guide as well. The United States did not assume any part of Great Britain's debt in 1783, nor apparently did Norway assume any part of Sweden's in 1905. The seceding Singapore and Bangladesh paid some part of the national debt of the country that they left.[417] The countries seceding from the former Soviet Union did pay a share of the USSR's national debt, but only after intense pressure from international bankers, who threatened to cut off future lending to non-payers.[418] Under similar pressure, each of the states emerging from Yugoslavia also agreed to accept its share of the parent nation's national debt.[419] However, the bankers surely issued a poker bluff: For if it is true that such debt would become the new nation's sovereign debt, then it should also be true that international banks never lend to those nations having defaulted on sovereign debt, which is absolutely false. A few of the dozens of sovereign debt defaults include Russia (1917, 1998), Mexico and a dozen other Latin American nations (1982), Ukraine (1999), Nicaragua and Ecuador (2008), Ecuador and Lebanon (2020), Argentina (2001, 2020, etc., etc.), and most famously, that paragon of states:

> The United States is famous for never having defaulted on its debt, except that it has. In 1862, the government defaulted on demand notes, in 1933 it defaulted on gold bonds. It also effectively defaulted in 1968 by refusing to redeem silver certificates and did so yet again in 1971 when it went off the gold standard.[420]

Academic attempts to establish a formula for apportioning national debt upon secession have failed. Daniel S. Blum offered several methods of calculating this apportionment: By per capita share, by State GDP share of national GDP, by the ratio of State benefits received versus State payments made, and by a detailed State versus national comparison of asset and liability classes.[421] But Blum solves nothing, since each method yields a different, equally "just" result. Indeed, reckoning by his third method would result in Texas paying nothing at all. Other equally plausible methods could be offered.

For example, a historical reckoning by the number of votes cast by the Texas Congressional delegation in favor of each debt increase, compared to the other States' votes in favor. Or again, if the borrowing that formed the national debt resulted in capital formation or redistribution that provided a net benefit to those outside Texas, then those recipients owe Texas a repayment for helping to effect it. If this borrowing provided a net benefit to the citizens of Texas, then those demanding some repayment must calculate what part of it went to the *exclusive* benefit of Texans, *at the expense and detriment of the larger economy*. Any amount resulting in mutual benefit requires no repayment.

The debt-to-GDP ratio of the United States currently stands above 100%, even if one takes the much lower percentage that considers only "debt held by the public" – as if debt held within the government magically "doesn't count."[422] The true debt-to-GDP stands above 136%.[423] This means that the government of the United States is in fact bankrupt. There can be no determination of the national debt until it is written down in a liquidation. This of course does not mean that the United States "goes out of business," any more than the bankruptcy of Puerto Rico in 2017, the largest in the history of the United States, meant that this territory "went out of business," since there is separate legal provision for governmental bankruptcy. However, it does mean that the government must come to terms with its bondholders, who must "take a haircut," just as the government must agree to follow legally imposed austerity measures. Until this reckoning is performed by the courts, any statement of proportional debt supposedly owing will be grossly overstated.

In any case, if as a practical matter a fair apportionment of the national debt of the United States could be determined – which cannot be done – it would not be payable to the government designated as the United States of America. It would be payable directly to the individual bondholders of that debt. If the goal is a proportional sharing of this debt, then the Republic of Texas is justified in awaiting the day when the United States begins to pay off these bondholders, when it might retire its share of the debt in like proportion. But who is fooling whom in this charade? Any reasonable person knows full well that the United States has no intention of ever attempting to pay off any part of its $30 trillion dollar debt, since this enormous sum *cannot* be repaid. Clearly, any clamor to impose upon Texas a "fair share" of the national debt is nothing more than an exit tax, whose sole purpose is not equity but confiscation, and furthermore an odious debt as previously defined.

But why should the central state *want* to shift off its national debt? According to the Keynesian and Modern Monetary ideologies that rule Federal economic policy, debt is a good thing; national debt creates wealth, creates jobs, and prospers economic activity in general. Under this prescription, a reduction of the national debt, to say nothing of its eventual elimination, was never contemplated. Texans therefore could not in good conscience impose their hillbilly household views of debt on a Federal government whose celebrated luminaries of Northeastern academe champion a robust national debt.[424, 425, 426, 427] Texans will magnanimously forgo any claim on this treasured debt. Logic, justice, and the big-hearted cowboy way demand that they must leave it as a parting gift.

Finally, one must not be blind to the elephant in the room: One of the very reasons for choosing secession in the first place is the fact that Texans wish to escape the destructive indebtedness of the United States. It is absurd that they should cast it off, only to pick it up again in the republic formed to escape it. It is duplicitous to assert that "the elected representatives of Texas voted to augment the debt," when every honest person is aware of the political framework that made that debt possible. That framework rests on "pork barrel" politics of majoritarian absolutism, on beggaring member States in the name of the "common good," and in general on the fiction that there exists a "society" that may be plundered without consequence to the individual members of which it is constituted.

But let us assume for completeness of argument that by their saber-rattling and intimidation the functionaries of the United States impose a part of its debt on the Republic of Texas. Very well: Any fictitious accounting may impose any number it pleases. The Republic of Texas does not fold to the poker bluff of international banking. Let the world know that the Republic of Texas cheerfully and in advance announces that it will repudiate every last penny of the exit tax of apportioned debt. The Gordian Knot of debt settlement is untangled with a single stroke.

❦

Secession is the only peaceful arbiter of intractable political disputes between large societies. It seeks not the domination of any existing government, but only to have its citizens go their own way to effect a new government to secure their happiness as they see fit, without a bloody and mutually destructive temporary resolution by force. Those who sincerely want to see an end to the polarization, extremism, and political strife in current society should champion secession, the only peaceful solution to irreconcilable group differences. Secession is the freedom of association writ large.

Conclusion

1.1.10 Given the sovereignty of the people as the foundation of free and prosperous societies; given that no republic based on the sovereignty of the people can exist without the principle of secession, a valid ultimate recourse for the symbiotic will; given that devolved associationism and sortition remedy the failure of elective oligarchy; given that the enumerated powers of republicanism are practicable under the proposed government; and given that the proposed government best employs the architectonic requirements for reason; we conclude that this government, called a dominium sortiens, *or a* kleristocracy, *or a* sortive democracy, *is the best prescription for a new Republic of Texas.*

[1] Rothbard, Murray, "Praxeology: Reply to Mr. Schuller," *American Economic Review* 61, no. 5 (1951): 945-46. Online at <https://cdn.mises.org/Praxeology%20Reply%20to%20Mr%20 Schuller_2.pdf> accessed February 23, 2022.

[2] von Mises, Ludwig; Greaves, Bettina Bien, *Human Action: A Treatise on Economics* (Liberty Fund, March 14, 2007, ISBN 978-0865976313, 1128 pages). Online: von Mises, Ludwig, *Human Action: A Treatise on Economics, The Scholar's Edition* (Henry Regnery, 1966, ISBN 0-94546624-2, 912 pages) <https://cdn.mises.org/Human%20Action_3.pdf> accessed February 24, 2022, PDF of *The Scholar's Edition* page 25.

[3] Ibid., page 11.

[4] Ibid., page 18.

[5] Ibid., page 20.

[6] Ibid., page 22.

[7] Ibid., page 24.

[8] Ibid., pages 25-6.

[9] Ibid., page 34.

[10] *Op.cit.*, Rothbard, "Praxeology: Reply to Mr. Schuller," 943-44.

[11] Ibid., page 943.

[12] Friedman, David D., *Law's Order: What Economics Has to Do with Law and Why It Matters* (Princeton University Press, November 1, 2001, ISBN 978-0691090092, 344 pages), page 9. Online at <https://portalconservador.com/livros/David-Friedman-Laws-Order.pdf> accessed April 6, 2022.

[13] Coulton, G. G., "Salimbene: On Frederick II, 13th Century," *Fordham University, Internet Medieval Source Book* (last edited June 15, 2021) <https://sourcebooks.fordham.edu/source/ salimbene1.asp> accessed February 27, 2022.

[14] von Mises, Ludwig; Raico, Ralph, translator, *Liberalism: In The Classical Tradition* (Cobden Press and The Foundation for Economic Education, Inc., third edition, January 1, 1985, ISBN 978-0930439231, 208 pages), page 35. Online at <https://mises.org/library/liberalism-classical-tradition/html> accessed February 19, 2022.

[15] Chesterton, G.K., "The Everlasting Man," public domain (published 1925) <https://d2y1pz2y630308.cloudfront.net/15471/documents/2016/10/G.K.Chesterton-The%20Everlasting%20Man.pdf> accessed November 10, 2021.

[16] Christakis, Nicholas A., *Blueprint: The Evolutionary Origins of a Good Society* (Little, Brown Spark, March 26, 2019, ISBN 978-0316230032, 544 pages), page xxi.

[17] Boehm, Christopher, *Moral Origins: The Evolution of Virtue, Altruism, and Shame* (Basic Books, May 1, 2012, ISBN 978-0465020485, 432 pages). Boehm (1931-2021) was an anthropologist and director of the Jane Goodall Research Center who believed that early hunter-gatherers were guided less by Darwinian struggle than by a gentler ethic of communalism and egalitarianism.

[18] *Op.cit.*, von Mises, *Human Action*, PDF of *The Scholar's Edition* page 34.

[19] Hobbes, Thomas, *Hobbes's Leviathan* (Oxford University Press, 1909 reprint from the 1651 edition, 557 pages), part 1, chapter 14, page 99 [of the 1929 reprint]. Online at <http://files.libertyfund.org/files/869/0161_Bk.pdf> accessed February 23, 2022.

[20] Harris, Sam, *The Moral Landscape: How Science Can Determine Human Values* (Free Press reprint of 2010 original, September 13, 2011, ISBN 978-1439171226, 320 pages), pages 201-202.

[21] Ibid., page 205.

[22] Solzhenitsyn, Aleksandr I.; Willets, Harry, translator, *The Gulag Archipelago: 1918-1956* (Harper Perennial, paperback reprint, February 1, 2002, ISBN 978-0060007768, 512 pages). Online excerpt at <https://www.goodreads.com/quotes/8365695-fire-fire-the-branches-crackle-and-the-night-wind-of> accessed February 23, 2022.

[23] Firing Line with William F. Buckley, Jr., "Is There a Case for Private Property?" (*YouTube*, length 59:38, published January 31, 2017; recorded November 7, 1977) <https://www.youtube.com/watch?v=p6FJR0Tf-Us> accessed March 12, 2022. Professor Friedrich August von Hayek at the 48:48 mark: "What you are suggesting – the whole theory of social justice is suggesting – is the government ought to treat the people very differently in order to put them in the same material position. That has nothing to do with your original claim for equality of the rules which government forces all people to apply. [...at 54:20:] Any redistributive policy requires a discriminating treatment of different people. You cannot so long as you treat all the people according to the same formal rules – forcing them to act only to observe the same rule – bring about any redistribution of incomes. Once you decide that government is entitled to take from some people in order to give it to others, this is automatically discrimination of a kind for which there can be no general rule. They are purely arbitrary. [...] Any rule where you know before who will be the gainers and who will be the sufferers is in that sense not a general rule. [...O]nce you authorize government to act arbitrarily there's no limit to it."

[24] Washington, George, "Washington's Farewell Address," *Yale Law School* (last edited February 21, 2022) <https://avalon.law.yale.edu/18th_century/washing.asp> accessed February 22, 2022. "All obstructions to the execution of the laws [...] serve to organize faction, to give it an artificial and extraordinary force; to put, in the place of the delegated will of the nation the will of a party, often a small but artful and enterprising minority of the community." My use of 'Interest' is similar to Washington's 'factions' and 'combinations,' except that it stresses the non-rational in supposedly "reasoned" public policy arguments.

[25] Young, Brian, "Life Before Roe: A Brief Survey of US Abortion Law Before the 1973 Decision," *Eternal Word Television Network* (published November 1, 2020) <https://www.ewtn.com/catholicism/library/life-before-roe-a-brief-survey-of-us-abortion-law-before-the-1973-decision-12100> accessed February 22, 2022. In 1967, abortion was a felony in all 49 states and a "high misdemeanor" in New Jersey; six years later the *Roe v. Wade* ruling struck down them all.

[26] Baker, Peter, "For Obama, Tricky Balancing Act in Enforcing Defense of Marriage Act," *The New York Times* (published March 28, 2013) <https://www.nytimes.com/2013/03/29/us/politics/for-obama-tricky-balancing-act-in-enforcing-defense-of-marriage-act.html> accessed February 22, 2022. The Obama administration initially supported the Defense of Marriage Act; within several years it had discarded it to advocate same-sex marriage.

[27] Ciancio, Susan, "Her Story: Norma McCorvey of 'Roe v. Wade'," *American Life League* (published October 1, 2020) <https://all.org/her-story-norma-mccorvey-of-roe-v-wade/> accessed February 22, 2022. Probably the most frequent argument advanced to legalize abortions was to protect the woman from 'back-alley, coat hanger' abortions; yet 87% to 90% of abortions before 1973 were performed by licensed physicians. Certainly other arguments can reasonably be advanced for legalization, but not this most prominent one.

[28] "Cartesian theater," *American Psychological Association Dictionary of Psychology* (published April 12, 2021) <https://dictionary.apa.org/cartesian-theater> accessed August 21, 2022.

[29] Kuehnelt-Leddihn, Erik Maria, Ritter von, *Leftism: From de Sade and Marx to Hitler and Marcuse* (Arlington House, July 15, 1974, ISBN 978-0870001437, 653 pages), page 360.

[30] Adam, Charles; Tannery, Paul; editors, *Oeuvres de Descartes*, 11 volumes, Paris: Librairie Philosophique J. Vrin, 1983, volume 5, pages 86-7. Cottingham, John; Stoothoff, Robert; Murdoch, Dugald; Kenny, Anthony; translators, *The Philosophical Writings of Descartes*, 3 volumes, Cambridge University Press, 1988, volume 3, page 326. Cited in Rutherford, Donald, "Descartes' Ethics," *Stanford Encyclopedia of Philosophy* (last edited July 27, 2017) <https://plato.stanford.edu/entries/descartes-ethics/> accessed December 3, 2021.

31 *Op.cit.*, Hobbes, Thomas, *Hobbes's Leviathan*, part 1, chapter 4, page 23 [of the 1909 reprint]. Asserting his radical empiricism: "For none of these things ever have, or can be incident to Sense; but are absurd speeches, taken upon credit (without any signification at all,) from deceived Philosophers, and deceived, or deceiving Schoolemen."

32 *Op.cit.*, Hobbes, Thomas, *Hobbes's Leviathan*, part 1, chapter 5, page 37-38 [of the 1909 reprint].

33 Calhoun, John C., *A Disquisition on Government, and a Discourse on the Constitution and Government of the United States* (A.S. Johnston, Columbia, SC, 1851, 406 pages), page 58. Online at <https://openlibrary.org/books/OL7010465M/A_disquisition_on_government> accessed March 1, 2022.

34 *Op.cit.*, Hobbes, Thomas, *Hobbes's Leviathan*, part 2, chapter 17, page 129 [of the 1909 reprint].

35 de Jasay, Anthony, *The State* (Liberty Fund, illustrated edition, March 31, 1998, ISBN 978-0865971714, 330 pages), pages 26, 31.

36 Rommen, Heinrich A.; Hanley, Thomas R., translator, *The Natural Law: A Study in Legal and Social History and Philosophy* from the 1936 *Ewige Wiederkehr des Naturrechts* (Liberty Fund, March 24, 1998, ISBN 978-0865971608, 278 pages), page xxvi.

37 Ibid., pages 31 and 117 both cite Romans 2:12-16: [12] For as many as have sinned without law shall also perish without law: and as many as have sinned in the law shall be judged by the law; [13] (For not the hearers of the law *are* just before God, but the doers of the law shall be justified. [14] For when the Gentiles, which have not the law, do by nature the things contained in the law, these, having not the law, are a law unto themselves: [15] Which shew the work of the law written in their hearts, their conscience also bearing witness, and *their* thoughts the mean while accusing or else excusing one another;) [16] In the day when God shall judge the secrets of men by Jesus Christ according to my gospel.

38 Ibid., page 223: "All men are born natural-law jurists."

39 Ibid., page xxiii.

40 Ibid., pages xxi-xxii.

41 Ibid., page 39.

42 Ibid., page 42.

43 Ibid., page 44.

44 Ibid., page 38.

45 Ibid., page 48.

46 Ibid., page 49.

47 Lovejoy, A.O., *The Great Chain of Being: The Study of the History of an Idea* (Harvard University Press, revised edition from 1933 original, October 1, 1971, ISBN 978-0674361539, 400 pages), page 40, citing Constantin Ritter's 1931 *Die Kerngedanken der platonischen Philosophie*, pages 56-57: "das Walten einer vernünftigen göttlichen Macht in allem Weltsein und Weltgeschehen".

48 *Op.cit.*, Rommen, page 51.

49 Ibid., page 53.

50 Ibid., page 52.

51 Ibid.

52 Ibid., page 53.

53 Alvarado, Ruben, *The Debate that Changed the West: Grotius versus Althusius* (Pantocrator Press paperback, October 11, 2018, ISBN 978-9076660516, 282 pages), page 14.

54 Ibid., page 61.

55 *Op.cit.*, Rommen, page 62.

56 *Op.cit.*, Alvarado, page 62: These two laws are restated in Grotius' 1604 *De Jure Praedae Commentarius* (*Law of Prize and Booty*).

57 Ibid., page 213.

58 Ibid., page 216.

59 Ibid.

60 Ibid., page 223, citing (book II, chapter I, §III-VIII).

61 Ibid., page 224, citing (book II, chapter I, §IX).

62 Ibid., pages 239-240, citing (book II, chapter XXII, §XI).

63 Ibid., page 200, citing (prologue, §11).

64 *Op.cit.*, Rommen, page 64.

65 Sommerville, Johann P., *Thomas Hobbes: Political Ideas in Historical Context* (Macmillan Education, July 13, 1992, ISBN 978-0333495995, 248 pages), page 17: Charles I dissolved parliament in 1629, raised money without parliamentary approval (by the Forced Loan in 1626-7) imprisoning refusers without cause, and billeted troops upon civilians.

66 Ibid., page 61.

67 *Op.cit.*, Hobbes, Thomas, *Hobbes's Leviathan*, introduction, page 8 [of the 1909 reprint].

68 Ibid., part 1, chapter 14, page 99 [of the 1909 reprint].

69 Ibid., part 2, chapter 17, page 128 [of the 1909 reprint].

70 Ibid., part 2, chapter 17, page 131 [of the 1909 reprint].

71 Strauss, Leo, *What Is Political Philosophy?* (University of Chicago Press, paperback reprint of 1959 original, October 15, 1988, ISBN 978-0226777139, 316 pages), pages 47-48. Strauss calls this Hobbes' hedonism: Passion over reason in the sense that fear of violent death spawns government, which spawns the desire for self-preservation, which spawns a "concern with solid comfort." Thus for Strauss, the ancestral "shivering poor devils" abandon concern for "justice or human excellence" to settle down to bourgeois comfort and maybe a plate of shepherd's pie on Sunday. As I see it, Strauss' use of the word "hedonism" rightly highlights Hobbes' magnification of Epicurean *aponia* (ἀπονία, absence of pain) to the complete suppression of Epicurean *ataraxia* (ἀταραξία, mental repose).

72 Gordon, David, "True Competition versus the Monopolist 'Minimal State'," *Mises Institute* (published December 31, 2021) <https://mises.org/wire/true-competition-versus-monopolist-minimal-state> accessed March 9, 2022. *Cf.*, his discussion of J. Roger Lee.

73 Friedman, David, *The Machinery of Freedom: Guide to a Radical Capitalism* (Createspace Independent Publishing Platform, third edition, February 28, 2015, ISBN 978-1507785607, 378 pages), pages 244-252: Discussion of Schelling Points.

74 Spooner, Lysander, *No Treason: The Constitution of No Authority* (Pine Tree Press reprint of 1870 original, January 1, 1966, ASIN B0006EQNWY, 71 pages).

75 Ibid., part 1, chapter 14, page 107 [of the 1909 reprint].

76 Ibid., part 1, chapter 14, page 108 [of the 1909 reprint].

77 Ibid., part 1, chapter 13, page 94 [of the 1909 reprint].

78 Ibid., part 2, chapter 24, page 193 [of the 1909 reprint].

79 *Op.cit.*, Sommerville, page 61.

80 *Op.cit.*, Rommen, page 79.

81 Locke, John, *Second Treatise of Government* (Project Gutenberg eBook #7370, last edited December 25, 2021) <https://www.gutenberg.org/files/7370/7370-h/7370-h.htm> accessed March 5, 2022. Chapter VII, "Of Political or Civil Society," Sect. 87.

82 Ibid.

83 *Op.cit.*, Rommen, page 79.

84 Rousseau, Jean-Jacques; Scott, John T., translator, *The Major Political Writings of Jean-Jacques Rousseau: The Two 'Discourses' and the 'Social Contract'* (University of Chicago Press, October 17, 2012, ISBN 978-0226921884, 320 pages), xxi.

85 Rousseau, Jean-Jacques; Bennett, Jonathan, translator, "The Social Contract," 1762 original, as translated and abridged by Dr. Bennett (published December, 2010) <https://www.earlymoderntexts.com/assets/pdfs/rousseau1762book1.pdf> accessed March 6, 2022. Book 1, chapter 2, page 1 [of Bennett pagination].

86 Rousseau, Jean-Jacques; Cole, G.D.H., translator, *The Social Contract and Discourses by Jean-Jacques Rousseau* (Everyman's Library, 1913, 287 pages) Online at <https://archive.org/details/in.ernet.dli.2015.100084/> and <https://oll.libertyfund.org/title/cole-the-social-contract-and-discourses> accessed March 6, 2022. "A Discourse on the Moral Effects of the Arts and Sciences," part 2. The citation is from his letter to Christophe de Beaumont, written November 18, 1762.

87 Ibid, from his discourse *On Inequality*.

88 Ibid.

89 Ibid.

90 Ibid.

91 *Op.cit.*, Bennett, book 2, chapter 7, page 19 [of Bennett pagination].

92 Ibid., book 2, chapter 7, page 21 [of Bennett pagination].

93 Hinde, Andrew, "Review of The Population of Europe, by Massimo Livi-Bacci, review no. 139," *Reviews in History* (published September, 2000) <https://reviews.history.ac.uk/review/139> accessed March 7, 2022.

94 Hume, David, *An Enquiry Concerning the Principles of Morals, Appendix I*, "Concerning Moral Sentiment" (Hume Texts Online edition of 1751 original, M App1.10, SBN 289). Online at <https://davidhume.org/texts/m/app1> accessed March 7, 2022.

95 *Op.cit.*, de Jasay, page 99.

96 Kant, Immanuel; Hastie, W., translator, *The Philosophy of Law* (T. & T. Clark, 1887 English edition from the 1796 original), "Introduction to the Science of Right, General Definitions and Divisions, C.: Universal Principle of Right." Online at <https://oll.libertyfund.org/title/hastie-the-philosophy-of-law> accessed March 7, 2022.

97 *Op.cit.*, Rommen, pages 89-90.

98 Popper, Karl R., *The Open Society and its Enemies* (Princeton University Press, fifth revised edition, February 1, 1971, ISBN 978-0314195210, 432 pages), page 31.

99 *Op.cit.*, de Jasay, page 161. "[*A Theory of Justice* is] the only fully fledged theory within the liberal ideology of the state as the prime instrument of the justice of rewards and burdens."

100 Rorty, Richard, *Objectivity, Relativism, and Truth*, Vol. 1 (Cambridge University Press, November 30, 1990, ISBN 978-0521358774, 238 pages), Part III, "The Priority of Democracy to Philosophy," page 185. "We read it [*A Theory of Justice*] as a continuation of the Enlightenment attempt to ground our moral intuitions on a conception of human nature (and, more specifically, as a neo-Kantian attempt to ground them on the notion of 'rationality')."

101 Rawls, John, *A Theory of Justice* (Belknap Press [Harvard University Press] revised second edition, September 30, 1999, ISBN 978-0674000780, 560 pages), page 10.

102 Ibid., page 124.

103 Ibid., page 118.

104 Ibid., pages 65-66.

105 Ibid., page 68.

106 Ibid., page 89.

107 Ibid., pages 280-281.

108 Ibid., page 125.

109 Scruton, Roger, "Living with a Mind," *First Things* (published December 2015) <https://www.firstthings.com/article/2015/12/living-with-a-mind> accessed July 25, 2022.

110 *Op.cit.*, de Jasay, page 273.

111 Surowiecki, James, *The Wisdom of Crowds* (Anchor, August 16, 2005, ISBN 978-0385721707, 336 pages).

112 Poundstone, William, *Gaming the Vote: Why Elections Aren't Fair (and What We Can Do About It)* (Hill and Wang, first edition hardcover, February 5, 2008, ISBN 978-0809048939, 352 pages).

113 "Details about Ranked Choice Voting," *FairVote* (last edited March 9, 2022) <https://www.fairvote.org/rcv#where_is_ranked_choice_voting_used> accessed March 10, 2022.

114 Cohen, Ethan; Levy, Adam Levy, "Why 'instant runoff' voting in New York doesn't mean instant results," *CNN* (published June 29, 2021) <https://www.cnn.com/2021/06/22/politics/new-york-ranked-choice-voting-explainer/index.html> accessed March 10, 2022.

115 Moore, Stephen, "Biden Wants to Regulate Everything – Even Your Air Conditioning," *Townhall* (published April 12, 2022) <https://townhall.com/columnists/stephenmoore/2022/04/12/biden-wants-to-regulate-everything%E2%80%93even-your-air-conditioning-n2605759> accessed April 12, 2022.

116 Schmitt, Carl, *Politische Theologie: Vier Kapitel zur Lehre von der Souveränität* (Duncker and Humblot, tenth edition of 1922 original, June 24, 2015, ISBN 978-3428147021, 72 pages), page 37: "Alle prägnanten Begriffe der modernen Staatslehre sind säkularisierte theologische Begriffe."

117 *Op.cit.*, Kuehnelt-Leddihn, page 54: "It is precisely this fact that the modern totalitarian ideologies – from simple leftism to national socialism, international socialism, and communism – have not only a pseudomonastic but also a 'heretical' aspect that make them so unacceptable and so incompatible with the great religions of the West: Christianity, Islam, and Judaism. They derive most of their strength [...] from the secularized version of a few Christian tenets. Therefore they are all *Religionsersatz* (substitutes for religion) and the parties representing them are secular 'churches'."

118 Siddique, Ashik, "The U.S. Spends More on Its Military Than the Next 10 Countries Combined," *National Priorities Project* (published April 30, 2020) <https://www.nationalpriorities.org/blog/2020/04/30/us-spends-military-spending-next-10-countries-combined/> accessed November 9, 2021.

119 Hoppe, Hans-Hermann, *A Theory of Socialism and Capitalism* (Kluwer Academic Publishers, December 31, 1988, ISBN 978-0898382792, 275 pages), page 136. Online at <https://www.hanshoppe.com/wp-content/uploads/publications/Soc&Cap7.pdf> accessed July 27, 2022.

120 Ibid., page 130.

121 Ibid.

122 Ibid., pages 130-131.

123 Ibid., pages 133-134.

124 Hoppe, Hans-Hermann, *The Economics and Ethics of Private Property: Studies in Political Economy and Philosophy* (Ludwig von Mises Institute second edition, ISBN 978-0945466406, August 12, 2010, 431 pages), page 406.

125 Bridges, Thomas, *The Culture of Citizenship: Inventing Postmodern Civic Culture* (SUNY Press, first edition, June 21, 1994, ISBN 978-0791420331, 267 pages), 14-15.

126 Aquinas, St. Thomas, "Summa Theologiae, Secunda Secundae Partis, Question 36," *New Advent* (last edited October 15, 2021) <https://www.newadvent.org/summa/3036.htm> accessed March 12, 2022.

127 Schoeck, Helmut, *Envy: A Theory of Social Behaviour* (Liberty Fund reprint of 1966 German original, December 1, 1987, *Der Neid: Eine Theorie der Gesellshaft*, ISBN 978-0865970649, 453 pages), chapter 1, "Man the Envier."

128 Crossman, Richard H. (editor); Engerman, David C. (foreword), *The God That Failed* (Columbia University Press reprint of 1949 original, September 15, 2001, ISBN, 272 pages), page 17.

129 Rand, Ayn, "The Age of Envy," *The Objectivist*, volume 10, number 8, August 1971.

130 Murawski, John, "Here Are the 90+ 'Equity' Plans Taxpayers Are Now Funding Across the Federal Government," RealClearInvestigations (published May 10, 2022) <https://www.realclearinvestigations.com/articles/2022/05/10/here_are_the_90_equity_plans_taxpayers_are_now_funding_across_the_federal_government_830643.html> accessed May 11, 2022. As part of their state-fabricated "gender rights," Democrats propose a Transportation Security Administration policy to reduce pat-downs of transgender travelers at airports.

131 Grossman, Hannah, "Rhode Island parents enraged at school board for removing honors classes in 'equity obsession'," *Fox News* (published May 9, 2022) <https://www.foxnews.com/media/rhode-island-parents-school-board-equity-obsession> accessed May 11, 2022.

132 Bettelheim, Bruno; Janowitz, Morris, *Social Change and Prejudice, Including Dynamics of Prejudice* (The Free Press of Glencoe, 1964, ISBN 978-0029034804, 337 pages), pages 52ff.

133 de Jasay, Anthony, *Against Politics: On Government, Anarchy, and Order* (Routledge, December 22, 1997, ISBN 978-0415170673, 256 pages), page 3.

134 Hoppe, Hans-Hermann, editor, *The Myth of National Defense* (Mises Institute, October 16, 2003, ISBN 978-0945466376, 453 pages), Radnitzky, Gerard, "Is Democracy More Peaceful than Other Forms of Government?" page 151.

135 Ibid., Hoppe, Hans-Hermann, "Government and the Private Production of Defense," pages 335ff.

[136] Bassani, Luigi Marco; Lottieri, Carlo, "The Rise of the Sovereign State," *Mises Institute* (published November 30, 2021) <https://mises.org/wire/rise-sovereign-state> accessed March 14, 2022.

[137] Gordon, David, "The Problem with Public Goods and So-Called Economic Power," *Mises Institute* (published January 21, 2022) <https://mises.org/library/problem-public-goods-and-so-called-economic-power> accessed March 12, 2022.

[138] Ibid.

[139] Serbu, Jared, "Senate passes 2022 federal spending bill, sends to Biden's desk," *Federal News Network* (published March 10, 2022) <https://federalnewsnetwork.com/congress/2022/03/senate-passes-2022-federal-spending-bill-sends-to-bidens-desk/> accessed March 14, 2022.

[140] "Dr. Rand Paul Calls on Congress to Read the Bills," *Senator Rand Paul website* (published March 10, 2022) <https://www.paul.senate.gov/news/dr-rand-paul-calls-congress-read-bills> accessed March 14, 2022.

[141] "GPO Produces U.S. Code with New Digital Publishing Technology," *United States Government Publishing Office* (published September 23, 2019) <https://www.govinfo.gov/features/uscode-2018> accessed March 14, 2022.

[142] "United States Statutes at Large," *United States Government Publishing Office* (last edited February 23, 2022) <https://www.govinfo.gov/app/collection/statute> accessed March 14, 2022.

[143] "Federal Register tops 70,000 pages (2020)," *Ballotopedia* (published December 9, 2021) <https://ballotpedia.org/Federal_Register_tops_70,000_pages_(2020)> accessed March 14, 2022.

[144] Bochsler, Daniel, "Duverger and the territory: explaining deviations from the two-party-competition-law," *Journal of Elections, Public Opinion and Parties*, DOI: 10.1080/17457289.2019.1658195 (published September 9, 2019) <https://www.tandfonline.com/doi/full/10.1080/17457289.2019.1658195> accessed March 16, 2022. Dr. Bochsler maintains that deviations between local and national constituencies do not invalidate the law.

[145] Fey, Mark, "Duverger's Law Without Strategic Voting," *University of Rochester, Department of Political Science* (published April, 2007) <https://www.rochester.edu/college/faculty/markfey/papers/Exit3.pdf> accessed March 13, 2022. Dr. Fey maintains that Duverger's Law applies regardless of whether strategic voting exists.

[146] Nast, Thomas, "That's What's the Matter," *Harper's Weekly* cartoon, page 944, column 1 (published October 7, 1871). The era was epitomized by the Nast cartoon of political boss William Marcy Tweed leaning against a ballot box saying, "As long as I count the votes, what are you going to do about it?"

[147] Alvarez, R. Michael; Hall, Thad E.; Hyde, Susan D. (editors), *Election Fraud: Detecting and Deterring Electoral Manipulation* (Brookings Institution Press, May 15, 2008, ISBN 978-0815701385, 255 pages), page 8. Online at <https://www.brookings.edu/wp-content/uploads/2016/07/electionfraud_chapter.pdf> accessed March 13, 2022.

[148] Abramson, Jill, "Campaign Finance; A Law Survives. Now, Let's Subvert It," *The New York Times* (published December 14, 2003) <https://www.nytimes.com/2003/12/14/weekinreview/the-nation-campaign-finance-a-law-survives-now-let-s-subvert-it.html> accessed March 13, 2022.

[149] Mann, Robert, "How the 'Daisy' Ad Changed Everything About Political Advertising," *Smithsonian Magazine* (published April 13, 2016) <https://www.smithsonianmag.com/history/how-daisy-ad-changed-everything-about-political-advertising-180958741/> accessed March 13, 2022.

[150] Criss, Doug, "This is the 30-year-old Willie Horton ad everybody is talking about today," *CNN* (published November 1, 2018) <https://www.cnn.com/2018/11/01/politics/willie-horton-ad-1988-explainer-trnd/index.html> accessed March 13, 2022.

[151] Jones, Bradley, "Most Americans want to limit campaign spending, say big donors have greater political influence," *Pew Research Center* (published May 8, 2018) <https://www.pewresearch.org/fact-tank/2018/05/08/most-americans-want-to-limit-campaign-spending-say-big-donors-have-greater-political-influence/> accessed March 13, 2022.

[152] "CITIZENS UNITED v. FEDERAL ELECTION COMM'N (No. 08-205)," *Cornell Law School, Legal Information Institute* (last edited March 8, 2022) <https://www.law.cornell.edu/supct/html/08-205.ZS.html> accessed March 13, 2022.

[153] Marra, Joey, "An Interesting History of Presidential Debates," *Libertarian Party* (published October 20, 2020) <https://ca.lp.org/an-interesting-history-of-presidential-debates/> accessed March 13, 2022.

[154] "2016 Post-Election Report," *Libertarian National Committee Ballot Access Committee* (published December 20, 2016) <https://www.lp.org/wp-content/uploads/2016/11/2016-12-10_LNC_Meeting_Ballot_Access_Committee_Report.pdf> accessed March 13, 2022.

[155] "The Sinister Attack on Ballot Access in New York," *The Libertarian Party* (August 26, 2021) <https://www.lp.org/the-sinister-attack-on-ballot-access-in-new-york/> accessed March 13, 2022.

[156] Kellermann, Donald S. (director), "On The Eve of '92: Fault Lines In The Electorate," *Pew Research Center* (published December 4, 1991) <https://assets.pewresearch.org/wp-content/uploads/sites/5/legacy-pdf/19911204.pdf> accessed March 13, 2022.

[157] "U.S. Term Limits, Inc. v. Thornton (93-1456), 514 U.S. 779 (1995)," *Cornell Law School, Legal Information Institute* (last edited March 10, 2022) <https://www.law.cornell.edu/supct/html/93-1456.ZS.html> accessed March 13, 2022.

[158] "UNITED STATES v. BUTLER et al.," *Cornell Law School, Legal Information Institute* (last edited March 10, 2022) <https://www.law.cornell.edu/supremecourt/text/297/1> accessed March 14, 2022.

[159] "NATIONAL FEDERATION OF INDEPENDENT BUSINESS v. SEBELIUS," *Cornell Law School, Legal Information Institute* (last edited January 16, 2022) <https://www.law.cornell.edu/supremecourt/text/11-393> accessed March 14, 2022.

[160] Siegel, Neil S.; Willis, Steven J., "The Taxing Clause," *National Constitution Center, Interactive Constitution* (last edited February 1, 2022) <https://constitutioncenter.org/interactive-constitution/interpretation/article-i/clauses/751> accessed March 14, 2022.

[161] Fancy, Tariq, "The Secret Diary of a 'Sustainable Investor' – Part 1," *Medium* (published August 2021) <https://medium.com/@sosofancy/the-secret-diary-of-a-sustainable-investor-part-1-70b6987fa139> accessed June 20, 2022.

[162] Mencken, Henry Louis, *A Mencken Chrestomathy* (Vintage annotated edition from 1949 original, April 12, 1982, ISBN 978-0394752099, 627 pages), page 622.

[163] *Op.cit.*, von Mises, *Liberalism: In The Classical Tradition*, page 46.

[164] Sahlins, Marshall, "Twin-born with greatness: The dual kingship of Sparta," (HAU: *Journal of Ethnographic Theory* 1 (1): 63–101, 2011, ISSN 2049-1115), page 64.

[165] Creveld, Martin van, *The Rise and Decline of the State* (Cambridge University Press, August 28, 1999, ISBN 978-0521656290, 448 pages), page 37.

[166] *Op.cit.*, Calhoun, page 393.

[167] Calabresi, Steven G.; Larsen, Joan L. Larsen, "One Person One Office: Separation of Powers or Separation of Personnel," (*Cornell Law Review*, Volume 79, Issue 5, July 1994, Article 1), page 1091. Online at <https://scholarship.law.cornell.edu/cgi/viewcontent.cgi?article=2522&context=clr;One> accessed March 17, 2022.

[168] Khatib, Lina; Wallace, Jon, "Lebanon's politics and politicians," *Chatham House* (published August 11, 2021) <https://www.chathamhouse.org/2021/08/lebanons-politics> accessed March 16, 2022.

[169] Dahl, Robert A., *Polyarchy: Participation and Opposition* (Yale University Press, September 10, 1972, ISBN 978-0300015652, 272 pages).

[170] Thommen, Marc, *Introduction to Swiss Law* (Carl Grossmann Verlag, September 1, 2018, ISBN 978-3941159235, 427 pages), page 11. Online at <https://www.open-ius.ch/literatur/thommen_introduction-to-swiss-law.pdf> accessed March 16, 2022.

[171] Buckley, F.H., *American Secession: The Looming Threat of a National Breakup* (Encounter Books, January 14, 2020, ISBN 978-1641770804, 184 pages), pages 53-54. Buckley argues that it is Roger Sherman, with his defense of States' rights, who deserves more credit for the idea of federalism, and that Madison furthermore took from David Hume his notion that factions were less likely in a large republic. But since these ideas were articulated in Federalist 51, which of course neither Hume nor Sherman authored, and likely not Hamilton, I think that the attribution properly belongs to Madison.

[172] Madison, James, "The Federalist Papers: No. 51," *Yale Law School* (last edited March 15, 2022) <https://avalon.law.yale.edu/18th_century/fed51.asp> accessed March 16, 2022.

[173] *Op.cit.*, Schoeck, page 25.

[174] Ibid., page 295.

[175] Griffith, Janelle, "House passes Crown Act banning discrimination against Black hairstyles," *NBC News* (published March 18, 2022) <https://www.nbcnews.com/politics/politics-news/house-passes-crown-act-banning-discrimination-black-hairstyles-rcna20617> accessed March 18, 2022. On March 18, 2022, the U.S. House passed with bipartisan support the "Creating a Respectful and Open World for Natural Hair" Act, aka the "CROWN" Act, officially H.R. 2116. The act exempts "people of African descent" from any employer's dress codes in regard to their wearing of "locs, cornrows, twists, braids, Bantu knots, or Afros."

[176] "Scientific Racism," *Harvard Library* (last edited May 9, 2022) <https://library.harvard.edu/confronting-anti-black-racism/scientific-racism>accessed May 23, 2022. "Contemporary scientific consensus agrees that race has no biological basis".

[177] Shea, John, "Is Race Real?" (*American Scientist*, July-August 2011, Volume 99, Number 4, page 276, DOI: 10.1511/2011.91.276). Online at <https://www.americanscientist.org/article/is-race-real> accessed May 23, 2022. Dr. Shea: "Race is folk taxonomy, not science." The term 'folk taxonomy' has a ring of snooty, learned archness to it, but it is indisputable that there exists a group that by its own "taxonomy" labels itself "black," just as other groups label themselves "Hispanic" or "Asian." If this is merely cultural "taxonomy," then are non-blacks racists for exercising their freedom of expression by disparaging that culture? Are they racists for exercising their freedom of association by segregating themselves from exponents of that culture? The truth is that "race" is less a *folk* taxonomy, and more a *state* taxonomy, arbitrarily defined to favor one group over another. It is a contradiction to demolish the notion of race on the one hand while simultaneously enforcing protections for it on the other.

[178] "Education secretary says he's spoken with schools defying mask mandate bans," *ABC News* (published August 17, 2021) <https://www.connectradio.fm/2021/08/17/education-secretary-says-hes-spoken-with-schools-defying-mask-mandate-bans/> accessed March 18, 2022. Education Secretary Miguel Cardona spoke directly to local school superintendents in Texas and Florida, indicating the central state's support for their defiance of the laws of their State. On March 18, he made a similar unspecified "got your back" pledge directly to LGBTQ students and their parents, outside the purview of the State.

[179] *Op.cit.*, Washington.

[180] *Op.cit.*, de Jasay, *The State*, pages 96-103. Page 102: "Therefore, the balancing [of consequences] intrinsically depends both on *foresight* and on *interpersonal comparisons.* Treating it as a pragmatic question of factual analysis, one of information and measurement, is tacitly taking the prior and much larger questions as having been somehow, somewhere resolved." [emphasis in original]

[181] Rector, Robert, "The War on Poverty: 50 years of failure," *The Heritage Foundation* (published September 23, 2014) <https://www.heritage.org/marriage-and-family/commentary/the-war-poverty-50-years-failure> accessed March 18, 2022.

[182] Coyne, Christopher J.; Hall, Abigail R., "Four Decades and Counting: The Continued Failure of the War on Drugs," *The CATO Institute*, Policy Analysis No. 811 (published April 12, 2017) <https://www.cato.org/policy-analysis/four-decades-counting-continued-failure-war-drugs#> accessed March 18, 2022.

[183] Thiessen, Marc A., "Biden's war on fossil fuels has strengthened Putin and weakened America," *American Enterprise Institute* (published February 25, 2022) <https://www.aei.org/op-eds/bidens-war-on-fossil-fuels-has-strengthened-putin-and-weakened-america/> accessed March 18, 2022.

[184] Rammos, Aleksander, "Love, Fear, and the Law of Good Intentions," *Mises Institute* (published March 24, 2022) <https://mises.org/wire/love-fear-and-law-good-intentions> accessed March 26, 2022. Rammos: "In the West, the political ideologies of the last two centuries have long been replaced by a collective raving love and fear delirium orchestrated by the privileged bureaucrats. In the center of it, there is a muddle of regulations regarding identity issues, climate change, energy efficiency, health and social threats, safeguard of democracy, etc. The subjects must follow all legislation religiously, not for its *doubtful results* (external) but to prove their *moral alignment* (internal) with the state in its fight against a vague emergency." [emphasis added]

[185] "ArtI.S8.C1.1 Taxing Power," *Cornell Law School, Legal Information Institute* (last edited March 7, 2022) <https://www.law.cornell.edu/constitution-conan/article-1/section-8/clause-1/taxing-power> accessed March 18, 2022.

[186] "Africa Report," *Global Slavery Index* (last edited February 12, 2022) <https://www.globalslaveryindex.org/2018/findings/regional-analysis/africa/> accessed March 19, 2022.

[187] Tennenhouse, Erica, "Modern-Day Human Cannibalism," *The Science Explorer* (published July 26, 2016) <http://thescienceexplorer.com/humanity/modern-day-human-cannibalism> accessed March 19, 2022.

[188] Dollinger, Philippe; Ault, D.S., Steinberg, S.H., translators, *The German Hansa* (Stanford University Press, January 1, 1970, ISBN 978-0804707428, oclc:record:1149171907, 474 pages). Online at <https://archive.org/details/germanhansa0000doll> accessed March 23, 2022. Dollinger dates the Hanseatic League from the founding of Lübeck in 1159 (page xviii) to the last Hanseatic diet (or *Hansetag*) at Lübeck in 1669 (page xix), writing that modern historians see the early merchant Hansa and the later powerful League as integral parts (page xxi).

[189] Blackburn, Robert, "Britain's unwritten constitution," *British Library* (published March 13, 2015) <https://www.bl.uk/magna-carta/articles/britains-unwritten-constitution> accessed April 12, 2022.

[190] Smith, Daniel J., "Constraining Elites: The Self-Enforcing Constitution of the Patricians of Venice," *Social Science Research Network* (last edited February 21, 2017), page 4. <https://papers.ssrn.com/sol3/papers.cfm?abstract_id=2851157> accessed March 15, 2022.

[191] Roncal, Antonio Manuel Moral, "Un carlista singular: Juan Vázquez de Mella y el sociedalismo," *El Obrero Periodismo Transversal* (published April 29, 2020) <https://elobrero.es/historalia/47876-un-carlista-singular-juan-vazquez-de-mella-y-el-sociedalismo.html> accessed March 21, 2022. While we must reject de Mella's assumptions regarding the state, this kernel expression of his idea of *sociedalismo* must be attributed here.

[192] MacIntyre, Alasdair, *After Virtue: A Study in Moral Theory* (University of Notre Dame Press, third edition of 1981 original, March 6, 2007, ISBN 978-0268035044, 978-0268035044, 286 pages). If his alternative to deontology could be expressed in one word, it would be his neologism "situatedness." From page xii: "What historical enquiry discloses is the situatedness of all enquiry, the extent to which what are taken to be the standards of truth and of rational justification in the contexts of practice vary from one time to another."

[193] Scruton, Roger, *On Human Nature* (Princeton University Press paperback reprint of 2017 original, October 16, 2018, ISBN 978-0691183039, 160 pages). Here Scruton maintains that deontology and virtue ethics are compatible – unconvincingly, in my view.

[194] *Op.cit.*, Rommen, page 223.

[195] Ibid., page 228.

[196] Smith, George H., "John Locke: Some Problems in Locke's Theory of Private Property," *Libertarianism.org* (published October 30, 2015) <https://www.libertarianism.org/columns/john-locke-some-problems-lockes-theory-private-property> accessed August 18, 2022.

[197] Cathey, Boyd, "Can the South Rise Again?" *Abbeville Institute* (published August 16, 2021) <https://www.abbevilleinstitute.org/can-the-south-rise-again/> accessed March 21, 2022.

[198] Matthew 22:37-39; Mark 12:30-31; Luke 10:27.

[199] Rand, Ayn, *The Virtue of Selfishness* (Signet 50th anniversary paperback of the 1964 original, ISBN 978-0451163936, 173 pages), page viii.

[200] "In U.S., Decline of Christianity Continues at Rapid Pace," *Pew Research Center* (published October 17, 2019) <https://www.pewforum.org/2019/10/17/in-u-s-decline-of-christianity-continues-at-rapid-pace/> accessed October 5, 2021.

[201] Ott, Michael, "Pope Pius IX," *New Advent* (last edited March 21, 2022) <https://www.newadvent.org/summa/3036.htm> accessed March 22, 2022.

[202] Bowring, Kelly, "Open Letter to Pope Francis: Are You Planning to Redefine Church Doctrine?" *Two Hearts Press* (published October 1, 2014) <https://twoheartspress.com/open-letter-to-pope-francis-are-you-planning-to-redefine-church-doctrine/> accessed March 22, 2022.

[203] Saler, Robert, "A Reader's Guide to Bonhoeffer Biographies," *Lutheran Forum* (last edited November 20, 2020) <https://www.lutheranforum.com/blog/a-readers-guide-to-bonhoeffer-biographies> accessed March 22, 2022.

[204] Bolz-Weber, "Hang out with Nadia in the Corners," *The Corners* (last edited March 18, 2022) <https://nadiabolzweber.com/> accessed March 22, 2022.

[205] Gordon, James, "Newly-ordained Lutheran pastor hosts DRAG Bible study class for children at woke Chicago church," Daily Mail (published December 19, 2021) <https://www.dailymail.co.uk/news/article-10327339/Woke-Chicago-Lutheran-church-invites-newly-ordained-pastor-hold-drag-queen-story-hour-kids.html> accessed April 8, 2022. Aaron Musser is an ordained Lutheran pastor at St. Luke's Lutheran Church of Logan Square, Chicago, in spite of being openly homosexual. On December 12, 2021, before the altar of his church he dressed as a woman and held a "drag queen story hour" for children under 10 years old, which was also broadcast over Zoom. According to Reverend Musser, "Queerness is sacred. [...] If you vote red, you vote against me and my rights."

[206] "John Knox: Scottish Reformer," *Presbyterian Historical Society* (last edited August 4, 2021) <https://www.history.pcusa.org/history-online/exhibits/john-knox-scottish-reformer-page-8> accessed March 22, 2022.

[207] Scanlon, Leslie, "Achtemeier charts spiritual journey on homosexuality at Covenant Network gathering," *Presbyterian Church USA* (published November 10, 2009) <https://www.pcusa.org/news/2009/11/10/achtemeier-charts-spiritual-journey-homosexuality-/> accessed March 22, 2022.

208 Olinger, Danny E., "Christianity and the Emergent Church," *The Orthodox Presbyterian Church* (published January 2009) <http://www.opc.org/nh.html?article_id=589> accessed March 22, 2022.

209 McClaren, Brian D., "About Brian McLaren," *Brian D. McClaren Blog* (last edited January 10, 2022) <https://brianmclaren.net/about-brian/> accessed March 22, 2022.

210 Dow, Darrell; Kirkwood, R. Cort, "Even At Church, It's Us Vs. Them," *American Remnant* (published September 27, 2020) <https://www.american-remnant.com/even-at-church-its-us-vs-them/> accessed November 9, 2021. For example,
• in 2012, the SBC approved members relabeling themselves as "Great Commission Baptists" to avoid the word "Southern";
• in 2015, it passed a resolution on "racial reconciliation" to increase non-white church leadership;
• in 2016, it repudiated the Confederate Flag, a clear rejection of its own founding;
• in 2017, it denounced the "Alt Right" and "white supremacy," without defining the terms;
• in 2018, the Ethics and Religious Liberty Commission, SBC's public policy arm, held a conference lionizing Martin Luther King Jr. without noting his activities that flouted Christian beliefs;
• and in 2019 the Convention adopted a resolution endorsing the use of Critical Race Theory and Intersectionality as analytical tools.

211 Smith, Sydney, "Union of Christendom," *The Catholic Encyclopedia*, Vol. 15, Robert Appleton Company (last edited October 4, 2018) <http://www.newadvent.org/cathen/15132a.htm> accessed November 14, 2018.

212 Pope John XXIII, "Mater et Magistra," paragraph 34 (*The Holy See*, published May 15, 1961) <http://www.vatican.va/content/john-xxiii/en/encyclicals/documents/hf_j-xxiii_enc_15051961_mater.html> accessed October 25, 2020.

213 Horn, Trent, "Can a Catholic Be a Capitalist?" (*Catholic Answers*, published February 18, 2020) <https://www.catholic.com/magazine/online-edition/can-a-catholic-be-a-capitalist> accessed October 25, 2020.

214 Alessandro, "Liberation theology finds new welcome in Pope Francis' Vatican," *The Washington Post* (published September 9, 2013) <https://www.washingtonpost.com/national/on-faith/liberation-theology-finds-new-welcome-in-pope-francis-vatican/2013/09/09/5265002e-198a-11e3-80ac-96205cacb45a_story.html> accessed March 22, 2022.

215 von Kuehnelt-Leddihin, Erik, *Leftism Revisited: From De Sade and Marx to Hitler and Pol Pot* (Gateway Books, February 1, 1991, ISBN 978-0895265371, 520 pages), page 95.

216 Grözinger, Robert, *Jesus, der Kapitalist: Das christliche Herz der Marktwirtschaft* (Finanz Buch Verlag, 2012, ISBN 978-3898797115, 192 pages), page 35. Online at <https://www.amazon.com/Jesus-der-Kapitalist/dp/3898797112> accessed September 1, 2020.

217 Ibid., page 44.

218 Ibid., page 42.

219 Ibid., page 32.

220 Reed, Lawrence W., "Rendering Unto Caesar: Was Jesus A Socialist?" (*Foundation for Economic Education*, published March 03, 2015) <https://fee.org/resources/rendering-unto-caesar-was-jesus-a-socialist/> accessed November 3, 2018.

221 Schoeck, Helmut; Hulsey, Terry L., translator, *Twelve Delusions of Our Time* (from the 1985 *Die 12 Irrtümer unseres Jahrhunderts*, Stagirite Press, January 1, 2011, ISBN 1883853036, 337 pages), page 31. Schoeck suggests that hereditary monarchy's immunity from envy is rooted in a profound human need. His masterwork, *Envy, op.cit. supra*, is the authoritative study of that subject.

222 Voegelin, Eric, *The New Science of Politics: An Introduction* (University of Chicago Press, first edition, paperback, August 15, 1987, ISBN 978-0226861142, 210 pages), page 120.

223 *Op.cit.*, Rothbard, Murray, "Karl Marx as Religious Eschatologist."

224 Wallace, R. Jay, "Practical Reason," *The Stanford Encyclopedia of Philosophy* (Spring 2020 Edition, Edward N. Zalta, editor) (last edited January 14, 2020) <https://plato.stanford.edu/archives/spr2020/entries/practical-reason/> accessed March 23, 2022.

225 Ibid.

226 Ibid.

227 Ibid.

228 Seckel, Al, "The Man Who Could Read the Grooves," *Los Angeles Times* (published October 19, 1987) <https://www.latimes.com/archives/la-xpm-1987-10-19-me-10336-story.html> accessed March 24, 2022. The article references Dr. Arthur Lintgen of Pennsylvania, who possessed the ability to identify classical music by looking at the grooves of an LP disk. Similar documentation could be produced for Ilker Yilmaz of Turkey, who could inhale milk and squirt it from his eyes; or the American Kim Goodman, who could pop her eyes from their sockets; or Ani K of Kerala, India, who painted murals with his tongue; or the Dutchman Wim Hof, who climbed Mount Everest wearing just shorts and sandals. It is not known whether any of them has run for elective office.

229 Fukuyama, Francis, *The End of History and the Last Man* (Free Press, reissue edition, March 1, 2006, ISBN 978-0743284554, 464 pages), pages 11, 48.

230 Dollinger, Philippe; Ault, D.S., Steinberg, S.H., translators, *The German Hansa* (Stanford University Press, January 1, 1970, ISBN 978-0804707428, oclc:record:1149171907, 474 pages). Online at <https://archive.org/details/germanhansa0000doll> accessed March 23, 2022.

231 Ibid., page 118.

232 Ibid., page 393.

233 Ibid., pages 72-73.

234 Smith, Daniel J., "Constraining Elites: The Self-Enforcing Constitution of the Patricians of Venice," *Social Science Research Network* (last edited February 21, 2017) <https://papers.ssrn.com/sol3/papers.cfm?abstract_id=2851157> accessed March 15, 2022, page 18. Note that, like the Hansa, the decline of Venice began with the rise of the state.

235 Ibid., pages 4-5.

236 Ibid., page 1.

237 Ibid., pages 6-7.

238 Ibid., page 8.

239 Matthew 22:37-39; Mark 12:30-31; Luke 10:27.

240 Pasternack, Lawrence; Rossi, Philip, "Kant's Philosophy of Religion," *The Stanford Encyclopedia of Philosophy*, Fall 2014 Edition, Edward N. Zalta, editor (last edited May 26, 2019) <https://plato.stanford.edu/archives/fall2014/entries/kant-religion/> accessed February 1, 2020.

241 Sauvage, George, "Fideism," *The Catholic Encyclopedia*, Vol. 6, Robert Appleton Company (last edited August 29, 2018) <http://www.newadvent.org/cathen/06068b.htm> accessed November 11, 2018.

242 *Op.cit.*, MacIntyre.

243 Hauerwas, Stanley; Willimon, William H.; *Resident Aliens: Life in the Christian Colony* (Abingdon Press, expanded 25th anniversary edition, April 15, 2014, ISBN 978-1426781902, 198 pages), page 61.

244 Ibid., page 90.

245 Pohle, Joseph, "Pelagius and Pelagianism," *The Catholic Encyclopedia*, Vol. 11, Robert Appleton Company (last edited March 22, 2022) <http://www.newadvent.org/cathen/11604a.htm> accessed March 27, 2022.

246 Ibid.

247 Rand, Ayn, *For the New Intellectual* (New American Library paperback reprint of 1961 original, 1964, OCLC Number 958368627, 192 pages), page 137.

248 Aristotle; Jowett, Benjamin, translator, *Politics of Aristotle* (Batoche Books, 1999, OCLC 229015989, 192 pages), Book IV, Section 9, page 93; Bekker 1294b. Online at <https://www.stmarys-ca.edu/sites/default/files/attachments/files/Politics_1.pdf> accessed March 28, 2022, PDF page 124.

249 Chen, Sophia, "Quantum Mechanics Could Solve Cryptography's Random Number Problem," *Wired* (published April 11, 2018) <https://www.wired.com/story/quantum-mechanics-could-solve-cryptographys-random-number-problem/> accessed March 28, 2022.

250 Shermer, Michael, *Why People Believe Weird Things: Pseudoscience, Superstition, and Other Confusions of Our Time* (Holt Paperbacks revised and enlarged edition, September 1, 2002, ISBN 978-0805070897, 384 pages), page xxvi: "Humans are pattern-seeking, storytelling animals, in search of deep meaning behind the seemingly random events of day-to-day life."

251 Dowlen, Oliver, *The Political Potential of Sortition* (Imprint Academic first edition hardcover, August 1, 2008, ISBN 978-1845401375, 264 pages), page 3.

252 Ibid., page 8.

253 Headlam, James Wycliffe, *Election by Lot at Athens* (Forgotten Books hardcover from 1891 original, ISBN 978-9333680820, 2016, 240 pages), page 2. Online at <http://www.archive.org/stream/electionbylotata00headuoft#page/78>, accessed January 29, 2019.

254 Smith, Graham, "Defining Mini-publics: Making sense of existing conceptions," *Political Studies Association*, Belfast conference (published April 3, 2012) <https://www.academia.edu/3999460/Defining_Mini_publics_Making_sense_of_existing_conceptions> accessed March 29, 2022.

255 "About CrowdLaw," *The Governance Lab* (published September 30, 2017) <https://crowd.law/crowdlaw-af1a9e1c9455> accessed March 29, 2022.

256 "What Is Deliberative Polling®?" *Stanford Center for Deliberative Democracy* (last edited March 8, 2022) <https://cdd.stanford.edu/what-is-deliberative-polling/> accessed March 29, 2022.

257 Landemore, Hélène; Lee, David T.; Aitamurto, Tanja, "Crowdsourcing for Participatory Democracies: Efficient Elicitation of Social Choice Functions," *Cornell University arXiv* (published September 7, 2020) <https://arxiv.org/ftp/arxiv/papers/1406/1406.7542.pdf> accessed March 29, 2022.

258 Marsh, Heather, "Stigmergy," Heather Marsh blog (published December 24, 2012) <https://georgiebc.wordpress.com/2012/12/24/stigmergy-2/> accessed March 29, 2022.

259 McKee, Rebecca, "The Citizens' Assembly behind the Irish abortion referendum," *Involve* (published May 30, 2018) <https://www.involve.org.uk/resources/blog/opinion/citizens-assembly-behind-irish-abortion-referendum> accessed January 29, 2019.

260 "France's citizen climate assembly: A failed experiment?" *Deutsche Welle Global Ideas* (last edited February 16, 2021) <https://www.dw.com/en/frances-citizen-climate-assembly-a-failed-experiment/a-56528234> accessed January 29, 2019.

261 Hotz, Julia, "Can an Algorithm Help Solve Political Paralysis?" *Scientific American* (September 18, 2020) <https://www.scientificamerican.com/article/can-an-algorithm-help-solve-political-

paralysis/> accessed January 29, 2019.

[262] Gov Futures, "Hélène Landemore - By the People? Crowdsourcing the Constitution in Iceland," (*YouTube*, length 5:03, published June 5, 2013) <https://www.youtube.com/watch?v=bmsXNTNCCbc> accessed January 29, 2019.

[263] Aitamurto, Tanja, "Democratic Participation and Deliberation in Crowdsourced Legislative Processes: The Case of the Law on Off-Road Traffic in Finland," *Communities and Technologies* 2013 conference (published June 29, 2013) <https://www.academia.edu/7176528/ Democratic_Participation_and_Deliberation_in_Crowdsourced_Legislative_Processes_The_Case _of_the_Law_on_Off_Road_Traffic_in_Finland> accessed January 29, 2019.

[264] DeGering, Nicea, "How much social media scrolling are you actually doing?" *ABC4 News, Good Things Utah* (published June 30, 2020) <https://www.abc4.com/gtu/how-much-social-media-scrolling-are-you-actually-doing/> accessed January 29, 2019.

[265] Davis, Iain, "Sorting Sortition," Iain Davis blog (last edited January 24, 2022) <https://in-this-together.com/sorting-sortition/> accessed March 29, 2022.

[266] Verger, Rob, "Newsweek Rewind: Debunking Global Cooling," *Newsweek* magazine (published May 23, 2014) <https://www.newsweek.com/newsweek-rewind-debunking-global-cooling-252326> accessed January 29, 2019.

[267] "Another Ice Age?" *Time* magazine (published June 24, 1974) <http://content.time.com/time/ subscriber/article/0,33009,944914,00.html> accessed January 29, 2019.

[268] "Experts Say a New Ice Age Is Imminent," *Science and Mechanics* magazine (published November, 1969). Archived at <https://www.worthpoint.com/worthopedia/vintage-november-1969-science-413700745> accessed January 29, 2019.

[269] Ebell, Myron; Milloy, Steven J., "Wrong Again: 50 Years of Failed Eco-pocalyptic Predictions," *Competitive Enterprise Institute* (published September 18, 2019) <https://cei.org/blog/wrong-again-50-years-of-failed-eco-pocalyptic-predictions/> accessed July 25, 2022. Some of the dooms-day predictions compiled by Ebell and Milloy: Dr. James P. Lodge, Jr., of the National Center for Atmospheric Research (NCAR), predicted a new ice age by the 21st century (*The Boston Globe*, April 16, 1970); Dr. S.I. Rasool, of the National Aeronautics and Space Administration (NASA), predicted a new ice age by 2021 (*The Washington Post*, July 9, 1971); Dr. George Kukla, of the Czechoslovakian Academy of Sciences, predicted a new ice age by 2072 (National Oceanic and Atmospheric Administration, citing his letter to president Nixon on December 3, 1972); Anthony Tucker, science correspondent for *The Guardian* in the U.K., predicted a new ice age "coming fast" (*The Guardian*, January 29, 1974); Dr. Stephen H. Schneider, of the National Center for Atmos-pheric Research (NCAR), predicted a new ice age following a drop in global temperature of more than 5°F by 2021 (*The New York Times Book Review*, July 18, 1976); Pentagon defense adviser Andrew Marshall in 2004 predicted a "Siberian" Britain by 2020 (*The Guardian*, February 21, 2004).

[270] Johnson, Scott, "1977 'coming ice age' Time magazine cover is a fake," *Climate Feedback* (published December 16, 2019) <https://climatefeedback.org/claimreview/1977-coming-ice-age-time-magazine-cover-is-a-fake/> accessed January 29, 2019. This article correctly documents an altered *Time* cover, but attempts to trivialize the authentic previously-cited 1974 *Time* article and a 1975 *Newsweek* article titled "The Cooling World."

[271] Ganz, Jami, "Sacheen Littlefeather, who refused Marlon Brando's Oscar, spent decades pretending to be Native American, say sisters," *Chicago Tribune* (published October 22, 2022) <https://www.chicagotribune.com/entertainment/ny-sacheen-littlefeather-pretended-native-american-20221022-5bg6we6jebgcpdaujpy3t6c4km-story.html> accessed October 24, 2022.

[272] "History of Women in the U.S. Congress," *Center for American Women and Politics* (last edited March 16, 2022) <https://cawp.rutgers.edu/facts/levels-office/congress/history-women-us-congress> accessed March 29, 2022.

[273] Ibid., Hotz, Julia, "Can an Algorithm Help Solve Political Paralysis?"

[274] Wehner, Peter, "In Defense of Social Justice," *Ethics and Public Policy Center* (published February 18, 2014) <https://eppc.org/publication/defense-social-justice/> accessed January 29, 2019.

[275] O'Sullivan, Domhnall, "'Parliaments project a distorted image of people and their problems'," *SWI* (SBC International) (published December 2, 2020) <https://www.swissinfo.ch/eng/politics/-parliaments-project-a-distorted-image-of-people-and-their-problems-/46196520> accessed November 8, 2021.

[276] Elbeshbishi, Sarah; Quarshie, Mabinty, "Fewer than 1 in 5 support 'defund the police' movement, USA TODAY/Ipsos Poll finds," *USA Today* (last edited March 8, 2021) <https://www.usatoday.com/story/news/politics/2021/03/07/usa-today-ipsos-poll-just-18-support-defund-police-movement/4599232001/> accessed March 30, 2022. Only 28% of blacks support defunding the police.

[277] Sutherland, Keith, "What Sortition Can and Cannot Do," *Social Science Research Network* (published September 18, 2011) <http://dx.doi.org/10.2139/ssrn.1928927> accessed January 29, 2019.

[278] Cassinelli, C.W., "The Law of Oligarchy," *American Political Science Review*, Volume 47, Issue 3, September 1953, pages 773-784. Online at <https://doi.org/10.2307/1952904> accessed January 29, 2019.

[279] Gonzalez-Ricoy, Inigo; Gosseries, Axel (editors), *Institutions For Future Generations* (Oxford University Press hardcover, February 22, 2017, ISBN 978-0198746959, 432 pages) pages 214-227. The pages reference Kristian Skagen Ekeli's chapter, in which he also discusses a second model, his *sub-majority rule model*. According to it, a minority of at least one-third of the legislators should be granted two procedural rights in order to protect future interests. The first empowers a minority to delay legislation. The second grants a minority the right to require referendums.

[280] Bouricius, Terrill, "Why Hybrid Bicameralism is Not Right for Sortition," *Politics & Society* 2018, Vol. 46(3) pages 435–451. Online, revised, at <https://www.academia.edu/37578530/Why_Hybrid_Bicameralism_is_Not_Right_for_Sortition> accessed January 29, 2019.

[281] Glück, Judith; König, Susanne; Naschenweng, Katja; Redzanowski, Uwe; Dorner-Hörig, Lara; Strasser, Irene; Wiedermann, Wolfgang, "How to measure wisdom: content, reliability, and validity of five measures," *Frontiers in Psychology*, Vol. 4, 2013, DOI 10.3389/fpsyg.2013.00405, ISSN 1664-1078. Online at <https://www.frontiersin.org/article/10.3389/fpsyg.2013.00405> accessed April 27, 2022. After subjecting a test group to five current measures of wisdom, this exhaustive Austrian study found that "none is entirely convincing as a measure of wisdom."

[282] Zimmerman, Martin, "TV REVIEW : 'Scaring' Raises Interesting Questions," *Los Angeles Times* (published April 21, 1994) <https://www.latimes.com/archives/la-xpm-1994-04-21-ca-48373-story.html> accessed March 29, 2022. In his ABC News report, John Stossel illustrates how alarmism and fear inspired misjudgments about alar, DDT, crime, and other issues.

[283] Kennan, George Frost, *Around the Cragged Hill: A Personal and Political Philosophy* (W.W. Norton & Co., January 1, 1993, ISBN 978-0393034110, 272 pages), page 240.

[284] Ibid., pages 244-245.

[285] Ibid., page 257.

[286] Brinkhoff, Thomas, "Switzerland: Cantons and Cities" *City Population* (last edited March 22, 2022) <https://www.citypopulation.de/en/switzerland/cities/> accessed March 31, 2022.

[287] "Texas Counties by Population," *Cubit Planning, Inc.* 800-939-2130 (last edited February 1, 2022) <https://www.texas-demographics.com/counties_by_population> accessed March 31, 2022.

[288] Grant, Adam, "How to Build a Culture of Originality," *Harvard Business Review* (published March, 2016) <https://hbr.org/2016/03/how-to-build-a-culture-of-originality> accessed April 5, 2022.

[289] Kahneman, Daniel; Sibony, Oliver; Sunstein Cass R., *Noise: A Flaw in Human Judgment* (Little, Brown Spark hardcover, May 18, 2021, ISBN 978-0316451406, 464 pages).

[290] "e-Governance," Estonian government (last edited March 25, 2022) <https://e-estonia.com/solutions/e-governance/e-democracy/> accessed April 2, 2022.

[291] *Op.cit.*, Alvarado, pages 53-54 and 123.

[292] Ibid., page 80.

[293] Rothbard, Murray N.; Hoppe, Hans-Hermann (2003 introduction), *The Ethics of Liberty* (NYU Press paperback from 1982 original, February 1, 2003, ISBN 978-0814775592, 308 pages), page 152.

[294] Gordon, David, "Carl Schmitt and Murray Rothbard," *Mises Institute* (published April 1, 2022) <https://mises.org/library/carl-schmitt-and-murray-rothbard> accessed April 2, 2022.

[295] *Op.cit.*, Rommen, page 219.

[296] Ibid., page 205. Rommen insists that there is no duality, that this principle of natural law is accepted by every jurist, even positivists. But then he notes the positivist distinction between this "mere fact" and "legal effects" attached to it by the state. It seems to me that the hairsplitting is avoided by simply establishing property as intuitively known, the denial of which results in an absurdity.

[297] Bentham, Jeremy, *Principles of the Civil Code* (Bowring edition of 1843, digitized by the Classical Utilitarianism Web Site) Objects of the Civil Law, Chapter 8, Of Property <https://www.laits.utexas.edu/poltheory/bentham/pcc/pcc.pa01.c08.html> accessed April 5, 2022.

[298] Pilon, Roger, "Can American Asset Forfeiture Law Be Justified?" *New York Law School Review*, Vol. 39, page 313. Online at <https://www.cato.org/sites/cato.org/files/articles/can_american_asset_forfeture_law_be_justified.pdf> accessed April 5, 2022.

[299] *Op.cit.*, Thommen, page 11.

[300] Barnett, Randy E., *The Structure of Liberty: Justice and the Rule of Law* (Oxford University Press, paperback second edition, February 19, 2014, ISBN 978-0198700920, 400 pages), page 341.

[301] *Op.cit.*, Benson, page 297.

[302] Eisenberg, Theodore; Lanvers, Charlotte, "What is the Settlement Rate and Why Should We Care?" *Journal of Empirical Legal Studies*, Volume 6, Issue 1, 111–146, March 2009), page 111. Online at <https://scholarship.law.cornell.edu/cgi/viewcontent.cgi?article=1202&context=facpub> accessed April 7, 2022. Data and definition problems muddle the numbers: "Of major case categories, tort cases tend to have the highest settlement rates [up to 87.2%], then contract cases, then employment discrimination cases [40-50%], followed by constitutional tort cases."

[303] Weatherford, Lisa, "History of the Texas ADR Act," *Alternative Resolutions*, Summer/Fall 2007, page 30. Online at <http://www.stcl.edu/wp-content/uploads/2016/02/Texas-ADR-Act-Legislative-History.pdf> accessed April 7, 2022. "[ADR] changed the face of Texas jurisprudence."

[304] Smith, Jeffrey Q.; MacQueen, Grant R., "Going, Going, But Not Quite Gone: Trials Continue to Decline in Federal and State Courts. Does it Matter?" *Judicature*, Vol. 101, No. 4, Winter, 2017. Online at <https://judicature.duke.edu/articles/going-going-but-not-quite-gone-trials-continue-to-decline-in-federal-and-state-courts-does-it-matter/> accessed April 7, 2022.

[305] Stone, Katherine V.W.; Colvin, Alexander J.S., "The arbitration epidemic: Mandatory arbitration deprives workers and consumers of their rights," *Economic Policy Institute* (published December 7, 2015) <https://www.epi.org/publication/the-arbitration-epidemic/> accessed April 6, 2022.

[306] "SOUTHLAND CORPORATION, et al., Appellants v. Richard D. KEATING et al.," *Cornell Law*

School, Legal Information Institute (last edited February 26, 2022) <https://www.law.cornell.edu/supremecourt/text/465/1> accessed April 6, 2022.

[307] Bingham, Lisa Blomgren; Nabatchi, Tina; Senger, Jeffrey M.; Jackman, Michael Scott, "Dispute Resolution and the Vanishing Trial: Comparing Federal Government Litigation and ADR Outcomes," *Ohio State Journal on Dispute Resolution*, Vol. 24:2, 2009, page 225. Online at <https://www.sidley.com/~/media/files/publications/2009/01/dispute-resolution-and-the-vanishing-trial-compa___/files/view-article/fileattachment/govlitadroutcomes.pdf> accessed April 6, 2022.

[308] Boyce, John K., III, *Dispute Resolution Texas Style* (State Bar of Texas Alternative Dispute Resolution Section, third edition, January, 2006), page 4. Online at <https://www.texasbar.com/AM/Template.cfm?Section=Our_Legal_System1&Template=/CM/ContentDisplay.cfm&ContentID=23458> accessed April 6, 2022.

[309] "Texas Arbitration Act," *ADR Times* (published September, 2021) <https://www.adrtimes.com/texas-arbitration-act/> accessed April 6, 2022.

[310] Fuller, Lon L.; Winston, Kenneth (editor), *The Principles of Social Order: Selected Essays of Lon L. Fuller* (Hart Publishing revised edition, February 1, 2002, ISBN 978-1841132341, 344 pages), page 144.

[311] Benson, Bruce L., *The Enterprise of Law: Justice Without the State* (Pacific Research Institute paperback, March 15, 1990, ISBN 978-0936488301, 397 pages), page 227.

[312] *Op.cit.*, Friedman, *Law's Order*, page 104.

[313] Ibid., page 305.

[314] Ibid., page 11.

[315] Ibid., page 45.

[316] Ibid., page 11.

[317] "Plea bargain," *Cornell Law School*, Legal Information Institute (last edited February 28, 2022) <https://www.law.cornell.edu/wex/plea_bargain> accessed April 7, 2022.

[318] *Op.cit.*, Nisbet, page 93.

[319] Ibid., page 78.

[320] Ibid., page 161.

[321] *Op.cit.*, Benson, page 321.

[322] Ibid., page 23.

[323] Ibid., page 2.

[324] Hoppe, Hans-Hermann, editor, *The Myth of National Defense* (Mises Institute, October 16, 2003, ISBN 978-0945466376, 453 pages), Bassani, Luigi Marco; Lottieri, Carl, "The Problem of Security: Historicity of the State and 'European Realism'," page 36: In the Middle Ages, "crime was never considered a social problem, a wound inflicted on the collective body. This, in turn, implied that the victims were the center of any lawsuit; redress was done from the point of view of the victims, never of a supposedly wounded collectivity."

[325] Ibid., page 21.

[326] Ibid., page 50.

[327] Ibid.

[328] Ibid., page 62.

329 Ibid., page 71.

330 Ibid., pages 71-72.

331 Jouvenel, Bertrand de; Huntington, J.F. (translator), *Sovereignty: An Inquiry into the Political Good* (Liberty Fund translation from the 1957 *De la souveraineté*, April 30, 1998, ISBN 978-0865971738, 416 pages), pages 212-213. The first English king to acquire standing armies was Edward III (1327-1377), for the Hundred Years War (1337-1453).

332 Ibid., page 211.

333 *Op.cit.*, Benson, page 146.

334 Ibid.

335 Ibid., page 115.

336 "Texas Property Taxes 2022," *Tax-Rates.org* (last edited April 2, 2022) <http://www.tax-rates.org/texas/property-tax> accessed April 9, 2022.

337 "Property Tax Bills," *Texas Comptroller of Public Accounts* (last edited January 21, 2022) <https://comptroller.texas.gov/taxes/property-tax/bills/index.php> accessed April 9, 2022.

338 Graham, John Remington; Livingston, Donald (foreword), *A Constitutional History of Secession* (Pelican Publishing, October 31, 2002, ISBN 978-1589800663, 464 pages), page 96.

339 "Biden: Insurrectionists 'need nukes' to take on US government," *BBC News* (published June 24, 2021) <https://www.bbc.com/news/av/world-us-canada-57590483> accessed September 6, 2021. Biden: "If you think you need to have weapons to take on the government, you need F-15s and maybe some nuclear weapons."

340 Hostelley, Darwin, "Future of the World Reserve Currency – What happens if the US dollar loses its status?" *Gold Alliance* (published May 26, 2021) <https://goldalliance.com/blog/if-the-dollar-loses-its-status-as-the-worlds-reserve-currency/> accessed April 11, 2022.

341 Brockman, Katie, "Is Social Security Going Bankrupt? 3 Reasons Not to Worry," *The Motley Fool* (published September 9, 2021) <https://www.fool.com/retirement/2021/09/09/is-social-security-going-bankrupt-3-reasons-not-to/> accessed April 11, 2022.

342 Tilford, Cale; Rennison, Joe; Noonan, Laura; Smith, Colby; Greeley, Brendan, "Repo: How the financial markets' plumbing got blocked," *Financial Times* (published November 25 2019) <https://ig.ft.com/repo-rate/> accessed April 11, 2022. One should note that neither the "Fed funds rate" nor its repo rate is enforced by statute, as if that were even possible. They are "enforced" by Federal Reserve buying and selling out of its own account, and thus subject to market forces. Those forces are no more subject to the whim of the Fed than were the tides subject to whim of King Canute.

343 Brugen, Isabel van, "America Races to Avert the 'Quantum Apocalypse'," (published February 5, 2022) *Newsweek* magazine <https://www.newsweek.com/america-races-avert-quantum-apocalypse-1676366> accessed April 11, 2022. Not only would the breaking of current cryptography be fatal for Internet-connected infrastructure, it would render worthless that increasingly popular store of personal wealth in cryptocurrency. According to Deloitte's 2021 Global Blockchain Survey, 76% of respondents believe digital assets will serve as a strong alternative to, or outright replacement for, fiat currencies in the next 5-10 years.

344 Bassani, Luigi Marco, *Chaining Down Leviathan: The American Dream of Self-Government 1776-1865* (Abbeville Institute Press, March 28, 2021, ISBN 978-1733407519, 380 pages), page 207.

345 2EyesnEars, "Judge Andrew Napolitano on Texas Secession" (*YouTube*, length 4:41, published November 14, 2012) at the 3:35 mark <https://www.youtube.com/watch?v=mOAcrluoteY> accessed October 25, 2021.

346 Hamilton, Alexander, "Federalist 32, January 3, 1788," *Library of Congress*, Federalist Papers:

Primary Documents in American History (published January 30, 2022) <https://guides.loc.gov/federalist-papers/text-31-40> accessed April 12, 2022.

347 "Ratification of the Constitution by the State of New York; July 26, 1788," *Yale Law School* (last edited April 12, 2022) <https://avalon.law.yale.edu/18th_century/ratny.asp> accessed April 12, 2022.

348 "Ratification of the Constitution by the State of Rhode Island; May 29, 1790," *Yale Law School* (last edited February 14, 2022) <https://avalon.law.yale.edu/18th_century/ratri.asp> accessed April 12, 2022.

349 "Ratification of the Constitution by the State of Virginia; June 26, 1788," *Yale Law School* (last edited January 10, 2022) <https://avalon.law.yale.edu/18th_century/ratva.asp> accessed April 12, 2022.

350 *Op.cit.*, Buckley, page 134.

351 Ibid., page 32.

352 Ibid., pages 41-42.

353 Gordon, David (editor), *Secession, State & Liberty* (Transaction Publishers, February 28, 2002, ISBN 978-0765809438, 360 pages), page xi. Online at <https://cdn.mises.org/secession_state_liberty.pdf> accessed May 1, 2021.

354 Hummel, Jeffrey Rogers, *Emancipating Slaves, Enslaving Free Men: A History of the American Civil War* (Open Court, second edition paperback, December 10, 2013, ISBN 978-0812698435, 448 pages), pages 293-294.

355 Downs, Jim, *Sick from Freedom: African-American Illness and Suffering during the Civil War and Reconstruction* (Oxford University Press reprint edition, January 1, 2015, ISBN 978-0190218263, 280 pages). Page 4: "The Civil War [sic], however, produced the largest biological crisis of the nineteenth century, claiming more soldiers' lives and resulting in more casualties than battle or warfare and wreaking havoc on the population[.]"

356 *Op.cit.*, Graham, John Remington, pages 18, 90.

357 Ibid., page 91.

358 Lolme, Jean Louis De; Lieberman, David (editor), *The Constitution of England; Or an Account of the English Government* (Liberty Fund, paperback reprint of 1771 original, November 24, 2007, ISBN 978-0865974654, 396 pages), page 101. Online at <https://oll-resources.s3.us-east-2.amazonaws.com/oll3/store/titles/2089/DeLolme1449_Bk.pdf> accessed April 12, 2022.

359 *Op.cit.*, Graham, John Remington, page 74.

360 Ibid., pages 90-91.

361 Ibid., page 99.

362 *Op.cit.*, Bassani, *Chaining Down Leviathan*, page 232.

363 "The Treaty of Annexation - Texas; April 12, 1844," *Yale Law School* (last edited March 23, 2022) <https://avalon.law.yale.edu/19th_century/texan05.asp> accessed April 14, 2022.

364 "Constitutions of Texas," *Tarlton Law Library* (last edited February 10, 2022) <https://tarlton.law.utexas.edu/c.php?g=787754> accessed April 14, 2022. The current Texas Constitution, adopted February 15, 1876, places the identical wording in Article I, Section 2, with the insertion of the following phrase between "benefit" and "they have at all times": "The faith of the people of Texas stands pledged to the preservation of a republican form of government, and, subject to this limitation only,".

365 "History of Texas Public Lands," *Texas General Land Office*, page 15 (last edited March 2018)

<https://www.glo.texas.gov/history/archives/forms/files/history-of-texas-public-lands.pdf> accessed January 29, 2020.

[366] *Op.cit.*, Napolitano, at the 1:14 mark.

[367] "The U.S. Constitution," *National Constitution Center, Interactive Constitution* (last edited April 13, 2022) <https://constitutioncenter.org/interactive-constitution/full-text> accessed April 14, 2022.

[368] "TEXAS v. WHITE ET AL.," *Cornell Law School, Legal Information Institute* (last edited January 23, 2022) <https://www.law.cornell.edu/supremecourt/text/358/1> accessed February 7, 2022.

[369] Robinson, Warren C., "D.C. within South's grasp after early rout," *The Washington Times* (published July 20, 2002) <https://www.washingtontimes.com/news/2002/jul/20/20020720-034512-5745r/> accessed April 14, 2022. After the Confederate victory at First Manassas on July 21, 1861, General "Stonewall" Jackson said to president Jefferson Davis, who was on the battlefield, "Give me ten thousand men and I will take Washington tomorrow." Davis declined. Thus the War Between the States could not possibly have been a "civil war": A civil war is contention over a single government; secession is separation to establish a second government indifferent to the first.

[370] *Op.cit.*, Buckley, page 41.

[371] Brown, Ed, "The United Nations, Self-Determination, State Failure and Secession," *E-International Relations* (published May 29, 2020) <https://www.e-ir.info/2020/05/29/the-united-nations-self-determination-state-failure-and-secession/> accessed April 14, 2022.

[372] "History of the UN," *The United Nations* (last edited March 19, 2022) <https://www.un.org/un70/en/content/history/index.html> accessed April 14, 2022.

[373] "Who are the current members of the United Nations?" *The United Nations* (last edited March 28, 2022) <https://ask.un.org/faq/14345> accessed April 14, 2022.

[374] Nwaubani, Adaobi Tricia, "Remembering Nigeria's Biafra war that many prefer to forget," *BBC News* (published January 15, 2020) <https://www.bbc.com/news/world-africa-51094093> accessed April 11, 2022.

[375] Remnick, David, "The Lincoln-Gorbachev Debate at Moscow State U.," *The Washington Post* (published March 24, 1990) <https://www.washingtonpost.com/archive/politics/1990/03/24/the-lincoln-gorbachev-debate-at-moscow-state-u/1a7824a2-e271-4325-bd82-42911da422f6/> accessed April 15, 2022.

[376] Abbeville Inst, "The Disintegration of Lincolnian America by Donald Livingston" (*YouTube*, length 52:51, published April 12, 2018) <https://www.youtube.com/watch?v=oC5vlcjWzpk> accessed April 15, 2022.

[377] *Op.cit.*, Bassani, *Chaining Down Leviathan*, page 260.

[378] Woodard, Colin, *American Nations: A History of the Eleven Rival Regional Cultures of North America* (Penguin, September 25, 2012, ISBN 978-0143122029, 384 pages), page 2.

[379] Kreitner, Richard, *Break It Up: Secession, Division, and the Secret History of America's Imperfect Union* (Little, Brown and Company, August 18, 2020, ISBN 978-0316510608, 496 pages), page 14.

[380] Ibid., page 8.

[381] Brougham, Henry Lord, *Political Philosophy*, second edition (London, 1849), Vol. 3, page 336. This reference is taken from Livingston, "The Secession Tradition in America," page 13, where he quotes from Brougham's magisterial, multi-volume study of constitutions: "It is plainly impossible to consider the Constitution which professes to govern this Union, this Federacy of States, as any thing other than a treaty."

[382] *Op.cit.*, Kreitner, page 19.

[383] Ibid., page 23.

[384] Ibid., page 32.

[385] Ibid., page 36.

[386] Ibid., page 40.

[387] Ibid., page 43.

[388] Ibid., page 57.

[389] Ibid., page 67.

[390] Ibid.

[391] Ibid., page 153.

[392] Ibid., page 189-190.

[393] Naylor, Thomas H.; Sale, Kirkpatrick (introduction), *Secession: How Vermont and All the Other States Can Save Themselves from the Empire* (Feral House, first edition, April 1, 2008, ISBN 978-1932595307, 240 pages), pages 47-52.

[394] Herbert, Hilary Abner, LL.D., *The Abolition Crusade and Its Consequences: Four Periods of American History* (Project Gutenberg eBook #39720, published May 17, 2012) <https://www.gutenberg.org/files/39720/39720-h/39720-h.htm> accessed April 16, 2022. The reference is to pages 25-26 of Herbert's 1912 original, where a footnote references Gaillard Hunt's *Disunion Sentiment in the Congress in 1794.*

[395] Quincy, Edmund, *Life of Josiah Quincy of Massachusetts* (BiblioBazaar paperback reprint of 1867 original, November 23, 2009, ISBN 978-1117393773, 578 pages), page 213 from Josiah Quincy: "The bonds of this Union are virtually dissolved; that the States which compose it are free from their moral obligation; and that, as it will be the right of all, so it will be the duty of some, to prepare definitely for a separation, amicably if they can, violently if they must."

[396] Davis, Jefferson, *The Rise and Fall of the Confederate Government, Volume One* (Project Gutenberg eBook #19831, published November 16, 2006) <https://www.gutenberg.org/files/19831/19831-h/19831-h.htm#footnotetag24> accessed April 16, 2022. The reference is to page 72 of the 1881 original, where Davis cites Pickering's letter of December 24, 1803: "A Northern confederacy would unite congenial characters and present a fairer prospect of public happiness; while the Southern States having a similarity of habits, might be left to manage their affairs in their own way. If a separation were to take place, our mutual wants render a friendly [...] intercourse inevitable[. ...The separation] must begin in Massachusetts."

[397] Adams, Charles, *When in the Course of Human Events: Arguing the Case for Southern Secession* (Rowman & Littlefield paperback first edition, December 23, 2004, ISBN 978-0847697236, 257 pages), page 13.

[398] *Op.cit.*, Graham, John Remington, pages 138-140.

[399] Brown, Charles Raymond, "The Essex Junto," *Abbeville Institute* (published May 4, 2018) <https://www.abbevilleinstitute.org/the-essex-junto/> accessed April 16, 2022.

[400] Adams, John Quincy, *The Jubilee of the Constitution* (Samuel Colman, 1839, 136 pages), page 69, from Adams' speech given April 30, 1839 on the 50th anniversary of the inauguration of George Washington: "But the indissoluble link of union between the people of the several states of this confederated nation, is after all, not in the *right*, but in the *heart*. [Friendship and "conciliated interests and kindly sympathies" are what form the union. Failing that,] "far better will it be for the people of the disunited states, to part in friendship from each other, than to be held together by constraint. Then will be the time for reverting to the precedents which occurred at the formation

and adoption of the Constitution, to form again a more perfect union, by dissolving that which could no longer bind, and to leave the separated parts to be reunited by the law of political gravitation to the centre." [emphasis in the original]

[401] Garrison, William Lloyd, *The Liberator*, May 31, 1844, Vol. XIV, No. 22, Whole No. 699, page 86. Online at <http://fair-use.org/the-liberator/1844/05/31/the-liberator-14-22.pdf>, accessed April 16, 2022. Garrison wrote "Address to the Friends of Freedom and Emancipation in the United States". In this strongly disunionist editorial, Garrison maintained that the Constitution had been created "at the expense of the colored population of the country". With Southerners continuing to dominate the nation because of the Three-Fifths Compromise, it was time "to set the captive free by the potency of truth" and "secede from the government." On the same day that this issue was published, the New England Anti-Slavery Convention endorsed the principles of secession from slaveholders by a vote of 250-24.

[402] Livingston, Donald; Gordon, David (editor), "The Secession Tradition in America" in *Secession, State & Liberty* (Transaction Publishers, February 28, 2002, ISBN 978-0765809438, 360 pages), page 13. Online at <https://cdn.mises.org/secession_state_liberty.pdf> accessed May 1, 2021.

[403] Mussomeli, Vito, "The Secession Movement in the Middle States," *Abbeville Institute* (published October 29, 2019) <https://www.abbevilleinstitute.org/the-secession-movement-in-the-middle-states/> accessed April 16, 2022. William C. Wright lists Maryland, Delaware, New Jersey, Pennsylvania, and New York. Note the overlap with Border State secessionists and the "Central Confederacy."

[404] *Op.cit.*, Kreitner, page 92.

[405] *Op.cit.*, Kennan, pages 149-150.

[406] Sale, Kirkpatrick, *Dwellers in the Land: The Bioregional Vision* (University of Georgia Press, April 13, 2000, ISBN 978-0820322056, 248 pages), page xiii. The "ecoregions" that he advocates conform basically to the 63 "Ecoregion Provinces" of the U.S. Forest Service, as he acknowledges.

[407] Jefferson, Thomas; Foley, John P. (editor), *The Jeffersonian Cyclopedia: A Comprehensive Collection of the Views of Thomas Jefferson*, "Letter to John Tyler, May 26, 1810" (Funk & Wagnalls Co., 1900, 1009 pages), page 212. Here advocating Anglo-Saxon "hundreds," Jefferson writes: "I have indeed two great measures at heart, without which no republic can maintain itself in strength. That of general education, to enable every man to judge for himself what will secure or endanger his freedom. To divide every county into hundreds, of such size that all the children of each will be within reach of a central school in it. But this division looks to many other fundamental provisions. Every hundred, besides a school, should have a justice of the peace, a constable and a captain of militia. These officers, or some others within the hundred, should be a corporation to manage all its concerns, to take care of its roads, its poor, and its police by patrols, &c., (as the select men of the Eastern townships.) Every hundred should elect one or two jurors to serve where requisite, and all other elections should be made in the hundreds separately, and the votes of all the hundreds be brought together. Our present Captaincies might be declared hundreds for the present, with a power to the courts to alter them occasionally. These little republics would be the main strength of the great one. [...] Could I once see this I should consider it as the dawn of the salvation of the republic [...]."

[408] Jefferson, Thomas; Foley, John P. (editor), *The Jeffersonian Cyclopedia: A Comprehensive Collection of the Views of Thomas Jefferson*, "Letter to Samuel Kercheval, 1816" (Funk & Wagnalls Co., 1900, 1009 pages), page 216. Here advocating "wards," six years after the John Tyler letter, Jefferson writes: "The article, nearest my heart, is the division of counties into wards. These will be pure and elementary republics, the sum of all which, taken together, composes the State, and will make a true democracy as to the business of the wards, which is that of nearest and daily concern [...]. [The division into wards...] enables them by that organization to crush, regularly and peaceably, the usurpations of their unfaithful agents, and rescues them from the dreadful necessity of doing it insurrectionally. In this way we shall be as republican as a large society can be; and secure the continuance of purity in our government, through salutary, peaceable, and regular control [by] the people."

409 *Op.cit.*, von Mises, *Liberalism: In The Classical Tradition*, pages 109-110.

410 Ibid.

411 "Brexit: How much disruption has there been so far?" *BBC News* (published February 1, 2021) <https://www.bbc.com/news/55831263> accessed April 16, 2022.

412 Mauldin, John, "Your Pension Is a Lie: There's $210 Trillion Of Liabilities Our Government Can't Fulfill," *Forbes* magazine (published October 10, 2017) <https://www.forbes.com/sites/johnmauldin/2017/10/10/your-pension-is-a-lie-theres-210-trillion-of-liabilities-our-government-cant-fulfill/> accessed April 16, 2022. Note that figures cited in this article are from four years ago, so therefore understate the true amounts.

413 Howse, Robert, "The Concept of Odious Debt in Public International Law," *United Nations Conference on Trade and Development*, Discussion Papers, No. 185, July 2007, page 3. Online at <https://unctad.org/system/files/official-document/osgdp20074_en.pdf> accessed April 17, 2022.

414 Ibid.

415 Ibid., page 5.

416 Ibid.

417 Blum, Daniel S., "The Apportionment of Public Debt and Assets during State Secession," *Case Western Reserve Journal of International Law*, Volume 29, Issue 2, 1997, page 271. Online at <https://scholarlycommons.law.case.edu/cgi/viewcontent.cgi?article=1537&context=jil> accessed April 16, 2022.

418 Parks, Michael, "Ukraine Agrees to Pay Its Share of Soviet Debt," *Los Angeles Times* (March 14, 1992) <https://www.latimes.com/archives/la-xpm-1992-03-14-mn-3134-story.html> accessed April 16, 2022.

419 Acquaviva, Guido, "The Dissolution of Yugoslavia and the Fate of Its Financial Obligations," *Denver Journal of International Law & Policy*, Volume 30, Number 2, Spring, January 2002, Article 5, page 209. Online at <https://digitalcommons.du.edu/cgi/viewcontent.cgi?article=1470&context=djilp> accessed April 16, 2022.

420 Boyle, Michael J.; Schmitt, Kirsten Rohrs, "Sovereign Default," *Investopedia* (last edited March 03, 2022) <https://www.investopedia.com/terms/s/sovereign-default.asp> accessed April 17, 2022.

421 *Op.cit.*, Blum, page 267.

422 "Financial Report of the United States Government," *Bureau of the Fiscal Service* (last edited July 25, 2021) <https://www.fiscal.treasury.gov/reports-statements/financial-report/government-financial-position-and-condition.html> accessed October 28, 2021.

423 Hennerich, Heather, "Debt-to-GDP Ratio: How High Is Too High? It Depends," *Federal Reserve Bank of St. Louis* (published October 07, 2020) <https://www.stlouisfed.org/open-vault/2020/october/debt-gdp-ratio-how-high-too-high-it-depends> accessed October 28, 2021. "U.S. federal debt-to-GDP ratio was 107% late [2019], and it went up to nearly 136% in the second quarter of 2020 with the passage of a coronavirus relief package."

424 Krugman, Paul, "Debt Is Good," *The New York Times* (published August 21, 2015) <https://www.nytimes.com/2015/08/21/opinion/paul-krugman-debt-is-good-for-the-economy.html> accessed April 17, 2022.

425 Whittaker, John, "Modern monetary theory: the rise of economists who say huge government debt is not a problem," *The Conversation* (published July 7, 2020) <https://theconversation.com/modern-monetary-theory-the-rise-of-economists-who-say-huge-government-debt-is-not-a-problem-141495> accessed April 17, 2022.

[426] Kelton, Stephanie, *The Deficit Myth* (PublicAffairs paperback reprint, March 9, 2021, ISBN 978-1541736191, 352 pages).

[427] Wray, L. Randall, *Modern Money Theory: A Primer on Macroeconomics for Sovereign Monetary Systems* (Palgrave Macmillan paperback second edition, September 22, 2015, ISBN 978-1137539908, 322 pages).

[Love of the Union] grows out of the affections, and has not, and cannot be made to have, anything universal in its nature. Sir, I confess it, the first public love of my heart is [my State]. There is my fireside, there are the tombs of my ancestors. [...] The love of this Union grows out of this attachment to my native soil, and is rooted in it.[1]

This was the meaning of patriotism for the founders of the American States. Now, are these the words of a secessionist, or a Texan, or a Southerner? – A secessionist, possibly; but definitely not a Texan or a Southerner. The actual text reads not [my State], but "the Commonwealth of Massachusetts," and the quote is from the quintessential Yankee, Josiah Quincy III. Patriotism is proper and ineradicable as the love of the near and familiar community that gives us identity; when misconceived, it is the chauvinistic worship of an ideology of state absolutism.

For the patriot of Texas, there is no need to await a promised glory: For in its sea of bluebonnets on its hills gently undulating to the far horizon, under the hard, glittering sunlight of its summer skies, its prairies dotted with cattle, mesquites, and chaparrals, its fragrant Piney Woods, its soaring Big Bend sky, its curlews crying along its coast, and in its best of peoples, generous, direct, and open, championed the world over yet most feared on any battlefield – in all of this one sees the face of almighty god, and one hears the word he whispers when he smiles and recollects the moment he outdid himself in the act of creation: "*Texas.*"

2. INSTANTIATION
The Constitution of the Republic of Texas
The Texas Legislature, more powerful than the Executive or Judicial branches, is instructed by the current Texas Constitution to meet at noon the second Tuesday in January of each odd-numbered year, for 140 calendar days. The Senate has 31 members; the House of Representatives has 150. The Lieutenant Governor, who is elected by popular vote, presides over the Senate; the Speaker of the House is elected by members of that body. Each appoints committee heads to his chamber.[2]

The current Constitution would require amendment by referendum to accommodate a kleristocracy.

The posts of Governor and Lieutenant Governor would be abolished, replaced by the previously described (1.2.5, page 127) 10-member Consilium. References in statute to those two posts would read "Consilium" instead.

As previously described (1.2.4, page 120), the sortition process would provide 312 legislators from the 254 current Texas counties. The Consilium appoints the House committee chairs, and from the 312, the members of the

Senate, increased from 31 to 50. From the remaining 262 résumés, the Consilium selects at least 50 and no more than 100 administrators for the posts described below, according to their abilities, to current needs, and to their willingness to serve[xxx] as administrators, leaving the remainder (162 to 212) as members of the House. Those House members then vote to approve or strike individually each of the 50 Senators selected by the Consilium. Any Senator receiving more than a simple majority to strike is replaced by the Consilium from someone among the 162 to 212 House members and returned to the House. The Senate approval vote takes place one time only. The House then votes on the slate of judiciary candidates offered by the Consilium, accepting each one separately, or demanding a replacement (if available) from others applying for the same post. The next business of the House is to examine the provided agenda. Although it cannot remove agenda items, it can by simple majority vote submit additions, which if denied by the Consilium can be added notwithstanding by a two-thirds vote of the chamber. The last item of business of its 140-day session, as previously described, is to elect at least two new Consuls by majority vote, whose only qualifications are that the person be at least 30 years of age, a citizen of Texas, and not a member of the current legislature.

The Consilium has two major functions: A consultative function in even-numbered years for the legislature's work in odd-numbered years, and a year-round administrative function like the Swiss Federal Council. To fulfill the consultative function, during even-numbered years it studies to provide the following:
• the selection of the slate of judiciary candidates to be approved by the House,
• the selection of House committee chairs from the 312 résumés provided by sortition in September,
• the selection of 50 Senators from the 312 résumés provided by sortition,
• the selection of 50 to 100 administrators as needed from the 312;
• the agenda for the legislature, which among other items includes the biennial budget, initiatives and county nullifications (both detailed on page 185), and two lists:
• the list of laws to be removed from effect (to be "sunset"),[3]
• the list of State services to be privatized.

The current Governor has 303 appointments in his gift.[4] As described below, some should remain, at least during the transition to kleristocracy, others should be modified or moved, while many others should be abolished, either outright or over a period of transition. A few might be added, and all reordered for their more efficient administration among the 10 Consuls of the Consilium.

[xxx] Selection as an administrator would be regarded as a mark of distinction, especially since it would mean a term of employment beyond the 140-day legislative session.

Remaining:
Legal: Remains as is, with the addition of the new *Legislative Services* office, which provides the law drafting expertise to the legislature.
Natural Resources: Existing Authorities remain; the office acquires the Environmental Quality, Parks and Wildlife, and Water Development Boards.

Modified or moved:
Financial: The School Land Board and Permanent School Fund merge as one board in the new *Home Affairs* office; the six pension and retirement boards also merge as one board in the new Home Affairs office.
Public Education: All boards related to the education of the deaf, blind, special needs, and disabled merge as one board named *Public Restorative Education*; the remaining boards and their functions are abolished.
Public Safety: Crime Stoppers, Emergency Communications, Emergency Management, and One-Call merge as one board named "Communications" in the new *Technology* office; the remaining boards are abolished.
Regulatory-Industry: Credit Union and Finance Commissions merge as one board named "Finance" in the new Home Affairs office; Lottery Commission moves to the new Home Affairs office; Forensic Science and Radiation Advisory move separately to the new Technology office; Securities Board moves to the new Home Affairs office; Law Enforcement moves to the new *Defense* office; Public Utility Commission moves to the new *Energy* office; the remaining boards are abolished.
State Oversight: Criminal Justice is moved to the new Defense office; Energy Plan Advisory and Energy Reliability move separately to the new Energy office; Environmental Quality moves to the existing Natural Resources office; ERCOT moves to the new Energy office; the Insurance Commission and Mutual Insurance merge and move to the new Home Affairs office; Military Preparedness moves to the new Defense office; Motor Vehicles and Public Safety merge as one board named "Motor Vehicles" and move to the new Home Affairs office; Parks and Wildlife moves to the existing Natural Resources office; Preservation Board moves to the new Home Affairs office; the Transportation Commission moves to the new Home Affairs office; the Veterans' Land Board merges with the School Land and Fund Board; the Water Development Board moves to the existing Natural Resources office.

Abolished:
Economic Development: Its various economic "incentivizations," "incubations," "developments," "advisories," and "researchings" are fully within the functions of the free market.

Financial: Affordable Housing Corporation Board, Work Group on Blockchain Matters, Housing and Community Affairs, Land Banks study committee, Opioid Abatement Fund Council, and the Public Finance Authority are abolished.

Healthcare: Its various medical "advisories" are fully within the functions of the free market.

Higher Education: The 10 university Boards of Regents are sufficient management for their respective institutions; the remaining five offices are devolved to the counties.

Human Services: Its various "advisories" are fully within the functions of private charities and the free market.

Humanities: Its various cultural, artistic, historical, and other commissions intrude on areas that are properly the choice of individuals.

Regulatory-Professional: Its various "examiners," "oversight," and other boards are all abolished.

Transportation: Its various functions are subsumed under the Transportation Commission, a part of the new Home Affairs office.

New:

Home Affairs: The School Land and Fund Board, Public Pension and Retirement Board, Finance, Securities Board, Insurance Commission, Mutual Insurance, Lottery Commission, Preservation Board, Motor Vehicles, Transportation Commission.

Technology: Communications (Crime Stoppers, Emergency Communications, Emergency Management, One-Call), Forensic Science, Radiation and Nuclear Advisory. A new function to be added would be Sortition Integrity.

Defense: Law Enforcement, Criminal Justice, Military Preparedness. An office is added: Cyber Defense.

Energy: Public Utility Commission, Energy Plan Advisory, Energy Reliability/ ERCOT.

Public Restorative Education: All boards related to the education of deaf, blind, special needs, and disabled citizens.

Thus one Consul of the Consilium will be assigned to each of the following functions: Legal, Natural Resources, Technology, Defense, Energy, Public Restorative Education, and Foreign Affairs. Two Consuls will manage Home Affairs – one managing The School Land and Fund Board, Public Pension and Retirement Board, Finance, Securities Board, Insurance Commission, and Mutual Insurance; the other managing the Lottery Commission, Preservation Board, Motor Vehicles, and Transportation Commission. The remaining Consul will be the Consilium's biennially rotating chief administrator, who will manage the day-to-day affairs of the Consilium, generally supervise the other nine, and – very importantly – evaluate the reports of whistleblowers from every part of the administration. The offices and boards listed above will change; they will be abolished or reassigned as power devolves to the counties.

By no later than September 7 of any even-numbered year, the Consilium will have received the résumés of all 312 sortitions offered for service to the Republic. On Wednesday before the fourth Thursday of November (Thanksgiving Day) of the even-numbered year, the Consilium will announce assignments from these résumés for its administrative appointments and for House committee chairs (the Senate electing its own), and also on that date publish the legislative agenda for the term of the odd-numbered year beginning in the following January. There must be included in that agenda any popular initiative that has by petition received 100,000 or more signatures from citizens of Texas, and a reconsideration of any law that has been formally nullified by any county. Such a nullified law may be redrafted, but in any case must receive a supermajority vote of two-thirds of the House to survive as law. The re-promulgated law remains in force unless again nullified, in which case the process repeats. It should go without saying that the agenda must include a bill to accept or modify the Consilium's budget, to be balanced without borrowing against receipts by the Republic, and include a bill to set the rate of the Republic's sales tax, or value added tax (VAT) if that is adopted instead. This tax will provide the primary source of revenue to the Republic, which will be sufficient given the removal of former Federal mandates, given the removal of all redistributive schemes, and given the reduction in government functions, especially regarding "the general welfare," above the county level.

Republic-wide referenda are mandatory as specified under current State law, to approve any constitutional reform, to approve an issue of national importance (as determined either by the Consilium or by a supermajority vote of two-thirds of the House), or to approve any treaty between the Republic and a foreign government.

2.1 Devolution of Power

The locus of government in the kleristocratic Republic of Texas is the county. As detailed in the section on sortition (1.2.4, page 120), the 254 current counties in Texas form 312 communities of about a quarter million or less.

The devolution of power from the current State government applies as well to municipalities, which have become sprawling Bantustans of government within the State government. After division into the more humane 312 communities of about a quarter million or less, municipal government devolves to become a county government – or governments in the case where the large municipality currently constitutes a county unto itself. For example, the enormous current Harris County that contains the city of Houston would become 24 counties. In the more frequent case where municipalities exist within a larger county, municipal law would still apply, but with an important amendment of their power and independence from their county: Any exercise of municipal government – whether it be a law, promulgation, rezoning, administrative decree, or any act whatsoever – would be subject to nullification by a vote of the county commissioners, and any city councilman or mayor could be removed by a vote of the county commissioners, which would immediately summon a special Consilium sortition to replace those so removed. The divided but adjacent municipalities certainly would cooperate on matters of common municipal interest, but no longer will a rogue city council be able to impose procrustean mandates on tens of thousands of citizens.

A devolution away from the newly-empowered counties is also required: It is accomplished by the institution of allodial land ownership. On the allod rests the empowerment of the families for which the county symbiotically exists. As previously given in the section on property (1.2.5, page 135), allodial title establishes possession of real property to be held free and clear of any superior landlord, not subject to taxation, eminent domain, or any assertion of superior right.

Currently in the United States allodial title does not exist. Holders of the common fee simple absolute title are said to hold the right to enjoy, use, and exploit[yyy] their property as they see fit. However, the government where the property resides has the power to tax it at any rate jointly set by the county and State, to place liens against it for unpaid taxes and to ultimately foreclose on it, to take it by eminent domain, to access fines against it for violation of its codes, to declare and enforce easements, and to otherwise restrict the property rights of the "owner."

The great benefit of allodial title is removal of the property from the county's property tax roles and its exemption from eminent domain. But additionally, the allodial title holder will have the option of replacing county property codes with those of the homeowners' association of at least 30 separately-owned contiguous properties in which he finds himself, and utility easements will be removed as public utilities are replaced by private utilities. As mentioned, this great benefit is only given to citizens of Texas counties. Allodial title reverts to fee simple on the sale of the property, unless the property is acquired by someone who has held within a year of the sale allodial title on some other property within the county, or unless acquired by an heir who is also a citizen of Texas according to the property county's requirements for citizenship.

The allod is the ultimate devolution of power to the sovereign people.

[yyy] Primarily in name only do they currently hold the *ius fruendi, utendi, et abutendi* – the power to dispose of the property as they will.

2.2 The County

In fact, the current locus of Texas government could be said to be county government, for it is here that citizens actually feel most of the promulgations from the State legislature, administered for the most part wisely and frugally by five remarkable persons: The County Judge and his four County Commissioners. It is they who maintain the infrastructure of the county in the broadest sense, look after the general welfare of its citizens, and collect and administer the State's property tax.

Some insight into their duties is offered by a meeting of the County Judges and Commissioners Association of Texas in October, 2021. There, a number of resolutions were adopted, especially objecting to unfunded mandates (for indigent care, indigent criminal defense, juvenile probation, mental health care, emergency services, holding of inmates up to 45 days, voting machines), objecting to encroachments on their authority (revenue capping, diversion of dedicated funds, special utility districts, homestead exemptions, sex offender regulation, lack of representation on regional water planning boards), and objecting to lack of consideration of county needs (groundwater effects of uranium mining, sludge and biosolid disposal, oil and gas waste disposal, delay in returning the State's forensic lab results).[5]

The County Judge, who presides over the four members of the Commissioners' Court, need only be "well informed in the law of the State", according to Article 5, Section 15 of the Texas Constitution. That is, he need not be a member of the State bar or be a licensed attorney. This should not be surprising, considering the broad range of his duties, in which he might well be said to hold competence, with his mastery being in practical wisdom. Those main duties are stated in the approved guide describing them:

> The county judge is both presiding officer of the commissioners court (Tex. Const. Art. V, Sec. 18) and judge of the county court (Tex. Const. Art. V, Sec. 15). As such, the judge is often thought of as the chief executive officer of the county.[6]

Furthermore, the County Judge serves "as budget officer in counties with fewer than 225,000 residents" and has "broad judicial duties, such as presiding over misdemeanor criminal and small civil cases, probate matters and appeals from the Justice of the Peace Court" and "[s]erves as head of emergency management".[7] Under kleristocracy, the "225,000 residents" restriction will no longer apply for county offices. Whenever any county has acquired 400,000 or more permanent residents as determined by the Texas decennial census, the Consilium will within six months of the publication of the census provide three different redrawn maps of the one county into two counties. The majority choice of one map by the voters in that county, voting in a referendum held within six months of the publication of the maps, shall define the two counties. The current officials shall hold office until the date of the next State-wide sortition for positions in the two distinct counties.

Election of county officers

The County Judge and Commissioners are currently elected individually to a four-year term, and they have almost identical qualifications for office. These qualifications would be modified to require the following:

- Texas citizenship for at least five years;
- Primary residency in the county for at least three years uninterrupted;
- Being at least 30 years of age for County Judge; 25 for Commissioner;
- Passing a test, as devised by the Consilium, demonstrating good understanding of Texas law, to be taken online when the candidate's résumé is submitted for sortition, unless the candidate is a current or retired member of the State bar, in which case no test is required.

The Consilium, with its Technology office of Sortition Integrity, would select the County Judge and Commissioners as in the previously described two-round sortition (1.2.4, page 123). That is, candidates submitting résumés meeting the above qualifications would be assigned a true random number. One additional random number would be drawn to provide a tell to determine three to five electors of the first sortition, that is, by selecting those candidate numbers nearest to the tell. These electors would become ineligible for office but would *separately and without consulting the other electors* provide a blind evaluation of the remaining candidates, whose résumés would be divided equally among them, rejecting at least 40% of them but no more than 60%. From that pool, a final sortition would select the County Judge and four Commissioners. Now, there are currently 92 Texas counties with populations of less than 10,000. Since any county of that size would not provide a pool of sufficient size for effective sortition, there must not be a doctrinaire insistence on its application: Either the Consilium would choose, or their County Judge and Commissioners would continue to be elected by the current process, but with the new requirements of office.

County revenues

The acquisition of Texas citizenship, and the satisfaction of other county requirements such as militia service and minimum term of residency, entitle property held by owners residing within the county to allodial title status, and thus removal from the county's property rolls. Although the property tax is currently the basis of all county funding, its crippling burden on true property ownership must be ended.

Well over half[8] of the burden of the current property tax is eliminated by the complete abolition of public schooling, as detailed below (section 2.9.4). Current events surrounding totalitarian school boards[9] that have long replaced local Parent Teacher Associations should provide sufficient evidence for the necessity of this abolition. But this is another example of a lesson given on the hides of citizens that could have been avoided by heeding the consequences foreseen by a philosopher, in this case by John Stuart Mill, over a century and a half ago:

> A general State education is a mere contrivance for moulding people to be exactly like one another; and as the mould in which it casts them is that which pleases the predominant power in the government, whether this be a monarch, a priesthood, an aristocracy, or the majority of the existing generation, in proportion as it is efficient and successful, it establishes a despotism over the mind, leading by natural tendency to one over the body.[10]

The property tax still applies for those who are not citizens of the county. Citizenship in the county confers another benefit: Voluntary direct taxation at the county level. Despite being voluntary, once the citizens commit to an amount, it must be enforced. Quarterly or monthly pre-payment directly from a bank account could be arranged, but once in default the citizen is subject to liens against his salary or other property, and even removal of the allodial status of his property within the county. The operation of the voluntary tax is most simply defined by the county budget calendar that would be instituted along with kleristocracy.

On January 1 of any even-numbered year, the Commissioners' Court publishes online its two-year budget exclusively to citizens of the county. To provide sufficient but not overwhelming detail, the online budget will offer between 20 and 40 budget items, with a blank input field alongside each of the Court's recommended expenditures. None of these items may fund any kind of welfare or redistributive scheme. The citizen will enter his determination for each item, whether higher or lower, with an automatic total provided. To prevent gaming of the system, each citizen's entries must total no less than the absolute floor budget total set by the Commissioners' Court. And to prevent the Court from gaming the will of its constituents with an arbitrarily high floor, Texas statute provides several means for removal of any member of that Court.[11] In addition, there will be two other sections for citizen input: The section for how the *bonum sociale* is to be distributed, with about six fields for a percentage entry, for example, for homelessness relief, drug rehabilitation, unemployment relief, etc. – and with an entry for non-distribution, as "rainy day savings," with an automatic validation that the total is 100%; and a section for entry of the official statute number of any existing law that the citizen wants removed – a nullification provision that must enter the aforementioned January agenda of the Republic if a simple majority of any county's citizens so indicate. The *bonum sociale* (sure to acquire the familiar name of "bonus") is funded entirely by voluntary contributions, entirely apart from the budgeting calendar. There will be no distribution in the very first budget, since there will not as yet have been any accumulation; however, preferred distributions should still be entered for purposes of planning and discussion.

On March 1 of any even-numbered year, the Commissioners' Court posts online the January budget, showing citizens' determinations and showing its agreement or modification of citizen entries, along with its reasoning for such modification. The citizens vote again, either confirming or modifying the Commissioners' amounts.

On May 1 of any even-numbered year, the Commissioners' Court posts online the budget as modified in March, and again showing its agreement or modification of citizen entries, along with its reasoning for such modification. The citizens vote a third and final time, either confirming or modifying the Commissioners' amounts, with no further changes admitted.

On September 1 of any even-numbered year, the Commissioners' Court posts online the final two-year budget, which must accept the final third vote of its citizens for each of the budget entry fields. The Court also posts (after the first two-year budget) the amounts to be spent from the *bonum sociale* in each of its posted categories. On September 7 the Court publishes the winner(s) of the sortitions for office, conducted during the first week of the month, and immediately forwards the résumés of the same to the Consilium.

The county *Landesgemeinde* occurs beginning on the third Saturday in September. This is essentially a series of town halls at which the winner(s) of the sortitions present themselves and accept questions from their constituents, and at which the members of the Commissioners' Court describe the effects of the adopted budget and – if their absolute floor budget total is too high – face calls for impeachment. It is to be hoped that the *Landesgemeinde* has an air something like the many Oktoberfests that take place in Texas when the heat begins to break at the end of September – a moment of celebration for what the community has achieved together.

Of course the moronic objection must be answered here: 'Why won't the community give themselves a free ride with picayune taxes, and impeach the Commissioner's Court until they get members to fix the absolute floor budget at next to nothing?' The question assumes the existence of a community so stupid as to foul their own nest by letting their county go to ruin. It assumes that there might exist in Texas a community like San Francisco or Seattle.

Other county powers

Among the county's new powers other than defining its conditions of citizenship and allodial title status are the power to outlaw a citizen or non-citizen, the power to banish the same, and the power to organize its county militia. Outlawry simply means that the outlaw must submit to the private court as chosen solely by the plaintiff and approved by the county, with no choice of courts by the outlaw. Banishment simply means that the banished person's property in the county is sold according to the laws of eminent domain as given by the Republic of Texas, with future acquisition of property within the county forbidden. Details on how the county might organize its militia are given in section 2.5.2, below.

In all administrative senses, unless otherwise stated, "county" signifies the county Commissioners' Court, or any of its delegated offices.

2.3 Law and the Courts
The Constitution of the State of Texas requires the popular election of judges throughout the State. Although this method of selecting judges makes them directly answerable to the public, one might wonder in what sense those who come before the bench are elective "constituents." Majoritarian elections introduce all of the faults of that system into what should be an impartial administration of justice. For example, regarding the issue of elective "name recognition," although he proved to be a capable and highly respected judge, one wonders whether Ron Chapman, a former Dallas County State District Judge and Appellate Court Judge for the State of Texas, gained office because his name was the same as that of a popular announcer for radio station KVIL in Dallas.

In the kleristocratic system, the Consilium draws up the slate of candidates for every judicial post from the résumés submitted for each post, eliminating those not committed to an orderly expansion of arbitration and private law, or not committed to an orderly privatization of criminal law, or not committed to the reduction of public goods; the Republic's legislature either confirms each candidate, or demands that the Consilium select another candidate (if available) from those applying for the stricken candidate's post.

Otherwise, the current qualifications would prevail, with the additional requirement that each judicial candidate be a Texas citizen for at least five years.

The Enumerated Powers of Republican Government
The Texas Constitution, at over 85,000 words, is more than 19 times longer than the U.S. Constitution. While it does preserve a republican government with all political power inherent in the people, the kleristocratic government of the new Republic of Texas is a radical departure from the centralized state model represented by the current Constitution, and thus cannot be grafted upon it by amendment or other editing. It must be rewritten.

The kleristocratic Constitution of the new Republic of Texas must incorporate the salient features of a republican government described in this section.

2.4 National Borders

The new Republic of Texas makes no claims beyond its current territorial boundaries as a State within the United States, except that as an independent nation it reclaims the larger Federal territorial waters as recognized by current international law.

The Republic of Texas assumes full commitment to The Treaty of 23 November 1970 ("1970 Treaty")[12] as the ruling document defining the border between itself and the United Mexican States, and entirely replaces any references to or obligations of the United States – a new dispensation that will be formalized in a new treaty, along with other accords that formalize the friendship between the two nations and their peoples.

It is hoped that free movement of people and of trade between the United States and the Republic of Texas can be maintained as at present. However, possession of a United States passport, of a driver's license from any of its administrative units, or of any other "official" identification entitles the holder to no special benefits beyond the basic rights described in the Texas Constitution, as re-written.

The driver's license currently held by any Texan complies with the United States Real-ID standard, to be enforced May 3, 2023.[13] Therefore, this identification might well suffice for air travel between the two countries. If not, it would seem reasonable that the U.S. Visa Waiver program would apply. As for cross-border vehicular traffic between the two countries, current technology, which Texas would most certainly use, will make it practicable to identify visitors without the need for manned roadblocks.

2.4.1 Citizenship, Immigration, and Naturalization

Citizenship in the Republic of Texas is exclusive, requiring renunciation of all others. It is the prerequisite of county citizenship, previously defined.

To restate, the prerequisite citizenship of the Republic is conferred on the basis of *ius sanguinis* and not *ius soli*; that is, its citizenship is conferred on anyone who has lived in any Texas county for a total of 35 years, disregarding any hiatus, or on anyone who can document lineal descent to, or adoption by, an ancestor who has lived in any Texas county for a total of 35 years, disregarding any hiatus. It is given even if the recipient is born abroad, outside Texas, provided he renounces any other citizenship upon reaching the age of 21. With this residency requirement and with the oath of citizenship in the Republic of Texas below, citizenship is automatic, unlike the conditional county citizenship.

As a practical matter, anyone possessing a valid Texas driver's license or valid Texas ID card will be assumed to be a citizen of the Republic up until the first anniversary of the formal date of secession, after which time the Texas driver's license or Texas ID card must bear an indication as to whether citizenship has been validated by the initial process above, with the oath of citizenship, and must bear an indication of the county where he has been granted its citizenship, if he has received it. When issued, the Texas passport for travel outside the Republic of Texas designates only citizenship in the Republic.

Other details of immigration and naturalization will be provided by statute as determined by the legislature of the Republic of Texas, but not to impair those who were provisional citizens during the year after the formal date secession. During that year there may be a provisional dual citizenship between citizens of the Republic of Texas and citizens of the United States, as determined in the Secession Agreement.

A special consideration might be made for Texans who serve in the U.S. armed forces, and who wish to complete their term of service. There were some 16,500 non-citizens serving in the U.S. military as of 2010, although officers are required to be U.S. citizens.[14] While those details might be accommodated, conflicting oaths of service would remain, since soldiers of both nations pledge to protect one nation to the exclusion of all others.

The passport of the Republic of Texas, its driver's license, and other official IDs shall contain the following printed oath or affirmation, which must be pronounced aloud to, and signed in the presence of,[zzz] an immigration official of the Republic of Texas, or his official delegate:

> By accepting citizenship in the Republic of Texas, I hereby declare that
> - I place the political sovereignty of the Republic of Texas above all others, and will defend its Constitution against all enemies, foreign and domestic, and will support its county militias;
> - I will not support any public policy that initiates violence against others;
> - I will not support any public policy that would be unethical were an individual alone to follow it;[15]
> - I will not support any public policy that would extract or borrow funds for any redistributive scheme.
> - I will not consider religious arguments as final reasoned support for any public policy;
> - And that I make this declaration freely, without any mental reservation or purpose of evasion.

A test for citizenship at the national level,[16, 17, 18] while not opposed in principle, should not be necessary, since there is no need to weed out ignorant voters in a system where no voting takes place.

[zzz] Of course, with appropriate accommodation for the disabled.

2.5 National Defense and War Powers

The Republic of Texas declares itself to be a neutral country, with military alliances or obligations to no one. The secession agreement with the United States will secure the removal, not the leasing, of Fort Hood[19] and other military bases, as well as the Pantex nuclear weapons[20] assembly site near Amarillo.

The mighty defensive shield of the United States, the greatest military machine on earth, whose accounted spending as of 2020 is over $778 billion a year, or more than the military spending of the next ten countries combined[21] – what exactly does this enormous national defense spending purchase for Texas? Exactly what nation directly imperils the lives of Texas citizens? What nation on earth would derive any advantage from an armed invasion or nuclear attack upon Texas? Clearly the only danger to Texas from nuclear attack is through its association with the aggressive provocations of the United States against China[22, 23] and Russia[24, 25] – a danger easily eluded by ending military association with that nation and avoiding any entangling alliance with it.

Let the reader multiply the many provocations at his leisure. He might list the Navy EP-3E spy plane downed on Hainan Island on April 1, 2001, the presence of American military providing training in Taiwan, and the constant saber-rattling against China by those in uniform with their abettors in the fourth estate.

Let the reader himself puzzle over the quivering alarm of America's military leaders before Russia, when the military budget is over half the entire GDP[26] of that country; let him evaluate Russia's responsible handling of its nuclear arsenal by comparing, for example, the behavior of General Curtis LeMay with that of Vasily Arkhipov during the Cuban Missile Crisis of October, 1962.

The sole threat to the citizens of Texas from any foreign country in recent times has been the threat at its southern border from the millions of illegal immigrants who harbor among them violent criminals, the diseased, and a culture and language not easily assimilated with those of Texas – an invasion not stemmed by the Biden administration, but actively encouraged by it.[aaaa] In this most important duty of any nation, that of protecting its citizens – a duty supposedly too staggering for any but a national military – the United States has in effect turned its weapons against Texans, and coerced them into paying for their own humiliation.

This is the vaunted buckler of the United States? *This* is the mess of pottage purchased with the blood and treasure of Texas patriots?

[aaaa] Previously detailed at the outset, in the section "Historical Context."

2.5.1 Armies and Navies

The fear of standing armies by the Founders of the United States is well known,[27] and even their staunch supporter Alexander Hamilton[bbbb] conceded that they must be under legislative control. Thus Article I, Section 8 of the U.S. Constitution insists that only the legislature may "raise and support Armies, but no Appropriation of Money to that Use shall be for a longer Term than two Years" – a quickly forgotten restriction on state power.

In contrast, the Governor of the State of Texas commands the Texas State Guard, the Texas Army National Guard, and the Texas Air National Guard, consulting the legislature only when their provisional funding is exhausted. While these forces are scarcely to be feared as agents of an imperial Governor, one may well question their usefulness. Governor Abbott's declaration of Operation Lone Star in March, 2021, called up thousands of Texas Army National Guard troops to address the invasion of the Rio Grande border. Federal interference quickly frustrated this operation, forbidding deportations and limiting arrests and detentions only for violations of State law, and its minions in the fourth estate swarmed in to ensure punctilious observance of detainee conditions and indigent legal care, so that in a year's time some $4 billion had been spent, funded primarily by raiding other State agencies.[28]

Certainly with independence, the problems caused by the state would not be present, but Operation Lone Star nevertheless exposes the failure of these militaries. The Texas National Guard proved itself to be frankly a nonserious war machine, with many of its soldiers engendering low morale with complaints about lack of delicious food and pleasant accommodation, and grousing that their voluntarily signed commitment had actually taken them from their day jobs.[29]

The ineffectiveness of Operation Lone Star demonstrates the principle that in the modern age, a professional army must be an all-or-nothing affair. That is, a part-time army lacks the vocational commitment to endure the hardships that are actually useful for inspiring high morale and unit cohesion. A part-time army stands no chance against full-time professional war-fighters. And yet, history amply corroborates the fear of such standing professional armies expressed by the Founders of the United States. As the saying goes, if your only tool is a hammer, every problem looks like a nail. In foreign affairs, the United States has repeatedly dismissed possibly more tedious tools to resolve international crises, and reached for the primed and ready hammer of violence, which does not resolve the problem but instead transforms it into a more serious one.

[bbbb] In The Federalist Papers, numbers 8, 24, 26, and 29.

The neutral Republic of Texas therefore maintains no army, navy, or air force. It offers to any invading aggressor no target force whose defeat or surrender would signify the defeat or surrender of the Republic as a whole. In the unlikely event of an aggressive invasion, the Republic of Texas defends itself with a highly trained and patriotic militia, and with a mercenary response aimed at decapitating the aggressor's command, as far down the leadership pyramid as necessary to stop the attack, starting at the top. Those first to fall will not be the deluded grunts on the battlefield, but those sending the sons and daughters of *other* families into harm's way, in smug fatuity that their remote bunkers might protect them from the consequences of their meddling with the free and independent Republic of Texas.

These two arms of defense are discussed in the next two sections.

2.5.2 Militias

Instead of an army, navy, or air force, the county militia defends the Republic of Texas, along with the mercenary response (2.5.3 below) within the Republic's Defense office. Although the public servants of the Republic are by oath and kleristocratic incentive urged to privatization, such a policy must not be considered for its institution of defense against foreign aggression:

> The problem is that private security will almost always choose to work for the highest bidder. And the highest bidder is almost always going to be the bidder with the monopoly on piracy, brigandage, and graft: the state (or the socialists, who are just the state in training).[30]

The vital necessity of the militia is indicated by its being a part of the initial clause of the oath of citizenship in the Republic. The oath states support in general terms for the Republic's county militias. The Republic of Texas will define exemptions from militia service for both conscientious objection or incapacity, and will define the terms under which the county candidly accepts payment in lieu of service. Beyond that, the county establishes further conditions and exemptions as it sees fit. The county might also provide incentives for those who serve, possibly out of the *bonum sociale*, although they should not be necessary: The compelling incentive is that militia service is a requirement for county citizenship, unless exempted. This service is *not* compulsory; however, unexempted refusal to participate must result in the loss of county citizenship. Those who initially voluntarily refuse service may reconsider, so that the loss is not permanent. Thus, as in other cases, a person may be a citizen of the Republic without citizenship in any Texas county.

The Republic's Defense department performs the initial establishment of county militias. Its foremost task is to provide instruction for the creation of an acephalous militia proficient in asymmetrical warfare. Although there should be provision for cooperation among the militia of the many Texas counties, there should be no strategy for mass battlefield formations.

The militia will have no uniforms, no military ranks, no badges, insignia, or distinctions of any formal kind. During the two calendar years of the 18th and 19th birthdays of each Texas citizen, both male and female, six weeks during the months of June and July shall be spent in military readiness training in the citizen's county of residence, under the direction of the militia commander for that county, with the assistance of the chief law enforcement officer of that county and any functionary of the Defense department. On at least one weekend in every year thereafter, the militia must have readiness training, possibly in separate units at different times of the year. It is inevitable that this training establishes a close bond among all the citizens within each Texas county, especially so that each one recognizes his superior not by badges, but by commanding presence and ability.

In case anyone has forgotten the lesson of Afghanistan, one must remember that after 20 years, over 6,000 American dead, and over two trillion dollars expenditure,[31] the most powerful army on earth was humiliated by a few lightly-armed, illiterate goatherds.[32] Consider the fate of this great army when instead confronted by intelligent, highly trained, and angry Texans whose families have been threatened.

To paraphrase the unsubstantiated quote, "Any invader of the Republic of Texas would find a rifle behind every blade of grass."

2.5.3 Letters of Marque and Reprisal

The mercenary response within the Republic's Defense office consists of its director and the few officials within the former Military Preparedness office. Beyond these few, there is no full-time employee performing military services, not even if offered *pro bono*, although consultants with no connections to the United States would be occasionally contracted.

Although the term "privateering" is more accurate, the term "letters of marque and reprisal" is used here because it is specifically mentioned in Article I, Section 8 of the U.S. Constitution as an important part of the war-making powers of Congress, and because bills reaffirming its applicability have been introduced recently in Congress, in 2001 and 2022.

On October 10, 2001, U.S. House member Ron Paul of Texas introduced H.R. 3076, a bill that

> authorizes the President to issue letters of marque and reprisal to all appropriate parties to capture Osama bin Laden and other members of al Qaeda or any other persons involved in the September 11 terrorist attacks [and] to establish a bounty for the capture of Osama bin Laden.[33]

On February 28, 2022, U.S. House member Lance Gooden of Texas introduced H.R. 6869, a bill that

> authorizes the President to issue letters of marque and reprisal to privately armed individuals and entities to seize the assets of certain Russian citizens [and] to employ all means reasonably necessary to seize any asset, such as a yacht or plane, outside of the United States that belongs to a Russian citizen on the Office of Foreign Asset Control's List of Specially Designated Nationals and Blocked Persons.[34]

These bills, and privateering bills in general, do not violate the just war requirement that hostilities be conducted by a public authority, since the private agents – mercenaries if you like – are operating under the direct sanction of a government.

The effectiveness of privateering is a matter of historical record. According to one scholar:

> in Europe between 1600 and 1815, privateers "probably contributed much more than warships to the actual harm done the enemy".[35]

And:

> without the presence of the American privateers in the Revolutionary War and the War of 1812, the United States would never have been able to hold off the British Navy.[36]

Is the mercenary principle effective today? In the recent U.S. wars in the Middle East and elsewhere, mercenaries eventually constituted fully half the deployment.[37] Clearly their contribution was part of the U.S. military failure, but the fact illustrates that the use of mercenaries is neither trivial nor embarrassing.

The mercenary response of the Republic of Texas, having no money-printing capability, would not be so spendthrift. Its Defense department would be engaged in constant research to identify resources for targeted assassination of the leadership of any attacker, from the top to any deterrent depth, and the means for clandestine payment for their services. The measures prepared by the Defense department would be triggered automatically, under strict conditions, so that no public official could be bribed or threatened to remove a fatal reprisal by the Republic. Without being provocative, these measures should be openly and frankly advertised as a program of targeted assassination *but only as a defensive response to aggression* against the neutral Republic, and *only after a formal declaration by its legislature of that aggression*.

Any aggressor against the Republic of Texas might well ask himself: Has that random soldier in the honor guard, that limousine driver, that carpenter, that personal pilot been bought for his service to the Republic of Texas?

Can that armed drone swarm be neutralized before reaching its target? Is every inch of that ground between your state desk and your bunkered home certain to be free of explosive devices? Yahya Ayyash should not have answered his cell phone... – should you answer yours?[38] Are you suffering from a passing headache, or might it be a permanent unpleasantness from microwaves? In short: Do you really want to mess with the Republic of Texas?

2.6 Revenues: Duties, Imposts and Excises, Taxes

Article 8 of the Texas Constitution describes the "Taxation and Revenue" specifics for the State. Local governments currently impose property taxes as their main source of tax revenue – the removal of which has been previously discussed (section 2.2, page 188).

As for the general government, over half the revenue of the State of Texas comes from the sales tax. For the $119.12 billion in revenues extracted for the 2020-2021 biennium,[39] the sales tax provided 54.5%. The other sources were as follows:

- 11.7% fees, investments and other non-tax revenue;
- 10.2% all other State taxes;
- 8.1% motor vehicle sales and rental taxes;
- 6.1% oil production tax;
- 5.0% franchise tax;
- 2.7% natural gas production tax;
- 1.7% motor fuel taxes.

Article I, Section 10 of the U.S. Constitution forbids States from laying "any Imposts or Duties on Imports or Exports" – a provision that would no longer apply with independence. Coincidentally matching the current sales tax percentage, during its nine years as a Republic, Texas had derived more than half of its total income – $1,273,280 out of $2,186,982 – from import duties.[40]

However, the Republic of Texas should avoid the tariff as an instrument of revenue or of any public policy, and instead pursue free trade – indeed, should constitutionally prohibit tariffs. Considering the mutual benefits currently deriving from the generally free trade provisions of the United States-Mexico-Canada Agreement (which slightly modified the 1994 North American Free Trade Agreement, or NAFTA, on July 1, 2020),[41] one would expect Texas to enjoy terms at least as beneficial as that agreement. However, the complete absence of tariffs – not only between the Republic of Texas and the United States, but between it and all nations – would be best of all.

Should a nation resort to "dumping" of its goods in Texas at below-market prices, Texans should rejoice that the exporter has showered a gift upon them at the expense of its own citizens.[42] Should nations impose trade barriers against us for political reasons, the economic loss will be theirs, as Texans find market partners elsewhere.

The most plausible case for "anti-dumping" tariffs is the attempt by a powerful government (e.g., China) to destroy a foreign market by subsidizing the below-cost losses of its domestic supplier. Even if we implausibly assume that the government can sustain those losses forever, the retaliatory tariff still should not be imposed, for several reasons: 1) the tariff often becomes a state revenue source, in disregard of the market it meant to save, 2) every unprofitable domestic market could be justified in its claim to receive such protection, and 3) there is a ready free alternative, in that the affected market could save itself with a campaign of labeling and advertising, convincing consumers to patriotically bear a slightly higher price for the domestic product.

Relying on free trade, there is no need for the Republic of Texas to impose a tariff regime of the World Trade Organization, or any other organization, nor is there any need to enter into a customs union with any country beyond the routine need for establishing standards of uniform and safe product.

With the devolution of power and duties from the central government, with the kleristocratic program of reduction of public goods, and with the disappearance of Federal mandated spending, current taxation should likely prove in need of reduction. One biennial budget cycle as a Republic should provide sufficient data to justify that reduction.

However, as previously suggested (section 1.2.5, page 134), funding of the transition to an independent Republic might err on the side of caution by requiring of citizens a one-time payment of the amount of their last Federal IRS personal income tax to the Republic of Texas in the year of its re-founding, with that amount progressively halved in the following three years, and eliminated in the fourth. If this fund provides a surplus – as it should – it should go into the State's current "rainy day fund."[43]

2.7 Commerce

With a GDP of $1.9 trillion, Texas is the ninth largest economy in the world, according to data from January, 2021[44] – just behind Brazil, France, and the United Kingdom, at $2.054, $2.583, and $2.638 trillion, respectively.[45] Prestigious *Forbes* rankings pronounced the State "first for its growth prospects" in 2019.[46]

For nearly two decades Texas has been the leading exporter among U.S. States, whose $279.3 billion in global export value in 2020 was greater than that of the next three largest U.S. exporting States combined. Although crude petroleum oils account for nearly a quarter of the total, the State is the leading cotton exporter in the U.S. as well as the leading sheep and goat exporter; it ranks second in both beef and wheat exports, and is among the top five U.S. States in the exportation of pecans, sorghum, rice, and dairy products. 37% of the State's agricultural exports go in trade to Mexico. Unsurprising to most Texans, the State has been the United States' leading exporter of technology products. In 2020, the State had $44.8 billion in technology-related exports, leading second-place California's $37.5 billion.[47]

Until very recently, whether administered by the Democrat or Republican party, Texas has enjoyed a relatively frugal government, and as a result has prospered economically.

The more recent administrative offices of the State government reflect a hankering to direct the economic development of the State. This is a fatal conceit[48] that supposes bureaucrats can pick economic winners and losers better than the market. All of the State boards abolished by kleristocracy (Economic Development, Financial, Healthcare, Higher Education, Human Services, Humanities, Regulatory-Professional, Transportation, and others) make presumptive choices, backed by force, that are fully within the functions of the free market. The greatest spur to commerce, the material foundation of the happiness of our grandchildren, and the greatest bond of friendship and peace between nations, is trade, and the wisest policy is for government to stand out of its way.

With independence, the commercial interests of Texas will look outward. As mentioned, Texas has led the United States in exports for nearly two consecutive decades,[49] of which over a third has been with Mexico. The most immediate and natural expansion of its trade will come with that nation, which currently supplies 35% of the orange juice[50] imported into the United States, about 50% of its imported vegetables, and about 40% of its imported fruit.[51] But South Korea also has become an important trade partner because of the advances of Texas in its technology sector, which will certainly a key driver of the Republic's future growth.

2.7.1 Money and Banking

Enacted in 1913, the U.S. Federal Reserve bank of the centralized state has the statutorily declared objective of promoting "maximum employment, stable prices, and moderate long-term interest rates."[52] It has never reliably achieved those objectives. In fact, the worst damage inflicted by the state in peacetime over the last hundred years has been through its manipulation of money and credit in the financial markets through the Federal Reserve. Even *Politico*, a journal almost always favorable to a large and active state, points to the Fed as the very cause of recessions:

> Nine times since 1961, the [U.S.] central bank has embarked on a series of interest rate increases to rein in inflation. Eight times a recession followed. The only true "soft landing" – as significant rate hikes with no subsequent slumps are called – occurred in 1994[.][53]

From a high Federal Funds effective rate of 20% in June, 1981,[54] the Fed has steadily lowered interest rates to the current .75% of May, 2022.[55] This

artificial cheapening of credit occurs primarily in two ways: By the Fed's purchase of Treasury debt and by its setting of the interbank Fed funds rate. When
the Fed buys Treasury debt (the short- and long-term borrowing of the Federal
government for bombers, national parks, Federal office computers, etc.), it
creates money out of thin air by creating a credit for its purchase on its account
in the bank that sold it – typically one of the "primary banks," the largest private banks in the New York Fed's region. This private bank can now lend out
that money up to the limit of the reserve requirement, thereby stimulating economic activity through its borrowers. When the Federal Reserve Board votes to
lower the Fed funds rate (the rate feverishly watched by financial media at the
Fed's eight annual meetings), bank rates linked to it (principally, the prime
rate) attract more borrowers, with loans to them stimulating economic activity.

This artificial cheapening of credit is like the blood-letting of ancient
medicine: With every failure it has caused, the remedy has always been more of
the same traumatic "cure." The low interest rate of about 3% in the 1990s
fueled the "dot-com" or technology stock bubble of 2000-2001; after a rate hike
to 6.5% in May, 2000, the rate fell to 1% in 2003 and was kept there for a year,
stoking the "housing bubble" that burst in 2006;[56] after an attempt at a more
realistic 5.25% rate in 2006 and 2007,[57] the shareholder-owned but state-
backed mortgage lenders Fannie Mae and Freddie Mac, the two largest in the
country, failed amid the 2008 financial crisis and were seized by the Federal
government as it bailed out banks and other institutional investors, eventually
swelling the Federal Reserve balance sheet to its current $8.5 *trillion*,[58] and
lowering interest rates to near zero – with open discussion of making them negative,[59] in effect placing a fine on investment and saving – and igniting inflation
to a 40-year high[60] of well over 8%.[cccc]

The price of an ounce of gold when president Nixon permanently suspended conversion of the U.S. dollar to that "barbarous relic" in August, 1971,
was $290.69. Today an ounce of gold approaches $2,000.00 – an increase in
value of 688%.[61] Over that same period of time, the inflation caused by the
central state's money-printing has dropped the value of a U.S. dollar to 15 cents
– a decline of 85%.[62] It is true that the price of gold fluctuates over the short
term, *as measured by the fiat money that it takes to buy it*; yet its value dramatically increases in comparison with state fiat money over the near and long
term – an objective illustration of the failure of the credit-manipulating regime
of central banking.

This is "stable prices, and moderate long-term interest rates"? *This* is
the means for avoiding recessions?

[cccc] The official Bureau of Labor Statistics rate has understated true inflation since 1990, when it
switched from being a cost of goods index (COGI) to a cost of living index (COLI).

Central bank management of money and credit is in fact a prescription for recessions; it is in fact, like all central state manipulation of money and credit in the financial markets, a prescription for economic collapse – always to be paid for by the taxpayers held at the mercy of the state's financial "experts."

The kleristocratic constitution of Texas, for these reasons, must forbid central banking, and in general forbid all fraudulent manipulations of the supply of money and credit, whether by a state monetarist policy or by private banking. As economist Murray Rothbard stated: "all quantities of money are optimal"[63] in the absence of these manipulations; there is no need to "adjust" the money supply.

It is important to note that the business cycle, with its alternating swings from boom to bust, is not some event external to the system of money and credit that supposedly needs to be "controlled" by a central bank. However, the creation of credit occurs not only by the Federal Reserve – typically by its buying of Treasury debt, as described above – but also by private commercial banks in a fractional reserve system. Rothbard:

> [I]t is not true [...] that central banking is necessary in order to generate this cyclical process. Any bank credit expansion in commercial loans is sufficient to generate the business cycle, whether a central bank exists or not.[64]

Thus a bank with a 10% reserve requirement can create demand deposits of 1 minus 10%, or 90% in excess of its reserves, with the summation of all such banks creating the inverse of the requirement, or 10 times their reserves.[65] In actuality, given the loosening of the definition of what constitutes "reserves," given the authorization of sweep accounts in the 1990s, and given other creative innovations, today's Federal reserve requirement is much lower than 10%,[66] and consequently an even more explosive engine of credit creation.

Thus the re-imposition of a gold standard – while it certainly would prevent inflation and reduce the severity of recessions – would not prevent boom-bust business cycles. There are only two ways to prevent them: Either eliminate fractional reserve banking, or

> arrive at a system where any bank, at the slightest hint of nonpayment of its demand liabilities, is forced quickly into bankruptcy and liquidation. While the outlawing of fractional reserve as fraud would be preferable if it could be enforced, the problems of enforcement, especially where banks can continually innovate in forms of credit, make free banking an attractive alternative.[67]

Digital advances since that writing in 1962 make the enforcement of 100% reserve banking more practicable, so that the catastrophic alternative of bank runs and bankruptcy necessarily associated with free banking can now be avoided. Enforcement of the 100% reserve requirement need not mean a central bank enforcer, as some might fear; enforcement would simply mean an administrative agent for the ordinary legal prohibition of force and fraud.[68]

So then, if a bank can no longer create credit up to the limit of a reserve requirement, how is it to make money? – By the interest on loans based on savings (its loan function), by fees for warehousing depositors' money (its deposit function), and by fees for selling the Republic's bonds (its underwriting function). More speculative resources will not disappear – hedge funds and venture capital funds will still exist – but banks will cease to be a source of speculative investment and cease to be a driver of cyclic recessions.

With the elimination of the recessions associated with the business cycle, there would be no need for the Republic to offer deposit insurance. First, deposit insurance does not work anyway. The Federal Savings and Loan Insurance Corporation did nothing to prevent the savings and loan crisis in the United States in the late 1980s, despite the fact that "FSLIC was precisely to savings and loan banks what the FDIC is to the commercial banking system".[69] Second, such government insurance increases the moral hazard of speculative banking and thus makes the system weaker.[70]

What is to be the money that constitutes the reserve requirement of the Republic of Texas? Gold; gold redeemable on demand in exchange for any currency that the Republic might issue. Thanks to the wisdom of State Representative Giovanni Capriglione, who first proposed establishing a Texas State bullion depository during the 2013 session, and who detailed its creation in HB 3505, the Republic now has its own gold bullion depository, located in Leander, Texas, 28 miles north of the State capitol building.[71] If banks choose to safely store their reserves in Leander, it might be reasonable to require a redemption delay of several days, in consideration of the logistics of transporting gold across the 800-mile depth and breadth of the Republic.

The money of the Republic of Texas in the sense of medium of exchange may circulate as silver coins or hard-to-counterfeit paper bills; but more important is that the Republic's money in the sense of unit of account be based in gold. This money of the Republic of Texas is to be not an independent entity, but a unit of measure: That unit is to be the Texas Mil. A Mil becomes the permanent measure of one one-thousandth of an ounce of 99.9% fine gold. While a unit of the metal of course has an exchange value determined by the market, incapable of any fixing by the government, the unit itself is not an entity that can be handled, any more than a pound or a gram can be handled. To determine an exchange value, supposing an ounce of 99.9% fine gold to have a current market value of $2,000, a Texas Half-Mil would exchange for $1; a Texas Mil for $2; a Texas 10 Mil for $20; and a Texas 100 Mil for $200. Bills larger than this would not be printed since they would be too great an attraction for counterfeiters. If there is to be paper currency for the Republic, these four denominations will constitute it, but again, not as value in themselves but as mere warehouse receipts redeemable on demand at its charter banks for the indicated weight of 99.9% fine gold.

Although it is not absolutely necessary that this gold circulate as the medium of exchange, coins might be struck for 1/4 Mil (50 cents), 1/8 Mil (25 cents), 1/16 Mil (12.5 cents), and 1/32 Mil (7.25 cents). But should they be minted, they would simply be the clearly designated weight of 99.9% fine gold or pure silver, and not some token amalgam of base metal marked with a fiat value (although some base metal ring might be used for convenience to surround a tiny gold piece). Note that if minted in silver, these coins must never state, nor be given to state, a fixed exchange rate between its silver and gold, in order to avoid the arbitrage pitfalls of bimetallism. While the Republic may have a mint, it is not to enjoy a monopoly on the minting of coins in circulation. Any number of private firms may produce the Republic's coins for sale, subject only to government inspection for fineness and uniformity of size and design with specifications provided by statute, with the fees for inspection and compliance not so large as to constitute a franchise. The sale price to retailers, determined by market competition among the providing firms, will provide a small profit to cover their administration, secure transport, and integrity of service. For retail shops accepting the coin, there exist reliable verification devices. For example, Sigma Metalytics sells a small detector that verifies silver, gold, palladium, and platinum in less than a second without damaging the metal.[72] It is inexpensive, but sure to become even less expensive with mass production for retail shops.

As previously stated, the price of gold fluctuates over the short term. But note: *This fluctuation is strictly in terms of the fiat money needed to buy an ounce of gold.* That fluctuation has nothing to do with the function of gold in reckoning market values, which is a key function of stable money, since the price as a unit of gold remains unchanged regardless. For example, a pair of shoes may be valued at 1/20th an ounce of gold or at $100 on Monday; on Friday that same pair of shoes remains valued at 1/20th an ounce of gold, *ceteris paribus*, regardless of whether they now cost $250 in dollar terms.

Several objections must be addressed. One is the belief among central bankers that without their valuable service of providing "some" inflation by adding to the money supply, deflation would result, signifying "a collapse of aggregate demand" and a death spiral of price cutting as producers sought to attract buyers. But this thinking is contrary to the evidence of the deflationary rise in the standard of living from the nineteenth century up to the First World War, when the general fall in prices increased the purchasing power of everyone holding a unit of the deflated currency, conferring the benefits of greater capitalization over the whole society.[73] Another objection is the possibility of a gold drain in the event that Texas introduced gold coins into general circulation, as those outside the Republic bought up those coins. But this would not constitute a "drain," since the introduction of the coins in every case would be accomplished by exchanging them for another currency, say dollars, at the dollar price per ounce of gold plus an amount for seignorage that would constitute a profit for the mint. The exchange would only mean that the mint or mints producing the Texas gold coins would be very busy buying gold with the exchanged currency so as to strike new coins. Texas would welcome such a "drain," since it would mean that its currency was gaining wide acceptance.

As a member of the global financial community, Texas institutions would remain members of the Society for Worldwide Interbank Financial Telecommunications (SWIFT), a system used by over 11,000 institutions to send secure instructions for the movement of money among its members around the world.[74] Although the SWIFT system is not a government entity, central banks have been able to exert influence upon it to impose political sanctions. In 2012, SWIFT disconnected sanctioned Iranian banks, and in 2022, it disconnected certain Russian banks over Russia's invasion of Ukraine. Alternatives to at least some of SWIFT functions are VisaNet, operated by Inovant for VISA credit card transactions, with 21,000 member financial institutions; the Visa International Base II system, providing international transaction processing for 180 currencies; MasterCard International, providing similar services; Clearstream International, operating under Luxembourg law since its founding in 2000, and providing clearing services for securities and precious metals transactions.[75] Alternatives explicitly created with the aim of avoiding the politicization of the SWIFT system are Russia's SPFS (System for Transfer of Financial Messages) and China's CIPS (China International Payments System).[76] All of these alternatives should be mastered by negotiators of Texas secession, in the event that the United States threatens to politicize the financial system to influence those negotiations.

As for the possibility of the United States freezing bank accounts during secession negotiations, the Republic of Texas could not claim sovereign immunity from such an action, since it would have no central bank to represent its sovereign financial standing.[77] Thus the United States could only freeze the accounts of particular banks, or more likely, simply threaten to do so. The current lawlessness of the regime would not prevent such an action. However, the selection of sanctioned banks would present an insurmountable problem, since they are not political agents and since their operations are so deeply enmeshed throughout the United States banking system that the action would severely disrupt its own economy.

Some mention must be made of Bitcoin, to preclude any temptation to officially recognize it by the Republic of Texas. Certainly any proposal to decouple money from government manipulation deserves very sympathetic and serious consideration. However, the following objections prohibit its adoption:

• The key goal in Bitcoin's adoption from the perspective of Austrian economics is its demolition of fractional reserve banking. And yet Mt.Gox, the largest and (formerly) most trusted Bitcoin exchange was accused of doing this very thing before its failure in 2014. There is nothing to prevent fractional banking in the exchanges on a Bitcoin base.

• Bitcoin *can* be hacked, and not only at its most vulnerable point of failure, the exchanges. The 2017 hack of Ethereum resulted in a completely new fork off the point of failure, creating the current Ethereum and Ethereum Classic from the old version. Trust in Bitcoin will be forever undermined by the threat of quantum supercomputing breaking its encryption. In that event – or even the credible threat of that event – all Bitcoin would become worthless overnight.

• The exchanges illustrate another weakness in owning cryptocurrency like Bitcoin. Owners can hold their Bitcoin in a personal wallet, but since transactions and passwords are difficult to manage, many owners rely on the exchanges to simplify their use. Once in an exchange, not only can the cryptocurrency be hacked, as just noted, but it can be confiscated as part of the bankruptcy proceedings of the exchange, should that happen. The first quarter 2022 Coinbase loss of $430 million and 19% drop in monthly users illustrated this possibility.[78] Depositors are not insulated from the institutional failure in another way: There is no deposit insurance.

• At the retail level, Bitcoin must overcome the increasing lag in finalizing transactions as they propagate through an ever-growing distributed ledger.

• At the wholesale level, Bitcoin must become a medium of exchange widely accepted enough to, say, seal a contract for a million barrels of oil without fear of catastrophic loss should Bitcoin lose value.

• Bitcoin use at both the retail and wholesale level is crippled by its speculative volatility. Even supposing that Bitcoin becomes the de facto cryptocurrency, speculation in non-serious competitors undermines its adoption. Having witnessed the Bitcoin mania, deracinated from any notion of value that a commodity basis might provide, dozens of other competitor cryptos foster their own bubbles – easily done with promotion by a media figure like Elon Musk, who has promoted Dogecoin, originally created as a spoof but now a money candidate, or Shiba Inu, another spoof that now contends as money. But more importantly, because it is currently only a speculative medium, nothing can overcome the reluctance to put down a fraction of a Bitcoin for a slice of pizza when tomorrow that fraction might double in value. For larger wholesale transactions, the reluctance is even greater. Ironically, its success has doomed Bitcoin to remain a speculative instrument rather than a money medium.

• Bitcoin must controvert Austrian monetary theory that says all money originates in, and must be ultimately convertible to, some commodity. Austrian economist Frank Shostak: "An object cannot be used as money unless it already possesses an exchange value based on some other use."[79] This is the statement of von Mises' Regression Theorem. Laura Davidson offers a solution to this problem, saying that some price structure, and not commodity status, has priority, and furthermore:

> If the regression theorem says that money can only arise out of a commodity, and 'commodity' means tangible good, then that theorem is wrong. Assuming bitcoin is a money (it is not yet generally accepted, although one day it might be) the regression theorem is wrong because bitcoin is not, and was never, a commodity. On the other hand, if the regression theorem says that money must arise out of something that is of value, then the regression theorem is correct.[80]

While one must emotionally cheer the success of cryptocurrencies like Bitcoin, prudence demands that they first overcome these difficulties before any national adoption.

2.7.2 Borrowing on the Credit of the Republic

As previously noted, Texas has been blessed for the most part by wise and frugal administration of its public finances, regardless of political affiliation. Enforcing that wise administration are the State's balanced budget requirement (mandated by its Constitution in Article 3, Section 49),[81] the Governor's Office of Budget, Planning, and Policy (GOBPP) that sets guidelines and goals for administrative agencies, the Legislative Budget Board (LBB) that evaluates the budget requests of all those administrative agencies and marks with fiscal notes the probable cost of any bill by the legislature (LBB being created in 1949 by Senate Bill 387, and becoming law in that year),[82] the Governor's power of line item veto to reject parts of the State budget, and the limitation of the legislature's threat to the commonwealth in only odd-numbered years.[83] Under kleristocracy, the Governor's powers would be assumed by the Consilium.

There are two types of State debt, according to the way it is secured: General obligation (GO) bonds, secured by the full faith and credit of the State; and revenue bonds, secured by specific revenue sources. In 2020, GO bonds made up about 29% of the total debt; 64% of the total was self-supporting, meaning that they were not funded out of general revenues.[84] The about 2/3 total for self-supporting is good, in that it does not subtract from general revenues, and might well be enforced by statute, except that it seems to be observed as a practical matter anyway. Upon becoming a Republic some restriction upon burdening its full faith and credit might be revisited. Counties, cities, school districts, and college districts are able to issue debt, which the counties, at least, have done responsibly. The recent increase in county indebtedness is largely owing to unfunded mandates imposed by the State, which should be addressed.

2.8 Infrastructure, Capital

Texas has been blessed with many natural advantages, particularly the life blood of the industrialized West, oil. It has 43% of the U.S. crude oil production, 25% of the U.S. marketed natural gas production, 32% of the U.S. refining capacity,[85] its own independent power grid, its own gold bullion depository, deep water ports, robust agricultural and technological sectors, as previously described (section 2.7, page 200), and a powerful tradition of private property, given the fact that over 95% of property is privately owned, with less than 2% "owned" by the Federal Union and its bureaucrats.[86]

"Infrastructure" should signify plant and long-term capital investment, but somehow, when the term enters public policy discussion it becomes a bag of Christmas toys for countless political interests.[87] Direction of economic activity cannot be the business of government: It cannot have the information to determine the "true" needs of its citizens – only the price determinations of the free market can do that. Free enterprises that misinterpret that information go out of business; governments never go out of business, and as previously shown, tend to double down on their errors, throwing good money after bad. Kleristocracy limits governmental policy interference on market determinations by confining those policies to the smallest possible unit of government, the county, where direct supervision by local citizenry can correct policy errors. Furthermore, the system of sortition at the heart of kleristocracy limits the lust for spending by self-aggrandizing politicians by making them disinterested, temporary servants of the government, following as much as possible the Swiss model, which has succeeded in encouraging that vital patriotic impulse of service from its most capable citizens.

2.8.1 Transportation

One of the biggest infrastructure expenditures for the vast expanse of Texas is for roads and bridges. This infrastructure is primarily the responsibility of the counties, which have no ability to concoct ostentatious State-wide schemes such as a high-speed rail or that perennial boondoggle to make the Trinity River navigable to the city of Dallas. From 2009 to 2011, Texas allocated 82% of its budget to its road funding on expansion.[88] This is surely a misallocation: The transportation infrastructure problem is really a maintenance problem. As one observer put it:

> We build without seeming to appreciate that every mile of fresh new road will one day become a mile of crumbling old road that needs additional attention.[89]

Certainly experts at the national level can provide valuable instruction for methods that reduce the maintenance costs associated with transportation infrastructure while simultaneously foreseeing future needs. But their planning must be constrained by the fact that the counties bear the burden of putting it into effect.

2.8.2 Power Grid

Texas is the only State among the 48 contiguous States with its own independent power grid. 90% of the State's population gets electricity from the Electric Reliability Council of Texas (ERCOT) grid, which operates solely within the State, therefore is subject not to interstate regulation by the Federal Energy Regulatory Commission (FERC) but is subject only to regulation by the Public Utility Commission (PUC) of Texas. The remaining 10% of Texans get electricity from the Western Electricity Coordinating Council (WECC), the Southwest Power Pool (SPP), and the Southeastern Electric Reliability Council (SERC), which because they also operate in other States, are fully subject to FERC regulation. The grid itself is separate, managed by six transmission and distribution utilities (TDU). The more than 710 power stations of all four electricity producers generated 473,880 gigawatt-hours (1 GWh = 1 million kWh) of electricity for Texans in 2020.[90]

No serious discussion of the Texas power grid can fail to address the outages that resulted from the ice storm that struck the State in mid-February, 2021. Indeed, the event is a perfect microcosm proving the necessity of secession to form an independent republic. The event perfectly illustrates the fatal characteristics of the centralized state: Its almost hysterical animus against any institution independent of its power; its reflexively offered solution of ever more state power; and its dogmatically asserted infallibility, demanding that all rival solutions be rejected on the standard of perfect hindsight, while its own solutions be evaluated solely on dubious future proof, beyond empirical scrutiny.

At the beginning of the ice storm, ERCOT, despite being free of one Federal tentacle, the FERC, nevertheless had to beg permission from the Department of Energy to increase natural gas production that might conceivably have exceeded Federal pollution regulations.[91] Yet in the middle of that storm, before all the data was available for a reasoned evaluation of the causes of the outage, New York Senator Chuck Schumer immediately flew to Texas to harangue its citizens that they needed not less, but *more* Federal regulation to enforce its crusade against "climate change."[92] The echo chamber of the fourth estate also immediately leapt into action before the ice storm concluded, howling the boilerplate tropes that more regulation would of course have foreseen all the issues[93] and that corporate greed was to blame for everything.[94]

A mature and fact-based assessment of causes was delivered the following April by the Reason Foundation.[95] While Texas leads the United States in the production of renewable energy (of the State's generation, wind power is 23%, nuclear 11%, and solar 2%),[96] the researchers found that it was not true that power outages were due to the failure of any one of these alone. Their study found that ERCOT administrators had acted reasonably, given the environmental conditions prevailing in Texas, and given its necessary reliance upon natural gas for about half its energy production. Some of their findings:

• "All types of power plants failed: wind, natural gas, coal, and nuclear." (page 3)

• "Natural gas wells and pipelines began freezing up" and with industrial electricity reduced to relieve stress on the grid (since homes get priority), they could not pump more gas to meet demand. (page 2)

• "While natural gas pipelines can obtain critical load designation, protecting them from rolling outages, many pipelines had failed to submit the information needed to their local power delivery company. At its worst, as much as 9,000 MW of generation was sidelined by the lack of gas supplies, in part due to power cut offs at gas pipelines." (page 10)

• "At its low point, natural gas production in Texas was as much as 45% below week-earlier levels according to the Energy Information Administration, even as demand for gas was soaring." (page 10)

• "[T]he loss of natural gas generation capacity was the biggest error in ERCOT's winter season resource adequacy analysis. Had natural gas capacity performed as assumed, the scale and duration of outages would have been dramatically smaller." (page 11)

• "Some winterization techniques employed farther north would reduce summer power plant reliability in Texas. For example, enclosing portions of Texas power plants now exposed to the weather would have protected them against freezing, but would make summer operations more challenging." (page 22)

In contrast to the Reason Foundation research, it is hard to find a difference on climate policy between the emotional screaming of an ignorant Swedish teenager and the Biden administration, which six months after the ice storm offered a candidate for the Office of the Comptroller of the Currency, Saule Omarova, who said, "We want them [the oil, coal and gas industries] to go bankrupt if we want to tackle climate change."[97] This is dogmatic ignorance, and membership in the Federal Union enforces obedience to it.

While it is true that fossil fuel combustion has contributed to the rise in global temperatures of about 1°C since 1870,[98] and that CO_2 enrichment of the atmosphere is affecting its chemistry and that of the oceans, the fact is that modern industrial society can be powered in just two ways: By fossil fuels and by nuclear power.[99] No other energy source can match their energy density and reliability. No alarmist state "war on climate change" can change these facts; denial can only lead to an exacerbation of the problems and to an extravagant waste of money.[100] The deontological war footing so reflexively demanded by the state to justify yet another expansion of its power is ballyhooed by its sycophant fourth estate using anecdotal sensationalism about the weather, with no basis in statistical fact.[101]

At the root of the current of counterproductive energy policy afflicting virtually all Western democracies is the failure to see the necessity for *more* economic development, the subordination of reasoned policy to apocalyptic alarmism, the hysterical ignorance about the safety of nuclear power, and most pervasively of all, the dogmatic insistence on state-enforced policies to be adopted with complete blindness to the fact that all solutions have costs.

Thanks to economic development, there has been a 92% decline in the death toll from natural disasters since its peak in the 1920s – and that during a period when world population quadrupled.[102] Thanks to economic development, the United Nations Food and Agriculture Organization (FAO) forecasts crop yields increasing 30% by 2050, with the poorest parts of the world, like sub-Saharan Africa, increasing by 80 to 90%.[103] The rise in global temperatures must be saluted for part of that increase:

> Wheat yields increased 100 to 300% around the world since the 1960s, while a study of 30 models found that yields would decline by 6% for every one degree Celsius increase in temperature.[104]

And how is alarmism justified, for example, when even the Intergovernmental Panel on Climate Change (IPCC) offers skepticism on estimates that the sea level could rise two feet (0.6 meters) by 2100?[105] Will the problem be addressed by some despotically imposed globalist scheme, or by localized solutions based on sound economics? Some parts of the Netherlands are *seven meters* below sea level;[106] are its citizens paralyzed by fear of a relatively miniscule rise over the course of a century?

All solutions have costs. State-imposed solutions presume to ignore this inescapable truth because they are in fact based on deontological moral imperatives (see page 90), not on a consideration of economic trade-offs. Old solar panels and lithium-ion batteries are toxic waste. They are harmful to the poor who scavenge them in the Third World countries that have increasingly become the dumping grounds of the West. A recent study by the *Harvard Business Review* (HBR) found that "the waste produced by solar panels will make electricity from solar panels four times more expensive than the world's leading energy analysts thought",[107] and produce an amount of waste 50 times greater in just four years than International Renewable Energy Agency (IRENA) projections.

The lithium in the lithium-ion batteries that are supposed to replace gasoline-powered automobiles is toxic and requires huge amounts of groundwater to extract. In Chile, mining activities in the dry Salar de Atacama region consume 65 per cent of the area's water. Lithium-ion batteries are prone to fires that are difficult to put out. For that reason, Dell recalled four million lithium-ion batteries in 2006; Samsung discontinued its Note 7 in 2016; Hewlett-Packard recalled over 100,000 laptops in 2019. Fires originating in the battery in Chevrolet Bolt vehicles are estimated to have cost General Motors around $2 billion; and Audi recalled its E-Tron SUV because of battery fires.[108]

The proposal to have biofuels replace petroleum products fails to consider a very important trade-off:

> Even the most efficient biofuels, like those made from soybeans, require 450 to 750 times more land than petroleum. The best performing biofuel, sugarcane ethanol, widely used in Brazil, requires 400 times more land to produce the same amount of energy as petroleum.[109]

The policy issue probably most immune to reasoned discussion is that of nuclear energy.[110] The paradigm of proof of that view is the March, 1979 Three Mile Island incident in Pennsylvania, which killed no one yet which the fourth estate managed to turn into a toxic cloud of anti-nuclear hysteria.[111]

> Anti-nuclear activists have long claimed that there is a trade-off between nuclear safety and economics when it comes to the operation of plants, when in reality the opposite is the case. With improved performance came far higher income from electricity sales. [...] The question is not how humans can gain absolute mastery, since that's impossible, but rather which machines, on balance, deliver the most good with the least harm. On that metric, nuclear power has always been, inherently, the safest way to power civilization.[112]

Thanks to François Mitterrand's wonderful political duplicity, France embarked upon a national program of nuclear electrification in 1981.[113] Its success was based on a single design that featured simplicity and safety, repeated all over the country, unlike the American policy of complex installations unique to every location, creating headaches for inspection, maintenance, and operator training.

Currently France stands apart from all of Europe in generating over 70% of its electric power from nuclear,[dddd] and is the only G7 country that invests more in nuclear energy than renewables. President Macron plans to add

---

[dddd] In autumn 2022, over half of France's 56 reactors were taken offline temporarily to perform maintenance (against corrosion) that had been postponed during the pandemic. Anti-nuclear activists tried to raise an outcry that this somehow demonstrated a "failure" of nuclear energy.

six more conventional nuclear reactors by 2044. With equal ambition, the nation is developing small modular reactors:

> Basically they're teeny reactors that can generate 300 MW – enough to power 126,000 homes – and can be pre-manufactured and assembled on site (meaning the technology has high export potential, which is why major firms in China, Russia, the US, and Japan are working on prototypes).[114]

These modular reactors seem ideally suited for deployment in Texas counties, and the new kleristocratic Technology office should immediately explore that possibility, with the hope of giving France the first large national contract for their installation – a fitting recompense to the first nation to recognize the original Republic of Texas in 1839.[115]

There are other exciting innovations in prospect for nuclear energy, for example the non-light water nuclear reactors,[116] and the Technology office of the Republic of Texas certainly will have the expertise to evaluate them for the safety of all its counties.

2.8.3 Technology

Given the expansion of citizen participation in kleristocracy, a robust and secure online government presence is vital. The nation of Estonia has done this (see page 124), and certainly Texas has the talent to realize this indispensable part of its infrastructure as one of its very first priorities.

While the importance of the future new Technology office was emphasized in the just-cited section, such expertise has always been vital to the people of Texas, as witness its role in providing technical support for Crime Stoppers, Emergency Communications, Emergency Management, and One-Call. The Consilium is certain to prioritize its funding in the legislative agendas that it presents to the biennial legislature.

2.9 Infrastructure, Human

Texas has been blessed with many natural advantages, and many advantages that might be classified as capital infrastructure. But as former Lieutenant Governor Bill Hobby wisely observed:

> If Texas was going to be important in the future, it would depend on what came out of people's heads, and not what came out of the ground.[117]

It will doubtless be the human infrastructure, the human capital of Texans, that leads its transformative restoration as an independent republic, when "Texas will again lift its head and stand among the nations."[118]

2.9.1 The General Welfare

The Republic of Texas must not be deluded by any expansive construction of "the general welfare," whether from its several mentions in its Constitution, or from any other source. It is the county, not the national government, that has the best knowledge of what promotes the welfare of its citizens. The national government of the Republic best fulfills its function in this regard by a consistent enforcement of its laws, by its non-interference with commerce, and by the oath of its public servants to reduce the number of public goods.

As part of the accurate measure of the "general welfare," Texas will conduct its own national decennial census, with no references as in its current Constitution to "decennial census of the United States," "United States census," "Federal census," or the like.

2.9.2 Social Security

Possibly the greatest source of concern from ordinary Texans about secession is the threat of losing their Federal Social Security benefits. It is a sad testament to the servile dependency indoctrinated in its subjects by the central state that there is such a fear of loss of what will be for many their only source of retirement income – a picayune amount that will keep them in bondage to the end of their days.

To understand the precarious and frankly immoral state of the Social Security funds, one must first understand that this "trust fund" is not a trust fund at all. As the Office of Management and Budget explained in 1999:

> These [trust fund] balances are available to finance future benefit payments and other trust fund expenditures – but only in a bookkeeping sense. These funds are not set up to be pension funds, like the funds of private pension plans. They do not consist of real economic assets that can be drawn down in the future to fund benefits. Instead, they are claims on the Treasury, that, when redeemed, will have to be financed by raising taxes, borrowing from the public, or reducing benefits or other expenditures.[119]

Thus there were only IOUs from the start, and never any real assets in the fund – it was always "stuffed full of IOUs."

To clarify: Social Security (OASDI) is funded by the payroll tax, which rate is the 6.2% paid out of wages that employees and employers each pay (a total of 12.4%) into the Federal Treasury. (The fund also earns about 7% of its income on interest from securities and about half that on taxes on benefits.) But the Social Security trust fund does not get any of that money: The government spends the "real" money, and this is what constitutes its "raiding" or "looting" of the fund. The fund merely gets an accounting "credit" – an IOU – from the Treasury in the form of an exclusive bond issued only to the fund. This exclusive character is what really defines these bonds as IOUs. When the fund needs the money to pay benefits, it redeems the bonds, which are paid by the Treasury out of general revenues.[120] Therefore, the trust fund is really just an accounting device to indicate how much the government has borrowed from Social Security, without providing resources to finance future benefits. Taxation is the true revenue source. The most recent annual report of this balance states:

> The Old-Age and Survivors Insurance (OASI) Trust Fund, which pays retirement and survivors benefits, will be able to pay scheduled benefits on a timely basis until 2033, one year earlier than reported last year. At that time, the fund's reserves will become depleted and continuing tax income will be sufficient to pay 76 percent of scheduled benefits.[121]

This digression should provide sufficient evidence that the only honest way to assure a retirement fund is to create a true trust fund; and since the free market is fully capable of providing that service, with severe penalties for frauds like those just described, government meddling in offering it adds only one thing: The possibility of theft, under the moral cloak of "helping the aged and infirm."

Benefits earned up to the moment of secession would be guaranteed by "totalization agreements" between the Federal government and the new Republic. The U.S. Social Security Administration defines these agreements as

> benefit protection for workers who have divided their careers between the United States and another country. Agreements to coordinate Social Security protection across national boundaries have been common in Western Europe for decades.[122]

Thus ordinarily if a Texan has worked 20 years in the United States, then works 10 years in, say, Spain, the Federal government would pay 20/30, or 2/3 of his retirement benefit and Spain 1/3. Totalization with Texas would be much the same, *with one very important difference:* The remaining third of the benefit would be paid not by the Republic of Texas, but by a private trust established for that purpose, assuming that the Republic required every worker to establish a retirement trust, possibly seeded by the Republic. There would be no other meddling by the government other than the inspection of solvency of the trust provider, the enforcement of a minimum contribution by employer and employee, and enforcement of rules for access of funds so that they remain available for retirement. The banks or other fiduciary agents might well provide this service of creating and maintaining the trust, which would travel with the worker.

2.9.3 Healthcare

National health care rests on the egalitarian assumption that a poor man is entitled to as much healthcare as a rich man. This assumption prompts the measurable policy question: To what extent are citizens financially responsible for the bad healthcare decisions of their fellow citizens? Mortal flesh is heir to disease and injury, which often strikes at random, and against those possibilities insurance pools the risk. But for the chain smoker, the man who drinks a liter of vodka every week, or the one who refuses moderate exercise – are all their fellow citizens to pay the health consequences? The truth is that whatever our genetics or financial situation, conscious choices and good habits influence much of our health; aside from random disease and injury, good health is a function of managed care.

Given the importance of managed care, who is to manage it? Government must always apply universal rules for its distribution of public healthcare goods, or else it must resort to their distribution by agents empowered to make arbitrary choices. The citizen can't shop bureaucrats to find the one to write a government check to suit his needs. In the free market, he most certainly can shop around to find the provider most suitable for his lifestyle and financial situation. The provision of healthcare as a public good simply cannot overcome the problem of the commons (see page 133), and it is more subject to the problem of moral hazard than private providers.

Government, however, can help overcome some of the knowledge problem associated with selecting healthcare. That is, although the current Healthcare board is abolished, the Republic of Texas might create an office within the Public Education board for the dissemination of several defined levels of care, and inspect compliance among those private insurers who advertise that they offer the described level.

As for Federal Medicare coverage, it is currently financed jointly by employer and employee from payroll, much like Social Security: The rate is 1.45% each, for a 2.9% total.[123] Certainly temporary transition coverage must be provided to those who have come to depend on Medicare. The fund for this transition might come from the savings to Texas from the removal of Federal mandates, from the temporary IRS diversion (see page 134), and from a slight increase in the rate. The fund must have a "sunset" provision by which it dissolves after transition to private coverage.

Texas veterans of the U.S. military will continue to receive benefits for service-connected disabilities through the Veterans Administration's Foreign Medical Program, no matter where they live.[124]

To those who complain that Medicare and similar state-provided services are "too important" to be left to the private sector, one observation should be sufficient: What could be more important than food? Would you like the state to be in complete command of providing it? Or would continuation of the current "Wild West" provision by the free market be all right with you?

2.9.4 Public Schools

School and state must be separated, just as church and state are separated, and for the same reasons. Every family's spiritual values are projected into the future by means of the education of its children. The results of foolishly entrusting to state officials so important a task as schooling are now manifest. All across the country kindergarteners and elementary school children are now being subjected to "transgender story hour,"[125] to instruction in "gender fluidity,"[126] to denial of biology,[127] and even instruction in how to masturbate.[128] At the secondary level, boys' restrooms in Oregon must now by force of law supply free feminine hygiene products;[129] and at the university level, students are taught that pederasty is not a mental disease.[130] The state cannot even provide the most basic assurance of physical safety to students.[131, 132, 133]

Current events demonstrate that it is completely false to suppose that any school can teach some "value-neutral" set of civic values, or even "value-neutral" instruction in reading, writing, and arithmetic when the instructor stands before students as a flamboyant role model for sexual perversity. In every case, instruction conveys spiritual value, or in the current culture, the lack of it:

> The quality of virtue, meaning that some things and some doings are recognizably better than others, was deceitfully replaced by the equity of nothing being allowed to be better than anything else. Truth and beauty have gone outlaw. Bad faith and wickedness rule, led by a Party of Chaos.[134]

Texas currently spends over $33 billion dollars annually on elementary and secondary public schools, or about $6,000 per student.[135] It should be evident that any parent can better educate his children, especially in spiritual instruction, with $6,000 available each year for each of them.

In comparison with the relatively frugal State and county spending, public school districts – and cities, it might be noted – have been irresponsibly profligate. Although more than 98.4% of school district debt outstanding is voter-approved, with debt service limited to a maximum of $0.50 per $100 of valuation (Texas Education Code, Section 45.0031),[136] nevertheless school districts have managed to impose $5,011 of the total $8,500 per capita debt[137] ($375.7 *billion* overall) of local government in the State. Since this debt is financed through local property taxes, it is no surprise that Texans live under the sixth-most burdensome property tax system in the United States.[138] However, in November, 2021, a majority of school district bonds failed voter approval for the first time since 2011. Doubtless this awakening was due to the

State legislature's passage of two bills in 2019: House Bill 3, which requires on every school bond proposition the statement: "THIS IS A PROPERTY TAX INCREASE"; and Senate Bill 30, which requires bonds for construction unrelated to teaching (e.g., football stadiums,[139] swimming pools, performing arts buildings, etc.) to be voted upon separately, instead of as a "take it or leave it" package deal.[140] Much of the profligate public school spending has been financed by capital appreciation bonds (CABs), by which the entire principal and interest are deferred until maturity – an instrument outlawed in some States because of its risk and its option of rolling into yet another CAB at maturity. Alarmed at the practice, State legislators passed House Bill 114 in 2015, disallowing a district with more than 25% of its debt in CABs to issue more. At the time of the bill's passage, some districts' CAB debt was over 70%.[141]

In spite of this extravagance in school spending, the performance of Texas high school students remains mediocre at best, whether using national[142] measures or its own STAAR testing standard.[143] It should be obvious that the current system is more a feeding trough for public school bureaucrats (see page 31) rather than an educational system. Texans can do better than this.

By the third anniversary of the formal date of secession, there shall exist no public funding whatsoever for elementary and secondary public schooling nor for any agency related to the same within the Republic of Texas.

On the first anniversary of the formal date of secession, the Texas Education Agency shall be abolished, and all its functions (with the exception of services related to personnel transition described below), along with the temporary administration of each of its over one thousand elementary and secondary public school districts, shall then pass to the Commissioners' Court in the county within which the principal area of its district exists at the date of secession. Each Court so charged with at least one district shall appoint a sixth member, not of their number, without voting rights, and serving at their pleasure, who shall administer the sale and shall administer these school functions until the sale out of public ownership of all school properties under the Court's administration, with the purely advisory, nonbinding counsel of the elected school board of each district charged to the Court's administration. The office of this additional sixth member expires on second anniversary of the formal date of secession, or on the completion of the sale of all the county's public school properties, whichever occurs first. If on the second anniversary of the formal date of secession the Commissioners' Court has not effected the sale of all its elementary and secondary public school properties, then the temporary administration of the unsold district, and the administration of its sale, shall be effected by the Republic of Texas, as specified by statute, to be completed within one year of being charged with this duty.

The Republic of Texas, as specified by statute, shall create an agency, existing for no more than three years and not composed of any member of the

Texas Education Agency or of any former public school teacher, for the purpose of assuring orderly disbursement of proceeds from the sale of its elementary and secondary public schools and agencies. All Texas Education Agency capital and all services related to the dismissed school administrators and teachers such as credit unions shall be sold, with the total proceeds divided proportionally among the school districts according to enrollment, and added to the proceeds of each school's sale, forming a unique total for each school district. From each unique total, pensions, severance packages, and other remuneration for teachers and administrators shall be disbursed frugally, with no former school district administrator in total receipt of an amount greater than the highest total receipt of any full-time classroom teacher of that same district. Also from each unique total, disbursement shall be made to each district property owner having paid an assessed school tax at the date of the district's sale, disbursed in proportion to the tax paid. None of these disbursements is lump-sum, but according to the period specified for receipt of proceeds in the district's terms of sale. After provision for county administrative expenses, for former Texas Education Agency employees, for former elementary and secondary public school employees, and for former property tax payers, no elementary and no secondary public school funds shall exist.

There can be no independent Texas without the independence of parents to fully direct the private schooling of their own children.

As for the State post-secondary schools, all tenure will be revoked. All schools and colleges of the humanities (including education, public affairs, all social sciences, political science, and every program listed under Liberal Arts in the 1922 bulletin of the University of Texas at Austin) will be immediately dissolved and all instructors dismissed, although of course accrued benefits will honored upon retirement. The remaining schools and colleges of every type (including but not limited to junior colleges, community colleges, and vocational schools) will be privatized, although possibly 10 years might be allowed for the transition to private ownership to avoid a "fire sale" devaluation of the considerable capital investment, especially in state-funded science research facilities. The gain from privatization will go into the existing "rainy day fund."[144]

2.10 Excluded Powers

Insofar as possible, national and local governments of the Republic of Texas are denied monopoly powers for the performance of any public service when there is any reasonable private alternative. For example, there will be no government monopoly on the delivery of mail.

Similar to the U.S. Constitution's Article I, Section 10 limitations on the power of States, Texas counties are forbidden to engage in foreign diplomacy, conduct war, coin money, impair contracts, grant special favors or titles, interfere with commerce between or among counties, or interfere with the administration of justice throughout the Republic of Texas.

In general, current State law prevails except as detailed above to institutionalize kleristocracy.

[1] Quincy, Edmund, *Life of Josiah Quincy of Massachusetts* (Cambridge University Press, fifth edition, 1867), page 212. Online at <https://quod.lib.umich.edu/m/moa/ABP2687.0001.001?rgn=main;view=fulltext> accessed March 22, 2022.

[2] "Texas Constitution: Includes Amendments Through the November 2, 2021, Constitutional Amendment Election," *Texas Legislative Council* (last edited April 1, 2022) <https://tlc.texas.gov/docs/legref/TxConst.pdf> accessed April 28, 2022.

[3] "Laws and Rules, The Sunset Act," *Texas Sunset Advisory Commission* (last edited March 31, 2022) <https://www.sunset.texas.gov/about-us/laws-and-rules> accessed April 27, 2022. Effectively, the Consilium assumes governance of this commission.

[4] "Appointed Positions," *Office of the Texas Governor* (last edited March 23, 2022) <https://gov.texas.gov/organization/appointments/positions> accessed April 28, 2022.

[5] "County Judges and Commissioners Association of Texas 2021 Resolutions," *County Judges and Commissioners Association of Texas* (draft published October 13, 2021) <https://31j8fe2l56f122iue1wuvve1-wpengine.netdna-ssl.com/wp-content/uploads/2021/10/CJCAT21-Resolutions.pdf> accessed May 2, 2022.

[6] Brooks, David B., *Guide to Texas Laws for County Officials* (Texas Association of Counties, November 2021), page 64. Online at <https://www.county.org/TAC/media/TACMedia/Legal/Legal%20Publications%20Documents/2021/2021-Guide-to-Laws-for-County-Officials.pdf> accessed May 2, 2022.

[7] "Texas County Judge," *Texas Association of Counties*, referencing Vernon's Ann. Texas Const. Art. 5, §15; V.T.C.A., Election Code §141.001 (no publication date) <https://www.county.org/About-Texas-Counties/About-Texas-County-Officials/Texas-County-Judge> accessed May 2, 2022.

[8] "Property Tax Bills," *Texas Comptroller of Public Accounts* (last edited January 21, 2022) <https://comptroller.texas.gov/taxes/property-tax/bills/index.php> accessed April 9, 2022.

[9] O'Neill, Tyler, "Parents outraged after teacher mocks 'bigots,' 'evangelicals' in Dr. Seuss-style poem at school board meeting," *Fox News* (published December 24, 2021) <https://www.fox7austin.com/news/parents-outraged-after-teacher-mocks-bigots-evangelicals-in-dr-seuss-style-poem-at-school-board-meeting> accessed May 5, 2022.

[10] Mill, John Stuart, *On Liberty* (Project Gutenberg eBook #34901, published January 10, 2011) <https://www.gutenberg.org/files/34901/34901-h/34901-h.htm> accessed May 5, 2022. The reference is to pages 201-202 of the 1859 original.

[11] "LOCAL GOVERNMENT CODE; TITLE 3. ORGANIZATION OF COUNTY GOVERNMENT; SUBTITLE B. COMMISSIONERS COURT AND COUNTY OFFICERS; CHAPTER 87. REMOVAL OF COUNTY OFFICERS FROM OFFICE," *Texas Constitution and Statutes* (last edited March 8, 2022) <https://statutes.capitol.texas.gov/Docs/LG/htm/LG.87.htm> accessed May 5, 2022.

[12] "Rio Grande/Rio Bravo," *International Waters Governance* (last edited November 13, 2021) <http://www.internationalwatersgovernance.com/rio-granderio-bravo.html> accessed May 7, 2022.

[13] "REAL ID Frequently Asked Questions," *U.S. Department of Homeland Security* (last edited May 6, 2022) <https://www.dhs.gov/real-id/real-id-faqs> accessed May 10, 2022.

[14] Thompson, Mark, "Non-Citizens Make Better U.S. Soldiers," *Time* magazine (published April 06, 2012) <https://nation.time.com/2012/04/06/non-citizens-make-better-u-s-soldiers/> accessed May 8, 2022: "Non-citizens have to be legal permanent residents of the U.S., have a high school diploma, and speak English well enough to meet each service's requirements, in order to enlist. All regular U.S. military officers must be U.S. citizens. There were 16,500 non-citizens serving in uniform in mid-2010, constituting 1.4% of the enlisted force. There were 16,500 non-citizens serving in uniform in mid-2010, constituting 1.4% of the enlisted force."

[15] Hoppe, Hans-Hermann, ed., *The Myth of National Defense* (Mises Institute, October 16, 2003, ISBN 978-0945466376, 453 pages), page 24: Before Niccolò Machiavelli's *Il Principe* (1513) and Giovanni Botero's *La Ragion di Stato* (1589), "the viciousness of a double morality – one limited to those acting in the name of the State and the other suitable for the general public – simply did not exist." In other words, this double morality is a characteristic of the state, born in the 17th century.

[16] Harsanyi, David, "We must weed out ignorant Americans from the electorate," *The Washington Post*, May 20, 2016 <https://www.washingtonpost.com/opinions/we-must-weed-out-ignorant-americans-from-the-electorate/2016/05/20/f66b3e18-1c7a-11e6-8c7b-6931e66333e7_story.html> accessed May 31, 2021.

[17] Caplan, Bryan, "A Cheap, Inoffensive Way to Make Democracy Work Better," *The Library of Economics and Liberty*, October 9, 2013 <https://www.econlib.org/archives/2013/10/a_cheap_inoffen.html> accessed May 31, 2021. Caplan proposes that governments give money rewards (A=$1000, B=$500, C=$100) for those who pass a citizenship test, without excluding the franchise from those who fail.

[18] Somin, Ilya, "Bryan Caplan's Voter Achievement Test," *The Volokh Conspiracy* (published October 10, 2013) <https://volokh.com/2013/10/10/bryan-caplans-voter-achievement-test/> accessed May 9, 2022.

[19] "Fort Hood Army Base Guide," *Military.com* (last edited June 3, 2022) <https://www.military.com/base-guide/fort-hood> accessed June 6, 2022. Fort Hood is home to the U.S. III Corps and First Cavalry (armored) Division, and is the largest military installation in the world, covering 214,968 acres, or about 340 square miles, in Coryell and Bell Counties.

[20] "Pantex Nuclear Weapons Facility ," *Texas Health and Human Services* (last edited March 3, 2021) <https://dshs.texas.gov/radiation/emergency-preparedness/pantex.aspx> accessed June 6, 2022. The Pantex Plant is the United States' only nuclear weapons assembly and disassembly facility. It is a 16,000-acre site in Carson County, 17 miles northeast of Amarillo, near the intersection of U.S. Hwy. 60 and Farm Road 2373.

[21] Tirpak, John A., "Strategy & Policy: The Next 10 Countries Combined," *Air Force Magazine* (published August 27, 2021) <https://www.airforcemag.com/article/strategy-policy-the-next-10-countries-combined/> accessed May 10, 2022.

[22] Ziezulewicz, Geoff, "How could the USS Connecticut sub crash into an undersea mountain?" *Military Times* (published November 3, 2021) <https://www.militarytimes.com/news/your-navy/2021/11/03/how-could-the-uss-connecticut-sub-crash-into-an-undersea-mountain/> accessed November 9, 2021.

[23] Yuandan, Guo; Xuanzun, Liu, "US military activities in S. China Sea in 2020 unprecedented," *Global Times* (published March 12, 2021) <https://www.globaltimes.cn/page/202103/1218193.shtml> accessed November 9, 2021.

[24] Isachenkov, Vladimir (The Associated Press); Litvinova, Daria (The Associated Press), "Putin says US and UK were behind Black Sea 'provocation'," *Military Times* (published June 30, 2021) <https://www.militarytimes.com/flashpoints/2021/06/30/putin-says-us-and-uk-were-behind-black-sea-provocation/> accessed November 9, 2021.

[25] Atlamazoglou, Constantine, "US warships went on another mission to a European hotspot, and Putin says they're in Russia's 'crosshairs'," *Business Insider* (published November 16, 2021) <https://www.businessinsider.com/us-navy-warships-in-black-sea-amid-nato-russia-tensions-2021-11> accessed November 17, 2021.

[26] "GDP (current US$) - Russian Federation," *The World Bank* (published April 30, 2022) <https://data.worldbank.org/indicator/NY.GDP.MKTP.CD?locations=RU> accessed May 10, 2022. The aforementioned $778 billion U.S. military spending divided by the Russian 2020 GDP of $1.483 trillion is .52.

[27] Preble, Christopher A., "The Founders' Foreign Policy," *The CATO Institute* (published March 4, 2019) <https://www.cato.org/blog/founders-foreign-policy> accessed May 10, 2022. The article references James Madison's address to the Constitutional Convention in June of 1787, and George Washington's Farewell Address.

[28] Griswold, Niki; Mekelburg, Madlin, "Texas allocates additional $495 million in funding for Operation Lone Star," *Austin American-Statesman* (last edited April 29, 2022) <https://www.statesman.com/story/news/2022/04/29/texas-governor-greg-abbott-adds-operation-lone-star-funding-title-42-border-policy-ends/9589052002/> accessed May 10, 2022.

[29] Winkie, Davis (Military Times); Barragán, James and Essig, Chris Essig (The Texas Tribune; Cohen, Rachel (Military Times), "'I hate it here': National Guard members sound off on Texas border mission in leaked morale survey," *The Texas Tribune* (published Februry 24, 2022) <https://www.texastribune.org/2022/02/24/national-guard-Texas-border-morale-survey/> accessed May 10, 2022.

[30] Morgan, Jason, "Private Security Isn't Enough: Why America Needs Militias," *Mises Institute* (published June 1, 2021) <https://mises.org/wire/private-security-isnt-enough-why-america-needs-militias> accessed May 11, 2022.

[31] "U.S. Costs to Date for the War in Afghanistan," *Watson Institute for International & Public Affairs* (last edited November 7, 2021) <https://watson.brown.edu/costsofwar/figures/2021/human-and-budgetary-costs-date-us-war-afghanistan-2001-2022> accessed November 8, 2021.

[32] Fox News, "Erik Prince issues stark warning: This is just the beginning" (*YouTube*, length 4:29, published August 13, 2012) <https://www.youtube.com/watch?v=VlO2NGF24ek> accessed November 8, 2021. Blackwater founder Erik Prince: "We've been beaten by weapons designed in the 1940s, carried by largely illiterate goat herders."

[33] Paul, Ron, "September 11, 2001 : Attack on America Air Piracy and Capture Act 2001," *Yale Law School* (published October 10, 2001) <https://avalon.law.yale.edu/sept11/speech_ron_paul_1010.asp> accessed May 11, 2022.

[34] "H.R.6869 - To authorize the President of the United States to issue letters of marque and reprisal for the purpose of seizing the assets of certain Russian citizens, and for other purposes," *Congress.gov* (last edited February 28, 2022) <https://www.congress.gov/bill/117th-congress/house-bill/6869/> accessed March 12, 2022.

[35] Sechrest, Larry J., "Privateers: An Example of Private-Sector Military Defense," *Mises Institute* (published July 10, 2019) <https://mises.org/wire/privateers-example-private-sector-military-defense> accessed May 11, 2022.

[36] Ibid.

[37] Schwartz, Moshe; Swain, Joyprada, "Department of Defense Contractors in Afghanistan and Iraq: Background and Analysis," *Congressional Research Service* (published May 13, 2011) <https://sgp.fas.org/crs/natsec/R40764.pdf> accessed May 11, 2022. "[I]n Iraq, Afghanistan, and the Balkans – the three largest military operations of the past 15 years – [...] contractors have comprised approximately 50% of DOD's combined contractor and uniformed personnel workforce in country."

[38] Schmemann, Serge, "Palestinian Believed to Be Bombing Mastermind Is Killed," *The New York Times* (published January 6, 1996) <https://www.nytimes.com/1996/01/06/world/palestinian-believed-to-be-bombing-mastermind-is-killed.html> accessed May 11, 2022. Despite the routine official denials, it was widely believed that the Mossad had rigged the explosive cell phone that decapitated Mr. Ayyash.

[39] "Biennial Revenue Estimate," *Texas Comptroller of Public Accounts* (last edited December 3, 2021) <https://comptroller.texas.gov/about/media-center/infographics/2019/bre2020-21/> accessed May 12, 2022.

[40] Johnson, John G., "Tariff Policies of the Republic of Texas," *Texas State Historical Association* (last edited April 27, 2019) <https://www.tshaonline.org/handbook/entries/tariff-policies-of-the-republic-of-texas> accessed May 12, 2022.

[41] "United States-Mexico-Canada Agreement," *Office of the United States Trade Representative* (last edited May 9, 2022) <https://ustr.gov/trade-agreements/free-trade-agreements/united-states-mexico-canada-agreement> accessed May 12, 2022.

[42] Alford, Jeremy, "Will local shrimpers ever benefit from tariffs?" *HoumaToday* (last edited December 2, 2005) <https://www.houmatoday.com/story/news/2005/12/03/will-local-shrimpers-ever-benefit-from-tariffs/26687705007/> accessed May 24, 2022.

[43] Costello, TJ; Green, David; Graves, Patrick, "The Texas Economic Stabilization Fund Saving for Rainy Days," *Texas Comptroller of Public Accounts* (last edited December 26, 2021) <https://comptroller.texas.gov/economy/fiscal-notes/2016/september/rainy-day.php> accessed May 28, 2022. Officially named the Economic Stabilization Fund, it was created in 1988 after an economic recession that forced the State to raise taxes. The amount fluctuates around $10 billion, and is commonly greater than that of other States with a similar fund.

[44] "Texas enters 2021 as world's 9th largest economy by GDP," *Texas Economic Development Corporation* (published January 27, 2021) <https://businessintexas.com/news/texas-enters-2021-as-worlds-9th-largest-economy-by-gdp/> accessed May 12, 2022.

[45] "GDP by Country," *Worldometer* (last edited May 12, 2022) <https://www.worldometers.info/gdp/gdp-by-country/> accessed May 12, 2022. This site uses 2017 GDP figures published by the World Bank, which seems to be using Purchasing Power Parity (PPP) Adjusted GDP. Rankings from various sources shift from year to year, and according to adjustments to the nominal GDP. Data from 2019 maintain Texas' ranking at eighth or ninth place.

[46] "Best States for Business 2019," *Forbes* magazine (last edited May 9, 2022) <https://www.forbes.com/places/tx/?sh=32a214d45fba> accessed May 12, 2022.

[47] "Texas tops all U.S. states in exports for 19th consecutive year: Natural resources, agricultural production among state's economic generators," *AgriLife Today* (published March 18, 2021) <https://agrilifetoday.tamu.edu/2021/03/18/texas-tops-all-u-s-states-in-exports-for-19th-consecutive-year/> accessed May 27, 2022.

[48] Hayek, F.A., *The Fatal Conceit: The Errors of Socialism*, Volume I of the Collected Works of F.A. Hayek (University of Chicago Press paperback, August 28, 1991, ISBN 978-0226320663, 194 pages), page 27. The conceit is "that man is able to shape the world around him according to his wishes" in contravention of economic laws.

[49] Green, David; Halbrook, Shannon, "Texas' International Trade," *Texas Comptroller of Public Accounts* (published July, 2020) <https://comptroller.texas.gov/economy/fiscal-notes/2020/july/trade.php> accessed May 12, 2022.

[50] "U.S. Citrus Processing Report," *Citrus Industry* (October 13, 2021) <https://citrusindustry.net/2021/10/13/u-s-citrus-processing-report/> accessed April 28, 2022.

[51] Gajanan, Mahita, "Half-Empty Shelves. Skyrocketing Prices. Here's What Would Happen to the Produce Aisle if Trump Closes the Mexico Border," *Time* magazine (published April 3, 2019) <https://time.com/5562656/mexico-produce-price/> accessed April 28, 2022.

[52] "Federal Reserve Act: Section 2A. Monetary policy objectives," *Board of Governors of the Federal Reserve System* (last edited February 13, 2017) <https://www.federalreserve.gov/aboutthefed/section2a.htm> accessed January 11, 2020.

[53] White, Ben, "8/9. That's the Fed's record on triggering a recession while trying to fix inflation," *Politico* (published March 29, 2022) <https://www.politico.com/news/2022/03/29/federal-reserve-recession-inflation-rates-00021119> accessed May 14, 2022.

[54] "FRED Graph: Interest Rates 1953-04-01 to 2022-04-01" *St. Louis Fed* (last edited January 12, 2022) <https://fred.stlouisfed.org/graph/?id=GS30,GS10,GS5,GS1,GS3M,FEDFUNDS> accessed May 14, 2022.

[55] "Effective Federal Funds Rate," *Federal Reserve Bank of New York* (last edited May 13, 2022) <https://www.newyorkfed.org/markets/reference-rates/effr> accessed May 14, 2022.

[56] Sabrin, Murray, "The Fed's Bubblenomics," *Mises Institute* (published November 15, 2017) <https://mises.org/wire/feds-bubblenomics> accessed May 14, 2022.

[57] Singh, Manoj; Cheng, Marguerita, "The 2007-2008 Financial Crisis in Review," *Investopedia* (last edited November 27, 2021) <https://www.investopedia.com/articles/economics/09/financial-crisis-review.asp> accessed May 14, 2022.

[58] "REPORT TO CONGRESS: Federal Reserve Balance Sheet," *The Federal Reserve* (published November 2021) <https://www.federalreserve.gov/monetarypolicy/files/balance_sheet_developments_report_202111.pdf> accessed May 14, 2022.

[59] Harrison, David, "Fed Has Many Tools to Deter Recession, Former Chairman Bernanke Says," *The Wall Street Journal* (published January 4, 2020) <https://www.wsj.com/articles/fed-has-many-tools-to-deter-recession-former-chairman-bernanke-says-11578184800> accessed January 5, 2020.

[60] Lopez, German, "Inflation's 40-Year High," *The New York Times* (published April 13, 2022) <https://www.nytimes.com/2022/04/13/briefing/inflation-forty-year-high-gas-prices.html> accessed May 24, 2022.

[61] "Gold Prices - 100 Year Historical Chart," *Macrotrends* (last edited May 11, 2022) <https://www.macrotrends.net/1333/historical-gold-prices-100-year-chart> accessed May 14, 2022.

[62] Bennett, Jeannette N., "A Dollar's Worth: Inflation Is Real," *St. Louis Fed* (last edited May 3, 2022) <https://research.stlouisfed.org/publications/page1-econ/2021/12/01/a-dollars-worth-inflation-is-real> accessed May 14, 2022.

[63] Rothbard, Murray N., "Aurophobia, Or: Free Banking On What Standard?" *The Review of Austrian Economics*, ISSN 0889-3047, Vol. 6, No. 1, 1992, page 97.

[64] Ibid., page 98.

[65] Rothbard, Murray N., *The Mystery of Banking* (Ludwig von Mises Institute, second edition hardcover, September 10, 2008, ISBN 978-1933550282, pages), page 164. Online at <https://mises.org/library/mystery-banking> accessed September 9, 2021.

[66] Bennett, Paul; Peristiani, Stavros, "Are Reserve Requirements Still Binding?" Federal Reserve Bank of New York, *Economic Policy Review*, Volume 8, Number 1, May 2002 issue. Online at <https://www.newyorkfed.org/research/epr/02v08n1/0205benn/0205benn.html> accessed May 25, 2022.

[67] Rothbard, *The Mystery of Banking*, page 261.

[68] Rothbard, Murray N., *The Case for a 100 Percent Gold Dollar* (Ludwig von Mises Institute, 2001, ISBN: 0-945466-34-X, 77 pages), page 51. Online at <https://mises.org/library/case-100-percent-gold-dollar-2> accessed October 16, 2021.

[69] Ibid., page 14.

[70] French, Doug, "Thanks to Bailouts, Wall Street Banks Are More Fragile than Ever," *Mises Institute* (published November 8, 2021) <https://mises.org/wire/thanks-bailouts-wall-street-banks-are-more-fragile-ever> accessed November 8, 2021.

[71] Mulverhill, Lauren, "The Texas Bullion Depository Its timing is golden," *Texas Comptroller of Public Accounts* (published September 2017) <https://comptroller.texas.gov/economy/fiscal-notes/2017/september/bullion-depository.php> accessed May 25, 2022.

[72] "Home," *Sigma Metalytics* (last edited May 13, 2022) <https://www.sigmametalytics.com/> accessed May 25, 2022.

[73] Shostak, Frank, "Forget What the 'Experts' Claim about Deflation: It Strengthens the Economy," *Mises Institute* (published May 7, 2022) <https://mises.org/wire/forget-what-experts-claim-about-deflation-it-strengthens-economy> accessed May 25, 2022.

[74] Seth, Shobhit; Khartit, Khadija; Jasperson, Hans Daniel, "How the SWIFT System Works," *Investopedia* (last edited March 14, 2022) <https://www.investopedia.com/articles/personal-finance/050515/how-swift-system-works.asp> accessed May 25, 2022.

[75] Padoa-Schioppa, Tommaso, *Committee on Payment and Settlement Systems Payment and settlement systems in selected countries* (Bank for International Settlements Red Book, April 2003, online ISBN 92-9197-646-6, 525 pages), pages 459-471. Online at <https://www.bis.org/cpmi/publ/d53p01.pdf> and <https://www.bis.org/cpmi/publ/d53p16.pdf> accessed May 25, 2022.

[76] Shira, Dezan, "Russian & Chinese Alternatives For SWIFT Global Banking Network Coming Online," *Russia Briefing* (published June 17, 2019) <https://www.russia-briefing.com/news/russian-chinese-alternatives-swift-global-banking-network-coming-online.html/> accessed May 25, 2022.

[77] Wuerth, Ingrid, "Does Foreign Sovereign Immunity Apply to Sanctions on Central Banks?" *Lawfare* (published March 7, 2022) <https://www.lawfareblog.com/does-foreign-sovereign-immunity-apply-sanctions-central-banks> accessed May 25, 2022.

[78] Gordon, Nicholas, "Coinbase earnings were bad. Worse still, the crypto exchange is now warning that bankruptcy could wipe out user funds," *Fortune* magazine (published May 11, 2022) <https://fortune.com/2022/05/11/coinbase-bankruptcy-crypto-assets-safe-private-key-earnings-stock/> accessed May 25, 2022.

[79] Shostak, Frank, "The Bitcoin Money Myth," *Mises Institute* (published April 17, 2013) <https://mises.org/library/bitcoin-money-myth> accessed May 25, 2022.

[80] Davidson, Laura; Block, Walter E., "Bitcoin, the Regression Theorem, and the Emergence of a New Medium of Exchange," *The Quarterly Journal of Austrian Economics*, Vol. 18, No. 3, 311-338, Fall 2015. Also: *Mises Institute* (published September 28, 2018) <https://mises.org/library/bitcoin-regression-theorem-and-emergence-new-medium-exchange> accessed October 22, 2021.

[81] "THE TEXAS CONSTITUTION: ARTICLE 3. LEGISLATIVE DEPARTMENT," *Texas Constitution and Statutes* (last edited March 11, 2022) <https://statutes.capitol.texas.gov/Docs/CN/htm/CN.3.htm> accessed May 12, 2022.

[82] "History of the LBB," *Legislative Budget Board* (last edited May 16, 2022) <https://www.lbb.texas.gov/History.aspx> accessed May 27, 2022.

[83] "Legislative Action: Spring Through Fall of Even-Numbered Years," *The Texas Politics Project* (last edited December 28, 2019) <https://texaspolitics.utexas.edu/archive/html/pec/features/0403_01/slide2.html> accessed May 26, 2022.

[84] "Debt at a Glance," *Texas Comptroller of Public Accounts* (last edited May 12, 2022) <https://comptroller.texas.gov/transparency/local/debt/texas.php> accessed May 26, 2022.

[85] "Texas State Energy Profile," *U.S. Energy Information Administration* (last edited May 19, 2022) <https://www.eia.gov/state/print.php?sid=TX> accessed June 6, 2022.

[86] "Federal land ownership by state," *BallotPedia* (last edited November 14, 2019) <https://ballotpedia.org/Federal_land_ownership_by_state#Federal_land_by_state> accessed January 29, 2020.

[87] Stern, Richard, "The Road to Ruin Is Paved With Gimmicks," *The Heritage Foundation* (published November 18, 2021) <https://www.heritage.org/budget-and-spending/commentary/the-road-ruin-paved-gimmicks> accessed May 26, 2022.

[88] Jaffe, Eric, "America's Infrastructure Crisis Is Really a Maintenance Crisis," *Bloomberg CityLab* (published February 12, 2015) <https://www.bloomberg.com/news/articles/2015-02-12/america-s-infrastructure-crisis-is-really-a-maintenance-crisis> accessed September 6, 2021. Re-thinking infrastructure spending toward maintenance means more than budgeting with that emphasis. It means reducing the factors that contribute to expansion and to the burdening of maintenance, as Columbia planning scholar David King has pointed out.

[89] Ibid.

[90] Pressler, Mary, "Texas Power Grid Explained," *Quick Electricity* (last edited May 22, 2022) <https://quickelectricity.com/texas-power-grid/> accessed May 27, 2022. Mary Pressler's concise and informed article is a highly recommended primer on the Texas power grid.

[91] Natter, Ari, "Texas Power Plants Get Emergency Clearance to Crank Up Output," *Bloomberg News* (published February 15, 2021) <https://www.bloomberg.com/news/articles/2021-02-15/pollution-limit-waived-for-texas-power-plants-in-emergency-order> accessed May 27, 2022.

"The Department of Energy issued an emergency order allowing several Texas power plants to produce as much electricity as possible, a move expected to violate anti-pollution rules"[.]

[92] Schumer, Chuck, "Millions across Texas are hurting," *Twitter* (published February 17, 2021, 4:07 PM) <https://twitter.com/senschumer/status/1362161758929113089> accessed May 27, 2022. The entire Tweet reads: "Millions across Texas are hurting/The Senate is ready to help/But Gov. Abbott & Fox News are trying to blame wind turbines?/This is a lie/And lying about the climate crisis and refusing to act on it are exactly what is exacerbating extreme weather in Texas and across America".

[93] Schwartz, Jeremy; Collier, Kiah; Davila, Vianna, "How Texas repeatedly failed to protect its power grid against extreme weather," *Salon* (published February 26, 2021) <https://www.salon.com/2021/02/26/how-texas-repeatedly-failed-to-protect-its-power-grid-against-extreme-weather_partner/> accessed May 27, 2022.

[94] Hirs, Ed, "Why Texans are cold and in the dark," *The Washington Post* (published February 18, 2021) <https://www.washingtonpost.com/opinions/2021/02/18/texans-grid-outage-deregulation/> accessed May 27, 2022.

[95] Giberson, Michael; Moore, Adrian T., "Texas Power Failures: What Happened in February 2021 and What Can Be Done," *Reason Foundation* (published April 2021) <https://reason.org/wp-content/uploads/texas-power-failures-what-happened-what-can-be-done.pdf> accessed May 27, 2022.

[96] Browne, Ed, "Graphic Shows What Percentage of Texas' Energy Is Renewable," *Newsweek* (published February 18, 2021) <https://www.newsweek.com/how-much-power-texas-renewable-coal-gas-wind-turbines-1570238> accessed May 28, 2022.

[97] Hume, Brit, "Biden nominee Saule Omarova," *Sovren Media* (published November 9, 2021) <https://sovren.media/video/biden-nominee-saule-omarova-294.html> accessed November 10, 2021.

[98] "Global Warming," NASA Earth Observatory (published June 3, 2010) <https://earthobservatory.nasa.gov/features/GlobalWarming/page2.php> accessed September 26, 2022. "The global average surface temperature rose 0.6 to 0.9 degrees Celsius (1.1 to 1.6° F) between 1906 and 2005, and the rate of temperature increase has nearly doubled in the last 50 years."

[99] Zubrin, Robert, "How We Can Get Clean Energy – Fuel and Human Progress," *Daily Caller* (published April 14, 2022) <https://quillette.com/2022/04/14/how-we-can-get-clean-energy-fuel-and-human-progress/> accessed May 26, 2022.

[100] Catenacci, Thomas, "Energy Department Burned Through Nearly $1 Billion On Failed Projects Intended To Cut Carbon Emissions," *Daily Caller* (published January 12, 2022) <https://dailycaller.com/2022/01/12/energy-department-billion-dollars-failed-projects-carbon-emissions/> accessed May 26, 2022.

[101] Alimonti, G., Mariani, L., Prodi, F. et al., "A critical assessment of extreme events trends in times of global warming," *The European Physical Journal Plus*, volume 137, 112 (2022). Online at <https://doi.org/10.1140/epjp/s13360-021-02243-9> accessed September 26, 2022. This Italian study of supposedly anomalous recent weather found "no evidence of a climate emergency in the records to date."

[102] Shellenberger, Michael, "Why Disasters Have Declined," *Forbes* magazine (published January 10, 2022) <https://www.forbes.com/sites/michaelshellenberger/2022/01/10/why-disasters-have-declined/?sh=1d8e54071897> accessed October 4, 2022.

[103] Shellenberger, Michael, "Why Apocalyptic Claims About Climate Change Are Wrong," *Forbes* magazine (published November 25, 2019) <https://www.forbes.com/sites/michaelshellenberger/2019/11/25/why-everything-they-say-about-climate-change-is-wrong/> accessed May 26, 2022.

[104] Ibid.

[105] Alexander, Ralph B., "No Evidence That Climate Change Is Accelerating Sea Level Rise," *Science Under Attack* (published September 23, 2019) <https://www.scienceunderattack.com/blog/2019/9/23/no-evidence-that-climate-change-is-accelerating-sea-level-rise-35> accessed October 4, 2022.
Climate apocalypse skeptic Judith Curry and the UN's IPCC (Intergovernmental Panel on Climate Change) both state that the average global rate of sea level rise from 1901 to 2010 was 1.7 mm (about 1/16th of an inch) per year, and that projections of an increase should take into account the natural fluctuations of sea level.

[106] Ibid.

[107] Shellenberger, Michael, "Dark Side To Solar? More Reports Tie Panel Production To Toxic Pollution," *Forbes* magazine (published June 21, 2021) <https://www.forbes.com/sites/michaelshellenberger/2021/06/21/why-everything-they-said-about-solar---including-that-its-clean-and-cheap---was-wrong/?sh=3eafb6e85fe5> accessed May 26, 2022.

[108] Orlowski, Andrew, "The truth about electric cars: They are far more environmentally damaging than normal cars," *Spiked Online* (published March 3, 2022) <https://www.spiked-online.com/2022/03/03/the-truth-about-electric-cars/> accessed May 26, 2022.

[109] Shellenberger, Michael, "New Michael Moore-Backed Documentary On YouTube Reveals Massive Ecological Impacts Of Renewables," *Forbes* magazine (published April 21, 2020) <https://www.forbes.com/sites/michaelshellenberger/2020/04/21/new-michael-moore-backed-documentary-on-youtube-reveals-massive-ecological-impacts-of-renewables/> accessed May 26, 2022.

[110] Bryce, Robert, "Another nuclear plant closes: Get ready for electricity shortages," *The Hill* (published May 29, 2022) <https://thehill.com/opinion/energy-environment/3503142-another-nuclear-plant-closes-get-ready-for-electricity-shortages/> accessed May 28, 2022. Without explanation, the Michigan Palisades nuclear power plant was taken offline on May 20 by the Biden administration, removing seven terawatt-hours of power per year from the grid – which will be replaced the by natural gas energy that the administration considers to be part of the "existential threat" posed by fossil fuels.

[111] Shellenberger, Michael, "It Sounds Crazy, But Fukushima, Chernobyl, And Three Mile Island Show Why Nuclear Is Inherently Safe," *Forbes* magazine (published May 11, 2019) <https://www.forbes.com/sites/michaelshellenberger/2019/03/11/it-sounds-crazy-but-fukushima-chernobyl-and-three-mile-island-show-why-nuclear-is-inherently-safe/> accessed May 26, 2022.

[112] Ibid.

[113] Girardet, Edward, "Mitterrand 'freezes' French nuclear energy program," *The Christian Science Monitor* (published June 1, 1981) <https://www.csmonitor.com/1981/0601/060151.html> accessed May 29, 2022.

[114] "France Invests in Small Nuclear Reactors Amid Europe's Energy Meltdown," *The Motley Fool* (published October 12, 2021) <https://www.fool.com/investing/2021/10/12/france-invests-in-small-nuclear-reactors-amid-euro/> accessed May 26, 2022.
India's "fleet reactors" is a similar concept: Small (220 to 700 MW) reactors built from start to finish within five years. *Vide*: "From 2023, India to start building nuclear power plants in 'fleet mode'," *Business Standard* (last updated March 27, 2022) <https://www.business-standard.com/article/economy-policy/from-2023-india-to-start-building-nuclear-power-plants-in-fleet-mode-122032700145_1.html> accessed July 25, 2022.

[115] Hafertepe, Kenneth, "French Legation," *Handbook of Texas Online* (last edited July 21, 2016) https://www.tshaonline.org/handbook/entries/french-legation> accessed May 29, 2022.

[116] Lyman, Edwin, "'Advanced' Isn't Always Better," *Union of Concerned Scientists* (published Mar 18, 2021) <https://www.ucsusa.org/resources/advanced-isnt-always-better#read-online-content> accessed November 18, 2021.

[117] BakerInstitute, "How Things Really Work: Lessons from a Life in Politics" (*YouTube*, length 54:28, published June 9, 2012) <https://youtu.be/wX0mzTxO90k?t=1800> accessed February 21, 2021.

[118] "This Day in History, September 05: Sam Houston elected as president of Texas, 1836," *History* (last edited March 24, 2022) <https://www.history.com/this-day-in-history/sam-houston-elected-as-president-of-texas> accessed May 12, 2022.

[119] John, David, "Misleading the Public: How the Social Security Trust Fund Really Works," *The Heritage Foundation* (published September 2, 2004) <https://www.heritage.org/social-security/report/misleading-the-public-how-the-social-security-trust-fund-really-works> accessed May 28, 2022.

[120] Amadeo, Kimberly; Rasure, Erika; Ernsberger, Emily, "What Is the Social Security Trust Fund?" *The Balance* (last edited October 17, 2021) <https://www.thebalance.com/social-security-trust-fund-history-solvency-how-to-fix-it-3305890> accessed May 28, 2022.

[121] "A Summary of the 2021 Annual Reports," *Social Security Administration* (last edited May 27, 2022) <https://www.ssa.gov/oact/TRSUM/> accessed May 28, 2022.

[122] "U.S. International Social Security Agreements," *Social Security Administration* (last edited May 7, 2022) <https://www.ssa.gov/international/agreements_overview.html> accessed May 28, 2022.

[123] "Topic No. 751 Social Security and Medicare Withholding Rates," *Internal Revenue Service* (last edited May 23, 2022) <https://www.irs.gov/taxtopics/tc751> accessed May 30, 2022.

[124] "Veterans Living Overseas," *U.S. Department of Veterans' Affairs* (last edited May 13, 2022) <https://www.benefits.va.gov/persona/veteran-abroad.asp> accessed May 30, 2022.

[125] Breeding-Gonzales, Lucinda, "Denton library cancels story time, citing safety concerns," *Denton Record-Chronicle* (published November 15, 2021) <https://dentonrc.com/news/denton/denton-library-cancels-story-time-citing-safety-concerns/article_51143d3b-d3f1-5bb4-86b5-c16eb0f6407d.html> accessed May 30, 2022. The reader is invited to read the article not only for the facts, which could not be disguised, but for the transparent dishonesty in presenting them.

126 Showalter, Brandon, "Gender-bending sex-ed curricula tells teachers to hide kids' gender confusion from parents," *The Christian Post* (published August 19, 2020) <https://www.christianpost.com/news/gender-bending-sex-ed-curricula-tells-teachers-to-hide-kids-gender-confusion-from-parents.html> accessed May 30, 2022. The article references efforts by the Gay, Lesbian, & Straight Education Network, the ACLU, the Human Rights Campaign, and the National Education Association to sexualize elementary schoolchildren – including "gender-inclusive puberty education" where male and female sexual differentiation, including normal bodily processes, is erased – while hiding it from their parents.

127 Rantz, Jason, "Rantz: Can a man get pregnant? Democrat state rep. says 'it depends'," *MyNorthwest* (published January 30, 2020) <https://mynorthwest.com/1692099/rantz-man-pregnant-sex-education-kindergarten/> accessed May 30, 2022. State Representative Monica Stonier (D-Vancouver) introduced legislation mandating sex education for public school students starting in kindergarten. The instruction? "By Grade 1, students read *My Princess Boy* by Cheryl Kilodavis (page 28). In Grade 6, students are taught about gender identity (page 191) with gender-neutral language like 'someone with a vulva vs. a girl or woman.'"

128 Kennedy, Dana, "Dalton parents enraged over 'masturbation' videos for first graders," *Fox News* (published May 29, 2021) <https://www.foxnews.com/us/dalton-parents-masturbation-videos-first-graders> accessed May 30, 2022.

129 Olin, Tiffany, "Free menstrual products coming to all public school restrooms in Oregon," *KTVL News10* (published May 9, 2022) <https://ktvl.com/news/local/free-menstrual-products-coming-to-all-public-school-restrooms-in-oregon-medford-school-district-tampons-pads-department-education-boys-girls-gender> accessed May 30, 2022.

130 Hammer, Alex, "Johns Hopkins child sex abuse center hires trans professor, 34, who was forced to resign from Virginia school for DEFENDING pedophiles as 'minor attracted persons'," *UK Daily Mail* (published May 13, 2022) <https://www.dailymail.co.uk/news/article-10813233/Trans-professor-DEFENDED-pedophiles-minor-attracted-persons-hired-Johns-Hopkins-center.html> accessed May 30, 2022. Beggaring belief, Johns Hopkins University representatives rejoiced on Twitter that the new hire, one Allyn Walker, was to work in the school's Moore Center for the Prevention of Child Sexual Abuse.

131 "Video shows parents begging officers to charge into Texas elementary school during shooting," *KABC Television* (published May 26, 2022) <https://abc7.com/uvalde-texas-school-shooting-police-response-robb-elementary/11897692/> accessed May 30, 2022.

132 Taylor, Scott, "Loudoun County assault victim's dad wants apology for being called 'domestic terrorist'," *WJLA ABC News* (published October 25, 2021) <https://wjla.com/features/i-team/loudoun-county-public-school-parents-called-domestic-terrorists-scott-smith-sex-assault-victim-father-wants-apology> accessed May 30, 2022.

133 Johnson, Tiana, "Teenager arrested following video of 'horrific incident' at West Brook High School, Councilman Mike Getz says," *KBMT 12 News* (published September 10, 2022) <https://www.12newsnow.com/article/news/crime/teenager-arrested-following-video-of-horrific-incident-at-west-brook-high-school/502-29c34599-1ad1-4475-8522-5fadac02c5f2> accessed September 26, 2022.

134 Kunstler, James Howard, "Childhood's End," *LewRockwell.com* (published May 28, 2022) <https://www.lewrockwell.com/2022/05/james-howard-kunstler/childhoods-end/> accessed May 28, 2022.

135 "Operating Budget: Fiscal Year 2020," *Texas Education Agency* (published December 2019) <https://tea.texas.gov/sites/default/files/2020-operating-budget.pdf> accessed October 25, 2021, PDF page 2.A,2.

136 "Independent School Districts," *Texas Bond Review Board* (last edited May 13, 2022) <https://data.brb.texas.gov/local/isd/> accessed June 28, 2022.

[137] Johnson, Brad, "Texas Local Governments Amass $8,500 per Citizen in Spending Debt: School districts account for the largest portion of the outstanding debt," *The Texan* (published January 5, 2022) <https://thetexan.news/texas-local-governments-amass-8500-per-citizen-in-spending-debt/> accessed June 28, 2022.

[138] Quintero, James, "Have Voters Reached Their Breaking Point with School District Debt?" *Texas Public Policy Foundation* (published November 11, 2021) <https://www.texaspolicy.com/have-voters-reached-their-breaking-point-with-school-district-debt/> accessed June 28, 2022.

[139] "Top 10 most expensive high school football stadiums in Texas: When it comes to building pigskin palaces, there's no comparison to the Lone Star State," MaxPreps.com (published June 18, 2019) <https://www.maxpreps.com/news/VFHT4UsAn0Kxjx_zXJeiow/top-10-most-expensive-high-school-football-stadiums-in-texas.htm> accessed June 28, 2022. The mania in Texas for football borders on the pathological, as measured in spending on football facilities. Here is a list of the top 10 most expensive high school – not collegiate, not professional – but *high school* stadiums in the State:
1. $80 million Cy-Fair FCU Stadium (2006, Houston area);
2. $70 million Legacy Stadium (2017, Houston area);
3. $70 million McKinney ISD Stadium (2018, far north Dallas area);
4. $60 million Eagle Stadium (2012, far north Dallas area);
5. $49 million Woodforest Bank Stadium (2008, Houston area);
6. $48 million Children's Health Stadium (2019, Houston area);
7. $47.3 million Beaumont ISD Memorial Stadium (2010, Houston area);
8. $41.4 million Alvin ISD Freedom Field (2018, Houston area);
9. $39 million Challenger Columbia Stadium (2016, Houston area);
10. $38 million Planet Ford Stadium (2019, Houston area).

[140] Ibid.

[141] Nuzback, Kara, "Leander ISD tackles debt," *Community Impact* (published September 14, 2016) <https://communityimpact.com/austin/leander-cedar-park/education/2016/09/14/leander-isd-tackles-debt/> accessed June 28, 2022.

[142] Anderson, Lindsey, "Texas falls to 43 in national education ranking," *El Paso Times* (published January 10, 2016) <https://www.elpasotimes.com/story/news/education/2016/01/10/texas-falls-43-national-education-ranking/78519596/> accessed June 28, 2022.

[143] Johns, Kasey, "New STAAR testing data shows Texas students slip in reading, math proficiency since 2019," *Talk Radio 1370* (published June 28, 2021) <https://www.audacy.com/talk1370/news/state/staar-test-shows-texas-students-slip-in-reading-math> accessed June 28, 2022.

[144] *Op.cit.*, Costello, TJ; Green, David; Graves, Patrick, "The Texas Economic Stabilization Fund Saving for Rainy Days."

Three things cannot be long hidden: The sun, the moon, and the truth.

– Buddha

3. THE FUTURE

Normalcy bias – the tendency to discount the possibility of a disaster that has never happened before[1] – becomes fatal in the absence of normalcy.

Does normalcy currently prevail in public life? Has the recent past illustrated its increase, or instead, its decline? Does the prospect of popular elections promise its return? This book has provided ample evidence of the recent dramatic erosion of the most basic social norms in the United States. It is a complete denial of reality to suppose that "everything will be fixed in the next election." It is a delusion akin to the Jews striving to be "good Germans" even as the death camps were being filled.[2] At some point the pretense of normalcy becomes a mass psychogenic illness where a zombified populace shuffles to disaster.

As a peaceful movement, secession can only advance through a campaign of education. This campaign can only succeed with the acceptance of the following truths by a great majority of citizens:

- The state cannot be the moral representative of its citizens. Any coerced action lacks moral value, since that value requires the voluntary will and intention of each individual.

- No political solution, whether public or private, is perfect. Because of its moral pretense of representing the "general will," the state makes the preposterous demand that private challengers perfectly satisfy *every* individual, while it claims perfect representation of the "general will" by satisfying only *some* of the majority that elected it.

- Elections are oligarchic; sortition is democratic.

- The smaller the community where choices are made collectively, the smaller will be the probability that any individual's preference gets overruled.

- Markets provide more goods tailored to individual needs than state-provided public goods.

- No individual right gives you a claim on others; no one and no government owes you anything.

A citizenry convinced of these truths is ready for secession. Unfortunately, there will be no final acceptance of its program until a catastrophic failure of the central authoritarian state provides an object lesson of real suffering. Therefore the long and patient campaign of instruction must be built with that catastrophe in mind. Before the crisis, supporters can demand that the Texas legislature form a small standing commission to study the prospects for secession and update its findings every year, addressing every proposition in this book by its numbering in the Instantiation chapters. Privately funded symposia and advertising campaigns will be key to the initial campaign. After the crisis, supporters in every county should know which county commissioners are sympathetic, and they should know in advance how to mobilize emergency relief. Thoughtfulness and adaptability will mitigate the suffering, and will open hearts and minds to the reasonable program for the inevitable separation.

Secession is the peaceful means of resolving intractable differences between societies, and so must be realized by convincing a supermajority of its truths and never by violent imposition. This task is easier than it may seem; the great majority of mankind are followers, and will always be led by a spirited and knowledgeable few. In fact the long campaign of education offers time for the architects of kleristocracy to complete the required detailed work yet to be done.

Although the inevitable collapse of the state will usher in a period of hardship, we must remember as we have stated previously (1.2.6, page 136) that secession is the essence of a free republic, and that with planning, the creation of a new government out of its ruins can be a cause of celebration.

Will Texans have the resolve to create a new government free of the failed state form? Here is what might well happen. Texas will secede, but will initially preserve the very defects of the union from which it separates, solely because its forms are familiar, because the proposals offered here seem radical, in spite of their incontrovertible truth.

Texas secession is not meant to destroy America, but to restore its non-state Jeffersonian form over the long run. Its success, using tools not available to Madison, will provide a paradigm for a distant future restoration of America as that loose confederation intended by its founders. If Texans have the resolve to re-institute the republic that is rightly theirs, it is certainly reasonable to hope for a re-confederation with the chastened but independent sovereignties of the United States in the distant future.

Other countries, especially those re-formed in Eastern Europe after 1991, might prove a more receptive home to kleristocratic government. Although they lack most of the advantages possessed by Texas, their combination of small size and their leadership with a demonstrated capacity to successfully implement radical reforms offer two advantages that, frankly, Texas does not possess.

Of The Kingdome of Darknesse

Instead of considering the reasoned benefits of secession to all parties, the United States' 'grief at another State's prosperity' may well desire nothing but ruin for that State, even at the expense of far greater collateral damage to itself. Equal to any nuclear Armageddon, this is the "Kingdom of Darkness," ruled by a junta of deceivers having no reasoned arguments, only threats of violence to preserve their parasitic eminence in the state.

Nevertheless, if a sufficient number of Texans truly want their independence and freedom, nothing can stop them. It must never be forgotten, as Étienne de la Boétie[3] observed in the 16th century, that the sovereign people are many, who obey the few only because they freely choose their bondage.

Of Utopias

No Spartacus Revolt can ever succeed. No revolutionary change can ever occur without the coherently reasoned program of an original thinker, promulgated by an intelligentsia as an ideal for the wider public. The more profound the change offered by such a program, the more likely it is to be called "utopian."

The great political thinkers Anthony de Jasay in *The State*, Robert Nisbet in *The Quest for Community*, and Martin van Creveld in *The Rise and Decline of the State* all demolished the pretensions of the state. However, none of them[eeee] provided a program for a government that might supplant it. Then there are the dilettante libertarians who are ideologically antagonistic to any planning whatsoever, who believe that some successor government will evolve "spontaneously" like the markets they hold in religious reverence – a form of magical thinking for which we have nothing but contempt.

A cursory glance at successful revolutions will illustrate that it is exactly such programs maligned as "utopian" that drive effective change. Even misguided programs triumph over more reasonable policy because the latter fail to provide a detailed "utopian" alternate program. Thus there would have been no French Revolution without the "utopian" Declaration of the Rights of Man and the Enlightenment philosophers, no Socialist Revolution without the "utopian" *Manifesto of the Communist Party* by Marx and Engels, no New Deal of the Roosevelt administration without the nostrums of John Maynard Keynes, no Federal takeover of the national money supply without Henry Parker Willis and Paul Warburg. Even wholly fatuous programs like the contemporary Green New Deal drive policy precisely because they do not shrink from the "utopian" nature of their appeal.

[eeee] Nisbet, on page 236 of *The Quest for Community*, weakly suggests a "new laissez faire," and even accepts its being called "utopian," but he provides no real program to specify its meaning or its realization.

It must never be forgotten: "Utopia" can mean "nowhere"; but it can also mean "a good place." It is only an idealistic, reasoned program – maligned as "utopian," and more viciously so in proportion to its threat to the state – that can take us from the "nowhere" of the failed state to tomorrow's free and prosperous "good place."

---

[1] Shermer, Michael, *The Believing Brain: From Ghosts and Gods to Politics and Conspiracies – How We Construct Beliefs and Reinforce Them as Truths* (Macmillan, May 24, 2011, ISBN 9781429972611, 400 pages), page 275.

[2] Bettelheim, Bruno, *Individual and Mass Behavior in Extreme Situations* (Irvington Publishers, paperback from 1943 original, October 1, 1991, ISBN 978-0829026214) Online at <https://pages.uoregon.edu/dluebke/HolocaustMemory407/Bettelheim1943.pdf> accessed April 27, 2022. Bettelheim describes how the longest-imprisoned Jews in a death camp "adapted" to acquire the beliefs and attitudes of their oppressors.

[3] Rothbard, Murray N., "The Political Thought of Étienne de la Boétie," *Mises Institute* (published July 20, 2005) <https://mises.org/library/political-thought-etienne-de-la-boetie> accessed February 17, 2022.

Appendix
A History of Secession in All 50 States

Secession movements have been initiated by both conservatives[1] and liberals,[2] in all 50 States, throughout the history of the United States. All 50 States listed petitions to secede from the United States in a 2012 Federal online forum.[3]

Some of the more recent examples of secession are better characterized as protest events rather than earnest, principled movements. Most of such examples rely on the U.S. Constitution's Article IV, Section 3, Clause 1 – a secession that requires "the Consent of the Legislatures of the States concerned as well as of the Congress", with the new State still under the jurisdiction of the United States. Nevertheless, these do represent assertions of the sovereignty of the people, however limited. Nor should there be any semantic hair-splitting that some of the examples are "cessions" and not secessions. The principle is clear: One society separated from another, to determine its political future according to the sovereign will of its own people.

It is important to remember that during the Jeffersonian period (1788-1861) secession was not only an integral part of the growth of the United States west of the Appalachians, but an option with the universally recognized power to assert full national sovereignty. Professor Donald Livingston argues that secession was a cornerstone of Jeffersonian democracy, which maintained that republics must be small in size and population in order to remain democracies and to avoid becoming empires. Whether by a State's secession of its western territories as settlers entered them, or by internal secession as its population grew beyond 300,000, Jefferson held that States must adjust to a size that could be administered by a democratic republic.[4]

Alaska
The Alaskan Independence Party, or AKIP, has been in existence since the 1970s, therefore quashing the temptation to associate it with UKIP, the British party driving the 2016-2020 Brexit. It advocates "an 'Alaska First' policy focused around the land and resource development."[5] It regularly holds party conventions.

Alabama
• Alabama was created by secession from western Georgia counties.
• It was one of the 11 Confederate States (1861-1865).

Arizona

• The "People of Arizona in Convention Assembled at La Mesilla, Arizona Territory, March 16, 1861," passed an ordinance of secession, and sent Granville Oury as its delegate to the Confederate Congress in Richmond.[6]

• In 2011, Paul Eckerstrom, the former Democratic Party chairman for Pima County, maintained a "Start Our State" Facebook site to make Pima County a State free of Right-wing politics.[7]

Arkansas

Arkansas was one of the 11 Confederate States (1861-1865).

California

• After 30 Americans declared California independent from Mexico in the Bear Flag Revolt of June 14, 1846, California existed as an independent nation for 25 days.[8]

• "There have been more than 200 secession efforts in California's history."[9] Just nine years after its becoming a State on September 9, 1850, its lawmakers attempted a breakup. The Yreka Rebellion of December 4, 1941, named after Siskiyou County's biggest town, Yreka, was the attempt of some Northern California counties to join southern Oregonians in the new State of Jefferson. On April 7, 1850, in Nevada County, The Great Republic of Rough and Ready seceded for almost three months. In 1965 and 1970, State legislators attempted to separate southern California along the Tehachapi Mountains. In the 1990s there was a ballot measure to split the State into three separate States, which was attempted again in 2018 with Silicon Valley billionaire Tim Draper, who in 2014 had wanted a split into six States. A 2009 plan would have created a coastal and an inland California – an idea floated again in 2011 by State Sen. Jeff Stone of Riverside County. In 2002, San Fernando Valley and Hollywood attempted secession from Los Angeles.[10]

• Louis Marinelli founded CalExit just after the victory of Republicans in the 2016 election. CalExit, or Yes California, under Marinelli's successor Marcus Ruiz Evans, in 2018 proposed combining secession, or "devolution,"[11] with the creation of an autonomous nation for American Indians within it.[12]

• The California National Party was formed in 2015, and remains viable and friendly to secession without explicitly supporting it. Scott Thompson, the Oroville, California Mayor, declared the city a constitutional republic – but rather confusedly denies that the declaration is an act of secession.[13]

• The California Freedom Initiative has done some earnest planning for the State's independence: It has drafted a constitution, with some details for the exit process.[14]

• Cascadia Now, a Seattle-based nonprofit founded by Brandon Letsinger, does not advocate secession, but instead advocates local "self-determination" on environmental matters for West Coast states.[15]

• Similarly, although it does not explicitly advocate secession, "The Cascadia Bioregional Party actively supports the break down [sic] and removal of arbitrary nation state borders within North America". "Cascadia" is a bioregion that "encompasses all or portions of Washington, Oregon, Idaho, California, Nevada, Wyoming, Montana, Alaska, British Columbia, and Alberta."[16]

Colorado

• In 2013 a proposal to form a new State from several northern Colorado counties failed, although it passed in five of the 11 Colorado counties where it appeared on the ballot.[17]

• As part of the 2013 northern county secession, the commissioners of the southern Colorado counties of Las Animas (principal city, Trinidad) and Huerfano (principal city, Walsenburg) considered the proposal of the 51st State Initiative.[18]

• In 2020 Christopher Richards registered the political committee Weld County Wyoming to have the county secede from Colorado because of the State's hostility to business and agriculture.[19]

Connecticut

On December 15, 1814, Federalists convened the Hartford Convention to debate seceding the State because of the local unpopularity of the War of 1812.[20] John Quincy Adams, Timothy Pickering, Fisher Ames, Elbridge Gerry, Theophilus Parsons, Josiah Quincy, and Joseph Story were among the leaders of the movement.[21]

Delaware

Delaware was a Border State and Middle Atlantic State during the War Between the States (1861-1865), with strongly divided sentiments for both North and South.[22]

Florida

• The State of Muskogee, around Tallahassee, was an independent nation from 1799 to 1803.

• The Republic of West Florida was an independent nation for about two months during 1810.

• Florida was one of the 11 Confederate States (1861-1865).

• On April 23, 1982, Key West mayor Dennis Wardlow briefly declared the Florida Keys the Conch Republic, mainly to protest Federal Border Patrol roadblocks. The event is still commemorated – facetiously, to promote tourism.[23]

• In 2008, Commissioner Rich Moyle of the south Florida county of North Lauderdale wanted his county and several Florida cities in the south to split to form South Florida. The proposal was revived in 2014.[24]

Georgia
• Georgia was one of the 11 Confederate States (1861-1865).
• In the 2018 primary, Pierce County Republicans voted 27% in favor of the following proposition: Should the counties south of Macon join together to "form the 51st state of South Georgia?"[25]

Hawaii
• In 2020, University of Hawaii Professor Stephen O'Harrow seriously addressed some of the difficulties confronting Hawaii secession.[26]
• For years The Nation of Hawaii, Hawaii's oldest independence organization, has been advocating independence under its leader, Dennis Pu'uhonua "Bumpy" Kanahele, who contends that the State's treaty with the United States is illegitimate.[27]

Idaho
• In 1852, Thornton F. McElroy published the *Columbian* newspaper to promote the creation of a State from what is now northern Oregon. His efforts led to the creation of Washington Territory in 1853.[28]
• In 1915, State Senator R.A. Hutchinson encouraged the Idaho legislature to create the State of Lincoln from Eastern Washington and Idaho Panhandle.[29]
• In 2015, chimney sweep Grant Darrow took up the idea, current since the 1960s, of moving Idaho's western boundary farther west to incorporate the rural counties of Oregon, which felt alienated from the liberal politics of Oregon's population centers. In the November 2020 election, four eastern counties were to move into Idaho; two counties approved the measure.[30]
• By 2021, the Greater Idaho movement had evolved into carving off about three-quarters of Oregon, with parts reaching to the Pacific Ocean.[31]

Illinois
• Illinois was originally part of the Northwest Territory, given in secession by the State of Virginia.
• In 1861, southern Illinois counties, or "Little Egypt," proposed secession.[32]
• After the State legislature refused to reapportion representatives after the 1910 and 1920 census, Chicago leaders advocated secession to make a separate State from Cook County, with possibly Lake and Dupage counties included.[33]
• Historical revenge would come a century later when "New Illinois, a secessionist movement founded in 2018 to lobby Congress to make Chicago the 51st U.S. state, [...] would allow the rest of Illinois to govern itself without the

influence of a major city." That is, in a novel variation on the theme of secession, a State would expel an unwanted area from itself. The movement is motivated by the State taxpayer-shouldered $221 million bailout for the Chicago pension system, among other policy differences.[34]

• In the early 1970s, 16 western Illinois counties upset over the allocation of State transportation funds inspired a student at Western Illinois University to declare the Republic of Forgottonia.[35]

• In 1981, the Chicago (or Cook County) secession idea revived with State Sen. Howard Carroll's passage of a bill for it in the State legislature, and again in 2011, with a proposal by State Representatives Bill Mitchell and Adam Brown, and again in 2019, with a resolution to the U.S. Congress to that effect by State Representatives Brad Halbrook, Chris Miller, and Darren Bailey.[36]

Indiana
• Indiana was originally part of the Northwest Territory, given in secession by the State of Virginia.
• In 2012, Indiana citizens endorsed the Federal online petition for secession.[37]

Iowa
In 2012, over 3,300 Iowans endorsed the Federal online petition for secession.

Kansas
In 1992, State Representative Gene Shore of Johnson City, Kansas, offered an amendment to allow counties to secede from the State in protest over State-wide property taxation to finance schools.[38, 39]

Kentucky
• Kentucky was created by secession from counties in western Virginia, whose enabling acts of 1788 allowed it to become a State four years later.
• Kentucky was a Border State during the War Between the States (1861-1865), having divided governments and being occupied by Federal troops.

Louisiana
Louisiana was one of the 11 Confederate States (1861-1865).

Maine
• Maine was created by secession from Massachusetts counties, becoming a State in 1820.
• From 1827 to 1842, the Republic of Madawaska existed as an unrecognized country along the Canadian border.[40]
• From the early 1880s to its most recent attempt in 2011, Peaks Island tried to secede from Portland, Maine at least eight times.[41]

• In 1997 and again in 2005, State representative Henry Joy proposed seceding the rural northern Maine from the south, which he blamed for the decline of traditional industries such as paper and forestry.[42]

• In 2015, the residents of Caribou, Maine, led by Paul Camping attempted secession, mainly because of over-taxation by the city of Portland.[43]

Maryland

• Maryland was the most strongly secessionist Border State and Middle Atlantic State during the War Between the States (1861-1865), but occupation by Federal troops prevented its joining the Confederacy.

• During the American Revolution, the State of Westsylvania was proposed, covering present-day West Virginia, the southwestern corner of Pennsylvania, the northeast corner of present-day Kentucky, and part of Maryland.[44]

• In the 1930s, nine counties of Maryland's Eastern Shore, the two counties of Virginia's Eastern Shore and the whole of Delaware proposed the State of Delmarva. In 1998, State legislators Richard F. Colburn and J. Lowell Stoltzfus managed to place secession for the East Shore before its citizens, and it passed; however, after internal dissention, the parts of the new State eventually seceded from Delmarva to rejoin their original States.[45]

• In 2009 and 2010, Frederick County Commissioner John L. Thompson Jr. attempted to have the county secede from Maryland.[46]

• In 2014, Scott Strzelczyk, Suzanne Olden and Rob Parr formed the Western Maryland Initiative to advance secession for western counties in the State.[47]

Massachusetts

• In 1803, U.S. Senator, former Secretary of State to Washington and Adams, and anglophile, Timothy Pickering, wrote: "I will rather anticipate a new confederacy, exempt from the corrupt and corrupting influence and oppression of the aristocratic Democrats of the South."[48]

• From 1778 until 1815, the Essex Junto was active as a group of ardent secessionists. Their discontent was rooted in their opposition to the Constitution, to Jeffersonian principles, to the Louisiana Purchase of 1803, to the Embargo of 1807, and to Southern leadership of national politics up to that time. They failed to enlist Alexander Hamilton in their plan to have New York secede, but did interest Aaron Burr. They were ardent supporters of the Hartford Convention.[49]

• On December 15, 1814, Federalists convened the Hartford Convention to debate seceding the State because of the local unpopularity of the War of 1812.[50] John Quincy Adams, Timothy Pickering, Fisher Ames, Elbridge Gerry, Theophilus Parsons, Josiah Quincy, and Joseph Story were among the leaders of the movement.[51]

• Even into the War Between the States, Essex County remained a hotbed of secession, when supporters of William Lloyd Garrison advocated its separation from Massachusetts.[52]

• In 1842, 46 businessmen of Haverhill, Massachusetts petitioned to dissolve the United States.[53]

• On April 13, 1857, the small town of Boston Corners in the southwestern part of Massachusetts seceded to join New York.[54]

• On July 23, 1919, State Representative James H. Brennan of Charlestown – angry with his constituents having to pay $600,000 in school taxes "of which not a cent's worth of benefit will be derived" – filed a bill to make a separate State of Boston, Chelsea, Revere, and the town of Winthrop.[55]

• In 1977, John Alley of West Tisbury and others proposed the secession of Martha's Vineyard and other neighboring islands from the State because proposed redistricting left them without representation.[56]

Michigan

• Michigan was originally part of the Northwest Territory, given in secession by the State of Virginia.

• In the 1830s, the U.S. Congress forced upon the new State of Michigan the Upper Peninsula, which did not have a bridge to connect it to Michigan until 120 years later. Its remoteness and unlikeness to the State have inspired many secession attempts as the State of Superior or the State of Ontonagon by its citizens, called "Yoopers," the latest of which occurred in 1975.[57]

• In 1844, James Jesse Strang declared himself monarch of the Mormon Kingdom of Beaver Island in Lake Michigan.[58]

• In 1979, Citizens for Secession attempted to secede Cass County to Indiana, with its name changed to "Michiana County."[59]

Minnesota

• Minnesota was originally part of the Northwest Territory, given in secession by the State of Virginia.

• In 1998, the Northwest Angle, Minnesota – that odd finger of land poking up from the State's 49° North Latitude border with Canada – saw its residents announce their desire to secede from the U.S. and join Manitoba.[60]

• In March, 2021, State Representative Jeremy Munson of Lake Crystal introduced HF-2423 to allow Minnesota counties to secede from the State and join South Dakota, particularly contending that western rural counties were no longer fairly represented in the State legislature. [61, 62]

Mississippi

• Mississippi was created by secession from western Georgia counties.

• It was one of the 11 Confederate States (1861-1865).

• From 1864 to mid-1865, a group of Confederate deserters led by Newton Knight hid in the swamps of the Leaf River in Jones County, where they seceded from the South as the Free State of Jones in allegiance with the U.S. government.[63]

Missouri
• Missouri was a Border State during the War Between the States (1861-1865), having divided governments and being occupied by Federal troops.
• In July, 1961, McDonald County briefly seceded to become McDonald Territory.[64]

Montana
• In 1939, counties in western South Dakota, northern Wyoming, and south-eastern Montana – all rural counties dissatisfied with their representation in remote urban capitals – joined to secede as the State of Absaroka.[65]
• In 2007 activist Russell Means, a Lakota Sioux advocate, proposed the creation of a Republic of Lakotah, comprising parts of North Dakota, South Dakota, Nebraska, Wyoming and Montana – currently Indian reservations defined by the 1851 Treaty of Fort Laramie.[66]

Nebraska
• In the 1860s, Nebraska panhandle leaders announced their intention to secede from Nebraska and join Wyoming in a dispute over water allocations.[67]
• In 2007 activist Russell Means, a Lakota Sioux advocate, proposed the creation of a Republic of Lakotah, comprising parts of North Dakota, South Dakota, Nebraska, Wyoming and Montana – currently Indian reservations defined by the 1851 Treaty of Fort Laramie.[68]

Nevada
A New Nevada movement was formed in 2018 by Robert Thomas III to secede rural counties from the rest of the State.[69]

New Hampshire
• The Indian Stream Republic, around Pittsburg, was an independent nation from 1832 to 1835.[70]
• On December 15, 1814, Federalists convened the Hartford Convention to debate seceding the State because of the local unpopularity of the War of 1812.[71] John Quincy Adams, Timothy Pickering, Fisher Ames, Elbridge Gerry, Theophilus Parsons, Josiah Quincy, and Joseph Story were among the leaders of the movement.[72]
• On March 10, 2022, the New Hampshire State House voted down CACR 32, a constitutional amendment that would have allowed voters to decide the

question of declaring peaceful independence from the United States. 13 members had supported the measure.[73, 74] Elliot Axelman had listed 12 benefits that he contends would have resulted from independence.[75]

New Jersey
• Although one of the Middle Atlantic States during the War Between the States (1861-1865), its secessionists had no political influence.[76]
• On November 4, 1980, five of six counties in southern New Jersey voted to secede. In all but one of the six counties where county lawmakers allowed the question on the ballot, the non-binding referendum was approved.[77]

New Mexico
The territory seceded from Mexico and separated from Texas in 1845, when Texas joined the Union.

New York
• New York was a Middle Atlantic State during the War Between the States (1861-1865), but with little secessionist sentiment. However, Fernando Wood, who was twice Mayor of New York City (1860-1861 and 1855-1857), advocated that the city to secede from both the Union and the State of New York.[78]
• In the 1969 New York City mayoral race, Norman Mailer and Jimmy Breslin (running for City Council President) ran on a platform that contained the proposal to have the city secede and become the 51st State — an idea partly rooted in mayor Fernando Wood's proposal from a century earlier.[79]
• In 1999, when the New York State legislature repealed the New York City's 0.45 percent tax on commuters' income, mayor Rudolph W. Giuliani and the City Council proposed statehood for the city. Upstate Senator John R. Kuhl Jr. obliged them by proposing that New York City, Long Island and Westchester and Rockland Counties became a separate State called New York, with the rest of the counties to be called West New York – a very popular idea throughout the State at the time.[80]
• In 2007, Cesidio Tallini proposed that Long Island — comprising Brooklyn, Queens and Nassau and Suffolk Counties — should secede from the United States and form the sovereign nation of Independent Long Island.[81]
• In 2009, 2013, and 2015, various State senators proposed non-binding referenda on the question of dividing the State in two.[82]
• In the 2010 State governor's race, Carl Paladino, running as a candidate for the Taxpayer Party, Rus Thompson, and James Ostrowski (the latter two being leaders of a Western New York secession movement) all ran as libertarians proposing the separation of upstate and downstate New York.[83]
• In 2015, the Upstate New York Towns Association explored the possibility of 15 southern New York State towns seceding to join Pennsylvania so that they

could profit from extracting natural gas in the Marcellus Shale, which New York had outlawed.[84]

• In 2020, State senator Robert G. Ortt sponsored a constitutional amendment to divide the State into three autonomous regions: The New Amsterdam Region, the New York Region, and the Montauk Region, with separate regional governors and regional legislators for each.[85]

North Carolina

• In 1789, the State of North Carolina gave its lands west of the Appalachians to the Federal government; the next year the U.S. created the Southwest Territory, from which the State of Tennessee was created in 1796.[86]

• North Carolina was one of the 11 Confederate States (1861-1865).

North Dakota

In 2007 activist Russell Means, a Lakota Sioux advocate, proposed the creation of a Republic of Lakotah, comprising parts of North Dakota, South Dakota, Nebraska, Wyoming and Montana – currently Indian reservations defined by the 1851 Treaty of Fort Laramie.[87]

Ohio

• The "Pontiac Rebellion" (1763-1766) represents a Native American secession from Britain, as well as a colonial nullification of The Proclamation of 1763, which forbade white settlement west of the Appalachians.[88]

• Ohio was originally part of the Northwest Territory, given in secession by the State of Virginia.

Oklahoma

Senator Joseph Silk proposed changing Section I-1 of Oklahoma's constitution to delete the word "inseparable" from the phrase "The State of Oklahoma is an inseparable part of the Federal Union, and the Constitution of the United States is the supreme law of the land." Although Silk did not propose immediate secession, he wanted to provide for the possibility "30-40 years from now."[89]

Oregon

• Although citizens of southern Oregon were involved in attempts by Northern California to form the State of Jefferson in 1852 and in the 1941 "Yreka Rebellion," (see California), current secession interest focuses on becoming part of Idaho instead.

• In 2015, chimney sweep Grant Darrow took up the idea, current since the 1960s, of moving Idaho's western boundary farther west to incorporate the rural counties of Oregon, which felt alienated from the liberal politics of

Oregon's population centers. In the November 2020 election, four eastern counties were to move into Idaho; two counties approved the measure.[90]
• By 2021, the Greater Idaho movement had evolved into carving off about three-quarters of Oregon, reaching to the Pacific Ocean.[91]

Pennsylvania
• During the American Revolution, the State of Westsylvania was proposed, covering present-day West Virginia, the southwestern corner of Pennsylvania, the northeast corner of present-day Kentucky, and part of Maryland.[92]
• Pennsylvania was a Middle Atlantic State during the War Between the States (1861-1865), but with only a very weak secessionist element.[93]

Rhode Island
On December 15, 1814, Federalists convened the Hartford Convention to debate seceding the State because of the local unpopularity of the War of 1812.[94] John Quincy Adams, Timothy Pickering, Fisher Ames, Elbridge Gerry, Theophilus Parsons, Josiah Quincy, and Joseph Story were among its leaders.[95]

South Carolina
South Carolina was one of the 11 Confederate States (1861-1865).

South Dakota
• In 1939, counties in western South Dakota, northern Wyoming, and south-eastern Montana – all rural counties dissatisfied with their representation in remote urban capitals – joined to secede as the State of Absaroka.[96]
• In 2007 activist Russell Means, a Lakota Sioux advocate, proposed the creation of a Republic of Lakotah, comprising parts of North Dakota, South Dakota, Nebraska, Wyoming and Montana – currently Indian reservations defined by the 1851 Treaty of Fort Laramie.[97]

Tennessee
• North Carolina seceded what would become the Southwest Territory (see North Carolina), from which Tennessee was created, with statehood in 1796.
• Tennessee was one of the 11 Confederate States (1861-1865).
• Despite the State joining the Confederacy, many counties in the east supported the Union, among them Scott County, where over 90% of its voters cast their ballots against secession. Furthermore, they declared themselves the Free and Independent State of Scott – a proclamation that remained in county law until its repeal in 1986.[98]

Texas

• Texas was one of the 11 Confederate States (1861-1865).

• Since its life as an independent republic from 1836 to 1845, it has seen countless proposals for secession. At least six other republics were independent nations before joining the Union: Vermont Republic, 1777-1791; State of Muskogee (around Tallahassee, FL), 1799-1803; Republic of West Florida, 1810; Republic of Fredonia (around Nacogdoches, TX), 1826-1827; Indian Stream Republic (around Pittsburg, NH), 1832-1835; and California Republic, 1846.[99]

• In 2012, Texas had over 100,000 citizen endorsements of the Federal online petition for secession, the largest number of all the 50 States.[100]

• The Texas Nationalist Movement (tnm.me) has been in existence almost 20 years. Founded by its president, Daniel Miller, it has over 425,000 dues-paying members and some 210,000 followers on Facebook.[101]

Utah

• In 1849, Mormons in Utah proclaimed the State of Deseret, a sprawling area encompassing present-day States of Utah and Nevada, as well as southern California, most of Arizona, and parts of five other States. "Deseret," a word made up by Joseph Smith to mean "honeybee," went out of existence with the creation of the Utah Territory by the U.S. Congress in 1850.

• In 1857-1858, Mormons fought the Utah War against the U.S. government for independence, before becoming a State in 1896.

• In 2006, after a five year effort, Wendover, Utah, failed to secede into West Wendover, Nevada: Utah did not want Wendover to take its airport, and Nevada did not want Wendover's $27 million public debt.[102]

• In 2008, the familiar urban-rural dispute prompted State representative Neal B. Hendrickson to file HJR006 to create "a separate state, with the boundary stretching east and west across the present state of Utah and along the southern border of Utah County."[103]

Vermont

• The Vermont Republic was an independent nation between 1777 and 1791.

• On December 15, 1814, Vermont sent one delegate to the Hartford Convention to debate seceding from the Union because of the local unpopularity of the War of 1812.[104] John Quincy Adams, Timothy Pickering, Fisher Ames, Elbridge Gerry, Theophilus Parsons, Josiah Quincy, and Joseph Story were among the leaders of the movement.[105]

• In 2003, Thomas Naylor founded the Second Vermont Republic, and in 2010, the party fielded 10 candidates for State office. Naylor summarized the party platform as "left-libertarian, anti-big government, anti-empire, anti-war, with small is beautiful as our guiding philosophy."[106]

• In 2005, the cities of Winhall and Killington considered proposals to secede and join New Hampshire, despite the fact that Winhall was not adjacent to that State. Both cities were frustrated by high taxes and lack of representation in the capital of Montpelier.[107]

Virginia

• During the American Revolution, the State of Westsylvania was proposed, covering present-day West Virginia, the southwestern corner of Pennsylvania, the northeast corner of present-day Kentucky, and part of Maryland.[108]
• Virginia was one of the 11 Confederate States (1861-1865).
• In 2020, Rick Boyer organized VEXIT, a movement to have counties in western Virginia secede and join West Virginia. Citizens of the counties were opposed to "the radical policies of Democrat Party leaders in Richmond."[109]

Washington

• Throughout the colonial period, Jefferson and other leading statesmen, James Monroe, James Madison, William Crawford, Henry Clay, Thomas Hart Benton, and Albert Gallatin supported an independent Pacific Republic.[110]
• Cascadia Now, a Seattle-based nonprofit founded by Brandon Letsinger, does not advocate secession, but instead a local "self-determination" on environmental matters.[111]
• Similarly, although it does not explicitly advocate secession, "The Cascadia Bioregional Party actively supports the break down [sic] and removal of arbitrary nation state [sic] borders within North America". "Cascadia" is a bioregion that "encompasses all or portions of Washington, Oregon, Idaho, California, Nevada, Wyoming, Montana, Alaska, British Columbia, and Alberta."[112]
• Eastern rural counties – all conservative, as rural counties typically are – have in recent years remained at odds with liberal policies imposed from the capital of Olympia. A sampling of some of the bills for secession:[113]
HB 1818 - 2015-16: "Creating a task force to determine the impacts of adjusting the boundary lines of Washington to create two new states with one state east and one state west of the Cascade mountain range."
HB 1832 - 2015-16: "Creating a task force to determine the impacts of adjusting the boundary lines of Washington and Oregon to create two new states with one state east and one state west of the Cascade mountain range."
HJM 4000 - 2017-18: "Petitioning for the creation of a new state in eastern Washington."
HB 1509 - 2019-20: "Establishing the new state of Liberty."

West Virginia

• During the American Revolution, the State of Westsylvania was proposed, covering present-day West Virginia, the southwestern corner of Pennsylvania, the northeast corner of present-day Kentucky, and part of Maryland.[114]

• In 1861, Lincoln recognized a new West Virginia government by personal fiat, and insisted that its two Senators and two Representatives be seated in Congress over the objections of some of its members. Lincoln's Secretary of State William Seward and Attorney General Edward Bates considered its admission into the Union to be unconstitutional, maintaining that the people in convention must vote to become a State – State creation being the unilateral power of neither the president nor Congress.[115]

Wisconsin

• Wisconsin was originally part of the Northwest Territory, given in secession by the State of Virginia.

• In April, 2014, Sixth Congressional Republican Caucus delegates passed a resolution reaffirming Wisconsin's right to secede from the union should it choose to do so. The measure passed through the GOP convention's Resolution Committee, but was voted down.[116]

• In 2017, Republican lawmakers threatened secession with a resolution that read: "BE IT FURTHER RESOLVED that we strongly insist our State representatives work to uphold Wisconsin's 10th Amendment rights, and our right to secede, passing legislation affirming this to the US Federal Government."[117]

Wyoming

• In 1939, counties in western South Dakota, northern Wyoming, and southeastern Montana – all rural counties dissatisfied with their representation in remote urban capitals – joined to secede as the State of Absaroka.[118]

• In 2007 activist Russell Means, a Lakota Sioux advocate, proposed the creation of a Republic of Lakotah, comprising parts of North Dakota, South Dakota, Nebraska, Wyoming and Montana – currently Indian reservations defined by the 1851 Treaty of Fort Laramie.[119]

[1] Failla, Zak, "New Poll Reveals Percentages Of Americans Who Want To Secede By Region," *White Plains Daily Voice* (published August 1, 2021) <https://dailyvoice.com/new-york/whiteplains/politics/new-poll-reveals-percentages-of-americans-who-want-to-secede-by-region/812724/> accessed February 5, 2022. The poll measured support for the respondent's home State seceding to join one of five regional unions. Pollsters found that "rather than support for secession diminishing over the past six months, as we expected, it rose in every region and among nearly every partisan group. [...] The jump is most dramatic where support was already highest (and has the greatest historical precedent) — among Republicans in the South."

[2] Buckley, F.H., *American Secession: The Looming Threat of a National Breakup* (Encounter Books, January 14, 2020, ISBN 978-1641770804, 184 pages), page x, writing of current trends: "[T]he states with the most active secession movements are progressive".

[3] Ryan, Danielle, "White House receives secession pleas from all 50 States," *Los Angeles Times* (published November 14, 2012) <https://www.latimes.com/politics/la-xpm-2012-nov-14-la-pn-white-house-secession-50-states-20121114-story.html> accessed February 5, 2022.

[4] Abbeville Inst, "The Disintegration of Lincolnian America by Donald Livingston," (*YouTube*, length 52:52, published April 12, 2018) <https://www.youtube.com/watch?v=oC5vlcjWzpk> accessed February 10, 2022. From 8:56 to 9:56.

[5] Collet, Christian, "Alaskan Independence Party Introduction," *AKIP* (last edited December 13, 2021) <http://www.akip.org/introduction.html> accessed April 23, 2022.

[6] Lee, Steve, "How Arizona Seceded from the Union," *Abbeville Institute* (published October 22, 2020) <https://www.abbevilleinstitute.org/how-arizona-seceded-from-the-union/> accessed April 23, 2022.

[7] "America's 51st state: Baja Arizona?" *NBC News* (published March 1, 2011) <https://www.nbcnews.com/id/wbna41858048> accessed April 23, 2022.

[8] Wood, Stephen, "When California (Briefly) Became Its Own Nation," *History* (published September 9, 2020) <https://www.history.com/news/california-independence-bear-flag-revolt> accessed October 4, 2022.

[9] Chea, Terry, "California secession fever is nothing new. There's a rich history of wanting to slice up the state or split it off," *Los Angeles Times* (published December 24, 2016) <https://www.latimes.com/politics/la-pol-ca-road-map-california-secession-20161224-story.html> accessed April 23, 2022.

[10] Ibid.

[11] Marinelli, Louis, "On the founding of CalExit and it's [sic] new meaning for 2022 and beyond," *Substack* (published January 5, 2022) <https://marinelli.substack.com/p/founding-calexit-and-new-meaning> accessed September 3, 2022. According to Marinelli, Evans insisted on the term "devolution" not to distinguish it from secession, but because "he was afraid of being associated with southern rednecks from the states of the former Confederacy if we were to use that dirty 'S' word".

[12] Panzar, Javier, "'Calexit' leaders are back with a new plan to set aside land for Native Americans," *Los Angeles Times* (published July 31, 2018) <https://www.latimes.com/politics/la-pol-ca-new-calexit-plan-20180731-story.html> accessed April 23, 2022.

[13] DeLeon, Kelly, "Oroville declares itself a Constitutional Republic," *KRCR ABC affiliate* (published November 3, 2021) <https://krcrtv.com/news/oroville-declares-itself-a-constitutional-republic> accessed March 14, 2022.

[14] "Draft Initiative: An Act Reaffirming the Sovereignty of California," *Free The Bear* (last edited April 28, 1998) <https://calrepublic.tripod.com/caplan.html> accessed April 23, 2022.

15 Griffin, Anna, "Far-fetched as they might seem, secession movements are thriving in the NW," *Oregon Public Broadcasting* (published March 23, 2017) <https://www.opb.org/news/article/pacific-northwest-secession-state-of-jefferson-cascadia/> accessed April 26, 2022.

16 "Indigenous Sovereignties," *The Cascadia Bioregional Party* (published January 24, 2019) <https://cascadiabioregionalparty.org/indigenous-sovereignty/> accessed April 26, 2022.

17 Colwell, Andy, "Weld County residents propose leaving Colorado again, this time to join Wyoming," *The Colorado Sun* (published January 27, 2021) <https://coloradosun.com/2021/01/27/weld-county-secession-wyoming/> accessed April 24, 2022.

18 Bonham, Nick, "51st State Initiative (secession)," *Coyote Gulch* (published September 10, 2013) <https://coyotegulch.blog/category/colorado-water/51st-state-initiative-north-colorado-secession/> accessed April 24, 2022.

19 Kiggins, Steve, "With Colorado 'at war' with small businesses, agriculture, and oil and gas, Weld County group seeks secession to Wyoming," *USA Today* (last edited January 29, 2021) <https://www.usatoday.com/story/news/nation/2021/01/28/colorado-weld-county-wyoming-secession/4304239001/> accessed April 24, 2022.

20 Janis, Mark, "The Hartford Convention and the Specter of Secession," *UConn Today* (published December 15, 2014) <https://today.uconn.edu/2014/12/the-hartford-convention-and-the-specter-of-secession/> accessed April 25, 2022.

21 Banner, James M., *To the Hartford Convention: the Federalists and the origins of party politics in Massachusetts, 1789-1815* (Alfred A. Knopf, January 1, 1970, ASIN B0006CK7KU, 378 pages), page 115: "From at least 1786, the [Massachusetts] Commonwealth had been the special spawning ground of disunionist schemes."

22 Mussomeli, Vito, "The Secession Movement in the Middle States," *Abbeville Institute* (published October 29, 2019) <https://www.abbevilleinstitute.org/the-secession-movement-in-the-middle-states/> accessed April 16, 2022.

23 "The Founding of the Conch Republic," *The Official Website of the Conch Republic* (last edited December 27, 2021) <https://conchrepublic.com/our-founding-in-1982/> accessed April 24, 2022.

24 Huriash, Lisa J., "North Lauderdale wants to split Florida into two states," *South Florida Sun-Sentinel* (published May 06, 2008) <https://www.sun-sentinel.com/news/sfl-flbnewstate0507pnmay07-story.html> accessed April 24, 2022.

25 Holmes, Aaron, "In Pierce County, hard times and a push to 'secede' from Georgia," *The Atlanta Journal-Constitution* (published June 18, 2018) <https://www.ajc.com/news/state--regional-govt--politics/pierce-county-hard-times-and-push-secede-from-georgia/eyJj2rF8NqcQ5HFdSdVlaL/> accessed April 24, 2022.

26 O'Harrow, Stephen, "If the goal is for Hawaii to form its own nation, many legal and political barriers block the way," *Honolulu Civil Beat* (published March 6, 2020) <https://www.civilbeat.org/2020/03/full-independence-for-hawaii-looks-unfeasible-for-now/> accessed April 24, 2022.

27 Timsit, Annabelle, "5 U.S. Independence Movements Inspired by Brexit," *Politico Magazine* (published July 04, 2016) <https://www.politico.com/magazine/story/2016/07/5-us-independence-movements-inspired-by-brexit-214010/> accessed February 5, 2022.

28 McClelland, John M. Jr., "Prelude to Statehood — The Remarkable Beginning of Washington Territory," *Columbia The Magazine of Northwest History*, Summer 1988 Vol. 2, No. 2. Online at <https://www.washingtonhistory.org/wp-content/uploads/2020/04/02-2_McClelland-1.pdf> accessed April 24, 2022.

29 Banel, Feliks, "Eastern Washington: Most likely to secede ever since 1861," *My Northwest* (last edited February 6, 2019) <https://mynorthwest.com/1259527/washington-secede-state-of-liberty/> accessed April 24, 2022.

[30] Hitchens, Antonia, "Modern America's Most Successful Secessionist Movement," *The Atlantic* (published December 23, 2021) <https://www.theatlantic.com/politics/archive/2021/12/oregon-secession-idaho-move-border/621087/> accessed April 24, 2022.

[31] Johnson, Kirk, "Their Own Private Idaho: Five Oregon Counties Back a Plan to Secede," *The New York Times* (published May 21, 2021) <https://www.nytimes.com/2021/05/21/us/oregon-idaho-secession.html> accessed April 26, 2022.

[32] Ibid.

[33] Gale, Neil, "Chicago proposes to secede from Illinois to form the 'State of Chicago'," *Digital Research Library of Illinois History Journal* (published November 25, 2019) <https://drloihjournal.blogspot.com/2019/11/the-state-of-chicago.html> accessed April 24, 2022.

[34] McClelland, Edward, "Activists are again asking Congress to split Illinois into two states: Chicago, and everything else," *Chicago* magazine (published October 15, 2020) <https://www.chicagomag.com/news/october-2020/illinois-secession/> accessed April 24, 2022.

[35] Ibid.

[36] Ibid.

[37] "Indiana Lawmakers Mixed On Secession Petition," *WSCH Wagon Wheel Broadcasting* (published November 14, 2012) <https://www.eaglecountryonline.com/news/local-news/indiana-lawmakers-mixed-on-secession-petition/> accessed February 5, 2022.

[38] Hanna, John, "House turns aside secession proposal," *Hutchinson News* (published April 12, 1991) <https://kgi.contentdm.oclc.org/digital/api/collection/p16884coll1/id/276/download> accessed April 24, 2022.

[39] McCormick, Peter J., "The 1992 Secession Movement in Southwest Kansas," *Great Plains Quarterly*, No. 994, 1995. Online at <https://core.ac.uk/download/pdf/188061153.pdf> accessed April 24, 2022.

[40] Morgan, James, "Neither American or Canadian: the Republic of Madawaska," *North Country Public Radio* (published July 10, 2016) <https://blogs.northcountrypublicradio.org/allin/2016/07/10/neither-american-or-canadian-the-republic-of-madawaska/> accessed April 25, 2022.

[41] Hurd-Forsyth, Holly, "Exploring Independence: A Brief History of Peaks Secession Movements," *Fifth Maine Museum* (published October 6, 2020) <https://www.fifthmainemuseum.org/2020/10/06/exploring-independence-a-brief-history-of-peaks-secession-movements/> accessed April 25, 2022.

[42] Donahue, Sean, "A separate peace | A conversation with Rep. Henry Joy, an Aroostook County Republican who advocates creating a new state in northern Maine," *Mainbiz* (published April 18, 2005) <https://www.mainebiz.biz/article/a-separate-peace-a-conversation-with-rep-henry-joy-an-aroostook-county-republican-who> accessed April 25, 2022.

[43] Sherwood, Dave, "Movement to break up tiny Caribou, Maine, takes step forward," *Reuters* (published March 31, 2015) <https://www.reuters.com/article/us-usa-maine-secession/movement-to-break-up-tiny-caribou-maine-takes-step-forward-idUSKBN0MR2AT20150331> accessed April 25, 2022.

[44] "The forgotten history of Westsylvania," *Observer-Reporter* (last edited May 8, 2021) <https://observer-reporter.com/publications/liwc/the-forgotten-history-of-westsylvania/article_41011b14-6ab5-11ea-bff9-57ff6679a38d.html> accessed April 25, 2022.

[45] Thompson, William L., "The Rise and Fall of Delmarva, the 51st State," *The Baltimore Sun* (published February 24, 1998) <https://www.baltimoresun.com/news/bs-xpm-1998-02-25-1998056159-story.html> accessed April 25, 2022.

[46] Stern, Nicholas C., "Commissioners reject proposal to secede from state," *The Frederick News-Post* (last edited March 11, 2016) <https://www.fredericknewspost.com/archive/article_7a0a9fc4-7bb4-5940-a722-7d0fa7952f8c.html> accessed April 25, 2022.

[47] Bubala, Mary, "Some Western Md. Residents Want To Form Their Own State," *CBS Baltimore* (published February 10, 2014) <https://baltimore.cbslocal.com/2014/02/10/some-western-md-residents-want-to-form-their-own-state/> accessed April 25, 2022.

[48] "Letter of Timothy Pickering to Richard Peters," in *Henry Adams, Documents Relating to New-England Federalism, 1800-1815* (Little, Brown & Co., 1877), page 338.

[49] Brown, Charles Raymond, *The Northern Confederacy according to the plans of the 'Essex junto', 1796-1814* (Library of Congress, December 31, 1915, ASIN B003TXT696, 140 pages), pages 25ff.

[50] Janis, Mark, "The Hartford Convention and the Specter of Secession," *UConn Today* (published December 15, 2014) <https://today.uconn.edu/2014/12/the-hartford-convention-and-the-specter-of-secession/> accessed April 25, 2022.

[51] Banner, James M., *To the Hartford Convention: the Federalists and the origins of party politics in Massachusetts, 1789-1815* (Alfred A. Knopf, January 1, 1970, ASIN B0006CK7KU, 378 pages), page 115: "From at least 1786, the [Massachusetts] Commonwealth had been the special spawning ground of disunionist schemes."

[52] Tuttleton, James W., "The many lives of Frederick Douglass," *The New Criterion*, Vol. 12, No. 6, February 1994. Online at <https://web.archive.org/web/20051217101513/http://www.newcriterion.com/archive/12/feb94/douglass.htm> accessed April 25, 2022.

[53] Kreitner, Richard, *Break It Up: Secession, Division, and the Secret History of America's Imperfect Union* (Little, Brown and Company, August 18, 2020, ISBN 978-0316510608, 496 pages), page 153.

[54] Ellis, Capt. Franklin, "Boston Corners and Weed Mine, Ancram, Columbia County, New York," from *History of Columbia County, New York*, 1878, pages 372-373.

[55] Trinklein, Michael J., "Altered states: The strange history of efforts to redraw the New England map," *boston.com* (published May 2, 2010) <http://archive.boston.com/bostonglobe/ideas/articles/2010/05/02/altered_states/?page=full> accessed April 25, 2022.

[56] Seccombe, Mike, "Talkin' About a Revolution," *Martha's Vineyard Magazine*, September-October 2007 edition. Online at <https://web.archive.org/web/20110714141528/http://www.mvmagazine.com/2007/september-october/secession.php> accessed April 25, 2022.

[57] Trinklein, Michael, "'Superior' could be our nation's 51st state," *Wisconsin State Journal* (published April 30, 2021) <https://madison.com/wsj/opinion/column/michael-trinklein-superior-could-be-our-nations-51st-state/article_c25fe178-79da-5c9a-84b1-fa4dbefdbb4a.html> accessed April 25, 2022.

[58] Ovitt, Nell, "New book documents the life of James Jesse Strang, self-professed Mormon monarch of Beaver Island," *Michigan Radio* (published July 24, 2020) <https://www.michiganradio.org/arts-culture/2020-07-24/new-book-documents-the-life-of-james-jesse-strang-self-professed-mormon-monarch-of-beaver-island> accessed April 25, 2022.

[59] "They 'want out of Michigan'," *Lansing State Journal*, October 25, 1979, page 1.

[60] Radil, Amy, "The Northwest Angle," *Minnesota Public Radio* (published August 17, 1998) <http://news.minnesota.publicradio.org/features/199808/17_radila_angle-m/> accessed April 25, 2022.

[61] Munson, Jeremy, "Minnesota lawmaker proposes secession to border states," *ABC KSTP News* (last edited April 2, 2021) <https://kstp.com/politics/minnesota-lawmaker-proposes-secession-to-border-states-2/> accessed April 25, 2022.

[62] "Minnesota lawmaker proposes bill to allow counties to join South Dakota," *ABC News 18, Eau Claire* (published March 28, 2021) <https://www.wqow.com/news/minnesota-lawmaker-proposes-bill-to-allow-counties-to-join-south-dakota/article_1bc4c09d-96a0-57f8-925c-134010034c68.html> accessed April 25, 2022.

[63] Bynum, Victoria, *The Free State of Jones: Mississippi's Longest Civil War* (The University of North Carolina Press, January 25, 2016, ISBN 978-1469627052, 350 pages).

[64] [no last name provided], Kaitlyn, "That time McDonald County seceded from Missouri," *Ozarks Alive* (published June 23, 2019) <https://www.ozarksalive.com/stories/that-time-mcdonald-county-seceded-from-missouri> accessed April 25, 2022.

[65] Pedersen, Nate, "The State of Absaroka: Redrawing our borders would have left us without the Badlands, Black Hills and Mount Rushmore," *South Dakota Magazine*, July/August 2009 issue (published 2017) <https://www.southdakotamagazine.com/article?articleTitle=the+state+of+Absaroka%20(1939)--1311951720--138--history> accessed April 25, 2022.

[66] Palet, Laura Secorun, "Americans for independence... from America," *USA Today* (published November 4, 2014) <https://www.usatoday.com/story/news/politics/2014/11/04/ozy-america-secessionist-movement/18457863/> accessed April 25, 2022.

[67] May, Robert, "Thinking About The Future," *Southwest Regional Group of the Nebraska Development Network* (published May, 1999) <https://web.archive.org/web/20060720150053/http://www.buffalocommons.org/docs/smenu1/divided_nebr.html> accessed April 25, 2022.

[68] Palet, Laura Secorun, "Americans for independence... from America," *USA Today* (published November 4, 2014) <https://www.usatoday.com/story/news/politics/2014/11/04/ozy-america-secessionist-movement/18457863/> accessed April 25, 2022.

[69] Appleton, Rory, "Longshot 'New Nevada' idea born of political frustration," *Las Vegas Review-Journal* (published December 18, 2020) <https://www.reviewjournal.com/news/politics-and-government/nevada/longshot-new-nevada-idea-born-of-political-frustration-2225079/> accessed April 25, 2022.

[70] "Indian Stream Republic," *Pittsburgh, New Hampshire* <https://pittsburg-nh.com/index.php/about-pittsburg/town-history/41-indian-stream-republic> accessed October 4, 2022.

[71] Janis, Mark, "The Hartford Convention and the Specter of Secession," *UConn Today* (published December 15, 2014) <https://today.uconn.edu/2014/12/the-hartford-convention-and-the-specter-of-secession/> accessed April 25, 2022.

[72] Banner, James M., *To the Hartford Convention: the Federalists and the origins of party politics in Massachusetts, 1789-1815* (Alfred A. Knopf, January 1, 1970, ASIN B0006CK7KU, 378 pages), page 115: "From at least 1786, the [Massachusetts] Commonwealth had been the special spawning ground of disunionist schemes."

[73] "CACR 32 Voted down by NH House March 10th 2022," *NHexit* (published March 12, 2022) <https://nhexit.us/> accessed April 25, 2022.

[74] Tracy, Paula, "N.H. could become its own nation under CACR 32," *The Conway Daily Sun* (edited January 21, 2022) <https://www.conwaydailysun.com/news/local/n-h-could-become-its-own-nation-under-cacr-32/article_79f62438-7afc-11ec-935d-b39bf17835d5.html> accessed January 24, 2022.

[75] Axelman, Elliot, "12 Benefits of New Hampshire Independence" *The Liberty Block* (published October 21, 2019) <https://libertyblock.com/12-benefits-of-new-hampshire-secession/> accessed April 25, 2022.

[76] Mussomeli, Vito, "The Secession Movement in the Middle States," *Abbeville Institute* (published October 29, 2019) <https://www.abbevilleinstitute.org/the-secession-movement-in-the-middle-states/> accessed April 16, 2022.

[77] Larsen, Erik, "South Jersey voted to secede from NJ," *Jersey Roots* (published March 5, 2016) <https://www.app.com/story/news/history/erik-larsen/2016/03/05/south-jersey-votes-secede-nj/81323914/> accessed April 16, 2022.

[78] Mussomeli, Vito, "The Secession Movement in the Middle States," *Abbeville Institute* (published October 29, 2019) <https://www.abbevilleinstitute.org/the-secession-movement-in-the-middle-states/> accessed April 16, 2022.

[79] Roberts, Sam, "Podcast: Remembering Mailer for Mayor," *The New York Times* (published November 14, 2007) <https://web.archive.org/web/20100115233532/http://cityroom.blogs.nytimes.com/2007/11/14/podcast-remembering-mailer-for-mayor/> accessed April 16, 2022.

[80] Tierney, John, "The Big City; The Moochers From Upstate? Cut 'Em Loose," *The New York Times* (published May 24, 1999) <https://www.nytimes.com/1999/05/24/nyregion/the-big-city-the-moochers-from-upstate-cut-em-loose.html> accessed April 16, 2022.

[81] Kilgannon, Corey, "What Has the Hamptons, 4 Airports and a Hankering for Independence?" *The New York Times* (published September 22, 2007) <https://www.nytimes.com/2007/09/22/nyregion/22secede.html> accessed April 16, 2022.

[82] McCarthy, Jimmy, "Another Bill Aims To Divide State," *Post-Journal* (published February 21, 2015) <http://web.archive.org/web/20150222050656/http://post-journal.com/page/content.detail/id/661644/Another-Bill-Aims-To-Divide-State.html?nav=5192> accessed April 16, 2022.

[83] Barrett, Wayne, "How Does Carl Paladino Get the 'Tea Party' Tag After Teabagging the Tea Partiers?" *The Village Voice* (published October 14, 2010) <https://web.archive.org/web/20101118093834/http://blogs.villagevoice.com/runninscared/2010/10/how_does_carl_p.php> accessed April 16, 2022.

[84] Goggin, Caroline, "Southern Tier towns looking to cut NY ties," *WBNG Binghamton* (last edited February 19, 2015) <https://web.archive.org/web/20150219175611/http://www.wbng.com/news/local/Southern-Tier-towns-looking-to-cut-NY-ties--292486411.html> accessed April 16, 2022.

[85] Ortt, Robert G. (sponsor), "Senate Bill S5416," *The New York State Senate* (last edited January 30, 2022) <https://www.nysenate.gov/legislation/bills/2019/s5416> accessed April 16, 2022.

[86] "Southwest Territory 1790-1796," *TNGen Web Project* (last edited February 6, 2022) <https://www.tngenweb.org/tnletters/territories/sw-terr.html> accessed April 25, 2022.

[87] Palet, Laura Secorun, "Americans for independence... from America," *USA Today* (published November 4, 2014) <https://www.usatoday.com/story/news/politics/2014/11/04/ozy-america-secessionist-movement/18457863/> accessed April 25, 2022.

[88] "Pontiac's Rebellion," *Ohio History Central* (last edited April 7, 2022) <https://ohiohistorycentral.org/w/Pontiac%27s_Rebellion> accessed April 26, 2022.

[89] "Lawmaker says proposed bill would allow Oklahoma to secede," *News 4* (last edited January 19, 2017) <https://kfor.com/news/lawmaker-says-proposed-bill-would-allow-oklahoma-to-secede/> accessed April 26, 2022.

[90] Hitchens, Antonia, "Modern America's Most Successful Secessionist Movement," *The Atlantic* (published December 23, 2021) <https://www.theatlantic.com/politics/archive/2021/12/oregon-secession-idaho-move-border/621087/> accessed April 24, 2022.

[91] Johnson, Kirk, "Their Own Private Idaho: Five Oregon Counties Back a Plan to Secede," *The New York Times* (published May 21, 2021) <https://www.nytimes.com/2021/05/21/us/oregon-idaho-secession.html> accessed April 26, 2022.

[92] "The forgotten history of Westsylvania," *Observer-Reporter* (last edited May 8, 2021) <https://observer-reporter.com/publications/liwc/the-forgotten-history-of-westsylvania/article_41011b14-6ab5-11ea-bff9-57ff6679a38d.html> accessed April 25, 2022.

[93] Mussomeli, Vito, "The Secession Movement in the Middle States," *Abbeville Institute* (published October 29, 2019) <https://www.abbevilleinstitute.org/the-secession-movement-in-the-middle-states/> accessed April 16, 2022.

[94] Janis, Mark, "The Hartford Convention and the Specter of Secession," *UConn Today* (published December 15, 2014) <https://today.uconn.edu/2014/12/the-hartford-convention-and-the-specter-of-secession/> accessed April 25, 2022.

[95] Banner, James M., *To the Hartford Convention: the Federalists and the origins of party politics in Massachusetts, 1789-1815* (Alfred A. Knopf, January 1, 1970, ASIN B0006CK7KU, 378 pages), page 115: "From at least 1786, the [Massachusetts] Commonwealth had been the special spawning ground of disunionist schemes."

[96] Pedersen, Nate, "The State of Absaroka: Redrawing our borders would have left us without the Badlands, Black Hills and Mount Rushmore," *South Dakota Magazine*, July/August 2009 issue (published 2017) <https://www.southdakotamagazine.com/article?articleTitle=the+state+of+Absaroka%20(1939)--1311951720--138--history> accessed April 25, 2022.

[97] Palet, Laura Secorun, "Americans for independence… from America," *USA Today* (published November 4, 2014) <https://www.usatoday.com/story/news/politics/2014/11/04/ozy-america-secessionist-movement/18457863/> accessed April 25, 2022.

[98] "The Free & Independent State of Scott," *Scott County Tennessee* (last edited April 6, 2022) <https://scottcounty.com/welcome/about-scott-county/the-free-independent-state-of-scott/> accessed April 25, 2022.

[99] Andrews, Evan, "6 Short-Lived Republics in the United States," *History* (last edited December 15, 2016) <https://www.history.com/news/6-short-lived-republics-in-the-united-states> accessed April 26, 2022.

[100] Fernandez, Manny, "White House Rejects Petitions to Secede, but Texans Fight On," *The New York Times* (published January 15, 2013) <https://www.nytimes.com/2013/01/16/us/politics/texas-secession-movement-unbowed-by-white-house-rejection.html> accessed April 26, 2022.

[101] Holley, Peter, "Are Texas Republicans Serious About Secession?" *Texas Monthly* magazine (published November 2022) <https://www.texasmonthly.com/news-politics/are-texas-republicans-serious-about-secession/> accessed November 14, 2022.

[102] "City merger looks dead in Wendover," *Deseret News* (published March 6, 2006) <https://www.deseret.com/2006/3/6/19941841/city-merger-looks-dead-in-wendover> accessed April 25, 2022.

[103] "Joint Resolution Consenting to Creation of New State Within Utah," *Utah State Legislature* (last edited January 2, 2008) <https://le.utah.gov/~2008/bills/hbillint/hjr006.htm> accessed April 25, 2022.

[104] Janis, Mark, "The Hartford Convention and the Specter of Secession," *UConn Today* (published December 15, 2014) <https://today.uconn.edu/2014/12/the-hartford-convention-and-the-specter-of-secession/> accessed April 25, 2022.

[105] Banner, James M., *To the Hartford Convention: the Federalists and the origins of party politics in Massachusetts, 1789-1815* (Alfred A. Knopf, January 1, 1970, ASIN B0006CK7KU, 378 pages), page 115: "From at least 1786, the [Massachusetts] Commonwealth had been the special spawning ground of disunionist schemes."

[106] Galloway, Anne, "Startup Republic: Small secessionist group stands up to big 'empire'," *VTDigger* (published February 23, 2010) <https://vtdigger.org/2010/02/23/startup-republic-small-secessionist-group-stands-up-to-big-empire/> accessed April 26, 2022.

107 Keese, Susan, "Winhall rejects secession, still unhappy with Vermont," *Vermont Public Radio* (published March 1, 2005) <https://archive.vpr.org/vpr-news/winhall-rejects-secession-still-unhappy-with-vermont/> accessed April 26, 2022.

108 "The forgotten history of Westsylvania," *Observer-Reporter* (last edited May 8, 2021) <https://observer-reporter.com/publications/liwc/the-forgotten-history-of-westsylvania/article_41011b14-6ab5-11ea-bff9-57ff6679a38d.html> accessed April 25, 2022.

109 "Vexit Leaders Announce Next Steps In Movement To Leave Virginia," *VEXIT* (published March 12, 2020) <https://www.prnewswire.com/news-releases/vexit-leaders-announce-next-steps-in-movement-to-leave-virginia-301022390.html> accessed April 26, 2022.

110 Livingston, Donald, "What Secession Is," *Abbeville Institute* (published March 21, 2022) <https://www.abbevilleinstitute.org/what-secession-is-3/> accessed March 22, 2022.

111 Griffin, Anna, "Far-fetched as they might seem, secession movements are thriving in the NW," *Oregon Public Broadcasting* (published March 23, 2017) <https://www.opb.org/news/article/pacific-northwest-secession-state-of-jefferson-cascadia/> accessed April 26, 2022.

112 "Indigenous Sovereignties," *The Cascadia Bioregional Party* (published January 24, 2019) <https://cascadiabioregionalparty.org/indigenous-sovereignty/> accessed April 26, 2022.

113 "Bill Summary," *Washington State Legislature* (last edited April 23, 2022) <https://app.leg.wa.gov/billsummary> accessed April 26, 2022.

114 "The forgotten history of Westsylvania," *Observer-Reporter* (last edited May 8, 2021) <https://observer-reporter.com/publications/liwc/the-forgotten-history-of-westsylvania/article_41011b14-6ab5-11ea-bff9-57ff6679a38d.html> accessed April 25, 2022.

115 Benner, Dave, "Secession Hypocrisy: The Case of West Virginia," *Abbeville Institute* (published March 28, 2016) <https://www.abbevilleinstitute.org/secession-hypocrisy-the-case-of-west-virginia/> accessed April 25, 2022.

116 Freedlander, David, "Wisconsin's GOP Secession Panic," *Daily Beast* (last edited July 12, 2017) <https://www.thedailybeast.com/wisconsins-gop-secession-panic> accessed April 25, 2022.

117 Ibid.

118 Pedersen, Nate, "The State of Absaroka: Redrawing our borders would have left us without the Badlands, Black Hills and Mount Rushmore," *South Dakota Magazine*, July/August 2009 issue (published 2017) <https://www.southdakotamagazine.com/article?articleTitle=the+state+of+Absaroka%20(1939)--1311951720--138--history> accessed April 25, 2022.

119 Palet, Laura Secorun, "Americans for independence... from America," *USA Today* (published November 4, 2014) <https://www.usatoday.com/story/news/politics/2014/11/04/ozy-america-secessionist-movement/18457863/> accessed April 25, 2022.

Index of section quotes

{front} It is only in the shadows, when some fresh wave, truly original, truly creative, breaks upon the shore, that there will be a rediscovery of the West.
— Jacques Barzun

Rothstein, Edward, "Jacques Barzun: A Sojourner in the Past Retraces His Steps," *The New York Times* (published April 15, 2000) <https://archive.nytimes.com/ www.nytimes.com/library/books/041500barzu n-book.html> accessed April 15, 2022.

{page 48} In Heaven there will be no law[;...] in Hell there will be nothing but law, and due process will be meticulously observed.
— Grant Gilmore

Gilmore, Grant; Bobbitt, Philip (foreword), *The Ages of American Law* (Yale University Press paperback second edition, January 13, 2015, ISBN 978-0300189919, 248 pages), page 99.

{page 49} So convenient a thing is it to be a reasonable creature, *since it enables one to find or make a reason for everything one has a mind to do.*
— Benjamin Franklin

Franklin, Benjamin, *Autobiography of Benjamin Franklin* (Project Gutenberg eBook #20203, published December 28, 2006) <https://www.gutenberg.org/files/20203/ 20203-h/20203-h.htm> accessed April 10, 2022.

{page 76} We believe that equality is of the devil, and that the Lord our God delights in multiplicity.
— Hermann Borchardt

Borchardt, Hermann; Mussey, Barrows (translator), *The Conspiracy of the Carpenters: Historical Accounting of a Ruling Class* (Simon and Schuster, January 1, 1943, ASIN B000V05FA4), p. 371.

{page 78} Belief in the existence of a common good prohibits almost nothing and permits almost anything.
— Anthony de Jasay

de Wolf, Aschwin, "Interview with Anthony de Jasay," *The Independent Review* (last edited December 10, 2021) <https://www.independent.org/pdf/tir/tir_16_ 02_7_dewolf.pdf> accessed March 8, 2022, PDF page 273.

{page 82} Government is force. Politics is a battle for supremacy.
— John James Ingalls

Ingalls, John James, *Selections from the Writings of John J. Ingalls* (Hudson Press, 1907, 110 pages), page 90.

{page 84} [T]he preservation of property [is] the end of government, and that for which men enter into society.
— John Locke

Locke, John, *Second Treatise of Government* (Project Gutenberg eBook #7370, last edited December 25, 2021) <https://www.gutenberg.org/files/7370/7370- h/7370-h.htm> accessed March 5, 2022. Chapter 11, Section 138. (Also Chapter 7, Section 85.)

{page 85} The sovereign power residing in the people [...] is not a principle of discord, rancour or war: it is a principle of melioration, contentment, and peace.
— James Wilson,
a representative of Pennsylvania at the 1787 Constitutional Convention

Wilson, James, *Collected Works of James Wilson*, Volume I, "PART I, CHAPTER I.: Introductory Lecture. Of the Study of the Law in the United States," (Liberty Fund, October 22, 2007, ISBN 978-0865976832, 1262 pages), page 443. Online at <https://oll.libertyfund .org/title/hall-collected-works-of-james-wilson- vol-1> accessed April 11, 2022.

{page 89} The left is not necessarily aiming at totalitarianism. But their know-it-all mindset leads repeatedly and pervasively in that direction.

– Thomas Sowell

Perry, Mark J., "Thomas Sowell quotations on the 'vision of the political left'," *AEIdeas* (published October 14, 2018) <https://www.aei.org/carpe-diem/thomas-sowell-quotations-on-the-political-left/> accessed April 23, 2022.

{page 91} [Society is] a partnership not only between those who are living, but between those who are living, those who are dead, and those who are to be born.

– Edmund Burke

Burke, Edmund, *Reflections on The Revolution in France*, 1790, transcribed by the McMaster University Faculty of Social Sciences (last edited January 31, 2022) <https://socialsciences.mcmaster.ca/econ/ugc m/3ll3/burke/revfrance.pdf> accessed February 19, 2022, PDF page 80.

{p. 97} This is the way the world ends, the world ends, the world ends:
Not with a bang nor a whimper
But with a snarl of envy.

– adapted from *The Hollow Men*, T.S. Eliot

Eliot, T. S., *The Waste Land, Prufrock, The Hollow Men and Other Poems* (Dover Thrift Editions paperback, February 16, 2022, ISBN 978-0486849065, 64 pages), page 52.

{page 103} Multiply your associations and be free.

– Pierre-Joseph Proudhon

Nisbet, Robert, *The Quest for Community: A Study in the Ethics of Order and Freedom* (Intercollegiate Studies Institute, July 5, 2010, ISBN 978-1935191506, 330 pages), page 247.

{page 109} The flourishing of the virtues requires and in turn sustains a certain kind of community, necessarily a small-scale community.

– Alasdair MacIntyre

MacIntyre, Alasdair, *After Virtue: A Study in Moral Theory* (University of Notre Dame Press, third edition of 1981 original, March 6, 2007, ISBN 978-0268035044, 978-0268035044, 286 pages), page xii.

{page 113} The pilot will judge better of a rudder than the carpenter, and the guest will judge better of a feast than the cook.

– Aristotle

Aristotle; Jowett, Benjamin, translator, *Politics of Aristotle* (Batoche Books, 1999, OCLC 229015989, 192 pages), Book III, Section 11; Bekker 1282a. Online at <https://www.stmarys-ca.edu/ sites/default/files/attachments/files/ Politics_1.pdf> accessed March 28, 2022, PDF pages 87-88.

{page 124} The personal being of man exists as a datum prior to all positive law.

– Heinrich A. Rommen

Rommen, Heinrich A.; Hanley, Thomas R., translator, *The Natural Law: A Study in Legal and Social History and Philosophy* from the 1936 *Ewige Wiederkehr des Naturrechts* (Liberty Fund, March 24, 1998, ISBN 978-0865971608, 278 pages), page 205.

{page 136} [T]he smaller the domain where choices among alternatives are made collectively, the smaller will be the probability that any individual's preference gets overruled.

– Anthony de Jasay

de Jasay, Anthony, *Against Politics: On Government, Anarchy, and Order* (Routledge, December 22, 1997, ISBN 978-0415170673, 256 pages), page 49.

Index

Other works by T.L. Hulsey:

No More Pictures
(Book III of *The Human Stigmergy* trilogy)
(forthcoming)

Kudzuland
(Book II of *The Human Stigmergy* trilogy)
(forthcoming)

Amid a Crowd of Stars
(forthcoming)

25 Texas Heroes
(2021, ISBN 978-1947660533)

A Birdless Silence
(2021, ISBN 978-1883853075)

A Murmuration of Humans
(Book I of *The Human Stigmergy* trilogy)
(2020, ISBN 978-1-883853-05-1)

The Art of Dying
(2013, ISBN 978-1-883853-04-4)

Twelve Delusions of Our Time
(2011, ISBN 1-883853-03-6)

Heroic Tales and Treasures of the Lonely Heart
(1993, ISBN 978-1-883853-00-6)

OVER 70 UNAPOLOGETICALLY SOUTHERN TITLES FOR YOU TO ENJOY

SHOTWELLPUBLISHING.COM

If no other in the world be aware I sit content,
And if each and all be aware I sit content.

One world is aware and by far the largest to me, and that is myself,
And whether I come to my own to-day or in ten thousand or ten million years,
I can cheerfully take it now, or with equal cheerfulness I can wait.

My foothold is tenon'd and mortis'd in granite,
I laugh at what you call dissolution,
And I know the amplitude of time.
– from Song of Myself, Walt Whitman

T.L. Hulsey

Made in the USA
Columbia, SC
19 November 2022

71756203R00153